Programming the Display PostScript® System with X

Adobe Systems Incorporated

WITHDRAWN

Addison-Wesley Publishing Company, Inc.

Reading, Massachusetts • Menlo Park, California • New York

Don Mills, Ontario • Wokingham, England • Amsterdam

Bonn • Sydney • Singapore • Tokyo • Madrid • San Juan

Paris • Seoul • Milan • Mexico City • Taipei

WILLIAM F. MAAG LIBRARY
YOUNGSTOWN STATE UNIVERSITY

Copyright © 1989-1993 by Adobe Systems Incorporated. All rights reserved.
ISBN 0-201-62203-3

No part of this publication may be reproduced, stored in a retrieval system, or transmitted, in any form or by any means, electronic, mechanical, photocopying, recording, or otherwise, without the prior written consent of the publisher. Any software referred to herein is furnished under license and may only be used or copied in accordance with the terms of such license.

PostScript, the PostScript logo, Display PostScript, Adobe Garamond, Trajan, Adobe Illustrator and the Adobe logo are trademarks of Adobe Systems Incorporated which may be registered in certain jurisdictions. XView is a trademark of Sun Microsystems, Inc. Motif and OSF/Motif are trademarks of Open Software Foundation, Inc. UNIX is a registered trademark of UNIX Systems Laboratory. Helvetica, Times, and New Caledonia are trademarks of Linotype-Hell AG and/or its subsidiaries. ITC Stone is a registered trademark of International Typeface Corporation. Lucida is a registered trademark of Bigelow & Holmes. X Window System is a trademark of the Massachusetts Institute of Technology. OI is a trademark of ParcPlace Systems. DECstation is a trademark of Digital Equipment Corporation. SPARCstation is a trademark of SPARC International, Inc., licensed exclusively to Sun Microsystems, Inc., and is based upon an architecture developed by Sun Microsystems, Inc. Macintosh is a registered trademark of Apple Computer, Inc. MS-DOS is a registered trademark of Microsoft Corporation. NeXTSTEP is a trademark of NeXT Computer, Inc. FrameMaker is a registered trademark of Frame Technology Corporation. Other brand or product names are the trademarks or registered trademarks of their respective holders.

This publication and the information herein is furnished AS IS, is subject to change without notice, and should not be construed as a commitment by Adobe Systems Incorporated. Adobe Systems Incorporated assumes no responsibility or liability for any errors or inaccuracies, makes no warranty of any kind (express, implied or statutory) with respect to this publication, and expressly disclaims any and all warranties of merchantability, fitness for particular purposes and noninfringement of third party rights.

1 2 3 4 5 6 7 8 9 10 - AL - 9796959493
First printing, March 1993

QA
76.73
.P67 D57
1993

Contents

WILLIAM F. MAAG LIBRARY
YOUNGSTOWN STATE UNIVERSITY

Programming Guide

Client Library Reference Manual

Client Library Supplement for X

pswrap Reference Manual

Display PostScript Toolkit for X

List of Figures

Programming Guide

Client Library Reference Manual

Client Library Supplement for X

Display PostScript Toolkit for X

List of Tables

Preface

Programming Guide

Client Library Reference Manual

Client Library Supplement for X

Display PostScript Toolkit for X

List of Examples

Programming Guide

Client Library Reference Manual

Client Library Supplement for X

pswrap Reference Manual

Display PostScript Toolkit for X

Foreword

The concept of using a device-independent computer language to drive displays actually predates the printer implementation of the PostScript™ language. Two early incarnations of the language that became PostScript were used to create graphics on minicomputers at Evans & Sutherland Computer Corporation and at Xerox PARC between 1976 and 1982.

In 1985, the year that our PostScript printers first appeared, Adobe began development of PostScript imaging technology for the screen—the Display PostScript™ system—as a joint project with NeXT Computer, Inc. The result of having the PostScript imaging model drive both the display and printer soon became clear: the Display PostScript system was able to produce the closest possible correspondence between the screen and printed page.

Our next challenge was to provide our powerful imaging model across many other UNIX® platforms, a need that our application developers at Adobe were experiencing firsthand. We based our solution on another industry standard, the X Window System™ from the Massachusetts Institute of Technology. Our implementation of Display PostScript as an extension to X, codeveloped with Digital Equipment Corporation, has been adopted by Digital, IBM, Integrated Computer Solutions, NCD, Silicon Graphics, Sun Microsystems and other workstation manufacturers and system integrators. The combination of the PostScript imaging model with a widely accepted windowing system is helping to provide a solid foundation for developing graphically sophisticated UNIX-based X applications.

We and our OEM partners believe that the imaging power and device independence of X with Display PostScript will keep UNIX at the forefront of industrial-strength operating systems and will make it a very attractive environment for application developers. In fact, at Adobe, we have been moving Adobe Illustrator™ and other of our major applications to X and Display PostScript.

This book, the X-specific successor to *Programming the Display PostScript System with NeXTstep*™, begins with a Programming Guide that contains advice on how to write robust, efficient Display PostScript applications. A new Toolkit manual and the standard Display PostScript reference manuals are bound right in, making *Programming the Display PostScript System with X* a one-stop resource and companion to the *PostScript Language Reference Manual*. Among the many people at Adobe and elsewhere who contributed valuable input to this book, foremost is Paul Asente, the principal author and engineer of the Programming Guide and the Display PostScript Toolkit.

We believe that *Programming the Display PostScript System with X* will greatly benefit any X application developer who follows the book's advice on how to get the best performance at the lowest development cost. To quick-start your own application, you can use the sample programs in the Programming Guide as building blocks. We hope that they will contribute to the fast development and superior performance of your application—and, in turn, will help it contribute to the growth and power of the UNIX platform.

John Warnock
February 1993

Preface

About This Book

The text and graphics imaging resources of the Display PostScript System provide the same imaging model for both printers and active computer displays. As a result, developers can more easily write programs that provide true WYSIWYG (what-you-see-is-what-you-get) imaging.

This book is a compilation of several manuals that describe how to write applications that make use of the Display PostScript System in an X Window System development environment. The following paragraphs briefly describe each manual.

Programming Guide explains how to render text and images by using facilities provided by the Display PostScript extension to X. Trade-offs between development efficiency and runtime performance are discussed, porting considerations are noted, and coding techniques are described in detail. This manual is a good overview for X Window System programmers with little knowledge of the PostScript language.

Client Library Reference Manual describes the application program interface to the Display PostScript system, including how to send programs and data to a PostScript execution context, how to handle context output, and how to create and terminate a context. It contains procedure definitions, programming tips, and a sample application program. It is the definitive reference for the Client Library.

Client Library Supplement for X contains information about the Client Library interface to the Display PostScript system implemented as an extension to the X Window System. It is the definitive reference for X-specific features of the Client Library.

pswrap Reference Manual describes ways to define C language-callable procedures that contain PostScript language programs. It details methods for declaring input arguments and output to be received from the interpreter. It documents the *pswrap* command line options and is the definitive reference for *pswrap*.

Display PostScript Toolkit for X is a collection of utilities for programmers who use the Display PostScript extension to the X Window System. The toolkit can be used for context management, user object management, user path handling, and file previewing. It also lets users preview and choose from currently available fonts by using the font selection panel and the font sampler. It is the definitive reference for the Display PostScript Toolkit for X.

About the Audience

This book is written for C programmers with some X Window System and Motif™ programming experience who want to incorporate Display PostScript technology into new or existing applications.

Related Documentation

The following additional manuals are useful to developers who are programming with the PostScript language or are developing in a Display PostScript environment.

PostScript Language Tutorial and Cookbook is an introduction to the PostScript language. It contains a collection of example programs that illustrate the PostScript language and imaging model. This book emphasizes examples rather than efficient programming strategies, to illustrate clearly many of the capabilities of the PostScript language.

PostScript Language Reference Manual, Second Edition, is the official reference for the PostScript language. It describes the imaging model, the interpreter, and the operators in detail. It is the definitive resource for all PostScript language programmers.

PostScript Language Program Design is a guide for advanced developers to use in designing and debugging PostScript language programs. Although its content focuses on printers, much of it is relevant to the Display PostScript system.

Adobe Type 1 Font Format describes the format and methods of construction for Adobe Type 1 font programs. Type 1 fonts give font developers the ability to create a single font program that can be rendered on a wide variety of devices and resolutions. They are useful for small graphical objects such as control points as well as text characters.

System-Specific Documentation

The term *system specific* refers to implementations of the Display PostScript system that are customized to fit a specific machine and operating system environment. *Client Library Reference Manual* and *pswrap Reference Manual* apply to all Display PostScript implementations. *Programming Guide, Client Library Supplement for X*, and *Display PostScript Toolkit for X* apply to all Display PostScript implementations under the X Window System.

Notes and comments throughout this book alert you to system-specific issues. For more information about system-specific aspects of your Display PostScript implementation, see the documentation provided by your Display PostScript system vendor.

Typographical Conventions

The following typographical conventions are used in this book:

Table 1 *Typographical conventions*

Item	Example of Typographical Style
file or executable	*<DPS/dpsXshare.h>, libdps.a*
variable, typedef, code fragment	*ctxt, x, y, DPSContextRec, cid, drawable*
code example	`typedef struct {`
procedure	**XDPSCreateSimpleContext**
PostScript operator or customop	**file, currentXgcdrawable**
new term or emphasis	"The toolkit procedures *must* be used…

Developer Resources

The following is a list of resources maintained by Adobe for developers:

Technical Publications. The manuals described in the section "Related Documentation" on page xxx can be obtained from Addison-Wesley Publishing Company, from a technical bookstore, or from the Adobe Developers Association.

Adobe Developers Association. Adobe provides a membership program for active developers. The literature and services provided by the association are designed to support developers and keep them up to date as they work with Adobe technology. For information about membership, publications, and services call the Adobe Developer Support Line.

Adobe Developer Support Line. You can call 1-415-961-4111 for the following kinds of support:

- To order Software Development Kits (SDKs).

- To order the code samples from *Programming the Display PostScript System with X* in machine-readable form.

- To receive information on training classes.

- To receive a free Technical Literature Catalog.

- To order technical literature.

- To receive a membership application for the Adobe Developers Association.

- To request technical assistance (for members of the Adobe Developers Association only).

Public Access File Server. Users who have access to Internet or UUCP electronic mail can use Adobe's public access file server to obtain the following information:

- Source code examples, including the sample applications discussed in this book.
- AFM (Adobe font metric) files.
- Documentation.
- PPD (PostScript printer description) files.
- Press releases.

The public access file server is a mail-response program. You send it a request by electronic mail and it mails back a response. (The "Subject:" line is treated as part of the message by the file server.)

To send mail to the file server, use one of the following addresses:

Internet: `ps-file-server@adobe.com`
UUCP: `...!decwrl!adobe!ps-file-server`

To receive detailed information on how to use the file server, send the following message:

`send Documents long.help`

To receive a listing of available documents, send the following message:

`index Documents`

To receive a listing of available example programs, send this message:

`index Programs`

To receive a listing of available press releases, send this message:

`index Updates`

The file server may take a few hours to respond, so consider sending all of the above messages at the same time. You will receive the fastest response if you mail each message separately.

The file server maintains several documents that describe the contents of Adobe Software Development Kits. These kits provide a set of documentation and tools that give application developers a head start with their PostScript and Display PostScript projects.

PostScript Language Software Development Kit. This comprehensive set of tools and reference materials helps application software developers take advantage of PostScript language technology. The PostScript SDK includes technical papers, manuals, sample code, fonts, and utilities.

Display PostScript Software Development Kit for X. This SDK includes current documentation on Display PostScript, PostScript, and Type 1 font design as well as software tools, libraries, code examples, and fonts.

POSTSCRIPT™
Software From Adobe

The Display PostScript System

Adobe Systems Incorporated

PG

Programming Guide

Preface to the Programming Guide

About This Guide

The *Programming Guide* explains how to render text and graphics with the Display PostScript™ extension to X. It uses several example programs to evaluate trade-offs between ease of development and runtime performance, to examine porting considerations, and to describe coding techniques in detail.

Because application development is tightly woven into the windowing environment, the operating system, and the imaging model, it is difficult to provide practical instruction without touching on all three areas. The applications described in this guide were developed with the UNIX® operating system, the X Window System™, and the OSF/Motif™ graphical user interface library. You can use other toolkits such as OLIT, XView™, OI™, Athena, or no toolkit at all. However, only Motif applications can use the font selection panel and other Motif dialogs included in the Display PostScript Toolkit for X.

What This Guide Contains

Chapter 1, "Introduction to the Display PostScript System," provides an overview of the Display PostScript system, architecture, and programming interface.

Chapter 2, "Overview of X and OSF/Motif," provides an overview of the X Window System and the OSF/Motif programming environment and discusses X and Motif programming issues that concern the Display PostScript system.

Chapter 3, "Building a Display PostScript Application," describes how to build a Display Postscript program in X and introduces the concept of drawing in a window.

Chapter 4, "The Coordinate System," describes how to achieve device independence through a device-independent coordinate system. It also discusses the concept of a path and its relation to pixels.

Chapter 5, "Single-Operator Procedures and Wraps," explores three mechanisms for communicating with the X server: using **DPSPrintf**, using single operator procedures from the Client Library, and using wraps created with the *pswrap* translator.

Chapter 6, "Path Construction and Painting," discusses issues of efficiency in rendering paths.

Chapter 7, "Managing Graphical Information," describes user objects and gstate objects, which allow efficient drawing in a display environment.

Chapter 8, "Drawing Small Objects," compares seven methods to display large numbers of small objects.

Chapter 9, "Hit Detection and Buffering," examines hit detection, zooming, and buffering.

Chapter 10, "Drawing and Scrolling," focuses on drawing issues and their effect on scrolling.

Chapter 11, "Displaying Text," discusses text management and display issues in the PostScript language.

Chapter 12, "Encapsulated PostScript Files," discusses how to import and export Encapsulated PostScript files.

About the Code Examples

The examples given in this guide were developed in the X Window System and OSF/Motif programming environment. The C language was used as the application programming language; imaging was performed using PostScript language code and Display PostScript Client Library procedures. Each code example is identified as C code, PostScript language code, or a PostScript wrap definition.

Performance is a critical aspect of developing an interactive application, and many of the examples in this guide explore the fastest and most efficient ways to handle specific drawing issues. However, performance is not the only factor a developer must consider when choosing an implementation method; ease of programming and portability are two other important considerations. Accordingly, the examples sometimes present several solutions to a given problem and provide performance figures to illustrate the trade-offs between methods. There are several reasons for providing multiple approaches instead of a single best solution:

- The various approaches give a better understanding of how the PostScript language and the Display PostScript system work.

- The best solution for one type of drawing might not be the best solution for other types of drawings. Other approaches might be faster under certain conditions or easier to implement for drawing routines that are infrequently called.

- Hardware or system differences may cause results to vary from one architecture to another.

- The ability to write an application easily may be more important than maximizing the application's performance.

The goal of this guide is to provide enough information to help the application programmer find an approach that balances performance with ease of programming. At times, the guide focuses more on explanation than on performance issues. Some chapters describe PostScript language characteristics, such as the coordinate system, while others deal with application programming techniques, such as offscreen buffering. The intent is to introduce the subject, provide an example, and carry the information into other areas and uses.

The sample applications in this guide are available in machine-readable form from the Adobe Developers Association. Portions of the source code are included as examples where they are relevant to the text. Not all chapters contain source code examples, and the examples themselves are not intended to show every aspect of the application.

Note: *To obtain complete listings for the applications, see "Developer Resources" on page xxxiii in this book.*

About Performance Timings

The applications provided in this guide are accompanied by performance statistics, where applicable, that illustrate the method that achieves peak performance. However, your timing numbers may differ from those shown in the guide. Hardware platforms, display architectures, and software architectures can affect the performance of a Display PostScript application.

The statistics presented in this guide were produced on an Adobe standard reference implementation of the Display PostScript system. Its server is based on the MIT X11R5 sample server on a simple, 8-bit color frame buffer. The programming techniques that produce the best performance on the reference implemention will perform well on most other platforms.

However, platform differences do exist. A technique based on drawing into pixmaps and copying them to the screen may be recommended in this guide, but on a workstation without a frame buffer it may be more efficient to draw directly to the screen. Some display architectures include special accelerators to speed up drawing lines or drawing characters and, in these cases, techniques that can use the accelerators may perform better than those that cannot. If you are targeting your application toward a specific hardware configuration, running the sample applications on that platform should indicate the techniques that are most efficient.

Note: *When obtaining timings for the applications, run the tests repeatedly to avoid transient effects that may occur in timing studies.*

CHAPTER 1

Introduction to the Display PostScript System

This chapter summarizes the text and graphics capabilities the Display PostScript system brings to X applications. It also describes the components that make up the Display PostScript system.

The Display PostScript system displays graphical information on the computer screen with the same imaging model and PostScript language that are the standards for printers and typesetters. Therefore, the same high-quality graphics that could once be rendered only on a printer can now be easily displayed on a screen.

The PostScript language makes it possible for an X application to draw lines and curves with perfect precision, rotate and scale images, and manipulate type as a graphic object. In addition, X applications that use the Display PostScript system have access to the entire Adobe Type Library.

Device and resolution independence are important benefits of PostScript printers and typesetters. The Display PostScript system extends these benefits to interactive displays. An application that takes advantage of the Display PostScript system will work and appear the same on any supported display without modification to the application program.

The Display PostScript system has several components, including the PostScript interpreter, the Client Library, and the *pswrap* translator. The Client Library is the link between an application and the PostScript interpreter. An application draws on the screen by making calls to Client Library procedures. These procedures generate PostScript language code that is sent to the PostScript interpreter for execution. In addition to the Client Library, the Display PostScript system provides the *pswrap* translator. It takes PostScript language instructions and produces a C language procedure—called a *wrap*—that can then be called from an application program.

WILLIAM F. MAAG LIBRARY
YOUNGSTOWN STATE UNIVERSITY

In addition to the PostScript interpreter, the Client Library, and the *pswrap* translator, the Display PostScript system includes the Display PostScript Toolkit for X. This X-specific toolkit provides a variety of high-level utilities for the developer using the X Window System, including an Encapsulated PostScript (EPS) file preview package and a Motif font selection panel.

1.1 How Applications Use the Display PostScript System

An application interacts with the Display PostScript system in the following manner:

1. The application creates a PostScript execution context and establishes a communication channel to the server. A *context* can be thought of as a virtual printer. It has its own set of PostScript stacks, input and output facilities, and memory space. The PostScript interpreter switches among contexts, giving multiple applications access to the interpreter.

2. The application then sends Client Library procedures and wraps to the context and receives responses from it.

3. When the application exits, it destroys the context and closes the communications channel, freeing resources used during the session.

1.2 Extensions to the PostScript Language

The Display PostScript system provides a number of extensions to the PostScript language. These extensions have been incorporated in PostScript Level 2, a 1991 revision of the PostScript language. Because the extensions are part of the PostScript language, they can be used on printers as well as computer screens. However, some language extensions (those that accommodate user feedback, for example) have no meaning to printers, and cannot be used with them.

The language extensions that are available on printers are present only in printers that support PostScript Level 2. In order for these extensions to work on Level 1 printers, your application must emulate them with PostScript Level 1 commands when it creates a printable file.

The language extensions fall into the following major categories:

- New path construction and imaging operations provide more convenient generation and optimized execution. User paths, **xyshow**, and **rectfill** are examples. They can be used on Level 2 printers.

- Operators such as user object operators and graphics state operators meet the demands of an interactive display environment, but they can also be used on Level 2 printers.

- Some operators such as view clipping operators were created only for interactive display environments and do *not* work with PostScript printers. These operators are available only in the Display PostScript system.

- Extended memory management and multiple processing capabilities accommodate the dynamic and unpredictable use of resources in interactive display environments. These language extensions may also be used on Level 2 printers.

This book focuses on language extensions important to application programmers and does not explain every extension to the PostScript language. A complete description of the PostScript language, including the Display PostScript system and Level 2 extensions, can be found in the *PostScript Language Reference Manual, Second Edition.* Of special interest is Appendix A, which summarizes the operators that are available on Level 1 printers, those available on Level 2 printers, and those available only in the Display PostScript system.

1.2.1 Using Display PostScript Extensions on Printers

You must perform some workarounds if your application uses Display PostScript extensions and prepares PostScript language files destined for printing. The workarounds fall into three basic categories:

Avoidance—avoid using the Display PostScript extensions when preparing output for printing. This technique requires taking a separate code path for the printing process.

Emulation—include definitions of PostScript language procedures that emulate the language extensions. Unfortunately, some of the operators in the extensions cannot be emulated efficiently.

Limitation—produce output that can be printed only on Level 2 printers. This is suitable if you know that your application will be used in a very restricted environment that excludes Level 1 printers.

Most applications use a combination of the first two workarounds, emulating the language extensions that can be emulated efficiently and avoiding those that cannot. Completely avoiding the use of the extensions, both on the screen and in the output for printing, is not recommended. In many cases these operators give substantial performance improvements and are important tools for making Display PostScript applications run quickly.

1.3   Advantages of the Display PostScript System

The PostScript language significantly speeds the development of high-quality applications by taking over many of their graphics responsibilities. The features itemized below emphasize the advantages of writing X applications that employ the Display PostScript system.

- Fonts are fully scalable to the resolution of the screen. The fonts can also be rotated or transformed arbitrarily, a capability not provided by X.

- PostScript language graphics are specified relative to a coordinate system that is independent of screen resolution.

- The default unit of measure is 1/72 of an inch. This unit is very close to a printer's point, which is 1/72.27 inch. The PostScript language default unit is often, though inaccurately, referred to as a point. The Display PostScript system automatically adjusts for screen resolution so that an application will appear the same on any screen.

- PostScript halftoning technology improves the appearance of text, graphics, and scanned images on the screen.

- Scanned images can be scaled, rotated, and adjusted for color.

- Drawing operators, including those that manipulate Bézier curves, are more extensive than those offered by the basic X Window System.

- Drawing in color is possible without concern for the capabilities of the screen. Whether the screen is monochrome, grayscale, or has a limited number of colors, the Display PostScript extension provides the closest possible approximation to the colors in the source image.

- Imported EPS files can be displayed in an application. EPS is an industry-standard format for included graphics.

- The Display PostScript system is a standard imaging system that makes it easier to port your application to a non-X environment such as NeXTSTEP.

The following sections describe in more detail several important features of the Display PostScript system.

1.3.1 Outline Fonts

Type 1 PostScript language fonts are mathematical representations of character outlines, implemented as programs. Therefore, text created by Type 1 font programs can be scaled, rotated, and rendered without requiring individual bitmaps for each point size and rotation. In addition, Type 1 font programs use a set of embedded hints to provide high-quality character rendering at small point sizes or coarse resolutions. Figure 1.1 illustrates a filled character and the Bézier curve segments that define its outline.

Figure 1.1 *Characters in an outline font*

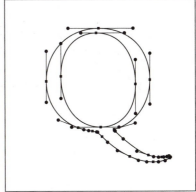

Filled character   *Outline description of a character*

1.3.2 Type 1 Font Library

There are thousands of typefaces available in the Type 1 font format. This large library of fonts provides a wide range of typographic weights and widths, including light, normal, semibold, bold, heavy, condensed, and compressed. The standard Adobe character set for Roman faces includes the ISO Latin-1 character set, which is also the standard set for the X Window System.

Many faces include additional characters such as small capitals and ligatures. Display faces for headlines and special fonts for music, math, and maps are also available. Some Display PostScript systems support the Kanji character set through the PostScript language composite font mechanism. Figure 1.2 illustrates some of the available Type 1 fonts.

Figure 1.2 *Type 1 fonts*

1.3.3 Device-Independent Coordinate System

All PostScript language graphics are specified relative to a coordinate system that is independent of the resolution of the screen. By using specific PostScript operators like **translate**, **rotate**, and **scale**, you can change or transform this coordinate system. Coordinate transformations are easy to implement because text, graphics, and scanned images are all drawn through this system. Figure 1.3 illustrates a graphic that has been transformed with the **scale** and **rotate** PostScript operators.

Figure 1.3 *Scaled and rotated graphic*

Normal   *Scaled*   *Rotated*

1.3.4   Halftoning

The appearance of text, graphics, and images is improved on monochrome, grayscale, and 8-bit color screens through PostScript halftoning technology. Colors are described in high-level color models such as red-green-blue (RGB), hue-saturation-brightness (HSB), and cyan-magenta-yellow-black (CMYK); the PostScript interpreter determines how to paint pixels on a given device. Users will see additional colors or shades of gray on their screens. PostScript language color models shield the developer from device-dependent color capabilities.

On a colormapped display, the PostScript interpreter requires a small number of entries in the color map and uses this fixed set of entries for halftoning (dithering) to achieve device independence. The application interface for color is completely independent of the color capabilities of any single device. Figure 1.4 shows an example of halftoning.

Figure 1.4 *Halftoning*

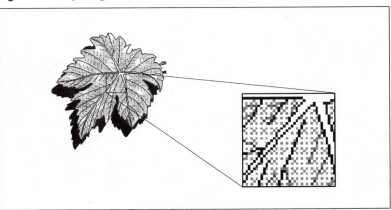

1.3.5 Bézier Representation of Curves

The Bézier representation of curves is compact and efficient. Because it describes complex curves in a device- and resolution-independent manner, the curves can be easily scaled for zooming effects—the interpreter adjusts the curves to accommodate device resolution. Bézier curves can also be joined in groups, either sharing a single endpoint or joined end-to-end to form a single continuous curve (see Figure 1.5).

Figure 1.5 *Bézier curves*

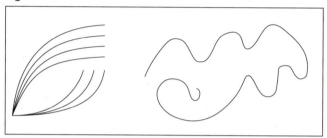

1.3.6 Scanned Image Manipulation

Scanned images, like other graphics can be displayed through a clipping region, scaled, rotated, and skewed. The Display PostScript system automatically displays color images in black and white on monochrome screens. If the resolution of the scanned image is different from the resolution of the screen, the image is automatically resampled to provide the best possible rendition of the image.

Figure 1.6 *Scaled, rotated, skewed and clipped scanned image*

1.3.7 Encapsulated PostScript Files

The EPS file format is a standard format describing single-page images containing text, graphics, and sampled images. Using the EPS format, you can import and export PostScript language files into different applications across computer system environments. EPS has become a standard in the desktop and commercial publishing industries.

Display PostScript applications automatically display EPS files at the highest resolution possible on any given screen. On other platforms, device-dependent bitmaps, frequently monochrome, appear on the screen. The quality of these images degrades significantly when bitmaps are resized or rotated. In the Display PostScript system, EPS files can be scaled and rotated with no loss in quality. Figure 1.7 illustrates EPS files being included into a page (the page is page PG-11, and the EPS files are shown in Figure 1.1).

Figure 1.7 *EPS graphic imported into a page of text*

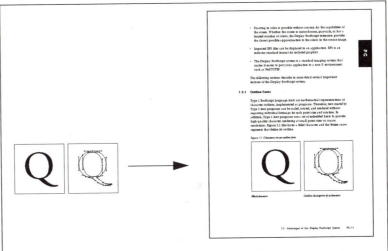

1.4 Summary

- The Display PostScript system is compatible with PostScript printers and provides a device-independent imaging model for displaying information on a screen.

- The Client Library contains procedures that allow an application to communicate with the PostScript interpreter.

- The *pswrap* translator enfolds PostScript language code in a C procedure interface so it can be called from an application program.

- The Display PostScript system provides a number of extensions to the PostScript language. Many of these extensions can be used on printers as well as computer screens.

- The Display PostScript system provides many capabilities that cannot be achieved with only the X Window System, such as:

  Arbitrary scaling, rotation, and transformation of text, graphics, and scanned images.

  Scaling of fonts to any point size.

  Automatically adjusting device color for color graphics and scanned images on black-and-white or grayscale screens.

  Rendering graphics that employ Bézier curves.

  Importing and displaying Encapsulated PostScript files (EPS) in an application.

  Automatically adjusting to screen resolution so that an application looks the same on any screen.

  Easy porting of your application to other Display PostScript environments.

CHAPTER 2

Overview of X and OSF/Motif

This chapter provides an overview of the X Window System and the OSF/Motif programming environment and discusses how the Display PostScript system fits into this environment. The chapter provides a basis for the examples and programs that appear in subsequent chapters of this guide.

The X Window System is implemented as a client-server network architecture. The server side of the architecture provides the user interface: output to the user in the form of graphic windows on a screen, and input from the user in the form of keyboard and mouse actions. The client side of the architecture is the application, including any libraries it calls.

Several toolkits have been developed to help implement an application's user interface by simplifying the interaction between the application and its X server. OSF/Motif is one such toolkit; it implements the Motif user interface.

2.1 X Window System

The X Window System is a client-server, network-based windowing system. The client, or application, runs in one process while the X server connected to the screen and keyboard runs in another. These processes can be either on the same computer or on different computers connected by a network. The communication between the client and the server is defined by the X protocol. This communication is transparent to the application.

As shown in Figure 2.1, the X Window System includes several layers above the X protocol. The X library provides a low-level interface to the X protocol. X Toolkit procedures, based on X library calls, build a framework for user-level components like menus, pushbuttons, and scroll bars. These components are known as *X widgets*. The OSF/Motif environment builds upon the X Toolkit calls to provide a set of widgets with a consistent look and feel. It also defines a user interface language to simplify the creation of user interfaces.

Figure 2.1 *X client-server architecture*

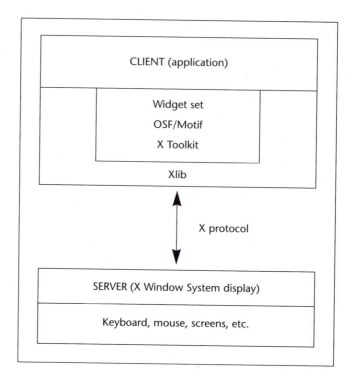

2.1.1   X Server

The X server runs on a computer with a screen, a keyboard, and a pointing device (typically a mouse). The X server handles all output to the screen based on requests from applications. It also handles user inputs and passes them back to the application in the form of *events*. Events are occurrences such as keyboard entries, pointing device movement, and messages between applications.

The X Window System is network-transparent. An application running on one computer can make calls to and receive calls from the X server, and therefore the display, on another computer. Although the X Window System supports a wide variety of screen display capabilities, it does so by exposing the capabilities to the client application. This requires that the developer not make device-dependent assumptions about screen resolution or color capabilities during implementation. To make sure that an application looks the same on any screen, the application must examine the screen's capabilities and produce images that match those capabilities.

2.1.2 X Protocol

The X protocol is asynchronous and bidirectional. Events can flow to the application at the same time that requests flow to the X server. The application usually sends a stream of requests without waiting for replies from the X server. Requests that require a reply should be kept to a minimum because the application must wait for the reply. The request and reply together are sometimes called a *round-trip*.

2.1.3 X Library

The X library, also called Xlib, is the lowest-level interface provided for C language programming. Xlib has routines that perform basic two-dimensional drawing and multifont text output to a window. Xlib does not provide standards for the appearance of the user interface. Although Xlib is too low level to be of much direct use in developing complex applications, it forms the basis for developing higher level toolkits, and Xlib calls can be freely mixed with calls to those toolkits. Xlib is also the component of the X Window System that provides the client-server interface routines that hide the X protocol from the application.

2.1.4 X Toolkit

The X Toolkit, also called the Xt Intrinsics (or simply Xt), contains routines that simplify application development by defining widgets and callback procedures. Widgets such as pushbuttons, scroll bars, and menus can be combined to form complex windows. When the user interacts with a widget, the X Toolkit calls a callback procedure to notify the application of the interaction. Most of the internals of a widget are hidden from the application.

The X Toolkit provides the set of routines and data structures for defining and using widgets but does not include the widgets themselves. It is normally used along with an existing widget set or toolkit. OSF/Motif is one of several such toolkits. Some applications also use the X Toolkit directly to define new, application-specific widgets.

2.1.5 OSF/Motif

The OSF/Motif environment consists of the Motif toolkit, a user interface language, and a window manager that implements a consistent user interface. The Motif toolkit includes such widgets as:

- Main windows
- Dialog boxes
- Menu bars
- Pull-down menus
- Pushbuttons
- Arrow buttons

The Motif toolkit contains a set of procedures that define the user interface appearance, callback procedures, and user interaction.

Motif also provides a user interface language called UIL. UIL permits the application's widget structure to be defined outside the C language source code. The UIL source code is separately compiled by a UIL compiler, which creates a user interface data (UID) file. The UID file is read by the application through C procedure calls.

UIL lets you separate almost all the user interface definition from the application source code. UIL compilation is much faster than C compilation and linking. You can use UIL to do rapid prototyping of the user interface with a minimum of application code in place. Different Motif user interfaces can be created for the same application in this way.

2.1.6 The Display PostScript Extension to X

The X Window System is extensible; that is, new features and technology can be added easily. The Display PostScript system is implemented as an extension to the X Window System; the extension is sometimes referred to as *DPS/X*. Figure 2.1 shows the components of the Display PostScript system and their relationship to X.

Figure 2.2 *X client-server architecture with Display PostScript extension*

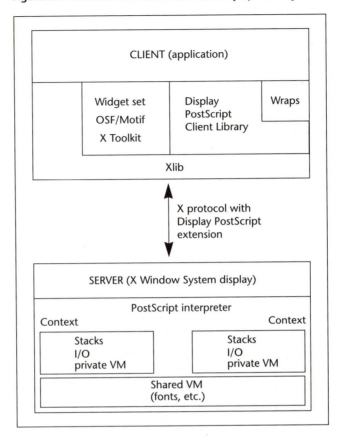

The Display PostScript extension is implemented as part of the X Window System client-server network architecture. The PostScript interpreter is implemented as part of the X server, and each application is a client. The application sends PostScript language code to the server through single operator calls or wraps. Data can be returned from the server in the form of *output* arguments. The Client Library implements Display PostScript client-server communication transparently using the low-level communication protocols provided by the X Window System.

Each application that uses the Display PostScript extension creates a *context*. A context can be thought of as a virtual PostScript printer that sends its output to a window or an offscreen pixmap. It has its own set of stacks, input/output facilities, and memory space. Separate contexts enable multiple applications to share the PostScript interpreter, which runs as a single process in the server.

Although the Display PostScript system supports multiple contexts for a single application, one context is usually sufficient for all drawing within an application. A single context can handle many drawing areas. There are exceptions, however, when it is preferable to use more than one context in a client. For example, a separate context might be used when importing Encapsulated PostScript (EPS) files. This simplifies error recovery if an included EPS file contains PostScript language errors.

The interpreter handles the scheduling associated with executing contexts in time slices. Each context has access to a private portion of PostScript *VM* (virtual memory space). An additional portion of VM, called *shared VM*, is shared among all contexts and holds system fonts and other shared resources. *Private VM* can hold fonts private to the context.

The structure of a context is the same across all Display PostScript platforms. Creating and managing a context, however, can differ from one platform to another. *Client Library Reference Manual* and *Client Library Supplement for X* in this book contain information on contexts and the routines that manipulate them, and *Display PostScript Toolkit for X* contains utilities for Display PostScript developers.

2.2 Development Environment

The development environment can be viewed as a hierarchy of layers (top to bottom), as shown in Figure 2.3. This ordering of layers is dictated by the order in which the libraries are loaded when the application is compiled.

Figure 2.3 *Library functions in the development environment hierarchy*

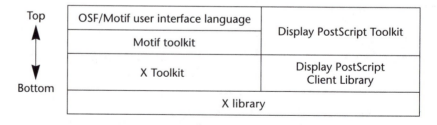

When an area of functionality is provided by more than one library, a good rule of thumb is to use the library function at the highest level of the hierarchy shown in Figure 2.3. In other words, use a Motif routine instead of an X library routine if the same functionality is provided by both.

Note: *Whenever there is a choice, using functionality from the Display PostScript column will usually create a more portable application.*

2.2.1 Programming Considerations

The X Window System client-server architecture divides a program's data into two separate sets, one on the server side and the other on the client side. Windows, pixmaps (offscreen buffers), clipping information, fonts, and graphics contexts are maintained in the X server. Widgets and scanned images are maintained in the application. The Display PostScript extension likewise separates the data into a set in the server and a set in the client, but it often lets you choose where to keep a particular piece of data. This guide provides guidelines to help you choose the partition that results in the most efficient application.

In the X Window System, all activity is event driven. The client does not display its graphics on the screen until it receives an Expose event. This action indicates that a new window has appeared or that a window that was completely or partially obscured by another window needs to be updated.

Note: *You can improve the execution time for an application by minimizing requests that require a response from the server. A network round-trip is required whenever the application sends a request that requires a response.*

2.3 Summary

- The X Window System is a device-independent, client-server, network-based windowing system.

- The server interacts with the user to provide input and output to the client application.

- The X library provides the application interface to the X server with the X protocol.

- The X Toolkit provides the application interface to widgets and callback procedures to simplify application development.

- To implement a user interface with a consistent look and feel, OSF/Motif provides the Motif toolkit (containing a library of routines and a set of widgets), a user interface language, development tools, and a window manager.

- The Display PostScript system is an extension to the X Window System. It is implemented through application-callable libraries on the client side and a corresponding extension on the X server side.

- Each application that uses the Display PostScript extension creates an execution context. Separate contexts enable multiple applications to share the PostScript interpreter, which runs as a single process in the server.

- The development environment can be viewed as a hierarchy of layers, ordered by the library loading sequence. For maximum portability, use routines in the Display PostScript Toolkit or Client Library.

- The Display PostScript extension separates its data into a set in the server and a set in the client. Often, you can choose whether to keep a particular piece of data in the client or the server.

CHAPTER 3

Building a Display PostScript Application

This chapter describes how to build a Display PostScript program in the X environment and introduces drawing in a window. The application *HelloWorld* illustrates the components needed to create a Display PostScript application. Some parts of the code in *HelloWorld* are specific to writing a Display PostScript application, but you could find most of the code in any Motif application.

Figure 3.1 illustrates the main window and pull-down menu for *HelloWorld*.

Figure 3.1 *HelloWorld main window and pull-down menu*

The main window of *HelloWorld* contains a menu bar and a drawing window. When the user chooses Commands from the menu bar, a pull-down menu appears with two checkbuttons, Write Text and Trace On, and one pushbutton, Quit. Selecting Write Text clears and displays the text "Hello World" in the window. Choosing Trace On turns on and off the Display PostScript text trace, which is a listing of all the PostScript language code the application uses.

3.1 Components of a Display PostScript Application

A Display PostScript application has the same flow as any other X application. The application first constructs its user interface by creating a set of windows that implement menus, pushbuttons, text fields, and so forth. It then waits for events from the X server and reacts to these events by executing code that implements the application's functionality. The only difference between Display PostScript applications and other X applications resides within this functionality code. A simple X application uses X functionality to display graphics or text on the screen, whereas a Display PostScript application uses a combination of X and Display PostScript functionality.

In a Motif application, the windows that make up the user interface are associated with abstract objects called *widgets*. To an application, a widget is a pointer to a data structure that contains information about the user interface object. The application creates, modifies, and finds information about widgets by calling procedures in the Motif library or in the underlying X Toolkit library.

The code that implements the application's functionality in response to user actions is contained in a set of procedures that will be called whenever events arrive from the X server. Motif and the X Toolkit provide a number of different types of procedures that are called in different circumstances, including event handlers, action procedures, and callback procedures.

3.1.1 Motif Widgets

A Motif application creates many widgets as part of its interface and provides many procedures to implement its functionality. Most widgets, like scroll bars, menu items, and pushbuttons, have their contents displayed automatically by Motif. This book concentrates on the Motif DrawingArea widget and its associated callback procedures. The DrawingArea widget is a general-purpose widget that is used for the main window in many graphical applications; it leaves displaying the contents to the application.

3.1.2 Exposure Handling

Exposure handling is an important concept in an X Window System application. When a portion of a window becomes visible, the X server sends Expose events to the client application so that the application can fill in the exposed areas. This also applies to the first time a window appears on the screen. Applications don't immediately display the contents of newly created windows; instead they wait for the first Expose event and respond by displaying the window contents.

Because Motif handles the redisplay of most kinds of widgets, the application itself doesn't need to handle the Expose events for them. Motif dispatches the Expose events to widget-specific Motif code. DrawingArea widgets, however, must be handled by the application, so Motif calls the *Expose callback*—a procedure the application has registered to handle the Expose event.

3.1.3 Resizing

Another important application procedure associated with the Drawing Area widget is the *Resize callback*. Motif calls this procedure to inform the application that the drawing area has changed size. A size change can occur because:

- A user changes the size of the application window and, in reapportioning the new area, Motif determines that the drawing area needs to become larger or smaller.

- The various widgets in the user interface have the opportunity to negotiate their sizes, which can result in some widget size changes. As a result of this negotiation, the actual size at which the widget first appears may not be the same as the size requested by the application. The Resize callback procedure notifies the application of this change.

Display PostScript applications must often do some work in response to resizing so they usually provide a Resize callback. The particulars of what the Resize callback does varies from application to application. Typical actions include reinitializing the clipping area, calculating a new position for graphics that should be centered, calculating new scale factors for graphics that should be scaled to the size of the window, and repositioning the origin of the coordinate system to keep it in the lower left corner of the drawing area.

3.1.4 Drawing

Unlike other Motif applications, Display PostScript applications use the PostScript language to do their drawing. They redraw the already existing parts of their drawings in the Expose callback. They react to user interactions by drawing new graphics and text in their drawing area.

The application finds out about user actions in many ways. The two most common are procedures the application has associated with widgets in the interface and procedures that the application has associated with events in the drawing area. An example of the first is a procedure that is called when the user moves a scroll bar. An example of the second is a procedure that is called when the user clicks a mouse button in the drawing area.

3.2 The HelloWorld Application

The following sections discuss the structure of *HelloWorld* application and provide source code examples of its implementation.

3.2.1 HelloWorld Widget Tree

The widgets in a Motif application's user interface make up a tree structure. Understanding this tree structure can help you understand how the user interface works. Figure 3.2 shows the widget tree for *HelloWorld*.

At the top of the tree is a special widget, the *Application Shell*. This widget holds the application's user interface much as an eggshell holds an egg: it wraps itself around the application's windows and separates the internal, self-managed world of the application from the external, chaotic world of the rest of the display. Within the tree there are two kinds of widgets:

- Composite widgets—internal nodes in the tree that act as containers to group, manage, and arrange other widgets

- Primitive widgets—the leaves of the tree

There are also two types of parent-child relationships in the widget tree:

- Simple containments

- Pop-up child relationships

Figure 3.2 *HelloWorld widget tree*

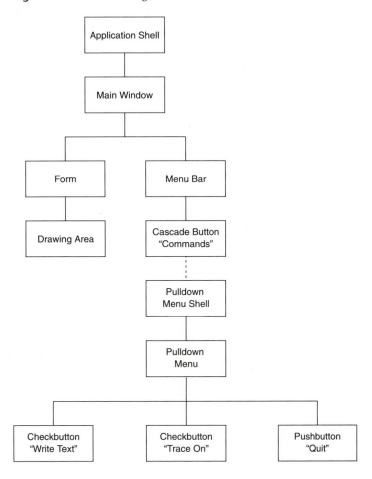

Most of the relationships between widgets, shown in Figure 3.2 as solid lines, are simple containments. If a widget contains another widget, the window for the child widget appears inside the window for the parent. The widget tree for *HelloWorld* shows that the Main Window widget contains a Menu Bar widget and a Form widget; the Menu Bar widget in turn contains a Cascade Button widget named Commands. The structure of the widget tree shows that the Menu Bar's window is inside the Main Window, and that the Commands Cascade Button widget is inside the Menu Bar.

The other type of parent-child relationship in the tree is the pop-up child relationship, shown in Figure 3.2 as a dashed line. The dashed line represents a logical relationship, not a visual one: the child's window is not inside the parent's window. Typically, the pop-up child is a menu or a dialog box—something that is logically related to its parent but not part of it. The widget tree for *HelloWorld* shows that the Commands Cascade Button widget is the pop-up parent for a Pulldown Menu widget.

3.2.2   Elements of a Display PostScript Application

Every Display PostScript application must contain the following elements:

- Global data declarations

- X and Motif initialization

- User interface creation

- Display PostScript initialization

- A main event loop

- Event processing procedures

- Exit processing

The global data declarations describe the data that the program will use. The initialization and creation steps are performed in the order listed, though the steps may be interleaved. The X Window System initialization procedures set up a connection to the X server and create a top-level application shell for the program. The creation of the user interface allocates the application windows in a Motif application by creating a tree of widgets. The Display PostScript system initialization procedures create a PostScript context, which can be thought of as a virtual printer that will send output to windows in the application instead of to paper. The main event loop waits for events from the X server and dispatches them to appropriate event-processing procedures. Some of these procedures perform imaging to the application drawing window using the PostScript context. The exit processing is the last step the application takes. Any application-specific initialization is normally done prior to Display PostScript initialization.

The application's user interface can be created in several ways. The most straightforward approach is to write code that calls procedures in the Motif library. The disadvantages to this method are that these procedures are complex, and you must modify the code to make changes to the user interface. Another approach is to employ interface building programs that let you interactively create the user interface and automatically generate the appropriate code. A third approach is to use a high-level user interface language to specify the user interface.

The programs in this book use the third approach, making use of UIL, the user interface language that accompanies Motif. The Motif programming environment includes a compiler that converts UIL files into a binary format called UID (user interface data). It also includes the Motif Resource Manager (MRM), which is a library that reads UID files and creates a user interface. Since UIL programming is independent of Display PostScript programming, it is not discussed in detail in this book; for information, see any of the books available on OSF/Motif.

3.2.3 HelloWorld Code Examples

The following sections discuss the code in the *HelloWorld* application, focusing on six areas that use Display PostScript functionality. These areas are listed below and are typical of all Display PostScript applications.

- PostScript execution contexts are created as part of the initial program setup (see Example 3.4).

- The **refreshWindow** procedure is the Expose callback for the main drawing area; it redraws the window depending on whether Write Text is toggled on or off (see Example 3.6).

- The **resizeWindow** procedure is the Resize callback for the main drawing area (see Example 3.8).

- The **writeProc** procedure is a callback associated with the Write Text menu item; it displays or erases "Hello World" in the main drawing area (see Example 3.9).

- The **traceProc** procedure is associated with the Trace On menu item; it calls procedures to enable or disable a text trace of the PostScript language code that the application executes (see Example 3.10).

- The **quitApp** procedure is associated with the Quit pushbutton; it destroys the PostScript execution context and exits the application (see Example 3.11).

Global Data Declarations

Example 3.1 shows the global data declarations for the *HelloWorld* application that are used in subsequent C code examples in this chapter.

Example 3.1 *Global data declarations*

C language code:

```
typedef struct {
  Widget      widget;   /* drawing area widget ID */
  DPSContext  dpsCtxt;  /* drawing DPS context */
  String      message;  /* message to display */
  Boolean     trace;    /* Send PostScript trace to stdout */
  Boolean     writeText; /* Toggle state to write the text */
} AppDataType, *AppDataTypePtr;

AppDataType AppData;
```

Initializing X Window System and Motif Components

When you initialize the X Window System, you must initialize
OSF/Motif and the X Toolkit also. The details are shown in Example 3.2,
which is followed by a description of each procedure.

Example 3.2 *X Window System initialization*

C language code:

```
void main (argc, argv)
  unsigned int argc;
  char **argv;
{
  XtAppContext appContext;
  Widget appShellWidget;
  Widget mainWindowWidget;
  /* Initialize MRM before initializing the X Toolkit */
  MrmInitialize ();

  /* Initialize the X Toolkit.
   * Get back an application shell widget. */
  appShellWidget = XtAppInitialize (&appContext, "Hello",
              (XrmOptionDescRec *)CommandLineOptions,
              XtNumber(CommandLineOptions),
              &argc, argv, (String *)FallbackResources,
              (ArgList)NULL, 0);

  XtGetApplicationResources (appShellWidget,
              (XtPointer)&AppData, Resources,
              XtNumber(Resources), (ArgList)NULL, 0);
```

```
/* Verify that DPS extension is present in the X server */
if (!XDPSExtensionPresent (XtDisplay(appShellWidget))) {
  fprintf (stderr, "%s: The Display PostScript system
          is not available\n", argv[0]);
  exit (1);
}
. . .
```

PG

The procedure **MrmInitialize** initializes MRM. This procedure notifies OSF/Motif that the application intends to use MRM to create the widgets that implement the user interface.

The procedure **XtAppInitialize** initializes the X Toolkit. This procedure initializes the Xt Intrinsics and the Motif toolkit, creates an X Toolkit application context, opens the display, and creates the Application Shell widget. The shell widget identifier is returned by the procedure.

Note: *Do not confuse an application context with a PostScript execution context. An application context has type* **XtAppContext** *and is an X Toolkit object. An execution context has type* **DPSContext** *and is a PostScript object.*

The procedure **XtGetApplicationResources** retrieves the customization settings that apply to the *HelloWorld* application.

The X Toolkit library procedure **XtDisplay** returns a pointer to the application's display and the Display PostScript Toolkit library procedure **XDPSExtensionPresent** determines whether the display supports the Display PostScript extension.

Creating the User Interface

Code to create the user interface varies depending on which method you use to define the user interface. Because the examples in this book use the OSF/Motif user interface language UIL, that method is briefly described here, but other methods are equally valid. Example 3.3 shows the user interface initialization in the *HelloWorld* application. This code continues the **main** procedure from the previous example.

Example 3.3 *User interface initialization*

C language code:

```
/* Open the UID files (the output of the UIL compiler) */
if (MrmOpenHierarchy (XtNumber(DbFilenameVec),
    DbFilenameVec, (MrmOsOpenParamPtr *) NULL,
    &SMrmHierarchy) != MrmSUCCESS) {
        fprintf (stderr, "Can't open hierarchy\n");
        exit (1);
}

/* Register the items MRM needs to bind for us.*/
MrmRegisterNames (RegList, XtNumber(RegList));

/* Get the main window for the application.*/
if (MrmFetchWidget (SMrmHierarchy, "MainWindow",
    appShellWidget, &mainWindowWidget, &DummyClass) !=
    MrmSUCCESS) {
        fprintf (stderr, "Can't fetch main window\n");
        exit (1);
}

/* Manage and realize the main window.
 * The interface comes up on the display now. */
XtManageChild (mainWindowWidget);
XtRealizeWidget (appShellWidget);

/* Do all the post-realization DPS/X processing here */
initDPSContext (appShellWidget);
    . . .
```

When a program uses UIL, the description of the user interface resides in separate files called UIL files, which must be compiled with the UIL compiler into UID files. Calling **MrmOpenHierarchy** opens the UID file for the application.

UIL files can contain named references to application objects like procedures. The application must associate real application objects with the UIL names; it does this by passing a table of name/value pairs to **MrmRegisterNames**.

Calling **MrmFetchWidget** creates the widget tree that was read in the earlier call to **MrmOpenHierarchy**. Calling **XtManageChild** informs the X Toolkit that the widget tree just created is the one the application wants to have visible. Finally, calling **XtRealizeWidget** makes that widget tree appear on the screen.

Display PostScript Initialization

After X Window System initialization is complete, the Display PostScript system must be initialized to create the PostScript execution context. Example 3.4 shows the Display PostScript initialization for the *HelloWorld* application.

Example 3.4 *Display PostScript initialization*

C language code:

```
void initDPSContext (shell)
  Widget shell;
{
  unsigned long mask = CWBitGravity;
  XSetWindowAttributes attr;
  Dimension height, width;

  /* Create the shared DPS context
   * in which rendering will occur */
  AppData.dpsCtxt = XDPSGetSharedContext (XtDisplay(shell));
  if (AppData.dpsCtxt == NULL) {
    printf ("Couldn't create a Display PostScript
            context.\n");
    exit (1);
  }

  /* Set the default DPS context */
  DPSSetContext (AppData.dpsCtxt);
  (void) XDPSSetEventDelivery(XtDisplay(shell),
        dps_event_pass_through);

  XtVaGetValues (AppData.widget,
                XmNwidth, &width, XmNheight, &height, NULL);

  if (XDPSSetContextDrawable(AppData.dpsCtxt,
    XtWindow(AppData.widget),height) != dps_status_success) {
    printf ("Couldn't set Display PostScript context
            drawable.\n");
    exit (1);
  }

  /* Change DPS origin to center of window and keep it there */
  PSsetXoffset(width/2, height/2);
  attr.bit_gravity = CenterGravity;
  XChangeWindowAttributes(XtDisplay(shell),
                          XtWindow(AppData.widget),
                          CWBitGravity, &attr);
```

```
        PSinitclip();
        PSinitviewclip();

        /* Create text context for trace option and
         * chain it if trace is on */
        XDPSChainTextContext (AppData.dpsCtxt, AppData.trace);
} /* end initDPSContext () */
```

The Display PostScript Toolkit procedure **XDPSGetSharedContext**
creates a PostScript execution context. Calling **DPSSetContext** sets the
new context as the one in which further drawing will occur, and calling
XDPSSetEventDelivery tells the client library that this application will
use pass-through event dispatching (see page CLX-28 in *Client Library
Supplement for X* for information on event dispatching).

The X Toolkit procedure **XtVaGetValues** gets the width and height of
the drawing area window with the parameters **XmNwidth** and
XmNheight. The Display PostScript Toolkit procedure
XDPSSetContextDrawable sets the execution context for use with a
particular drawable, in this example the main drawing area window.
The Display PostScript Client Library procedure **PSsetXoffset** sets the
origin of the PostScript language coordinate system to the center of the
drawing area widget. Calling **XChangeWindowAttributes** instructs the
X server to keep the origin in the center and to keep all graphics
centered if the window changes size. Calling **PSinitclip** and
PSinitviewclip initializes the window clipping areas to reflect the
window boundaries. Calling the Display PostScript Toolkit procedure
XDPSChainTextContext enables a debugging trace of all PostScript
language code that the application executes.

Handling Events with the Event Loop

After the initialization is complete, the application waits for events to
trigger any further action. Example 3.5 shows the callback event loop. It
is the conclusion of the **main** procedure that began in Example 3.2 and
continued in Example 3.3.

Example 3.5 *Callback event loop*

C language code:

```
    . . .
    /* Sit around forever waiting to process X and DPS events.
     * From here on, we only execute our callback routines. */
    while (1) {
      XEvent event;
      XtAppNextEvent(appContext, &event);
      if (!XDPSDispatchEvent(&event))
            (void) XtDispatchEvent(&event);
    }
}
```

The application never leaves its event dispatching loop. It repeats forever, waiting for events by calling **XtAppNextEvent** and dispatching them by calling **XDPSDispatchEvent** and **XtDispatchEvent**. If an event is a Display PostScript event, **XDPSDispatchEvent** will handle its dispatching and return true. Otherwise **XDPSDispatchEvent** returns false and the application passes the event to the **XtDispatchEvent** so the X Toolkit can dispatch it.

From this point onward, application flow is controlled by Motif and the X Toolkit. All subsequent activity in the application occurs in *callback procedures*—procedures invoked as a result of events dispatched through **XtDispatchEvent**.

Event Processing Procedures

The Expose callback is required in a Display PostScript application because drawing must not be done to a window until an Expose event has been received. If drawing is done before Expose event has been received, it may occur before the window appears on the screen and thereby fail to show up. The initial Expose event tells the application that it is safe to draw. In addition, an Expose event is received each time all or a portion of the drawing window becomes visible. The application must refresh the window at that time. Example 3.6 shows the Expose callback procedure **refreshWindow** for the *HelloWorld* application.

Example 3.6 *Expose callback procedure*

C language code:

```
void refreshWindow (w, clientData, callData)
  Widget w;
  XtPointer clientData, callData;
{
  register Display *dpy = XtDisplay(w);
  register Window window = XtWindow(w);
  XEvent event;

  /* Pseudo Exposure event compression
   * for the Drawing Area widget */
  if (XPending(dpy) > 0) {
    XPeekEvent(dpy, &event);
    if (event.type == Expose && event.xany.window == window)
      return;
  }

  /* Redraw if text is being shown */
  PSerasepage ();
  if (AppData.writeText) PSWDisplayText (AppData.message);
} /* end refreshWindow () */
```

When part of a window becomes visible, the X server sends the application a series of Expose events. Each Expose event contains one newly visible rectangular region of the window. Since the *HelloWorld* application is so simple, it redisplays its entire window any time part of the window becomes visible. To avoid multiple redisplays, it checks to see if there is another Expose event waiting in the event queue for the drawing window and doesn't redisplay if there is.

PSerasepage is a Display PostScript Client Library procedure that erases the display area. **PSWDisplayText** is a PostScript language wrap—a C-callable PostScript language procedure—that draws its message centered in the window. The procedure is defined for *pswrap* as shown in Example 3.7. Chapter 5 discusses wraps in detail.

Example 3.7 *Example pswrap definition*

Wrap definition:

```
defineps PSWDisplayText(char *text)
  /pointSize 72 def
  /Helvetica pointSize selectfont
  (text) stringwidth pop 2 div neg pointSize .3 mul neg
```

```
          moveto
   (text) show
endps
```

HelloWorld has a very simple Resize callback procedure. All it has to do is
reinitialize the clipping regions to reflect the new window size. It only
needs to do this if the widget is *realized* (has a window); otherwise the
call to the procedure is merely informational.

Example 3.8 *Resize event callback procedure*

C language code:

```
void resizeWindow (w, clientData, callData)
   Widget w;
   XtPointer clientData, callData;
{
   if (!XtIsRealized(w)) return;

   PSinitclip();
   PSinitviewclip();
} /* end resizeWindow () */
```

Other callback procedures are triggered when the user selects items
from the Commands menu. Motif calls the callback procedure
writeProc when the user toggles the Write Text checkbutton and the
callback procedure **traceProc** when the user toggles the Trace On
checkbutton. The callback procedures are shown in Example 3.9 and
Example 3.10.

Example 3.9 *Write Text toggle callback procedure*

C language code:

```
void writeProc (w, clientData, callData)
   Widget w;
   XtPointer clientData, callData;
{
   XmToggleButtonCallbackStruct *toggle =
                (XmToggleButtonCallbackStruct *)callData;

   AppData.writeText = toggle->set;
```

```
                          /* Draw the text to the drawing area window */
                          PSerasepage ();
                          if (AppData.writeText) PSWDisplayText (AppData.message);
                       } /* end writeProc () */
```

All callback procedures have the same parameters: *widget*, the widget
that the callback is being invoked for, *clientData*, a piece of data that the
application can specify, and *callData*, a piece of data sent by the widget
set. The documentation for each type of callback describes the format of
callData for that callback type. Callbacks associated with changes in
toggle buttons pass the address of an *XmToggleButtonCallbackStruct*
structure. The **writeProc** procedure casts the *callData* parameter into a
pointer to this structure and sets the application flag *AppData.writeText*
depending on whether the user set or cleared the Write Text
checkbutton. If the user set the checkbutton, **PSWDisplayText** is called
to show the text.

Example 3.10 *Trace On toggle callback procedure*

C language code:

```
  void traceProc (w, clientData, callData)
    Widget w;
    XtPointer clientData, callData;
  {
    XmToggleButtonCallbackStruct *toggle =
                  (XmToggleButtonCallbackStruct *)callData;

    /* Change the state of the toggle flag */

    AppData.trace = toggle->set;

    /* Chain text context for trace option if trace is on */

    XDPSChainTextContext (AppData.dpsCtxt, AppData.trace);
  } /* end traceProc () */
```

The **traceProc** procedure sets the *AppData.trace* flag in a similar way. The
procedure **XDPSChainTextContext** either enables or disables a text trace
depending on the value of the flag.

A text trace is the most important debugging tool in Display PostScript
development. It provides a listing of all the PostScript language code
that the application sends to the PostScript interpreter. This trace can
be quite voluminous for a complex application so the ability to turn it

on only around suspect code is a useful feature. Of course, the Trace On menu item is removed before the final version of an application is released.

Exit Processing

Display PostScript applications can exit by calling the Standard C Library procedure **exit**. All server resources (windows, fonts, pixmaps, PostScript execution contexts, and so forth) that the application was using are automatically reclaimed by the X server. Some applications have to continue on with other tasks after closing down one particular connection, so *HelloWorld* shows the steps involved in cleaning up a connection.

If an application uses **XDPSGetSharedContext** to create its PostScript context, the context should be destroyed with **XDPSDestroySharedContext**. Applications that create contexts directly with **XDPSCreateContext** or **XDPSCreateSimpleContext** should call

```
DPSDestroySpace(DPSSpaceFromContext(context));
```

to destroy the context and free all its associated memory.

Applications that need to close a display connection and still continue should call **XtCloseDisplay** to close the connection. To close all displays in an application context, call **XtDestroyApplicationContext**.

The Commands menu in *HelloWorld* contains the Quit pushbutton. Motif calls the **quitApp** callback procedure when the user chooses this button. Example 3.11 shows the callback procedure for exit processing.

Example 3.11 *Exit processing*

C language code:

```
void quitApp (w, clientData, callData)
  Widget w;
  XtPointer clientData, callData;
{
  if (AppData.dpsCtxt != NULL)
      XDPSDestroySharedContext (AppData.dpsCtxt);

  /* Close the X display and free all X resources. */
  XtDestroyApplicationContext (
                XtWidgetToApplicationContext (w));
  exit (0);
} /* end quitApp () */
```

3.3   Compiling a Display PostScript Application

A Display PostScript application is comprised of several types of source files: C language files, *pswrap* files, and sometimes UIL files.

To compile the C language file, use a command line like the following:

```
cc -c -D_NO_PROTO -I/usr/local/include HelloMain.c
```

where

-c indicates that only a compilation is to be performed.

-D_NO_PROTO

the _NO_PROTO preprocessor symbol controls whether the Display PostScript header files declare ANSI C function prototypes or the older, nonprototyped function declarations. When _NO_PROTO is asserted, the header files do not declare function prototypes.

-I...

this flag indicates the include directories to search (they vary from system to system). You only need to specify this flag if the X and Display PostScript header files are not installed in a directory that is searched by default.

Other machine-dependent flags may be necessary for a particular system.

To translate a *pswrap* source file into a C language file and compile it, use command lines similar to the following:

```
pswrap -o HelloWraps.c -h HelloWraps.h HelloWraps.psw
cc -c -D_NO_PROTO -I/usr/local/include HelloWraps.c
```

See Chapter 5 for a full explanation of the *pswrap* command line
options.

Once all the C language source files are compiled, link the object files
using a command line such as the following:

```
cc -o hello HelloMain.o HelloWraps.o -L/usr/lib
      -ldpstk -ldps -lMrm -lXm -lXt -lX11 -lm
```

where

-o indicates that the next entry is the output file. It is followed by the
   list of object files that are the linker input.

-L...
   indicates the directory containing the link libraries. You only need to
   specify this flag if the X and Display PostScript libraries are not
   installed in a directory that is searched by default.

-l...
   lists the link libraries. Include them in the order listed in Table 3.1.

Table 3.1 *Link libraries*

Library	Description
dpstk	Display PostScript Toolkit library
dps	Display PostScript Client Library
Mrm	Motif Resource Manager library
Xm	Motif toolkit library
Xt	X Toolkit (Xt Intrinsics) library
X11	X library (Xlib)

The order in which the link libraries are listed in the command line is
important because of calls from one library procedure to procedures in
another library down the hierarchy of layers. On many systems the
math library, *-lm*, is required by the Display PostScript Client Library.
Also, any application that uses the font selection panel must include
the Display PostScript Toolkit library for Motif *-ldpstkXm* and the
PostScript language resource location library *-lpsres*. In this case the link
order is as follows:

```
-ldpstkXm -ldpstk -lpsres -ldps -lMrm -lXm -lXt -lX11 -lm
```

The UIL file is compiled using a command line such as the following:

```
uil -o Hello.uid Hello.uil
```

The *-o* flag indicates that the next entry is the output file. The last entry is the input source file.

Note: *If you are using the* make *utility, it is best to have rules that compile* pswrap *files into objects and delete the intermediate C files. If you don't do this, the* make *utility will not automatically recompile* pswrap *files when they change. Here are the recommended Makefile rules for building* pswrap *objects:*

```
.psw.o :
    pswrap -o $*.c -h $*.h $<
    cc -c $(CFLAGS) $*.c
    rm $*.c
```

3.4   Summary

- Display PostScript applications use the PostScript language for drawing, but are otherwise identical to other X Window System applications.

- UIL provides an easy way to lay out the user interface and widget hierarchy, thus separating the form from the execution of the C language source code.

- Display PostScript applications must first initialize the X Window System environment and then the Display PostScript environment.

- X Window System initialization involves calls to procedures in the Motif toolkit and X Toolkit. Display PostScript initialization involves calls to procedures in the Display PostScript Toolkit and Display PostScript Client Library.

- Events from user interactions are attached to callback procedures in the C source code.

CHAPTER 4

The Coordinate System

An important advantage of the PostScript language is device independence. One way that device independence is achieved is through a coordinate system that is independent of the resolution of any screen. The PostScript interpreter maps paths defined in this coordinate system to device pixels as part of the rendering process. This coordinate system allows you to perform linear transformations such as scaling and rotating text and graphics. This in turn allows scalable fonts, text on a curve, and intricate objects rotated at any angle.

This chapter focuses on the coordinate system. It also discusses the relationship between a path, which determines where a line ideally would be displayed on the screen, and pixels, which determine where a line is actually displayed. Different path positions can affect the width of the line that is displayed. The PostScript interpreter can adjust lines to a uniform width regardless of path placement. This automatic stroke adjustment is the default behavior of the Display PostScript system, and it can be turned on and off.

The *StrokeAdjust* application is used to show the effect of stroke adjustment at the pixel level. Although stroke adjustment is not as much of an issue on high resolution devices, it often results in significant improvement in the appearance of graphics on low-resolution devices such as computer screens.

Note: *Automatic stroke adjustment is not available in PostScript Level 1 printers, so as a general rule applications should include stroke adjustment emulation procedures in their page descriptions when printing to PostScript Level 1 printers (see section 4.6).*

4.1 User Space and Device Space

The PostScript language coordinate system actually contains two coordinate systems: user space and device space. *User space* is used for all drawing. For example, in the statement **50 100 moveto**, the numbers refer to the point (50, 100) in user space, which is 50 units to the right and 100 units above the user space origin. The initial user space system is the same on any display or printing device. A drawn point appears in the same location in user space on any device.

Default user space attributes can be changed. Initially, the positive *y* axis extends vertically upward and the positive *x* axis extends horizontally to the right. The origin can be placed anywhere in the window, but it is usually in the lower left corner. The default length of a unit along the *x* axis and along the *y* axis is 1/72 of an inch. Some Display PostScript implementations use different default unit sizes because the true resolution of the workstation screen is not available to the PostScript interpreter. Because this is simply a uniform scale applied to the entire screen, it rarely presents any problems.

The second coordinate system, *device space*, is not device independent. A point in device space can, and most often will, appear in different locations on different devices. Device space is used to address actual pixels within the image area. Because devices vary in resolution and imaging direction, different device space coordinate system representations are necessary and contain different origins, axis orientations, and unit lengths. In the Display PostScript extension to X, the device space coordinates correspond to X's standard, pixel-based coordinate system.

Most of the time you do not need to be aware of how device space differs from one device to another because the PostScript interpreter performs the translation from user space to device space automatically. As a result, the application does not need to be concerned with printing or displaying to different types of devices. One set of drawing instructions relative to a single coordinate system is sufficient. The interpreter handles the translation from user space to device space for a given device, deciding which pixels are turned on and which are not.

In Figure 4.1, the user space is on the left and two different device spaces appear on the right. The first device space is from a typical X Window System display; the second is from a typical laser printer (300 dpi). Each has a different origin and a different unit length from those in the user space. In each case, the interpreter manages the mapping from user space to device space.

Figure 4.1 *User space to device space mapping*

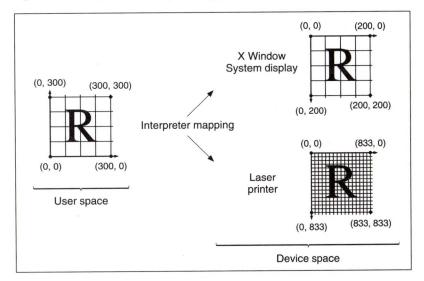

Displays used with the X Window System can vary considerably in device space unit size (the pixel size on the screen). Because a Display PostScript application must still deal with X Window System coordinates (for example, in mouse events), some knowledge of the X Window System coordinate system and its relation to PostScript user space is required. Coordinate system conversions are described in Section 4.3.

4.2 Transforming Coordinate Systems

The conversion from one coordinate system to another is specified by a transformation matrix called the *current transformation matrix* (CTM). This matrix is used to transform coordinates from user space to device space by mapping x and y values for a point in user space into the x and y values of the corresponding point in device space. The current transformation matrix can be changed to cause a different mapping from user space to device space.

One way to understand the alteration of the current transformation matrix is to visualize the user space changing, as shown in Figure 4.2.

Figure 4.2 *User space transformations*

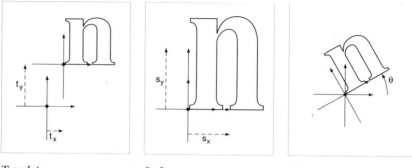

Translate   Scale   Rotate

- The **translate** operator moves the origin to a different location in device space, leaving the orientation of the axes and the unit size unchanged.

- The **scale** operator alters the units of the axes independently of each other, changing the length of a unit. For example, the coordinate system can be scaled so that a unit in the *y* direction is actually twice the size of a unit in the *x* direction.

- The **rotate** operator rotates the coordinate system around the origin by the specified angle and alters the angle of the axes.

These transformation types provide many ways to simplify drawing and produce interesting results. Examples include the following:

- The same path description can be used to display a path at any angle if the user space is rotated before the path is displayed.

- The same circle description can be used to display any type of oval if the circle is scaled or rotated before it is displayed.

- A drawing can be displayed at different magnifications by scaling the user space uniformly in the *x* and *y* directions.

For an explanation of the matrix mathematics involved in the current transformation matrix, refer to section 4.3 in the *PostScript Language Reference Manual, Second Edition.*

4.3   Converting Coordinates

In the X Window System, window sizes are specified in pixel units. The UIL code for the *Stroke* application creates two drawing areas that are 400 pixels high and 330 pixels wide. These pixels correspond to coordinates in device space. Because the program does all its calculations for spacing lines in user space, it needs to convert the window size from X Window System coordinates into user space.

To convert a user space coordinate into an actual pixel coordinate in an X window, the Display PostScript system transforms the coordinate by means of the current transformation matrix. It then adds in the offset between the X Window System origin and the device space origin. To reverse this conversion (that is, to convert X Window System coordinates back into user space), subtract the origin offset from an X Window System coordinate and transform the result by the inverse of the current transformation matrix.

Example 4.1 shows the code that implements this conversion. See section 5.2.2 on page PG-62 for details of the **PSWGetTransform** procedure.

Example 4.1 *Converting a window size to user space*

C language code:

```
#define A_COEFF 0
#define B_COEFF 1
#define C_COEFF 2
#define D_COEFF 3
#define TX_CONS 4
#define TY_CONS 5

void getTransform()
{
  Dimension width;
  float ctm[6], invctm[6];
  int xOffset, yOffset, x, y;

  /* Get the transform matrices */
  PSWGetTransform(ctm, invctm, &xOffset, &yOffset);

  /* Get the width of the drawing area in pixels*/
  XtVaGetValues(window1, XtNwidth, &width, NULL);

  /* Compute the height and width of the drawing area
   * in user space */
```

```
    x = (int) width;
    y = 0;
    x -= xOffset;
    y -= yOffset;
    width = invctm[A_COEFF] * x + invctm[C_COEFF] * y +
            invctm[TX_CONS];
    height = invctm[B_COEFF] * x + invctm[D_COEFF] * y +
            invctm[TY_CONS];
} /* end getTransform () */
```

This code converts the upper right corner of the window, (*width*, 0) in X Window System coordinates, into user space. Since the origin was previously set to the lower left corner, the result is the window size in user space units.

A full description of this conversion can be found on page CLX-13 and following pages in *Client Library Supplement for X*. However, you don't need to understand all the underlying mathematics to use the formulas from the example.

Another common use for the formulas is to convert the coordinates in X events into user space. Because the transformation matrices and offsets rarely change, you should save the results of **PSWGetTransform** to avoid the delay of sending a request to the server and waiting for it to return results. Eliminating such round-trips is one of the most effective ways to make any X application run faster. Have your application call **PSWGetTransform** only when the transform matrix changes—that is, when the coordinate system has been transformed or the origin moved.

You can also convert user space coordinates into X Window System coordinates. To do so, multiply the user space coordinates by the current transformation matrix and adding in the offset. This conversion is not nearly as common as converting in the opposite direction.

Table 4.1 summarizes the calculations required to convert between PostScript user space coordinates, X Window System coordinates, and PostScript device space coordinates.

Table 4.1 *Coordinate system conversion summary*

Start with...	And perform this calculation...	To find...
PostScript user space coordinates	Multiply by the current transformation matrix	PostScript device space coordinates
PostScript device space coordinates	Add the X Window System offset	X Window System coordinates
X Window System coordinates	Subtract the X Window System offset	PostScript device space coordinates
PostScript device space coordinates	Multiply by the inverse of the current transformation matrix	PostScript user space coordinates

4.4   Drawing with Paths

A *path* in the PostScript language is a set of line, arc, and Bézier curve segments. These segments can be continuous (having a single **moveto** operator) or disjoint (having multiple **moveto** operators interspersed within the set). The segments within a path have no width, and the shape formed by the path does not appear on the page until the path is rendered with a painting operator such as **stroke** or **fill**.

At the time the path is drawn, values for the current graphics state variables are used to determine which pixels to turn on. Line width or color settings are taken into account only when **stroke** or **fill** execute. For example, you cannot draw a multicolored path by changing the current color between path construction operators; each color must be a separately stroked path.

Executing **fill** fills the inside of the path with the current color. The fill does not extend outside the path, although any pixel that the path passes through is colored.

Stroking a path extends the width of the path by the current line width setting. One half of the line width extends on each side of the path. The line width is expressed in user space units so that any scaling operation has a corresponding effect on the line width.

The examples in Figure 4.3 show a path and its subsequent stroking and filling in an unspecified device space. The path is a mathematical representation of an arc. The stroked path and the filled path are the pixel representations in device space.

Figure 4.3 *Path, stroked path, and filled path*

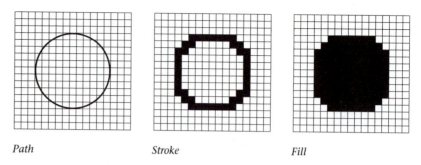

Path   *Stroke*   *Fill*

4.5   The StrokeAdjust Application

The placement of the path within a pixel is a factor in determining which pixels to turn on when stroking. Figure 4.4 shows four instances of a vertical path falling at different locations within a pixel column. In the first case, a line width setting equivalent to one pixel in device space results in a one-pixel line. In the second, third, and fourth cases, a line width setting equal to one pixel results in a two-pixel line. In the first case, the line width does not extend across pixel boundaries; in the others it does.

Figure 4.4 *Mapping line widths to device space*

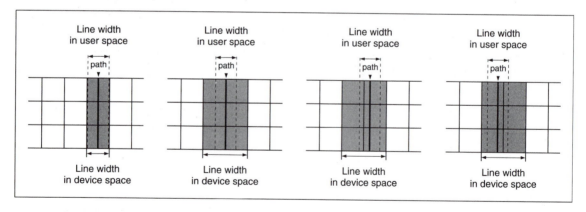

The *StrokeAdjust* application shown in Figure 4.5 illustrates the effect that line position has on the actual pixel width of lines. For high-resolution devices, the location of a path relative to the pixel grid is not important because the pixel size is so small that an additional pixel is difficult to detect. For lower resolution devices such as a computer screen or a 300-dpi printer, different positions of the path within a pixel can cause noticeable variation in the rendered stroke width. This behavior can cause unattractive results when a grid or another symmetrical group of lines is displayed. The improved look of the lines in the right drawing panel in Figure 4.5 is the result of stroke adjustment.

Figure 4.5 *StrokeAdjust main window*

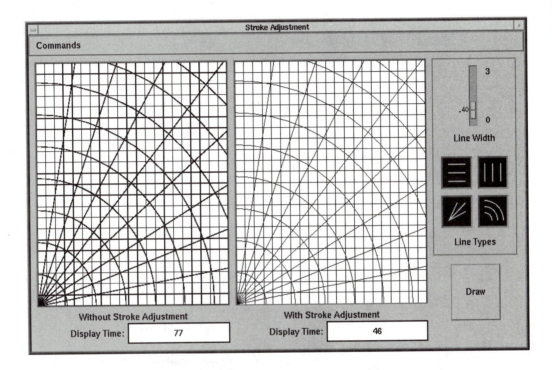

The Display PostScript system can adjust the location automatically to produce lines with a uniform pixel width. The system works by adjusting the placement of every path so the paths fall at precise locations within pixels. This adjustment is, by default, turned on in displays and turned off in Level 2 printers; it can be turned on or off with the **setstrokeadjust** operator.

The effect on performance of stroke adjustment depends on the line width. Stroke adjustment never slows rendering by more than a few percentage points, and it often speeds rendering considerably. Lines drawn with stroke adjustment turned on usually have fewer pixels rendered than the corresponding lines without stroke adjustment, and

---

Stroke Adjustment

Drawing times for line width of 0.40 in milliseconds

Without stroke adjustment	77
With stroke adjustment	43

this translates into better graphics performance. In particular, stroke-adjusted lines are more likely than nonadjusted lines to be one pixel wide, a width for which Display PostScript is highly optimized.

4.6 Printing

The Display PostScript system performs stroke adjustment automatically, producing lines of uniform width. In Level 2 printers, stroke adjustment is turned off by default, although turning it on is a simple matter of using the **setstrokeadjust** operator. Level 1 printers have no automatic stroke adjustment, so the functionality must be emulated.

For a complete description of how to emulate stroke adjustment, see Technical Note #5111, *Emulation of the setstrokeadjust Operator*, which is distributed as part of the PostScript Language Software Development Kit.

4.7 Summary

- The PostScript language imaging model achieves device independence by using two coordinate systems—device space, which is tied to the device, and user space, which is independent of the device and consistent across all interpreters. The unit size in device space corresponds to the resolution of the device, while the unit size in user space is a consistent 1/72 inch on all devices. The PostScript interpreter handles the mapping from user space to device space.

- The PostScript language allows linear transformations such as scaling, rotating, and translating of text, graphics, and images.

- X Window system coordinates must be translated into user space for use with a Display PostScript drawing.

- Stroke adjustment is a Display PostScript system feature that automatically adjusts paths to device space to produce consistent pixel widths for lines with the same line widths. This feature is also available on PostScript Level 2 printers.

- A similar stroke adjustment capability can be provided for in Level 1 printers by emulating the functionality and adjusting paths in device space.

CHAPTER 5

Single-Operator Procedures and Wraps

This chapter examines three mechanisms for communicating with the server: using **DPSPrintf** to send PostScript language code as text, calling *single-operator procedures* from the Display PostScript Client Library, and wrapped procedures, or *wraps*, created with the *pswrap* translator. Code examples taken from the sample application *LineDraw* show several ways to draw lines using each mechanism. Each example is accompanied by performance figures that give you a basis for comparing the methods used.

Additional examples illustrate the following techniques:

- Binding procedures in the wraps to speed up PostScript language execution.

- Postponing the drawing of a line until it changes width or color. This technique, called *delayed stroking*, is particularly effective when all lines have the same width and color. It can improve display time by 40% over a wrap that strokes every line and by 50% over single-operator procedures.

- Performing large amounts of data manipulation in the server. This is a technique to be avoided, as the example illustrates. Most computation and data manipulation should be done in the application.

- Drawing narrow lines. Lines that are one pixel wide in device space have been made a special case within the Display PostScript system. As a result, they display much more quickly than wider lines.

Using **DPSPrintf** to format the data is a method that will be familiar to you if you have ever written an application that generates a PostScript language file for printing. However, it is much slower than the other methods presented here and is not recommended for use with the Display PostScript system.

The use of single-operator procedures is straightforward. Wraps are more complex, are new to many readers, and are the most efficient way to communicate with the interpreter, so this chapter devotes greater space to explaining their use. A wrap contains a custom sequence of PostScript operations tailored to the needs of a particular application. The *pswrap* translator takes wrap source files and converts them into callable C procedures.

5.1   Single-Operator Procedures

The Client Library contains the procedures needed to communicate with the PostScript interpreter. One subset of the Client Library is a collection of C procedures called single-operator procedures, or *single-ops*. Each single-op executes a single PostScript operator. An example is **PSmoveto**, which is equivalent to the **moveto** operator. The **PSmoveto** procedure takes an (*x, y*) coordinate pair and makes it the current point in the graphics state. Every PostScript operator has a corresponding single-op.

The Client Library contains two sets of procedures that invoke single PostScript operators. These sets are identical except for the following differences:

- Members of the first group, defined in *<DPS/dpsops.h>*, take as their first argument an explicit execution context in which to execute the operator. Each procedure in this group begins with the letters DPS.

- Members of second group, defined in *<DPS/psops.h>*, do not take a context argument because the operators execute within the current context. Each procedure in this group begins with the letters PS.

Each PostScript operator has a corresponding single-op in *<DPS/dpsops.h>* and *<DPS/psops.h>*. Examples of each type for the operator **moveto** appear in Example 5.1.

Example 5.1 *Sample single-operator definitions*

C language code:

```
DPSmoveto(DPSContext ctxt; float x, y);

PSmoveto(float x, y);
```

Most PostScript operators take operands. These operands are usually specified as arguments to the corresponding single-op, as in the **DPSmoveto** and the **PSmoveto** procedures. However, some single-ops require operands even though they do not take arguments. Instead, they consume operands from the operand stack, a scheme that allows them to operate on a variety of data types. The **PSadd** procedure is an example. Although the **add** operator requires two operands, the corresponding **PSadd** procedure takes no arguments. The operands required by **PSadd** must be left on the stack by an operation or wrap that appears before the procedure.

One way to place data on the stack is by using the **PSsend...** set of single-ops: **PSsendboolean, PSsendchararray, PSsendfloat, PSsendfloatarray, PSsendint, PSsendintarray,** and **PSsendstring**. Each of these procedures takes an argument of the appropriate type and places it on the stack. Other procedures can then be used to perform operations on those arguments. You can use a corresponding set of **PSget...** procedures to retrieve objects from the operand stack.

Example 5.2 shows how to use the single-ops to compute $3.5 \times 4 + 1$ and return the result in the floating-point variable *answer*. Note the ability to mix floating-point and integer types in the calculation.

Example 5.2 *Using the stack*

C language code:

```
float answer;
PSsendfloat(3.5);              /*  Stack is 3.5 */
PSsendint(4);                  /*  Stack is 3.5 4 */
PSmul( );                      /*  Stack is 14.0 */
PSsendint(1);                  /*  Stack is 14.0 1 */
PSadd( );                      /*  Stack is 15.0 */
PSgetfloat(&answer);           /*  Stack is empty */
```

Note: *Example 5.2 illustrates one of the slowest ways to compute; it is included only to show how the **PSsend…** and **PSget…** procedures work and how to use procedures that consume operands previously placed on the stack. The PostScript language is better suited for imaging than for computation.*

Always look up the description of single-ops and check the argument types and the number of arguments. Passing incorrect arguments, especially integers in parameters that should be floating point, is a common error with single-ops.

5.1.1   Explicit and Implicit Contexts

Most applications use only one context. Therefore, the **PS…** versions of single-operator procedures with no context parameter are used most often. They execute in the context previously set by the procedure **DPSSetContext**. If you frequently switch between contexts, use the **DPS…** versions instead to avoid having to set explicitly each context before writing to it.

5.2   Wraps

The *pswrap* translator takes PostScript language code and turns it into a C-callable procedure. The procedure can pass arguments to and receive results from the PostScript interpreter. The advantage of *pswrap* is that it lets you group a set of PostScript operators into a single procedure that you can call from your application. This approach is similar to providing a C function interface to a FORTRAN library. The single-ops found in the Client Library are actually predefined wraps.

Because a wrap can receive results from the PostScript interpreter, it provides a convenient way for an application to query the server for information. A single wrap, which requires only one round-trip to the server, can receive multiple values. Retrieving the same information with single-ops can add up to a costly performance penalty because each single-op requires its own round-trip.

The *pswrap* translator is a standalone program that works like a compiler. The input file contains a text representation of PostScript language code. The output is two files: a source-level C file containing the wrap bodies and a header file containing the external declarations. See *pswrap Reference Manual* for complete command-line syntax and examples of how to use *pswrap*.

The C output file consists mainly of data structures that define the PostScript language code and calls to Client Library routines. The Client Library encodes any wrap arguments into a binary format at run time and sends them to the server along with the PostScript language code.

Figure 5.1 illustrates how wraps become part of the program, using the *LineDraw* application as an example.

- In step 1, the *pswrap* command is executed with arguments that translate the PostScript language source file *LineWraps.psw* into two C files: the source file *LineWraps.c*, which contains the wrap bodies, and the header file *LineWraps.h*, which contains external declarations for the wraps.

- In step 2, the C compiler is called to compile the C source files into object files. At least some of these files include the header files produced by *pswrap*.

- In step 3, the object files are linked to produce the executable output.

Figure 5.1 *pswrap translator process*

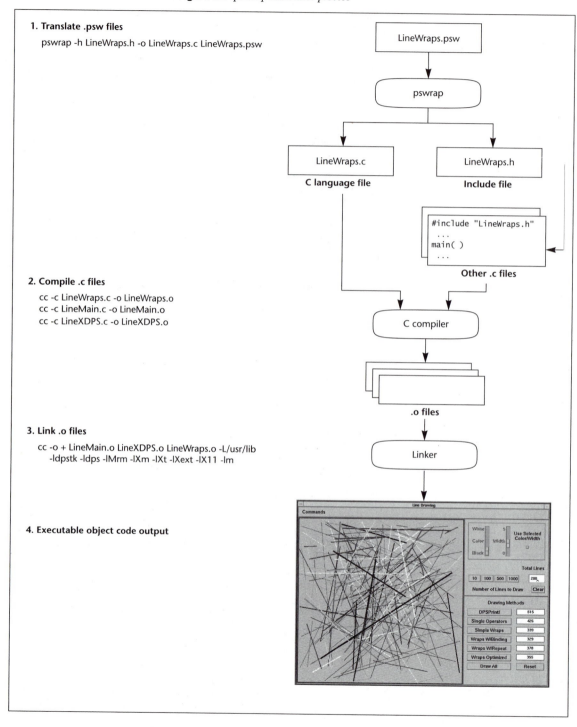

1. Translate .psw files

pswrap -h LineWraps.h -o LineWraps.c LineWraps.psw

LineWraps.psw

pswrap

LineWraps.c

C language file

LineWraps.h

Include file

```
#include "LineWraps.h"
...
main( )
...
```

Other .c files

2. Compile .c files

cc -c LineWraps.c -o LineWraps.o
cc -c LineMain.c -o LineMain.o
cc -c LineXDPS.c -o LineXDPS.o

C compiler

.o files

3. Link .o files

cc -o + LineMain.o LineXDPS.o LineWraps.o -L/usr/lib
-ldpstk -ldps -lMrm -lXm -lXt -lXext -lX11 -lm

Linker

4. Executable object code output

5.2.1 Wrap Definitions

This section briefly describes the syntax of a wrap definition. See the *pswrap Reference Manual* for a more comprehensive explanation of the wrap syntax.

Example 5.3 lists a sample *pswrap* source file, *examplewraps.psw*, and a call to the resulting C procedure, **PSWDrawLine**. The #include statement in the wrap invocation reads in the *examplewraps.h* file that was created when *pswrap* translated the wrap definition. This wrap takes two coordinates as arguments, constructs a path between the coordinates, and strokes the path to draw the line on the screen.

Example 5.3 *Sample wrap definition*

Wrap definition:

```
/* Wrap definition - examplewraps.psw */
defineps PSWDrawLine(float x1, y1, x2, y2)
    newpath
    x1 y1 moveto
    x2 y2 lineto
    stroke
endps
```

C language code (wrap invocation):

```
/* Wrap call in a C program */
#include "examplewraps.h"

main( )
{
    . . .
    PSWDrawLine(100.0, 100.0, 200.0, 200.0);
    . . .
}
```

Note that wrap definition files take the suffix *.psw* by convention, and wrap names take the prefix **PSW**.

As Example 5.3 illustrates, each wrap definition contains three parts:

- a *defineps/endps* pair
- a C procedure definition (including argument types)
- PostScript language code

Starting and Ending a Wrap Definition

Every wrap must be enclosed between *defineps* and *endps* keywords, and each keyword must start at the beginning of a new line. All the text between the pairing, except the procedure definition, must be PostScript language code. The *pswrap* translator processes the code and converts it into C code. All text not included between the pairings passes through to the source level C file untouched. Comments inside each *defineps/endps* pair must be PostScript language comments (% ....). Comments outside *defineps/endps* must be C comments (/* .... */).

C Procedure Definition for a Wrap

The procedure definition contains the procedure name and the argument list in parentheses. The procedure type is *void*, but this is implicit and should not be included as part of the definition. No other return type is possible. By default the procedure names are external, but they can be declared static if you place *static* on a separate line immediately before *defineps*.

Arguments can be passed to the server and returned from the server if included arguments are declared within parentheses immediately following the procedure name. Parentheses are required even for wraps without arguments. If the wrap has output parameters, they follow the input parameters, separated from them by a vertical bar (|). Example 5.4 on page PG-63 shows an example of this usage.

PostScript Language Code

All text between the keywords *defineps* and *endps* must be PostScript operators, comments, or arguments declared in the procedure definition. The *pswrap* translator converts the text into an efficient binary encoding but does not validate the operations. Errors in the body of a wrap are not caught during translation but instead cause exceptions at run time.

5.2.2 Returning Values in Wraps

Section 4.3 on page PG-49 described how to transform coordinates from the X coordinate system into PostScript user space using **PSWGetTransform** to find the current transformation matrix. The implementation of the wrap **PSWGetTransform** provides a good example of how wraps handle returned values. Example 5.4 shows its implementation.

Example 5.4 *PSWGetTransform*

Wrap definition:

```
defineps PSWGetTransform(DPSContext Ctxt | float Ctm[6],
                         Invctm[6]; int *XOffset, *YOffset)
    matrix currentmatrix dup Ctm
    matrix invertmatrix Invctm
    currentXoffset YOffset XOffset
endps
```

C language code:

```
float ctm[6], invctm[6];
int xOffset, yOffset;
PSWGetTransform(dpsCtxt, ctm, invctm, &xOffset,
                &yOffset);
```

The vertical bar (|) in the parameter list identifies *Ctm, Invctm, XOffset,* and *YOffset* as output parameters. Output parameters must be pointer or array types and must appear after any input parameters.

Each appearance of an output parameter in a wrap body generates code to remove the topmost value from the operand stack and store that value into the storage the parameter points to. For example, in the above wrap, the code

```
matrix currentmatrix dup
```

leaves two copies of the current transformation matrix on the operand stack. The following output parameter, *Ctm,* pops the top matrix from the stack and returns it to the application, where it is stored in the *ctm* array. Later, **currentXoffset** pushes first the *x* and then the *y* offset onto the stack, leaving the *y* offset on top. *YOffset* pops the top value from the stack and returns it to the application, then *XOffset* does the same with the new top value. Correct ordering is important when returning multiple values from a wrap.

Because an occurrence of an output parameter removes the top value from the stack, the value is no longer on the stack for further use. If the wrap needs to return a value and use it later on, it should use **dup** as shown in Example 5.4.

If an output parameter occurs more than once within the body of a wrap, the results depend on the parameter type. For full details, see *pswrap Reference Manual,* section 6, on page PSW-25.

5.3   The LineDraw Application

This section presents the *LineDraw* application, which draws randomly oriented lines of different colors and widths. The application compares three techniques for communicating with the PostScript interpreter: using **DPSPrintf** to write the data, using single-operator procedures from the Client Library, and using wraps created with the *pswrap* translator. To evaluate alternate approaches to writing wraps, *LineDraw* can draw with four different wraps.

The main window of the *LineDraw* application is shown in Figure 5.2.

Figure 5.2 *LineDraw application main window*

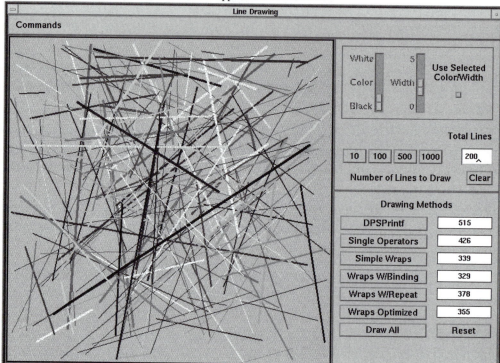

5.3.1   LineDraw User Interface

The main window of *LineDraw* contains a menu bar, a drawing area, a line width and color selection area, a lines-to-draw area, and a drawing methods area.

The color and width slide bars let the user choose the color and width of the lines to draw. When the user turns on the Color/Width toggle, *LineDraw* uses the color and width from the slide bar settings; otherwise, *LineDraw* randomizes both line width and gray value. The user can choose the number of lines to draw by clicking on 10, 100, 500, or 1,000. The user can also specify the number of lines to draw (up to 1,000) by entering the number in the command area. Clicking Clear clears the number of lines to draw.

The drawing methods area lets the user draw lines using six different methods:

- DPSPrintf—calls **DPSPrintf** to format the data and send it to the interpreter as text (see Example 5.6).

- Single-Operator Procedures—calls the Display PostScript Client Library directly and does not use a wrap (see Example 5.7).

- Simple Wraps—calls one wrap for every line drawn (see Example 5.8).

- Wraps with Binding—similar to Simple Wraps except that the wraps use PostScript language procedures instead of individual operators (see Example 5.9).

- Wraps with Repeat—passes in arrays of *x*, *y* coordinates, colors, and widths (see Example 5.10).

- Wraps Optimized—same as Wraps with Binding except that it groups together lines with the same color and width for stroking (see Example 5.11).

5.3.2   LineDraw Implementation Details

LineDraw defines six arrays of floating-point numbers, *X*, *Y*, *X1*, *Y1*, *C*, and *W*, to store the values that are used to draw the lines. The arrays store the starting *x* and *y* coordinates, the ending *x* and *y* coordinates, and the color and line width for each line. These arrays are filled when the user activates controls in the user interface.

Values for each line's starting and ending *x* and *y* coordinates are generated with the **random** procedure and are modified to fall within the bounding rectangle of the drawing area in the application. The color and line width can be set to specific values for each set of lines or generated randomly, again modified to fall within certain ranges. The performance results show that different methods are best depending on whether the application is drawing uniform lines or lines that vary in width and color.

Each method for displaying lines is contained in a separate C routine. *LineDraw* executes the appropriate routine when the user selects the button for a specific drawing operation. Each routine works from the same set of data. Example 5.5 shows some of the data declarations common to all routines.

Example 5.5 *Data declarations*

C language code:

```
DPSContext dpsCtxt;      /* drawing DPS context */
float width, height;     /* DPS size of the X Window */

float X[MAXARRAY];       /* X coordinate of start point*/
float Y[MAXARRAY];       /* Y coordinate of start point*/
float X1[MAXARRAY];      /* X coordinate of end point */
float Y1[MAXARRAY];      /* Y coordinate of end point */
float C[MAXARRAY];       /* gray scale color value */
float W[MAXARRAY];       /* line width */
```

5.3.3   DPSPrintf Method

DPSPrintf
Drawing times for 1,000 lines in milliseconds
Uniform width & color   2,283
Random width & color   2,605

DPSPrintf formats data like the C library **printf** procedure. The first argument is the context to send the data to, the second is the format string, and any further arguments are values to substitute into the format string. Example 5.6 shows the **drawDPSPrintf** routine, which uses **DPSPrintf** to communicate with the server.

Example 5.6 *Drawing with DPSPrintf*

C language code:

```
void drawDPSPrintf (nlines)
  int nlines;
{
  int i;

  /* Clear the screen */
  DPSPrintf(dpsCtxt, "%g setgray\n", BGCOLOR);
  DPSPrintf(dpsCtxt, "%g %g %g %g rectfill\n", 0.0, 0.0,
           width, height);
  DPSPrintf(dpsCtxt, "%g setgray\n", BGSTRCOLOR);
```

```
        DPSPrintf(dpsCtxt, "%g setlinewidth\n", BGSTRWIDTH);
        DPSPrintf(dpsCtxt, "%g %g %g %g rectstroke\n", 0.0, 0.0,
                    width, height);

        /* Draw the lines */
        for ( i = 0; i < nlines; i++) {
          DPSPrintf(dpsCtxt, "%g setlinewidth\n", W[i]);
          DPSPrintf(dpsCtxt, "%g setgray\n", C[i]);
          DPSPrintf(dpsCtxt, "%g %g moveto\n", X[i], Y[i]);
          DPSPrintf(dpsCtxt, "%g %g lineto\n", X1[i], Y1[i]);
          DPSPrintf(dpsCtxt, "stroke\n");
        }
    } /* end drawDPSPrintf () */
```

The drawing area is first cleared by drawing over the previous border with the background color and then stroking the border. The names in capital letters are predefined literals. The values used with **rectfill** and **rectstroke** are the origin and dimensions of the bounding rectangle for the drawing area.

The *for* loop draws one line for each iteration. Calls to **DPSPrintf** set the line width and color, create the path for the line, and stroke the line.

Notice in the calls to **DPSPrintf** that each string ends with a newline character. It's very important to include a newline, a space, or a tab at the end of each string to avoid having consecutive operator names incorrectly merged together. If the newline at the end of the **lineto** string were omitted, the interpreter would try to execute the nonexistent **linetostroke** operator.

While using **DPSPrintf** is very straightforward, it is about 20% slower than any other method in this chapter. The poor performance is a result of the way **DPSPrintf** communicates with the interpreter: the data is sent as a simple text string, which must be parsed in the PostScript interpreter. The other methods transparently use an efficient binary encoding that avoids this parsing overhead.

5.3.4 Single-Operator Procedures Method

The single-ops in the Client Library are called like other C procedures. Note how they are used in the **drawSingleOps** procedure shown in Example 5.7.

Single-Ops

Drawing times for 1,000 lines in milliseconds

Uniform width & color	1,925
Random width & color	2,175

Example 5.7 *Drawing with single-ops*

C language code:

```
void drawSingleOps (nlines)
  int nlines;
{
  int i;

  /* Clear the screen */
  PSsetgray (BGCOLOR);
  PSrectfill (0.0, 0.0, width, height);
  PSsetgray (BGSTRCOLOR);
  PSsetlinewidth (BGSTRWIDTH);
  PSrectstroke (0.0, 0.0, width, height);

  /* Draw the lines */
  for ( i = 0; i < nlines; i++) {
    PSsetlinewidth(W[i]);
    PSsetgray(C[i]);
    PSmoveto(X[i], Y[i]);
    PSlineto(X1[i], Y1[i]);
    PSstroke();
  }
} /* end drawSingleOps ( ) */
```

In Example 5.7, the names of procedures that begin with PS are single-ops in the Client Library, as defined in *<DPS/psops.h>*. The values passed to **PSrectfill** and **PSrectstroke** are the origin and dimensions of the bounding rectangle for the drawing area.

As in Example 5.6, the *for* loop in this example draws one line for each iteration. Some of the procedures in the loop, such as **PSsetgray**, take arguments. Others, such as **PSstroke**, do not. The number and type of arguments for each procedure are documented in the include files for the single-ops. For an explanation of the functions of the operators, see the *PostScript Language Reference Manual, Second Edition.*

5.3.5 Simple Wraps Method

Simple Wraps	
Drawing times for 1,000 lines in milliseconds	
Uniform width & color	1,578
Random width & color	1,817

You can also use simple wrap definitions to draw lines. The wrap definitions appear first, followed by their invocation in the C routine **drawSimpleWraps,** shown in Example 5.8. The first wrap clears the drawing area; the second creates and strokes a path that describes a line.

Example 5.8 *Drawing with wraps*

Wrap definitions:

```
/* Wrap definitions */
defineps PSWEraseView(float BGColor, BGStrColor, BGStrWidth
                      BGrect[4])
  BGColor setgray
  BGrect rectfill
  BGStrColor setgray
  BGStrWidth setlinewidth
  BGrect rectstroke
endps

defineps PSWDrawLine(float LineWidth, LineColor,
                     X, Y, X1, Y1)
  LineWidth setlinewidth
  LineColor setgray
  X Y moveto
  X1 Y1 lineto
  stroke
endps
```

C language code:

```
void drawSimpleWraps (nlines)
  int nlines;
{
  int i;
  float viewRect [4];

  /* Clear the screen */
  viewRect [0] = 0.0;
  viewRect [1] = 0.0;
  viewRect [2] = width;
  viewRect [3] = height;
  PSWEraseView (BGCOLOR, BGSTRCOLOR, BGSTRWIDTH,
               viewRect);

  /* Draw the lines */
  for ( i = 0; i < nlines; i++) {
    PSWDrawLine(W[i], C[i], X[i], Y[i], X1[i], Y1[i]);
  }
} /* end drawSimpleWraps ( ) */
```

The float array *viewRect* passes the bounding rectangle of the drawing area to the wrap as one structure rather than as four individual values, which simplifies the procedure. In the wrap declaration, the array is specified as a float array of size 4. The individual elements in an array can be accessed within a wrap by specifying an index, or the entire array can be specified by not including an index. Example 5.10 shows how to pass dynamically sized arrays to a wrap.

As in Example 5.7, the *for* loop draws one line per iteration. The end point coordinates of each line, its color, and its line width are passed to the wrap. The wrap sets the color and line width in the graphics state of the PostScript interpreter and creates and strokes the path.

5.3.6   Wraps with Binding Method

The wraps with binding method shown in Example 5.9 is similar to the simple wraps example shown in Example 5.8. However, in this example PostScript language *procedures* are defined and called instead of individual *operators* within the wrap. The necessary PostScript operators appear in the procedures.

Example 5.9 *Drawing with wraps (bind procedures)*

Wraps with Binding	
Drawing times for 1,000 lines in milliseconds	
Uniform width & color	1,507
Random width & color	1,753

Wrap definitions:

```
defineps PSWDefs( )
  % EVB is a mnemonic for "erase view, bind"
  /EVB { % BGrect BGStrWidth BGStrColor BGColor
    setgray 2 index rectfill
    setgray setlinewidth rectstroke
  } bind def

  % DLB is a mnemonic for "draw line, bind"
  /DLB { % X1 Y1 X Y LineColor LineWidth
    setlinewidth
    setgray
    moveto
    lineto
    stroke
  } bind def
endps

defineps PSWEraseViewBind(float BGColor, BGStrColor,
                              BGStrWidth, BGrect[4])
  BGrect BGStrWidth BGStrColor BGColor EVB
endps
```

```
defineps PSWDrawLineBind(float LineWidth, LineColor,
                         X, Y, X1,Y1)
  X1 Y1 X Y LineColor LineWidth DLB
endps
```

C language code:

```
void drawWrapsBind (nlines)
  int nlines;
{
  int i;
  float viewRect [4];

  /* Clear the screen */
  viewRect [0] = 0.0;
  viewRect [1] = 0.0;
  viewRect [2] = width;
  viewRect [3] = height;
  PSWEraseViewBind (BGCOLOR, BGSTRCOLOR, BGSTRWIDTH,
                    viewRect);

  /* Draw the lines */
  for ( i = 0; i < nlines; i++) {
    PSWDrawLineBind(W[i], C[i], X[i], Y[i], X1[i], Y1[i]);
  }
} /* end drawWrapsBind ( ) */
```

The wrap **PSWDefs** defines the PostScript language procedures. It is
called once when the application is initialized so the definitions are
known to the PostScript interpreter when the other wraps invoke them.
These procedures are created so they can be bound using the **bind**
operator. Binding replaces each executable operator name with its value
so that subsequent name lookups can be avoided. Binding eliminates a
level of indirection because the PostScript interpreter encounters a
pointer to the executable code that implements each operator rather
than the name of the operator. Eliminating this level of indirection
improves performance.

Whenever the interpreter encounters a name, it looks up its value in
the dictionaries on the dictionary stack. Although name lookups are
reasonably fast, they do represent noticeable processing overhead when
done repeatedly. Binding forces the lookup of the names of the
operators at definition time instead of every time the procedure is
executed.

Binding makes a greater difference for frequently called sequences of code. In this case, the drawing area is not erased frequently, so the saving is negligible for the PostScript language procedure **EVB** (erase view, bind). The saving is larger for **DLB** (draw line, bind), however, since this sequence is invoked many more times.

The procedures **EVB** and **DLB** have been assigned short names because the reduction in data communications overhead using short names can reduce processing time by up to 30% when sending data to a PostScript printer. In the Display PostScript system, the overhead of name length is insignificant because of *pswrap* name optimizations and the binary encoding scheme. If a stream might be converted to ASCII and sent to a printer, short procedure names are preferable.

The wrap names **PSWEraseViewBind** and **PSWDrawLineBind** have not been abbreviated. A wrap is a C procedure rather than an executable PostScript language name, and its name is not visible within the PostScript language code. Long wrap names make the application code easier to read and have no impact on performance.

While defining bound procedures speeds up Display PostScript execution slightly, its effect is much greater in PostScript language code for a printer. The amount of code required to draw a line with bound procedures is only 10% of the code required when each operator is specified in-line. This size difference makes output files smaller and significantly reduces the time needed to send a file to a printer. The definitions of the bound procedures should be included in the prologue section of the drawing's page description. See section 3.11.1 in the *PostScript Language Reference Manual, Second Edition,* for more information on binding.

5.3.7 Wraps with Repeat Method

Wraps with Repeat

Drawing times for 1,000 lines in milliseconds

Uniform width & color	1,668
Random width & color	1,926

Previous examples used a C loop to draw each line. In Example 5.10, the application passes the entire array of points to the wrap and uses a loop in the PostScript language. As the **DLRB** (draw line, repeat, bind) procedure shows, many stack operations such as **roll**, **dup**, and **exch** are necessary. The resulting drawing time shows that this method is slow when compared to other methods. Avoid extensive programming with the PostScript language, not only because of the slower performance but also because of the unnecessary complexity. The application should handle as much of the data manipulation as possible.

Example 5.10 *Drawing with repeat wraps (interpreter loop)*

Wrap definitions:

```
defineps PSWDefs( )
  % DLRB is a mnemonic for "draw line, repeat, bind"
  /DLRB { % i - number of times to loop
    0 1 3 -1 roll 1 sub { % for
      dup PSW exch get setlinewidth
      dup PSC exch get setgray
      dup PSX exch get PSY 2 index get moveto
      dup PSX1 exch get PSY1 2 index get lineto
      stroke pop
    } for
  } bind def
endps

defineps PSWDrawLineRepeatBind(float W[i], C[i], X[i], Y[i],
                                X1[i], Y1[i]; int i)
  /PSW W def
  /PSC C def
  /PSX X def
  /PSY Y def
  /PSX1 X1 def
  /PSY1 Y1 def
  i  DLRB
endps
```

C language code:

```
void drawWrapsRepeat (nlines)
  int nlines;
{
  int i;
  float viewRect [4];

  /* Clear the screen */
  viewRect [0] = 0.0;
  viewRect [1] = 0.0;
  viewRect [2] = width;
  viewRect [3] = height;
  PSWEraseViewBind (BGCOLOR, BGSTRCOLOR, BGSTRWIDTH,
                    viewRect);

  /*Draw the lines*/
  PSWDrawLineRepeatBind(W, C, X, Y, X1, Y1, nlines);
} /* end drawWrapsRepeat ( ) */
```

The drawing area is erased with the wrap **PSWEraseViewBind**, as was illustrated in Example 5.9. The wrap **PSWDrawLineRepeatBind** displays the lines. In this wrap, the six arrays that define the lines are passed to the server. In the **DLRB** procedure, the PostScript interpreter executes a loop with one iteration for each line. This case shows the use of dynamically sized arrays within wraps. The arrays and their size are passed as arguments. In the wrap declaration, the array size variable *i* is used to specify the size of the arrays.

This example seems to indicate that passing a dynamically sized array is inefficient and should be avoided. However, the real inefficiency results from the extensive stack manipulations the example uses to render the lines, not from passing the array. Chapter 7 provides an example in which passing large, dynamically sized arrays can provide significant time savings.

5.3.8 Wraps Optimized Method

Wraps Optimized	
Drawing times for 1,000 lines in milliseconds	
Uniform width & color	969
Random width & color	1,875

Wraps with optimized stroking are similar to wraps with binding, except that the lines are stroked only when the line width or color change. As long as the width and color are the same, the **moveto** and **lineto** operators are used to extend the path without stroking. If the width or color change, or the lines end, the resulting path is stroked and a new path is started. Example 5.11 lists the code used by the *LineDraw* application for wraps with optimized stroking.

Example 5.11 *Drawing with wraps (optimized stroking)*

Wrap definitions:

```
defineps PSWDefs( )
  % MLB is a mnemonic for "make line, bind"
  /MLB { % X1 Y1 X Y
    moveto
    lineto
  } bind def

  % SLB is a mnemonic for "stroke line, bind"
  /SLB { % LineColor LineWidth
    setlinewidth
    setgray
    stroke
  } bind def
endps
```

```
defineps PSWMakeLineBind(float X, Y, X1, Y1)
  X1 Y1 X Y MLB
endps

defineps PSWStrokeLineBind(float LineWidth, LineColor)
  LineColor LineWidth SLB
endps
```

C language code:

```
void drawOptimizedStroke (nlines)
  int nlines;
{
  int i;
  float viewRect [4];

  /* Clear the screen */
  viewRect [0] = 0.0;
  viewRect [1] = 0.0;
  viewRect [2] = width;
  viewRect [3] = height;
  PSWEraseViewBind (BGCOLOR, BGSTRCOLOR, BGSTRWIDTH,
                    viewRect);

  /* Draw the lines */
  for (i = 0; i < nlines; i++) {
    PSWMakeLineBind(X[i], Y[i], X1[i], Y1[i]);
    if (i == nlines - 1 ||
        C[i] != C[i + 1] || W[i] != W[i + 1])
        PSWStrokeLineBind(C[i], W[i]);
  } /* for */
} * end drawOptimizedStroke ( ) */
```

The PostScript operator **stroke** paints a line over the current path in the current color, using the current line attributes (width, line cap, etc.) in the graphics state. As long as the color or line attributes do not change, significant stroke overhead can be eliminated if the program collects a series of disconnected subpaths and performs a single stroke operation on the entire series.

If each line segment has a randomly determined width and color, optimized stroking shows no advantage over stroking every line; in fact, it is slightly slower. When lines can be grouped according to the same line attributes, however, optimized stroking is by far the fastest of all the methods explored in this chapter. When line attributes change for every line, this method requires two wraps for each line, which causes a performance penalty.

This method of drawing is useful when you are displaying grids, wire frame drawings, or other drawings with lines of uniform color and line attributes. Some applications may be able to gain a similar advantage by ordering lines according to similar line attributes within the application's data structures. However, this opportunity is fairly rare; other constraints usually dictate the order for drawing the lines.

Note: *The PostScript interpreter in most printers has a 1,500-point path length limit. For printer compatibility, place a ceiling on the number of points allowed when you draw a path. The limit is significantly larger in the Display PostScript system.*

The optimization method for stroking can also be used for filling, but there are important additional constraints (see section 10.5 on page PG-211 for details). However, it is always safe to combine filled rectangles in a single **rectfill** operation.

5.4 Performance Improvement Tips

This section summarizes some of the more important performance considerations. Some performance trade-offs were illustrated by the *LineDraw* application; others have not yet been stated explicitly.

5.4.1 Choosing Single-Ops or Wraps

Each wrap or single-op represents one request to the server, and each request incurs some small but fixed performance cost. This cost is the same whether the request was generated by a single-op or a wrap. Because a wrap usually contains several PostScript operators, it reduces cost and improves performance in proportion to the number of operators it contains. Therefore, you will improve performance if you use wraps instead of individual single-ops whenever a sequence of operators executes together. Performance improvement is typically 20%.

Single-ops are convenient for simple drawing such as filling in a rectangle or drawing a few lines. In these cases the performance penalty for not using wraps is very slight.

5.4.2 Performing Computation

As a general rule, avoid performing computations in the PostScript interpreter if the same computation can be done within the application. For example, to add two numbers, perform the addition in

C code instead of calling the **PSadd** procedure from the Client Library. Although **PSadd** provides the same answer, compiled code is more efficient than interpreted code.

5.4.3 Transforming Coordinates

A common task in Display PostScript applications is converting mouse events from X Window System coordinates to PostScript language coordinates. The following single-op call performs this conversion in the PostScript interpreter.

```
PSitransform((float) mouse_x, (float) mouse_y, &dps_x, &dps_y);
```

However, it is several hundred times more efficient to store a copy of the current transformation matrix in the application and to do the arithmetic there, as shown in Example 4.1 on page PG-46. The **PSitransform** version is particularly inefficient because it requires a round-trip to the server.

5.4.4 Setting Narrow-Width Lines

Narrow-width lines	
Drawing times for 1,000 lines in milliseconds	
0.15-point line width (uniform color)	555
2.0-point line width (uniform color)	969

Line widths equivalent to one pixel in device space display more quickly than wider lines because the PostScript interpreter is optimized for one-pixel lines. Setting a line width of zero guarantees a one-pixel line on any device, but this effect is not always desired. While a one-pixel line is clearly visible at screen resolution, it is barely visible on a 300-dpi printer and practically invisible on a 1200-dpi imagesetter.

Any line width less than 0.7 yields one-pixel lines on displays of up to 100-dpi resolution, and any line width less than 0.15 yields one-pixel lines on printers of up to 400-dpi resolution. If you want the same PostScript language code to display quickly on the screen and still produce visible lines on a 300-dpi printer, use a width between 0.7 and 0.15. If you want the very fastest print time and don't mind very thin lines on the printer, use a width of 0.15.

5.5 Comparison of Display Times

Figure 5.3 summarizes display times obtained from typical runs of the *LineDraw* application. To gather the data, *LineDraw* used each drawing method first to draw 1,000 lines of uniform width and color (width 2, black) and then to draw 1,000 lines of random width and color (width varying from 0 to 5, color varying from black to white). Note that **DPSPrintf** is by far the slowest method, reflecting the interpreter parsing overhead incurred when data is sent as text. This method takes 20% longer than single operators and 50% longer than wraps with binding. Single operator procedures are also relatively slow, reflecting the performance cost of many client-server requests when drawing large numbers of lines. Note also the much faster performance of the wraps optimized method when drawing uniform lines as compared to drawing random lines, an indication that this method improves performance only when many lines have the same width and color.

Figure 5.3 *Display times for 1,000 lines using six different methods*

Uniform Width and Color

Random Width and Color

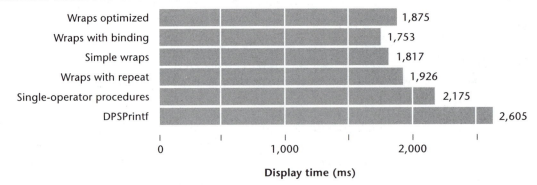

Display time (ms)

5.6   Summary

- Use wraps to group sets of PostScript operators and send them to the interpreter at one time.

- Define PostScript language procedures for frequently used series of imaging operations. Invoke the procedures in wraps to take advantage of the **bind** operator.

- Use the PostScript language and the Display PostScript extension for imaging but not for computation. Perform calculations in the application whenever possible, not in PostScript language code.

- Do not send text data to the PostScript interpreter when there are other alternatives. The binary encoding used by single-operator procedures and wraps is much more efficient.

- Delay stroking similar sets of lines until all the lines have been constructed. This method can dramatically reduce display time.

- For maximum speed in displaying lines, make the lines one pixel wide. However, note that such very narrow lines may be too light if the application sends the same PostScript language code to a high-resolution printer.

CHAPTER 6

Path Construction and Painting

Chapter 5 described how to paint paths using single operator calls and wraps. This chapter further explores the issue of efficiently painting paths using *user paths*, a Display PostScript system extension to the PostScript language.

A *user path* is a PostScript language procedure that is comprised of path construction operators and their corresponding operands, expressed as literal numbers. A user path is therefore a complete and self-contained path description. A number of painting operators can act on user paths to perform standard PostScript language operations such as stroking and filling. The highly structured nature of user paths allows an efficient alternate format that encodes the operators and operands into compact strings. Section 4.6 of the *PostScript Language Reference Manual, Second Edition*, covers user paths in depth.

User paths provide several important advantages:

- They are more efficient to interpret and execute than conventional paths.

- They provide a convenient way to send an arbitrary path to the PostScript interpreter.

- They are compact and minimize data transmission when the application and PostScript interpreter are on different machines.

- They can be cached.

In this chapter, the *Dial* application highlights four methods of drawing graduation marks around the inner edge of a dial. Two methods use standard path construction operators and the other two employ user paths.

The first method has one simple description for a single graduation mark and rotates the coordinate system to draw the mark at different orientations. The second method calculates the beginning and ending coordinates for the graduation marks using trigonometric functions. The third method is similar to the second, except that it uses user paths and the Display PostScript Toolkit procedure **DPSDoUserPath**. The fourth method is similar to the third, except that it stores the user path definitions in the server to avoid resending them each time they are used. In each case, graduation marks of the same width and color are combined into a single path, which reduces the number of operators sent to the server.

Note: *Performance for drawing stroked paths is improved when disjoint paths are combined into a single user path. However, combining filled paths can produce unexpected results when subpaths overlap; see section 10.5 on page PG-211 for details.*

A user path is the most efficient means of path construction in the Display PostScript system. You can send user paths to the server in a wrap or using the procedure **DPSDoUserPath.** This procedure provides a convenient interface to user paths and encodes the operands and operators into number strings, which is a more efficient format.

6.1   Using User Paths

User paths are especially useful when drawing a path that is known ahead of time. For example, the *Clock* application in Chapter 7 uses user paths to retain the descriptions of clock hands. Instead of drawing the hands using **moveto**, **lineto**, **curveto**, and so on, it draws the hands by retaining a user path in a static array and then sending it to the PostScript interpreter with **DPSDoUserPath**.

Even if the path is created dynamically, user paths can improve performance. The *Dial* application shows that it is faster to place a large path in a user path just before sending it to the server than it is to send the drawing instructions individually.

In short, user paths improve performance whether the application retains a user path definition for each object or converts an internal path representation to a user path immediately before drawing. The interface to **DPSDoUserPath** makes it easy to maintain two large buffers and accumulate a path description to send to **DPSDoUserPath**.

A limitation of user paths is that they can contain no more than 1,000 operators and 3,009 coordinates.

6.2 Defining a User Path

A user path is a procedure that consists of path construction operators and their operands expressed as literal numbers. The operators must be the standard PostScript language operator names and the operands must be literals. Therefore, the name **moveto** is a valid operator, but the name *MT* isn't, even if it is bound to the **moveto** operator. In addition, the name *moveto* in a user path is always a reference to the **moveto** operator, even if *moveto* is currently bound to a PostScript procedure. The number 100 is valid as an operand, but 50 50 **add** is not: 100 is a literal, but 50 50 **add** is an expression.

User paths are operated on by special user path painting operators such as **ustroke** and **ufill**. Each operator takes a user path as its argument and performs the appropriate painting operation.

6.2.1 Alternate Path Definition Formats

A user path description can be represented in two formats. The first format, illustrated in Example 6.1, consists of an ASCII path definition enclosed within { } braces. The { } braces create an executable PostScript language array—that is, a procedure. The four line segments at the left of the example show the visual result of executing the procedure with the **ustroke** operator.

Example 6.1 *ASCII user path description*

PostScript language code:

```
{
0 0 200 200 setbbox
175 100 moveto
200 100 lineto
100 175 moveto
100 200 lineto
25 100 moveto
0 100 lineto
100 25 moveto
100 0 lineto
} ustroke
```

While this format is easy to understand, it is not concise. Since only twelve possible operators are legal within a user path description, a more compact form is possible. The compact representation is based on assigning the twelve legal operators numeric codes from 0 to 11 and placing their operands in an associated data array. The complete representation is a two-element array; the first element contains the operands and the second element contains the operators.

Table 6.1 lists the path construction operators that are allowed in user paths. The second column lists the operands for each operator, the third column lists the corresponding encoding value for the operator, and the fourth column lists the Display PostScript literal definition for the encoding (contained in *<DPS/dpsXuserpath.h>*).

Table 6.1 *User path construction operators and encodings*

PostScript Operator	Operands	Encoding	Display PostScript Literal
arc	$x\ y\ r\ ang_1\ ang_2$	7	dps_arc
arcn	$x\ y\ r\ ang_1\ ang_2$	8	dps_arcn
arct	$x_1\ y_1\ x_2\ y_2\ r$	9	dps_arct
closepath		10	dps_closepath
curveto	$x_1\ y_1\ x_2\ y_2\ x_3\ y_3$	5	dps_curveto
lineto	$x\ y$	3	dps_lineto
moveto	$x\ y$	1	dps_moveto
rcurveto	$dx_1\ dy_1\ dx_2\ dy_2\ dx_3\ dy_3$	6	dps_rcurveto
rlineto	$dx\ dy$	4	dps_rlineto
rmoveto	$dx\ dy$	2	dps_rmoveto
setbbox	$llx\ lly\ urx\ ury$	0	dps_setbbox
ucache		11	dps_ucache

Example 6.2 uses the compact, encoded form of user path description to create the same user path as shown in Example 6.1. Again, the stroked path is shown to the left of the example. The outer [ ] brackets enclose the two-element user path array. The inner [ ] brackets enclose an array of operands. The second element of the array is a string enclosed in < > brackets that encodes the operators. Every two hexadecimal digits in the string is a single character encoding of an

operator as listed in Table 6.1. Each operator in turn uses operands from the list of operands, in order. There must be exactly as many operands supplied as are required by the specified operators.

Example 6.2 *Encoded user path description*

PostScript language code:

```
[
[
0  0  200  200  175  100
200  100  100  175  100  200
25  100  0  100  100  25  100  0
]
<000103010301030103>
] ustroke
```

A variation of Example 6.2 is shown in Example 6.3 along with the stroked user path it describes. Example 6.3 replaces the array of numeric arguments with a binary encoded number string. Encoded number strings are not easy to read, but they are very compact and efficient. An advantage of the **DPSDoUserPath** procedure is that it automatically generates number string encodings for its user path operands.

Example 6.3 *Encoded user path description with number string literals*

PostScript language code:

```
[<950000140000000000000000000000000c8000000c8000000af0000006400
0000c8000000640000006400000af00000064000000c800000019000000
6400000000000000064000000640000019000000640000000><00010301
0301030103>]ustroke
```

Note: *Number strings are much more compact in reality than they appear in Example 6.3. The data is actually stored and transmitted in binary, so each pair of hexadecimal digits only requires 8 bits.*

Although **DPSDoUserPath** is the most convenient way to use the number string encoding, there are other ways as well. The simplest is to use the *numstring* type in a wrap definition. The *pswrap* translator will generate code to translate conventional C language arrays into the binary number string format. See "Sending Encoded Number Strings" on page PSW-22 for a complete description of *numstring* parameters.

6.2.2   User Path Construction Operators

If you know the PostScript language, all the path construction operators shown in Table 6.1 except **ucache**, **setbbox**, and **arct** should be familiar. These operators are described below.

ucache Operator

The **ucache** operator, if included in a user path description, tells the PostScript interpreter to look for the path in a user path cache. If the search is successful, the cached value is used; if the search is unsuccessful, the path is entered into the cache. If **ucache** is present, it must appear as the first operator in the path description.

The user path cache is analogous to the font cache in that it retains the results of interpreting the path. If the PostScript interpreter encounters a user path that is already in the cache, it substitutes the cached results instead of reinterpreting the path definition. Note that the interpreter looks in the cache only if the user path contains **ucache**. This operator is both a directive to cache the path and a hint that the path may already be in the cache.

Additional processing is required to place the path in the cache, so you should limit caching to paths that are painted frequently. Caching is effective across translations of the coordinate system but not across other transformations like scaling or rotation. In such instances, the interpreter reinterprets and recaches the path. See Chapter 10, "Drawing Issues and Scrolling," for details about using cached user paths.

setbbox Operator

The **setbbox** operator is required in every user path. It immediately follows **ucache**, or is the first operator if **ucache** is not used. **setbbox** requires four operands that make up the bounding box enclosing the path. The operands specify the lower left and upper right coordinates of the bounding box.

Note: *The bbox argument describes the bounding box of the user path by specifying its lower left and upper right coordinates. The Display PostScript bounding box representation is different from the X Window System rectangle representation, which is an origin followed by a size.*

All coordinates specified as operands for successive operators must lie within the bounding box. Otherwise, a **rangecheck** error occurs. Including a bounding box reduces the number of calculations that the interpreter must perform and improves path painting performance.

A bounding box specification that is close in size to the actual bounding box of the user path performs slightly better than a bounding box that is larger. In the examples in this chapter, increasing the bounding box for **setbbox** by 1,000 points in each direction increases the execution time by a small amount—about 2%. An accurate bounding box improves program performance but is sometimes difficult to compute. In these cases, the improved performance may not be worth the programming effort required.

Note that the bounding box values are also used by the interpreter to determine when an image lies within a clipping region. In these cases, the difference in performance can be more significant.

arct Operator

The **arct** operator is the user path equivalent of **arcto**. The operators are identical except that **arct** does not push any results on the operand stack and **arcto** pushes four numbers. Because user paths must be completely self-contained and produce no side effects (except in raster memory), the operator **arcto**, which leaves results on the stack, cannot be used in a user path definition.

6.3 User Path Operators

The Display PostScript system extensions to the PostScript language include operators that interpret and operate on user paths. The operators are:

ufill	**inufill**
ueofill	**inueofill**
ustroke	**inustroke**
ustrokepath	
uappend	

Except for **uappend**, the operators in the first column perform the same functions on a user path that their corresponding operators perform on regular paths. Unlike **fill**, **eofill**, **stroke**, and **strokepath**, the user path operators do not change the current path. For example, **ufill** pops the user path off the operand stack, interprets it, and paints the area enclosed by the user path with the current color. The current path remains unchanged.

The **uappend** operator interprets a user path definition and appends the result to the current path in the graphics state. If you are painting, use a user path operator like **ustroke** directly rather than appending and then calling a regular path operator like **stroke**.

The operators in the second column are used for hit detection and are discussed in Chapter 9.

User path painting operators make a temporary adjustment to the user space by rounding the translation components of the current transformation matrix to the nearest integer values. This adjustment ensures that a single user path description produces uniform results, regardless of its position on the page or screen due to translation of the user space. However, this adjustment also means that drawing done with user paths may paint slightly differently from drawing done with regular paths. The differences are noticeable only in unusual cases, such as in trying to fill a shape using a regular path and then stroking its outline with a user path.

6.3.1   Clipping with a User Path

The list of painting operators does not include a user path clip operator. To clip with a user path, use the **uappend** operator to append the path to the current path and then use the **clip** operator to clip the current path, as follows:

> **newpath** *<user path>* **uappend** **clip**

6.3.2   Using DPSDoUserPath

The most convenient way to send a user path to the server is with the Display PostScript Toolkit procedure **DPSDoUserPath**. Refer to page TK-22 in *Display PostScript Toolkit for X* for the complete specification. Example 6.4 shows the calling sequence for this procedure.

Example 6.4 *DPSDoUserPath calling sequence*

C language code:

```
void DPSDoUserPath(
  DPSContext ctx,
  DPSPointer coords,
  int numCoords,
  DPSNumberFormat numType,
  DPSUserPathOp *ops,
  int numOps,
  DPSPointer bbox,
  DPSUserPathAction action)
```

The *coords* argument is a pointer to an array of coordinate points, with *numCoords* identifying the number of points in the array. The *numType* argument specifies the type of numbers in the *coords* array. The three possibilities are *dps_float*, *dps_long*, and *dps_short*, which indicate that the array *coords* is really *float*, *int*, or *short* respectively.

Note: *The dps_long tag refers to a 32-bit integer type, which may not be long on some machine architectures.*

The *ops* argument is a pointer to an array containing the user path construction operators, with *numOps* identifying the number of operators in the array. The *bbox* argument is a pointer to a four-element array that contains the values for the **setbbox** operator. The values in *bbox* must be the same type as those in the *coords* array. The *action* argument is an identifier for a user path painting operator. Examples are *dps_ufill* and *dps_ustroke*.

Example 6.5 uses **DPSDoUserPath** to draw the same four line segments as the previous three examples. The stroked user path is again shown at the left of the example.

Example 6.5 *User path with DPSDoUserPath*

C language code:

```
static short coords[ ] = {175, 100, 200, 100, 100, 175, 100,
                          200, 25, 100, 0, 100, 100, 25, 100, 0};
static short bbox[ ] = {0, 0, 200, 200};
static DPSUserPathOp ops[ ] = {dps_moveto, dps_lineto,
                          dps_moveto, dps_lineto, dps_moveto,
                          dps_lineto, dps_moveto, dps_lineto};

DPSDoUserPath (ctxt, (DPSPointer) coords, 16, dps_short,
                  ops, 8, (DPSPointer) bbox, dps_ustroke);
```

There is an alternative version of **DPSDoUserPath** called **PSDoUserPath**. It is identical in function, but operates in the current context and so does not take a context parameter.

6.4   The Dial Application

The *Dial* application shown in Figure 6.1 draws a dial with graduation marks around its inner edge.

Figure 6.1 *The Dial application*

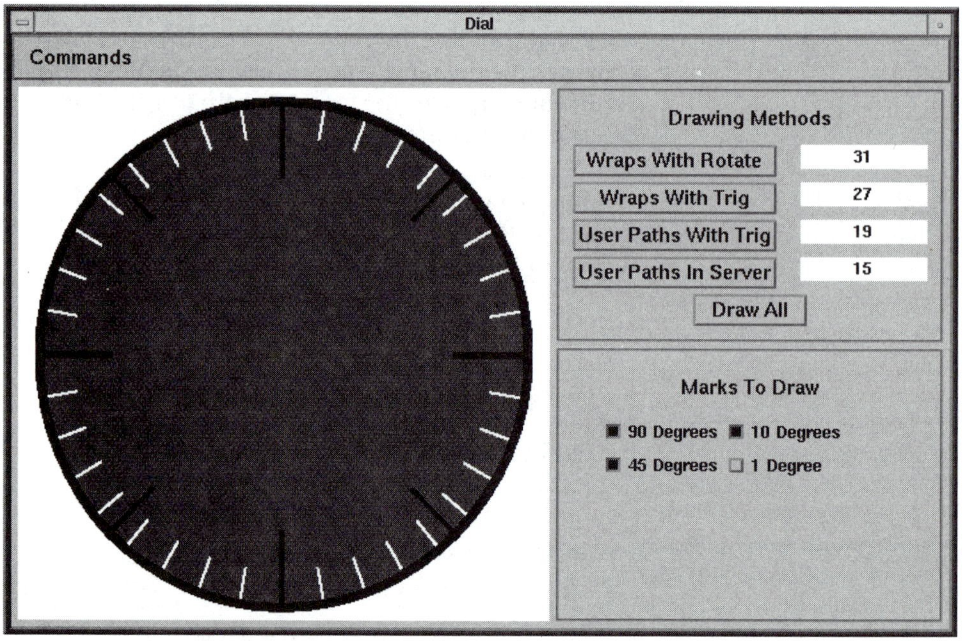

The user can specify how many graduation marks to draw with the 90-, 45-, 10-, and 1-degree check boxes; the settings shown in Figure 6.1 specify that marks be drawn at 90-, 45-, and 10-degree intervals. Four settings are used to evaluate performance for the *Dial* application. The four settings cause different numbers of graduation marks to be drawn, as shown in Table 6.2.

Table 6.2 *Dial application settings and number of lines drawn*

Degree Setting Combinations	Number of Lines Drawn
90	4
45, 90	12
10, 45, 90	40
1, 10, 45, 90	400

Four methods are used to draw the marks:

- Wraps With Rotate—rotates the coordinate system and calls a wrap for each line (see Example 6.6).

- Wraps With Trig—computes the line endpoints in the application and calls a wrap for each line (see Example 6.7).

- User Paths With Trig—computes the line endpoints in the application and sends the combined path to the server as a user path (see Example 6.8).

- User Paths in Server—stores the user path description of the lines in the server and uses these saved paths to display the lines (see Example 6.9).

Display times allow comparisons of the types of drawing and the number of graduation marks drawn. In the code segments, the wraps are shown first, followed by their invocations in the C language.

In the *Dial* application, each type of graduation mark has different color, size, length, and spacing attributes. The source code contains literal definitions for each attribute for the graduation marks, as follows, where *n* is the type of mark:

COLOR*n*	The color of the graduation mark
WIDTH*n*	The width of the graduation mark
LENGTH*n*	The length of the graduation mark
DEGREE*n*	The spacing between graduation marks

The length attribute is specified as the distance from the center of the dial to the beginning of the graduation mark. For example, a mark with a length attribute of 0.75 starts three-quarters of the way from the center and extends to the edge. The variable *radius* is the radius of the dial and is used to convert the length attributes into coordinates.

6.4.1   Wraps with Rotation

Wraps with Rotation

Display times in milliseconds

4 lines	3
12 lines	8
40 lines	27
400 lines	142

This method uses the same line description for each mark but rotates user space each time to paint the line at a different angle around the dial. The PostScript language procedure **RML** (rotate, moveto, lineto) in Example 6.6 rotates the user space by the specified angle and then adds a graduation mark to the current path using the **moveto** and **lineto** operators. The **PSWRotate_MakeLine** wrap calls the **RML** procedure. After all the lines have been constructed, the color and line width are set and the path is stroked by calling **PSWStrokePath**.

Example 6.6 *Wraps with rotation*

Wrap definitions:

```
defineps PSWDefs( )
  % RML is a mnemonic for rotate, moveto, lineto
  /RML { % X1 Y1 X0 Y0 Ang
    rotate moveto lineto
  } bind def
endps

defineps PSWRotate_MakeLine(float Ang, X0, Y0, X1, Y1)
  X1 Y1 X0 Y0 Ang RML
endps

defineps PSWStrokePath (float Color, Width)
  Color setgray Width setlinewidth stroke
endps
```

C language code:

```
float radius;            /* circle radius */
float width, height;     /* window dimensions in user space */

void drawRotateLines(color, linewidth, startlen,
                          endlen, degree)
   float color;
   float linewidth;
   float startlen;
   float endlen;
   float degree;
{
   int angle;

   for (angle = 0; angle < 360; angle += degree)
     /* Rotate user space and add line to current path */
     PSWRotate_MakeLine (degree, startlen, 0.0, endlen, 0.0);

   /* Stroke all the lines in the current path */
   PSWStrokePath (color, linewidth);
} /* end drawRotateLines ( ) */

void drawRotate( )
{

   ...
   /* Draw mark on 1 degree increments */
   drawRotateLines (COLOR1, WIDTH1, radius * LENGTH1,
                       radius, DEGREE1);
   ...
} /* end drawRotate ( ) */
```

This type of drawing is relatively easy to implement: one static path description can be used for all the drawings within a set. When only a few paths and rotations need to be painted, this method is acceptable because its relative slowness is not obvious to users.

6.4.2   Wraps with Trigonometric Calculations

Wraps with Trigonometric Calculations

Display times in milliseconds

4 lines	3
12 lines	7
40 lines	24
400 lines	129

This method performs trigonometric calculations in the application to find the precise coordinates for the line segments. The coordinates are then sent to the PostScript interpreter within a wrap to create the line. Again, stroking occurs after all the lines in the group have been made. This concept is shown in Example 6.7.

Example 6.7 *Wraps with trigonometric calculations*

Wrap definitions:

```
definps PSWDefs( )

  . . .
  /ML { % X1 Y1 X0 Y0
    moveto lineto
  } bind def
  . . .
endps

definps PSWMakeLine(float X0, Y0, X1, Y1)
  X1 Y1 X0 Y0 ML
endps
```

C language code:

```
void drawTrigLines(color, linewidth, startlen,
                        endlen, degree)
  float color;
  float linewidth;
  float startlen;
  float endlen;
  float degree;
{
  int angle;
  float x, y;

  /* Set the circle center coordinate points */
  x = width / 2;
  y = height / 2;

  for (angle = 0; angle < 360; angle += degree)
    /* Calculate the coordinate points for the ends of the
     * angled line using standard trigonometric
     * calculations and add the line to the current path */
    PSWMakeLine(x + (float) cos (angle * RADIANS)*startlen,
            y + (float) sin (angle * RADIANS) * startlen,
            x + (float) cos (angle * RADIANS) * endlen,
            y + (float) sin (angle * RADIANS) * endlen);
  /* Stroke all the lines in the current path */
  PSWStrokePath (color, linewidth);
} /* end drawTrigLines ( ) */
```

```
void drawTrig( )
{
  ...
  /* Draw mark on 1 degree increments */
  drawTrigLines (COLOR1, WIDTH1, radius * LENGTH1,
                 radius, DEGREE1);

  ...
} /* end drawTrig ( ) */
```

The display times produced by this method show some slight advantage over rotating a single path description. Rotating the coordinate system exacts an overhead penalty, but the overhead is not significant when you are only drawing a few lines. The disadvantage of calculating the coordinates is that it is significantly more complex than allowing the PostScript language to do the rotation.

This test case uses one of the simplest paths possible, a single line segment. A path with multiple line segments, curves, and arcs could be difficult to process in the application. Unless the performance advantage outweighs the complexity, rotating the user space is preferable to calculating the positions in the application.

6.4.3 User Paths with Trigonometric Calculations

User Paths with Trigonometric Calculations	
Display times in milliseconds	
4 lines	2
12 lines	6
40 lines	18
400 lines	66

This method takes the trigonometric approach a step further by adding each line segment to a user path. When the user path has all the line segments, it is sent to the interpreter. This method uses two arrays, one for coordinates and the other for operators. When the arrays are complete, **PSDoUserPath** sends the user path description to the interpreter.

The resulting execution time of a user path is significantly faster for a large number of lines because interpreter overhead during path construction is eliminated. User paths combine a restricted data format with an optimized painting pipeline to eliminate much of the data manipulation performed by such path construction operators as **moveto** and **lineto**.

The total processing time for drawing 12 graduation marks is not enough to produce a noticeable difference between user paths and wraps. For 400 graduation marks, however, user paths represent a time savings of more than 50% over the wrap method. For drawing large numbers of lines, the advantage of employing user paths to reduce the number of operators is large enough to outweigh the difficulty of performing complex calculations in the application. Note that the only reason these computations are necessary in this example is that elements with *different rotations* are being combined into a single user path. You can rotate an entire user path by rotating the coordinate system and then drawing the path (a technique used in Chapter 7 to rotate the hands of a clock).

Example 6.8 *User path with trigonometric calculations*

Wrap definition:

```
defineps PSWSetColorWidth (float Color, Width)
  Color setgray Width setlinewidth
endps
```

C language code:

```
void drawTrigUserPathLines(color, linewidth, startlen,
                                   endlen, degree)
  float color;
  float linewidth;
  float startlen;
  float endlen;
  float degree;
{
  int i, j, angle;
  float x, y;
  float pts[MAX_PTS];
  DPSUserPathOp[MAX_OPS];
  float bbox[4];

  /* Set the bounding box as the window size */
  bbox[0] = 0.0;
  bbox[1] = 0.0;
  bbox[2] = width;
  bbox[3] = height;

  /* Set the center coordinate point */
  x = width / 2;
  y = height / 2;
```

```
/* Initialize the array indices */
i = 0; j = 0;

for (angle = 0; angle < 360; angle += degree) {
  /* Calculate the coordinate points for the start
   * of the angled line. Place the 'moveto' operator
   * into the operator array. */
  pts[i++] = x + cos (angle * RADIANS) * startlen;
  pts[i++] = y + sin (angle * RADIANS) * startlen;
  ops[j++] = dps_moveto;

  /* Calculate the coordinate points
   * for the end of the angled line.
   * Place the 'lineto' operator into the operator array */
  pts[i++] = x + cos (angle * RADIANS) * endlen;
  pts[i++] = y + sin (angle * RADIANS) * endlen;
  ops[j++] = dps_lineto;
} /* end for */

/* Set the draw color and line width */
PSWSetColorWidth (color, linewidth);

/* Stroke all the lines in the user path */
PSDoUserPath ((DPSPointer) pts, i, dps_float, ops, j,
              (DPSPointer) bbox, dps_ustroke);

} /* end drawTrigUserPathLines ( ) */

void drawTrigUserPaths ( )
{
  ...
  /* Draw mark on 1 degree increments */
  drawTrigUserPathLines (COLOR1, WIDTH1, radius * LENGTH1,
                         radius, DEGREE1);
  ...
} /* end drawTrigUserPaths ( ) */
```

6.4.4 User Paths Retained in the Server

User Paths Retained in the Server	
Display times in milliseconds	
4 lines	2
12 lines	5
40 lines	15
400 lines	44

User paths are PostScript language objects so they can be stored in PostScript VM and quickly retrieved for use later. The last display method in the *Dial* application stores the user paths describing the graduation marks in PostScript VM.

Retrieving a user path object avoids the necessity of resending its description, and provides a 70% speed advantage over simple wraps. Chapter 7 discusses various issues involved in storing user paths and other information in PostScript VM.

The method shown in Example 6.9 places a name object on the stack. It then sends the user path description to the PostScript interpreter using **PSDoUserPath** with *dps_def* as the *action* argument, which assigns the user path description to the name object. The path can be drawn later by simply executing a user path drawing operator with the name object as the argument.

Example 6.9 *Server-retained user paths*

Wrap definitions:

```
defineps PSWPlaceName(char *str)
  /str
endps

defineps PSWDrawUserPath (float color, width; char *str)
  color setgray width setlinewidth
  str ustroke
endps
```

C language code:

```
/* The name of the user path array in the server. */
static char *upath1 = "upath1";
...
/* Define upath1 to be the computed path */
PSWPlaceName(upath1);
PSDoUserPath((DPSPointer) pts, i, dps_float, ops, j,
             (DPSPointer) bbox, dps_def);
...
/* Now draw the user path defined earlier */
PSWDrawUserPath (COLOR1, WIDTH1, upath1);
```

PostScript language trace:

```
/upath1
[<578 byte string><721 byte string>] def
...
1.0 setgray 0.5 setlinewidth upath1 ustroke
```

6.4.5   Comparison of Display Times

Figure 6.2 shows times in milliseconds for drawing graduation marks using the methods described in this chapter for the *Dial* application. Times are adjusted to remove the overhead of drawing the circle behind the dial. Note how the differences in display time between the four methods become more pronounced with increasing numbers of lines.

The performance numbers demonstrate that slower methods should not necessarily be discounted. For types of drawing that are different from those shown with the *Dial* application, these methods might be preferable, either because they are easier to implement or because the drawing is simple enough to mask the slower drawing rate.

Figure 6.2 *Display times for four methods of drawing 4, 12, 40, and 400 lines*

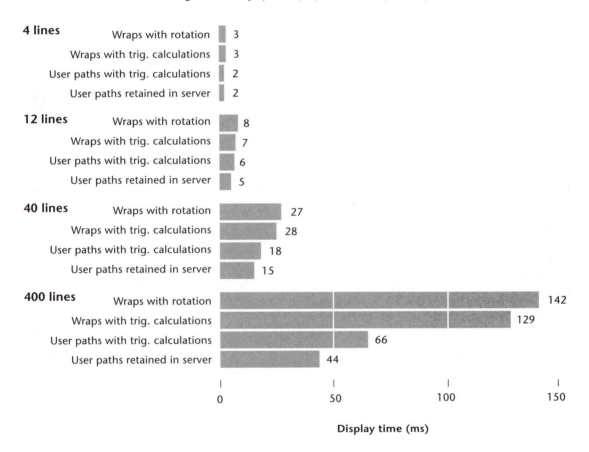

Display time (ms)

6.5   Summary

- A user path is a Display PostScript extension to the PostScript language that provides the most efficient way to construct and paint paths. User paths offer a compact and convenient way to paint previously existing or dynamically created paths.

- A user path is a complete and self-contained path description that consists of path construction operators and their coordinate operands expressed as literal numbers.

- The bounding box for a user path description consists of the lower left and upper right coordinates.

- Storing user paths in the server is the most efficient way to repeatedly draw objects that do not change.

- For simple, infrequent drawing, consider using techniques that are easy to implement even if they are not the fastest.

- Although it is sometimes faster to compute line segment endpoint coordinates in the application rather than with the PostScript interpreter, the code to do so can greatly increase application complexity.

CHAPTER **7**

Managing Graphical Information

This chapter explores two features of the Display PostScript system that are designed specifically for drawing in a display environment: user objects and graphics state objects, called *gstate* objects. These features allow a program to store frequently used information in the server and access it efficiently and conveniently. The chapter also discusses two additional ways to manage graphical information that are not specific to the Display PostScript system: offscreen buffers (pixmaps) and coordinate system transformations.

A *user object* is an integer that identifies an object in PostScript VM. A user object lets a program refer to objects by number rather than by object name. Any PostScript language object, such as an array, a string, a dictionary, or a graphics state, can be referenced by a user object. User objects are more convenient to store and manipulate in C than PostScript language variable names because names must be stored as strings.

Note: *A user object is different from a user path. A user object identifies an object in PostScript VM; a user path is a path description.*

The *graphics state* is a collection of parameters that determine how and where drawing occurs on a screen. Two mechanisms are used to store and retrieve the graphics state: a *graphics state stack* and a *gstate object*. The **gsave** and **grestore** operators move graphics states on and off the graphics state stack. This stack is used primarily in page descriptions for printing. The gstate object provides a more efficient means than the stack for storing graphics states in a display environment. A gstate object can be installed as the current graphics state by performing one **setgstate** operation, which avoids the stack-oriented semantics enforced by **gsave** and **grestore**.

Although gstate objects allow convenient switching between graphics states and can improve performance, they do use memory. Their principal use is as a way to refer to a device. The current device in the graphics state determines where imaging occurs: in a window or in a pixmap. Most applications render into different windows and pixmaps at different times. By managing a list of the gstate objects associated with each device, an application can easily switch among windows and pixmaps using the **setgstate** operator.

Offscreen buffers, also known as *pixmaps*, improve program performance by letting an application store parts of a drawing that do not change. Rather than repeatedly redrawing unchanged parts, the application stores them in a pixmap that is used as a background for further drawing. Pixmaps also allow smooth animation of rapidly changing graphics.

Coordinate system transformations allow an application to transform or scale a drawing without changing the coordinates of individual graphical objects. The application draws using normal coordinates and relies on coordinate system transformations to modify the size, shape, and orientation for viewing.

In this chapter, the *Clock* application employs user objects, gstate objects, pixmaps, and coordinate system transformations in the following ways:

- Path descriptions of the clock hands are stored as user objects. Whenever *Clock* draws a hand, it can refer to the user object instead of sending the hand coordinates to the PostScript interpreter (see Example 7.2).

- The drawing parameters for the clock hands are stored in gstate objects. The application can refer to the gstate object and does not have to set color, line width, and translation each time it redraws a hand (see Example 7.7).

- The clock face is stored in a pixmap. This scheme improves performance by letting the application update the clock without redrawing the background. *Clock* can also use a second pixmap to store the composite clock face, complete with hands. This double buffering eliminates flickering by keeping the hands from momentarily disappearing as the clock is copied into the window (see Example 7.10).

- Rotating the clock hands is done through coordinate system transformation. The application's description for each hand positions the hand at the horizontal, three o'clock orientation, defined as zero degrees of rotation. Displaying a hand at a different orientation is a simple process of rotating the coordinate system and drawing the hand.

- Scaling the clock is also done through coordinate system transformation. The application always draws the clock at one size and then uses coordinate system transformations to ensure that the clock appears scaled to fit the current window size (see Example 7.12).

7.1 Clock Application

The *Clock* application main window, shown in Figure 7.1, contains a menu bar above a drawing window in which the clock is displayed.

Figure 7.1 *Clock application user interface*

Timing window

Main window

When the user chooses Commands from the menu bar, a pull-down menu appears with three checkbuttons: Alarm On, Timing Window, and Trace On. The menu also contains one pushbutton, Quit.

Choosing Alarm On sets an alarm for a specific time   ng Trace
On turns the Display PostScript text trace on or off. This trace is a listing
of all the PostScript language code the application sends to the
interpreter. Choosing Timing Window brings up the performance
evaluation timing window, also shown in Figure 7.1. The timing
window lets the user choose among the following drawing methods:

- *Gstate Objects*—uses gstate objects to store the drawing parameters
  for the clock hands instead of setting the parameters each time they
  are drawn.

- *User Paths in Server*—employs user objects to store the user paths that
  define the clock hands instead of sending the paths each time they
  are drawn.

- *Double Buffering*—renders the clock into a pixmap and copies it into
  the window instead of rendering directly to the window.

- *Pixmap Background*—uses an image of the clock face stored in a
  different pixmap instead of redrawing the face each time the image
  must be updated.

At the bottom of the timing window is a Dismiss button, which closes
the window, and a number field that displays the elapsed time, in
milliseconds, for displaying the clock using the selected drawing
methods.

Figure 7.2 illustrates the clock's six visual components, which are drawn
in the main window below the menu bar.

Figure 7.2 *Clock components*

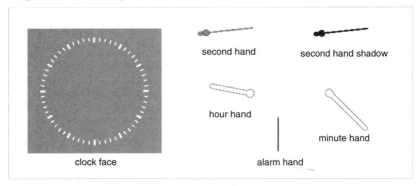

Each hand has a different offset from the center of the clock face and a different color and line-width attribute. *Clock* maintains the path descriptions as user paths and refers to them by means of user objects. The drawing positions, colors, and line widths for the hands are encapsulated in gstate objects that are also identified by user objects.

7.2 Object Identifiers

Often an application requires an efficient way to refer to objects stored in PostScript VM. If the information is a simple PostScript language object such as a number or a boolean value, it is easy to pass the object value to the application, keep it until it is needed again, and pass it back to the PostScript interpreter. However, passing the value of a composite object such as a procedure, a user path, a gstate object, or a dictionary is difficult and time consuming. An easier method is to pass an identifier that points to the object rather than the object value. Object identifiers take two forms: *names* and *user objects*.

7.2.1 Name Objects

Example 7.1, which is taken from the *Dial* application, uses a name object identifier. In the example, the static character string *upath1* refers to a user path in PostScript VM. The character string is sent to the server first to define the user path and then again to refer to the user path when rendering.

Example 7.1 *Defining a name object identifier for a user path*

Wrap definitions:

```
defineps PSWPlaceName(char *str)
  /str
endps

defineps PSWDrawUserPath (float color, width; char *str)
  color setgray width setlinewidth
  str ustroke
endps
```

C language code:

```
/* The name of the user path array in the server. */
static char *upath1 = "upath1";
...
/* Define upath1 to be the computed path */
PSWPlaceName(upath1);
PSDoUserPath((DPSPointer) pts, i, dps_float, ops, j,
             (DPSPointer) bbox, dps_def);
...
/* Now draw the user path defined earlier */
PSWDrawUserPath (COLOR1, WIDTH1, upath1);
```

PostScript language trace:

```
/upath1
[<578 byte string><721 byte string>] def
...
1.0 setgray 0.5 setlinewidth upath1 ustroke
```

The first two lines in the PostScript language trace (statements actually sent to the PostScript interpreter) associate the name *upath1* with the user path description. Later, the application can use the name to refer to the user path, as shown in the last line of the trace.

7.2.2 User Objects

While names work reasonably well as a way to indirectly refer to PostScript language objects, they are inconvenient to generate dynamically. User objects, on the other hand, allow you to tag objects with an integer instead of a name, thereby saving space and allowing you to provide identifiers dynamically in both the application and the server.

User objects are stored in the *userdict* dictionary in an array called *UserObjects*. This array is created in private VM and is defined as read-only. Specific operators (**defineuserobject**, **execuserobject**, and **undefineuserobject**) are available for placing, executing, and removing objects in the array.

The **defineuserobject** operator takes two arguments: a nonnegative integer index and the object to be defined. The object to be defined is placed in the array at the position specified by the index. If the index already exists, the new object replaces the existing one. If the index does not exist, the number of index entries in the array is extended to include the new object. When a user object index is assigned to another object, the first object is freed if there are no other references to it. The object does not need to be explicitly freed with the **undef** operator.

The **PSDefineAsUserObj** procedure ensures unique user object indices. Each time this procedure is called, it allocates a new index and associates the index with what is on top of the stack.

Note that it is not necessary to redefine a user object when the contents of the structure it refers to change. For example, if a user object refers to an array, changing entries in the array does not require changing the user object. In the *Clock* application, the gstate objects for the hands change whenever the clock changes size. However, the user objects that refer to the gstate objects can still be used because the gstate objects have changed only internally.

Figure 7.3 shows the *UserObjects* array for the *Clock* application. Entries 1-11 have been allocated by the *Clock* application for the gstate objects and user paths for the hands.

Figure 7.3 *UserObjects array for the Clock application*

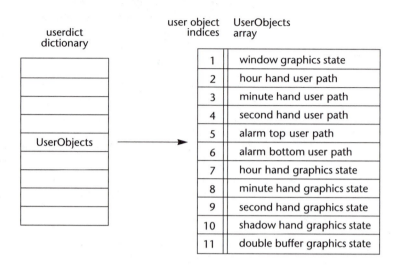

	user object indices	UserObjects array
	1	window graphics state
	2	hour hand user path
	3	minute hand user path
	4	second hand user path
	5	alarm top user path
	6	alarm bottom user path
	7	hour hand graphics state
	8	minute hand graphics state
	9	second hand graphics state
	10	shadow hand graphics state
	11	double buffer graphics state

The **execuserobject** operator takes a single number on the stack and replaces it with the corresponding entry from the UserObjects array. As shown in Figure 7.3, the sequence 2 **execuserobject** evaluates to the hour hand user path.

7.2.3   User Objects and User Paths

In the *Clock* application, user paths are retained as user objects. User objects provide an efficient way to refer to PostScript language objects in the server. Example 7.2 shows an example from the *Clock* application in which a user object refers to a user path.

Example 7.2 *Defining a user object*

Wrap definition:

```
defineps PSWUpathFill(userobject UPath)
  UPath ufill
endps
```

C language code:

```
/* User path operands and operators for the clock hands. */
static float ptsSec[] = {-1.5, 0, 0, 145, 3, 0, 0, -145,
                4, 0, 0, -20, 0, -20, 5.5, 360,
                180,0, 20, 4, 0, 0, 0, 0, 0, 10,
                360, 0};
```

```
static DPSUserPathOp opsSec[] = {dps_moveto, dps_rlineto,
            dps_rlineto, dps_rlineto, dps_rlineto,
            dps_rlineto, dps_arcn, dps_rlineto, dps_rlineto,
            dps_closepath, dps_moveto, dps_arcn,
            dps_closepath};

static float bboxSec[] = {-10, -30, 10, 170};

static int upathSec;

/* Set up second hand user path object. */
PSDoUserPath((DPSPointer) ptsSec, XtNumber(ptsSec),
            dps_float, opsSec, XtNumber(opsSec),
            (DPSPointer) bboxSec, dps_send);
pathSec = PSDefineAsUserObj();

...
/* Use user object defined before */
PSWUpathFill(pathSec);
```

PostScript language trace:

```
...
[<128 byte string> <14 byte string>]
4 exch
defineuserobject
...
4 execuserobject ufill
...
```

The parameters to **PSDoUserPath** describe an array that represents a user path. The operator *dps_send* leaves the user path on the operand stack.

PSDefineAsUserObj allocates a user object index, associates it with whatever is on top of the operand stack, and returns the index to the application. In Example 7.2, the user object index 4 was allocated and associated with the user path left by **PSDoUserPath**. All subsequent references to that user path use the object index 4. Even though **PSDefineAsUserObj** returns a result when it allocates a user object index, it does not require a round-trip to the server because the index is allocated in the client (in a manner similar to the way Xlib allocates window identifiers).

The last line in the PostScript language trace shows how to use a user object index. The **execuserobject** operator replaces the user object index (4) with the object that the index refers to (the user path). The *pswrap* translator automatically generates **execuserobject** for parameters declared with the *userobject* type, as in the wrap **PSWUpathFill**.

7.2.4 When to Use User Objects

User objects are recommended for data stored in the server such as gstate objects, dictionaries, large arrays or strings, user paths, and other objects whose elements are seldom used directly by the application. User objects can also identify PostScript language procedures, but procedures are usually called from within wraps and are rarely referred to by the client application directly.

Use names to refer to objects within wrap bodies and in other PostScript language code because the dictionary lookup mechanism is optimized for names. Use user objects when the objects will be referred to by the application.

If an identifier for a user object is passed to a single operator call or wrap as type *userobject*, the Client Library performs an implicit **execuserobject** on the identifier. Example 7.3 shows an example of a wrap with a **userobject** type parameter.

Example 7.3 *Sample userobject type*

Wrap definition:

```
defineps PSWUpathFill(userobject UPath)
    UPath ufill  % An execuserobject is unnecessary
endps
```

User Paths in Server	
Display times in milliseconds	
With user objects	148
No user objects	150

As the table of display times shows, user objects improve performance only slightly in the *Clock* application. The hand descriptions are not large, and the time required to transmit them is negligible. An application with more complex data to send to the server would show more improvement.

The real advantage of user objects lies in their convenience. It is much simpler to use the user object definition for a user path than to maintain all the data that defines the path. Calling **PSWUpathFill** is simpler than calling **PSDoUserPath** for each use of the path, and there is no performance penalty.

7.2.5 Emulating User Objects for Level 1 Printers

Some PostScript language development packages emulate user objects. Because the implementation is straightforward, it is provided here to show you how to write an emulation package. The emulation applies PostScript Level 1 document structure rules. A full description of the sections of a properly structured document are given in Appendix G, "Document Structure Rules," in the *PostScript Language Reference Manual, Second Edition*. Sections G.4.1, "Prolog," and G.4.2, "Script," are of special interest.

Document Prolog

The document prolog contains the PostScript language procedures that are used elsewhere in the document. This is the place to define procedures that emulate user object operations, as shown in Example 7.4.

Example 7.4 *Procedures to emulate user object operations*

PostScript language code:

```
/defineuserobject {
   userdict /UserObjects get 3 1 roll put
} bind def

/execuserobject {
   userdict /UserObjects get exch get exec
} bind def

/undefineuserobject {
   userdict /UserObjects get exch null put
} bind def
```

Document Setup

The document setup section contains initialization other than procedure definitions. This is the place to define data structures needed by the emulations, as shown in Example 7.5.

Example 7.5 *Data structures to emulate user object operations*

PostScript language code:

```
/MaxUserObjectIndex 30 def
/UserObjects MaxUserObjectIndex 1 add array def
```

The value assigned to MaxUserObjectIndex is the largest user object index used by the application; this value can normally be found by using the value of the global variable *DPSLastUserObjectIndex* in the Client Library.

The user object definitions do not exactly implement the semantics of the emulated operators. In this case, an upper limit has been imposed on the user object index that the emulations can use. Although the real operators expand the UserObjects array dynamically, emulating this behavior is complicated and would make all invocations of **defineuserobject** execute more slowly. Because the application can easily find and set an upper bound for the index, the emulation is able to use the more efficient static array.

7.3 The Graphics State

Painting operators such as **stroke** and **fill** and character-rendering operators such as **show** and **xyshow** cause graphical output to appear on the page or screen. These operators use implicit parameters to decide which pixels to paint. This set of parameters makes up the *graphics state*. The current graphics state defines the environment in which graphics painting operators execute. See section 4.2 in the *PostScript Language Reference Manual, Second Edition.*

Table 7.1 lists the device-independent parameters in the graphics state, together with their default values. An application typically modifies these parameters for drawing. Table 7.2 lists the device-dependent parameters in the graphics state, together with their default values. With the exception of device, which identifies the drawable to which the image is rendered, applications rarely modify these parameters.

Table 7.1 *Device-independent graphics state parameters*

Parameter	Definition	Default
clipping path	The path that defines the current boundary against which output is clipped.	Implementation-specific, but at least as large as the initial drawable size
color	The color that will be used during painting operations. Several color models can be specified.	0 (black)
dash pattern	A description of the dash pattern to be used when lines are rendered by the **stroke** operator.	A solid line
font	The set of graphics shapes (characters) that define the current typeface.	Undefined
line cap	A number that defines the shape of the endpoints of any open path that is stroked.	0 (square butt end)
line join	A number that defines the shape of joins between connected segments of a stroked line.	0 (mitered joins)
line width	The thickness in user space coordinates of lines to be drawn by the **stroke** operator.	1.0
miter limit	The limit of the length of line joins for line segments connected at a sharp angle.	1.0
path	The path that would be rendered by a **fill** or **stroke** operation.	Undefined
position	The current position in user space, also known as the current point.	Undefined
stroke adjustment	A boolean value that determines whether automatic stroke adjustment is on or off.	*true* (on)
transformation matrix	The matrix that maps positions from user space to device space.	A matrix that maps one PostScript language unit to 1/72 inch

Table 7.2 *Device-dependent graphics state parameters*

Parameter	Definition	Default
device	A set of internal primitives for rendering graphical objects in a particular area of raster memory. This parameter identifies the drawable to which the image is rendered.	Specified at context creation time
flatness	A number that reflects the accuracy with which curves are to be rendered. Smaller numbers give smoother curves at the expense of more computations.	1.0
halftone phase	A shift in the alignment of halftone and pattern cells in device space to compensate for window system operations that involve scrolling.	0, 0
halftone screen	A collection of objects that define the halftone screen pattern for gray and color output.	A Type 3 halftone dictionary
transfer function	Adjusts gray or color component values of devices to correct for nonlinear response in a particular device.	A PostScript language procedure

Initially, all graphics state parameters have default values. However, various PostScript operators change the parameters, and each PostScript operator executes with the graphics state left by its predecessors. Therefore, it is important to set the correct parameters before drawing.

Note: *Do not assume that commonly changing graphics state parameters retain their initial default value. A routine should explicitly set the color, position, path, font, and line width, unless the current state of a parameter is known to be appropriate. Routines that set parameters like the dash pattern or miter limit should restore the default values.*

7.3.1 Managing the Graphics State

Level 1 printers do not support gstate objects, so managing the graphics state involves moving the graphics state on and off a *graphics state stack* with **gsave** and **grestore** operations. The **gsave** and **grestore** operators isolate major changes in the current graphics state, with minor changes occurring when parameters are set and reset.

In many cases, a page description PostScript program temporarily replaces graphics state parameters, does some drawing, and then reverts to the previous graphics state. The **gsave** and **grestore** operators accomplish this by first pushing a copy of the entire graphics state onto the graphics state stack (**gsave**) and then restoring the entire graphics state to its former value when the drawing is done (**grestore**). At other times, the page description changes graphics state parameters as drawing proceeds without restoring the previous state. For example, a line drawing may interleave operators to draw lines with operators that change colors.

In some cases, it is more efficient to use the operand stack to save and reset previous parameter values than it is to use the graphics state stack. For example, a **currentlinewidth**/**setlinewidth** pair can encapsulate a change to the line width without a **gsave** and **grestore**, as shown in the following line of code:

```
currentlinewidth 0.5 setlinewidth stroke setlinewidth
```

The graphics state stack is useful for PostScript language programs that are page descriptions. This mechanism is difficult to use when the parameters of the graphics state change unpredictably, as in a display environment. In these cases, gstate objects are more useful.

7.3.2 Gstate Objects

In a display environment, a graphical object is drawn repeatedly, independent of other graphical objects, and within the same or different windows. Clipping paths, coordinate systems, and drawing attributes may differ from one window to another. Because so many graphics state parameters must be stored and recalled in a display environment, manipulating the graphics state stack to store the parameters is objectionably slow. It is more efficient to retain the graphics state for a frequently drawn object as a gstate object in PostScript VM.

Gstate objects store a copy of every graphic parameter, including the current path and clipping path. A single **setgstate** operation installs a gstate object, including all of its parameters.

Linking Gstate Objects to X Drawables

The most important use for a gstate object is as a link to an X drawable (window or pixmap). One component of the graphics state is the X drawable, as specified by the **device** graphics state parameter. This drawable is the destination of all current drawing operations. Because a gstate object describes the graphics state, it can be used to install a different drawable at different times.

A typical application uses the Display PostScript extension to draw into different windows or pixmaps at various times. PostScript operators like **setXgcdrawable** let you change the current drawable. Procedures in the Display PostScript Toolkit like **XDPSSetContextDrawable** provide an interface to these operators. However, these operators are relatively slow, and using them to switch among drawables is not recommended.

A more efficient method is to execute these operators once in order to install a drawable, and capture the current graphics state as a gstate object. Later, you can switch back to the drawable using this gstate object. A single gstate object operation establishes the drawable as the current output device and restores all graphics state parameters associated with that drawable. For example, using gstate objects, it is simple to display a drawing in several different windows concurrently, using different transformation matrices to reflect different zoom levels or different visible areas that result from scrolling. All the application has to do is install the gstate object for each window in turn and display the drawing.

The *Clock* application keeps two gstate objects for X drawables, one for the drawing window and one for a pixmap. If the user turns on double buffering, *Clock* installs the pixmap gstate object as the current graphics state; if the user turns off double buffering, *Clock* installs the window gstate object as the current graphics state. Example 7.6 shows the implementation.

Example 7.6 *Gstate objects for the pixmap*

C language code:

```
if (doubleBuffering && clockPixmap == None) {
    clockPixmap = XCreatePixmap(dpy, win,
                    Xwidth, Xheight, depth);
    PSWSetDrawable(clockPixmap, Xwidth/2, Xheight/2);
    XDPSCaptureContextGState(dpsCtxt, &gstateBuffer);
}

...

void setBufferRendering()
```

```
{
  if (doubleBuffering) {
    if (clockPixmap != None) {
      XDPSSetContextGState(dpsCtxt, gstateBuffer);
    }
  } else XDPSSetContextGState(dpsCtxt, gstateWindow);
}
```

The first section of code comes from the clock display procedure. If double buffering is enabled and the pixmap has not yet been allocated, **XCreatePixmap** is called to create it. **PSWSetDrawable** installs this newly created pixmap as the current drawable, and **XDPSCaptureContextGState** allocates a gstate object for it. (**PSWSetDrawable** is like **XDPSSetContextDrawable**, but it puts the origin in the middle of the window.) The pixmap remains the current drawable for future drawing operations.

When the user changes the double buffering setting in the Timing Window, *Clock* calls **setBufferRendering**. If double buffering is enabled and the pixmap already exists, the code installs the pixmap gstate object and future rendering is to the pixmap. If double buffering is disabled, the code installs the window gstate object and future rendering is to the window.

Disadvantages of Tracking Graphics Parameters with Gstates

In certain restricted situations, gstate objects can be used to keep track of graphics parameters for different components of a drawing. One example of such a situation is in the *Clock* application, which uses gstate objects to maintain the color and rotation of each clock hand in order to avoid setting these values explicitly before each hand is drawn.

In general, this method is not recommended; its performance advantages are few, and it has several disadvantages:

- A gstate object with an empty current path and an empty clipping path takes up about 200 bytes of VM. If either path is not empty, this size is potentially much larger. While it may not be a problem to save the graphics state for just a few objects, saving it for large numbers of objects is impractical. Typically, only a few of the many graphics state parameters differ between elements being drawn, so it is straightforward to set these parameters as necessary.

- While a gstate object can be used to store a painting path or a clipping path in the server, it is not efficient to do so. The user path mechanism, which was specifically designed for this purpose, is a much better choice.

- Gstate objects are difficult and inefficient to emulate on Level 1 PostScript printers. This does not present a problem when gstate objects refer to drawables, because the printed output of an application typically corresponds to the contents of one of the application's windows. If, however, an application uses gstate objects to set graphics state parameters within one window, it will have difficulty printing to Level 1 devices. The application can either use inefficient gstate object emulation or it can use the gstate objects only when drawing to the screen, not when sending to a printer. The latter technique involves creating multiple code paths, something to be avoided whenever possible.

- A final disadvantage is that installing a gstate object installs *all* the parameters in the graphics state. When a separate gstate object has been created for each graphical element, using the gstate objects later to create a composite drawing becomes impractical.

  Consider an application that keeps a gstate object with the drawing parameters (color, line width, font, etc.) for each picture element and draws the elements into multiple windows. The application can no longer just install a gstate object for each window and redraw its output, because installing an element's gstate object will restore the window that was in effect at the time the gstate object was captured. Similarly, the application can no longer scale or zoom its drawing by scaling the coordinate system, because installing an element's gstate object will restore the coordinate system in place when the gstate object was created. Each change to the coordinate system requires updating every gstate object.

Gstate Objects

Display times in milliseconds

With gstate objects	150
No gstate objects	150

The last disadvantage affects the *Clock* application when it uses gstate objects to store drawing parameters for the hands. If the user resizes the clock, each gstate object has to be updated to the new coordinate system. The table of display times shows no performance improvement when gstate objects are used for the hands.

7.3.3 Allocating and Initializing Gstate Objects for Drawables

The primary use for gstate objects is as a way of switching a context to different drawables (windows or pixmaps). There are two ways to associate a drawable with a context:

- An application can specify an initial drawable by creating a context with **XDPSCreateSimpleContext** or **XDPSCreateContext**.

- An application can install a new drawable using the operators **setXgcdrawable** or **setXgcdrawablecolor**. The Display PostScript Toolkit procedures **XDPSSetContextDrawable** and **XDPSSetContextParameters** provide a convenient interface to these operators. Example 7.7 shows how to create a gstate object for a drawable with **XDPSSetContextDrawable**.

Example 7.7 *Creating a gstate object for a drawable*

C language code:

```
DPSContext   dpsCtxt;
Window       win;        /* The destination drawable */
Dimension    winHt;      /* The height of the drawable */
DPSGState    winGstate;
int          status;
...
/* Set drawable in DPS context to window*/
status = XDPSSetContextDrawable (dpsCtxt, win, (int) winHt);

/* Initialize the graphics state parameters */
PSscale (0.5, 0.5);

/* Set up graphics state */
status = XDPSCaptureContextGState (dpsCtxt, &winGstate);
...
```

PostScript language trace:

```
currentXgcdrawable pop pop pop 37748784 0 400
                      setXgcdrawable
.5 .5 scale
1
gstate
defineuserobject
```

After installing the correct drawable, the application sets other graphics state parameters to the defaults for that drawable. In Example 7.7 the application scales the coordinate system by calling **PSscale**. It then creates a gstate object for the current graphics state by executing the **gstate** operator or the Display PostScript Toolkit procedure **XDPSCaptureContextGState**.

To restore the graphics state, simply execute the **setgstate** operator or call the Display PostScript Toolkit procedure **XDPSSetContextGState**, as shown in Example 7.8.

Example 7.8 *Setting the graphics state with a gstate object*

C language code:

```
status = XDPSSetContextGState (dpsCtxt, winGstate);
```

PostScript language trace:

```
1 execuserobject setgstate
```

An application sometimes needs to switch graphics states temporarily, draw, and then return to the previous state. The **setgstate** operation and subsequent drawing can be included within a **gsave/grestore** pair. **grestore** restores the drawable to its previous value. The Display PostScript Toolkit procedures **XDPSPushContextGState** and **XDPSPopContextGState** provide equivalent functionality. These procedures allow application code to temporarily draw into one window (a warning message, for example) and then restore the previous state without having to know what the previous state was.

A gstate object for a drawable should be captured only if you plan to return to that drawable later. The *Clock* application, for example, does not capture a gstate object for the clock face, which forms the background of the clock window. *Clock* draws the face into a pixmap rather than redrawing it directly in the window, but the face is never drawn twice in the same pixmap. The pixmap remains unchanged until the user resizes the window, at which time *Clock* must create a different pixmap because pixmaps cannot change size. Because the program does not have to return to the pixmap that stores the face, it has no need to save a gstate object for that drawable.

7.3.4 Multiple Screens, Colormaps, and Libraries

You can simplify installing a drawable in the graphics state if the following assumptions are true:

- All the drawables that will be installed are on the same screen and have the same depth.

- This screen is the default screen for the display.

- The default color cube and gray ramp are always sufficient.

If these assumptions are true (they usually are), then the only procedures required to install a drawable are **XDPSSetContextDrawable** and, occasionally, the single-operator procedure **DPSsetXoffset,** which sets the origin somewhere other than the lower left corner of the window.

However, if any of these assumptions is false, some additional work is required to install a new drawable in a context. If an application draws with multiple screens or depths, it must set up the context for the screen and depth of the new drawable. If an application does not use the default screen, it must initially set up the screen it intends to use. If an application installs special colormaps for some drawables, it must set them up and then reset them to return to the proper defaults.

Developers of library routines sometimes make false assumptions about the graphics state. The most common error occurs when a library routine uses a passed-in execution context to draw into its own drawable. To make a library routine fully portable and robust, do not assume that the execution context was set up with the correct screen, the correct depth, the correct color cube, and the correct gray ramp. To be safe, the routine should set all the parameters.

Three procedures similar to **XDPSSetContextDrawable** are available to set up the context correctly: **XDPSSetContextScreenDepth**, **XDPSSetContextRGBMap**, and **XDPSSetContextGrayMap**. In addition, a combined procedure **XDPSSetContextParameters** can simultaneously change any or all of these parameters.

Example 7.9 shows a call to **XDPSSetContextParameters** to set all context parameters.

Example 7.9 *Setting context parameters*

C language code:

```
DPSContext dpsCtxt;
Screen *screen;
int depth, height;
Drawable drawable;
status = XDPSSetContextParameters(dpsCtxt, screen, depth,
         drawable, height, (XDPSStandardColormap *) NULL,
         (XDPSStandardColormap *) NULL,
         XDPSContextScreenDepth | XDPSContextDrawable |
         XDPSContextRGBMap | XDPSContextGrayMap);
```

The *screen, depth,* and *height* parameters should hold the screen, depth, and height of *drawable*. Passing two *NULL* colormap parameters tells **XDPSSetContextParameters** to use the default color cube and gray ramps for the passed-in screen. The final parameter is a set of flags telling which of the context parameters to set; this example sets all of them. See sections 12.4, 12.6, and 12.9 for more examples of using **XDPSSetContextParameters**.

See the *Client Library Supplement for X* and the *Display PostScript Toolkit for X* manuals for more information on the default color cube and gray ramp.

7.3.5 Emulating Gstate Objects for Level 1 Printers

Gstate objects present difficulties when applications print on Level 1 printers because gstate objects are difficult to emulate using Level 1 operators. One solution is to represent the gstate object as an array containing all the graphics state parameters. The **gstate** operator, which creates a gstate object, stores all current graphics state parameters in the array. The **setgstate** operator, which installs a gstate object, sets each graphics state parameter to the value in the array.

This solution has memory and performance problems as well as being difficult to implement, so it is best to avoid using gstate objects in the printing process. Set graphics state parameters explicitly, and use the **gsave** and **grestore** operators when printing.

7.4 Storing Images in Offscreen Buffers

Complex drawings are simplified by isolating portions of an image that do not change and storing them in offscreen buffers. An application can copy them to a window as needed.

The *Clock* application provides an example. If the application's background pixmap is enabled, it draws the clock face into a pixmap at initialization and whenever the window is resized. For each movement of a clock hand, the face pixmap is copied into a second pixmap, where the hands are drawn on top of the face. When the drawing of the clock is complete, the composite pixmap is copied into the window drawing area.

Pixmaps are recommended for complex images that remain unchanged for long periods. A 400-by-400-pixel clock face takes approximately 80 milliseconds to draw. Because the image does not change unless the window is resized, a sensible approach is to draw the clock face into a pixmap once and then copy it into the drawable before drawing the hands. The table of display times shows that this approach reduces the time required to draw the clock by over 50%.

Pixmap Background	
Display times in milliseconds	
With pixmap background	70
No pixmap background	150

Creating pixmaps for the clock hands would not increase performance because each hand is rotated to a different position whenever it is displayed, and images can't be rotated easily as they are copied from a pixmap. In order to draw the hands without rotating them, a separate pixmap would be necessary for every position of each hand, a total of more than 200,000 pixmaps. Storing the user path descriptions for the hands in the server provides the best solution to imaging the hands.

Example 7.10 shows the C language code for drawing the clock face.

Example 7.10 *Drawing the clock face*

C language code:

```
void drawFace()
{
  float radius;

  /* Clear the page; add a little bit of slop */
  PSWErasePage (CLRPAGE, -CLOCKSIZE - 2, -CLOCKSIZE - 2,
                2*CLOCKSIZE + 4, 2*CLOCKSIZE + 4);

  radius = CLOCKSIZE * SIZEDASHES;
```

```
        /* Draw the filled circle that makes up the clock face */
        PSWDrawCircle (radius, CLRCIRC, True);

        /* Set the line cap parameter to round cap */
        PSsetlinecap (1);

        /* Draw the minute and hour tick marks around the face */
        drawUpathLines (CLRMIN, WIDMIN, radius * LENMIN,
                        radius, DEGMIN);
        drawUpathLines (CLRHOUR, WIDHOUR, radius * LENHOUR,
                        radius, DEGHOUR);
    }
```

Example 7.11 shows how *Clock* manages the pixmap for the clock face.

Example 7.11 *Handling the face pixmap*

C language code:

```
    if (pixmapBackground && facePixmap == None) {
        facePixmap = XCreatePixmap(dpy, win, Xwidth, Xheight,
                        depth);

        /* Temporarily render into face pixmap */
        PSgsave();
        PSWSetDrawable(facePixmap, Xwidth/2, Xheight/2);
        drawFace();
        PSgrestore();
        /* Wait for drawing to finish */
        DPSWaitContext(dpsCtxt);
    }
    ...
    /* Copy the face into the window, or draw it again */
    if (pixmapBackground) {
        XCopyArea(dpy, facePixmap, win, gc, 0, 0,
                    Xwidth, Xheight, 0, 0);
    } else {
        drawFace();
    }
    /* Draw the hands on top of the face */
    drawHands();
```

The code is taken from the procedure to redisplay the clock face. If a
pixmap background is being used and has not yet been allocated,
XCreatePixmap is called to create it. **PSgsave** saves the graphics state,

and **PSWSetDrawable** installs the pixmap for the face as the drawable. The **drawFace** procedure draws the face into the pixmap, after which **PSgrestore** restores the graphics state to its previous condition.

Example 7.11 continues by checking whether the pixmap background is enabled. If it is, **XCopyArea** copies the face pixmap into the window; if it is not, **drawFace** draws the face into the window. Note that **drawFace** draws using the current graphics state, whatever its current drawable may be. When the face pixmap is installed as the current drawable, **drawFace** renders into the pixmap; when the window is installed as the current drawable, **drawFace** renders into the window.

The Display PostScript extension executes PostScript language code somewhat independently of the rest of the X server. As a result, you must synchronize the activities of drawing into a pixmap and copying out its contents. **DPSWaitContext** provides this synchronization by flushing any information in the communication buffer and waiting until the drawing is complete before returning. If you don't use **DPSWaitContext**, the pixmap may be copied before the drawing is complete.

Applications should call **DPSWaitContext** only when necessary because unnecessary synchronizations slow system performance. Calling **DPSWaitContext** is not necessary after executing a wrap that returns a value because the value cannot be returned until all PostScript language code completes. However, do not use wraps that return values simply because you want to force a synchronization. Use these wraps only when you need to get new information from the server; overall, an application is most efficient if server information can be cached or calculated in the application.

7.4.1 Double Buffering

The *Clock* application uses double buffering to provide smooth animation to the window. Each second, the clock must be redisplayed with its hands rotated to new positions. Without double buffering, the image flickers as the clock background covers up the hands.

Double Buffering	
Display times in milliseconds	
With double buffering	168
No double buffering	150

When double buffering is disabled, *Clock* copies the background directly into the window and then draws the hands in the window. When double buffering is enabled, *Clock* copies the background into a second pixmap and draws the hands in the second pixmap. Only after a new clock image is ready does *Clock* update the window. The performance figures show that double buffering slows redisplay slightly. However, the elimination of flickering makes this time penalty acceptable.

7.4.2   Emulating Pixmaps for Level 1 Printers

Although graphics stored in pixmaps can be printed using the **image**
operator, they are limited to the resolution of the screen. To achieve the
highest quality results for each device, execute the PostScript operators
that describe each graphic or image. Use offscreen buffers only during
interactive display, not for the printing process. When printing, render
the graphics with PostScript operators.

7.5   Scaling a Drawing

The Display PostScript extension makes it easy to scale a drawing to any
width and height. The *Clock* application always draws the clock to
match the shape of its window, no matter how the user resizes it. Figure
7.4 shows *Clock* scaled to match various window sizes.

Figure 7.4 *Clock scaled to different window sizes*

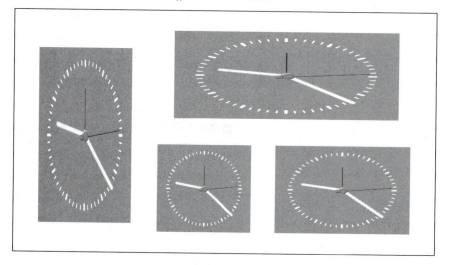

Clock does all its drawing in a coordinate system whose origin is in the
middle of the window and extends from –150 to +150 units in both the
x and *y* directions. The **PSscale** procedure scales this coordinate system
to match the current window size.

Figure 7.5 shows this process. The first drawing in the figure shows the
clock in its coordinate system as originally rendered. If the window is
resized so the clock measures 450 by 600 pixels, *Clock* scales the
coordinate system by 1.5 in the *x* direction and 2.0 in the *y* direction. In
this scaled coordinate system, the point (150, 150) in user space

corresponds to the upper right corner of the window. If a later change makes the clock dimensions 540 by 360 pixels, the coordinate system is scaled by 1.2 in the *x* direction and 0.6 in the *y* direction. In this case, too, the point (150, 150) corresponds to the upper right corner.

Figure 7.5 *Scaling to match the window size*

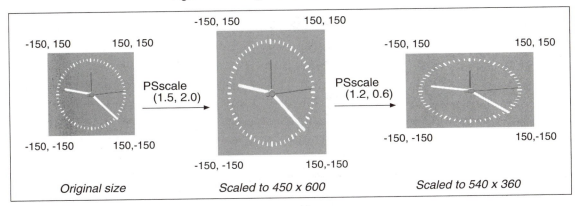

In the PostScript language, all coordinate system transformations take effect relative to the current coordinate system. For example, the net effect of a 10-degree rotation followed by a 20-degree rotation is a 30-degree rotation. *Clock* must compute the relative scale factors to convert its current scaled coordinate system to the new scaled coordinate system. The computation is simple:

1. Use the inverse transformation matrix to find the coordinates, in user space, of the new upper right corner of the window. The standard conversion from device space to user space, as shown in Chapter 4, can be used again.

2. Divide by the user space coordinates of the old upper right corner. This is a constant (150, 150) in the *Clock* application.

Figure 7.6 shows this computation during the last resizing in Figure 7.5. The new window size is shown as a hollow rectangle over the current window, and the coordinates of the upper right corner are (180, 90). Dividing these by 150 yields the scale factors 1.2 and 0.6.

Example 7.12 contains the code to do this scaling.

Figure 7.6 *Computing the scale factor*

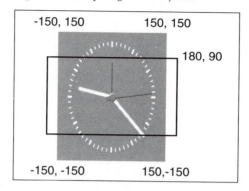

Example 7.12 *Reacting to a resized window*

C language code:

```
PSWSetOffset(newWidth/2, newHeight/2);

/* Compute coordinate of upper right corner */
/* in user space                            */
x = newWidth - newWidth/2;
y = 0 - newHeight/2;

newDPSWidth = Invctm[A_COEFF] * x + Invctm[C_COEFF] * y
                                  + Invctm[TX_CONS];
newDPSHeight = Invctm[B_COEFF] * x + Invctm[D_COEFF] * y
                                   + Invctm[TY_CONS];

/* Compute scale*/
xScale = newDPSWidth / CLOCKSIZE;
yScale = newDPSHeight / CLOCKSIZE;
PSscale (xScale, yScale);

/* Reinitialize clipping and get new matrix */
PSinitclip();
PSinitviewclip();
PSWGetTransform (Ctm, Invctm, &XOffset, &YOffset);
```

The conversion into user space uses the user space computation described in section 4.3 on page PG-49. After scaling the coordinate system, *Clock* reinitializes the clipping regions and gets the new transformation matrix corresponding to the scaled coordinate system.

When a window is resized, an application must perform several bookkeeping tasks. X pixmaps cannot change size, so *Clock* frees any pixmaps it was using and allocates new ones of the appropriate new size. The coordinate system is one of the elements in a gstate object. If gstate objects are associated with the clock hands, these objects must be updated to reflect the new coordinate system. If the gstate objects were not updated, the hands would continue to be drawn in their previous coordinate system.

7.6 Storing Data in the Server

Deciding which items make good candidates for storing in PostScript VM in the server is a matter of judgment. Gstate objects and dictionaries are not visible outside the server, so they must reside in the server. Data structures such as arrays, strings, and user paths can be retained in either the application or the server.

Sometimes it makes sense to store the data in the server rather than to keep passing it from the application, but in most cases structures do not belong in the server. When deciding whether to keep a structure in the server or the application, base your decision on the following factors:

- The size of the structure. Very large arrays are best kept in the application.

- The frequency of its execution. Structures that are called repeatedly usually belong in the server.

- The number of times the structure changes. To keep system overhead down, store structures that change often in the application. Interactive applications such as drawing programs and word processors are penalized when they store data in the server; the data changes so frequently that managing identical copies in the server and the application becomes a problem.

- How frequently the application needs access to the elements of the structure. Frequent calls to access a structure in the server increase system overhead.

- The client-server network transmission overhead. A fast network connection between the application and the server improves the time required to send data to the interpreter, but the overhead incurred accessing the data in the server remains high.

The hands of the clock are objects that can be profitably retained in the server. Their descriptions are not too large, they are called repeatedly, and they do not change. Once their user object descriptions have been sent to the server, the application has no need to access them. The application draws a hand by calling a wrap to draw the user path and passing the appropriate user object identifier to the server.

The declaration, definition, and invocation of user objects for the clock hands are shown in Example 7.2 on page PG-108.

7.7 Comparison of Display Times

Figure 7.7 displays times in milliseconds for displaying the clock using various combinations of the drawing methods in the *Clock* application. The combination of user paths, double buffering, and pixmap background provides the best combination of smooth animation, convenience in programming, and drawing speed. It is the recommended strategy for applications like *Clock*.

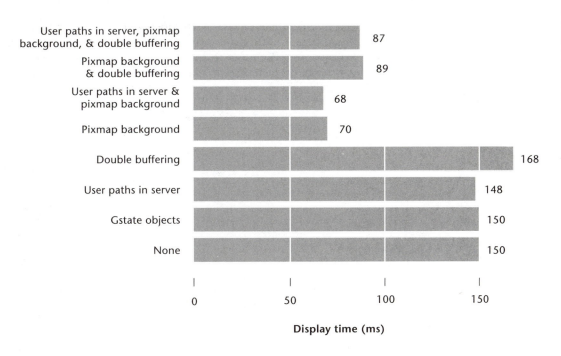

Figure 7.7 *Display times, in milliseconds, from the Clock application*

Drawing Method

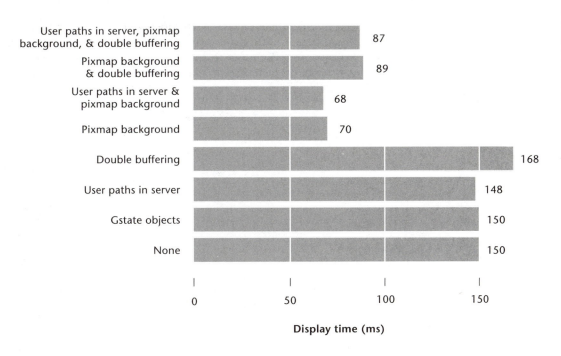

Display time (ms)

7.8   Summary

- User objects provide a convenient mechanism for referring to PostScript objects in the server using an integer identifier instead of a name.

- The graphics state is a collection of parameters that determine how and where a path is rendered.

- The gstate object is a PostScript language data type that encapsulates the values of a particular graphics state.

- Gstate objects allow efficient switching among drawing states and devices.

- You can simplify complex drawings by isolating portions of an image that do not change frequently, drawing them into offscreen buffers, and copying them to the main drawing window when needed.

- It is not always appropriate to store data in the server. Objects that are simple, unchanging, and used repeatedly make good candidates for storing in the server. If the application needs frequent access to data in the object, store the object in the application.

CHAPTER 8

Drawing Small Objects

This chapter uses the *ControlPoint* application to examine methods for displaying large numbers of control points. The term *control point* refers to a glyph that appears on the screen in multiple places, often in great numbers. The most common use of control points is in drawing programs where they are used to indicate selected objects, as shown in Figure 8.1.

Figure 8.1 *Control points on a drawing of a bicycle wheel*

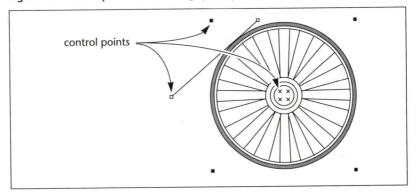

ControlPoint can draw four different control point glyphs: a filled square, an open square, a cross, and an X. The *ControlPoint* application uses the following drawing methods:

- *Basic drawing*—uses **rmoveto** and **rlineto** operators within wraps (see Example 8.4).

- *Cached user paths*—represents each control point as a cached user path and translates the path to each point location before drawing (see Example 8.6 and Example 8.7).

- *Combined user path*—creates a single large user path for multiple control points. Draws the control points with a single **ufill** or **ustroke** operator (see Example 8.8).

- *Rectangle operators*—used only for rectangular control points. Passes an array of rectangles to the **rectfill** and **rectstroke** operators (see Example 8.9 and Example 8.10).

- *Pixmap copying*—draws the control point into an offscreen buffer and then copies the image at each control point location (see Example 8.12, Example 8.13, and Example 8.14).

- **show** *operator*—takes advantage of the font-caching mechanism by turning the control point into a Type 3 font program. Displays the points with the **show** operator (see Example 8.15).

- **xyshow** *operator*—takes advantage of the font-caching mechanism by turning the control point into a Type 3 font program. Draws multiple points simultaneously by using the **xyshow** operator (see Example 8.16).

Figure 8.14 on page PG-173 summarizes the performance of each method for drawing each of the four control point types. Of the seven methods described, using rectangle operators is the fastest for drawing filled rectangular control points. The fastest way to draw other control points is to create a Type 3 font and use the **xyshow** operator.

Copying pixmaps is about two and one half times slower than **xyshow**. It is, however, the only method that can draw multicolored control points directly . The other methods require drawing each color separately. This method is the most efficient when control points have more than two colors.

The other methods used in the example application are all slower and offer no compensating advantages.

Note: *As with many types of drawing, you can use Xlib procedures such as* **XDrawLine**, **XDrawRectangle**, *and* **XFillRectangle** *to draw control point glyphs. However, the Display PostScript drawing techniques provide the advantages of display independence, color model independence, and a choice of available rendering operators.*

The same methods used to draw control points can be applied to drawing any small object. With small objects, consistent rendering and device independence are as important as efficiency. Control points are typically small; the control points in the *ControlPoint* application are four points across. At such small sizes, slight variations in the way the control points are rendered can have a significant effect on appearance.

8.1 Consistency and Device Independence

When drawing control points, you need to consider techniques for consistent rendering and device independence. *Consistent rendering* means that successive instances of the same control point or character look the same on a screen, regardless of the actual point location in device space. *Device independence* means that the same description produces the same results on displays with different resolutions.

Problems with consistent rendering or device independence can affect any type of drawing; however, problems are most noticeable when you are drawing small objects like characters or control points. Even a one-pixel difference can alter the appearance of a shape that is only four or five pixels across. The combination of the Type 1 font format's hinting mechanisms, which constrain character path descriptions to produce readable characters, and the PostScript interpreter's font caching scheme provides a solution for characters. You must use similar adjustment techniques to display control points correctly.

When rendering is inconsistent, as Figure 8.2 illustrates, the same control point description can produce different results when it is rendered to different locations on a screen. The inconsistency occurs when the paths fall at different locations within a pixel in device space.

Figure 8.2 *Inconsistent control points*

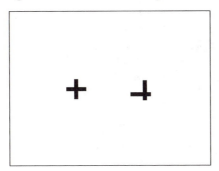

Same screen, different locations

Lack of device independence can be detected only with displays of different resolutions, as in Figure 8.3. Different mappings from user space to device space affect pixelization—that is, which pixels are turned on and which are turned off.

Figure 8.3 *Device-dependent control points*

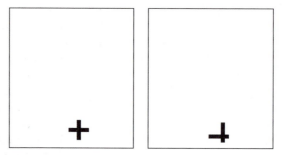

Different screens, same location

Figure 8.4 illustrates the source of these inconsistencies: the positioning of endpoints in the pixel grid. In the figure on the left, the endpoints fall into the centers of pixels, and the control point is drawn correctly. In the figure on the right, however, the endpoints fall into the corners of the pixel grid, and the control point is drawn poorly. This difference lies at the heart of inconsistency and device dependence. With inconsistency, different instances of a drawing fall in different positions relative to the pixel grid. With device dependence, each pixel grid may be a different size, leading to different positioning on different devices.

Figure 8.4 *Pixel placement differences*

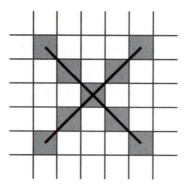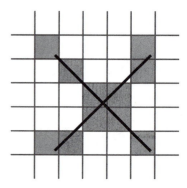

Crossing and endpoints on pixel centers   *Crossing and endpoints near pixel boundaries*

8.1.1 Rendering Consistent Characters and Control Points

Ensuring consistency involves trading off accuracy of display position for appearance. This trade-off occurs in several other places in the execution of the PostScript language.

- Chapter 4 discussed stroke adjustment. A line drawn without stroke adjustment has a width that closely approximates the correct line width, but the results can be uneven and inconsistent. Lines drawn with stroke adjustment have widths that may be further from the correct width, but the resulting lines are rendered more consistently.

- Chapter 6 discussed user paths and mentioned that the translation components of the current transformation matrix are temporarily rounded to integer values when user paths are being drawn. This rounding guarantees that a user path description looks the same no matter where it appears on the screen.

To display characters correctly, the Type 1 font description contains hints to rasterize fonts. For example, one common hint is that the three vertical lines of a lower case "m" must be evenly spaced. Depending on the way a particular "m" lies on the pixel grid, the font rasterizer may move a vertical line left or right by one pixel to create the even spacing. The resulting line is not exactly where it should be according to the character outline, but the results are more visually pleasing. Another rasterization technique ensures the consistent appearance of a character that is rendered repeatedly by moving each character slightly so the character origin always falls at the same spot relative to a pixel.

To create a consistent appearance for control points, adjustment routines similar to the character adjustment routines must be used directly. Each instance of a control point has its origin moved slightly, or *snapped*, to correspond to the center of a pixel. This adjustment guarantees that all control points are displayed consistently, as in the left of Figure 8.4.

Note: *The* **setstrokeadjust** *operator does not guarantee that all executions will be the same or the results symmetrical. Stroke adjustment guarantees only that line width is consistent.*

It is important to apply this snapping technique to the correct point in the control point glyph. Figure 8.5 illustrates the results of snapping the left endpoint of a cross to the pixel center at two different resolutions.

The cross on the left has the correct pixelization, but the arms of the cross on the right are different lengths. In this case, the wrong point was picked for snapping.

Figure 8.5 *Results of snapping the left endpoint of a cross*

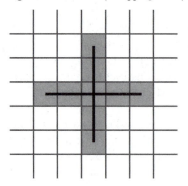   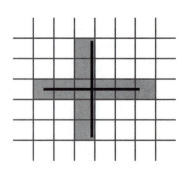

Correct alignment at one resolution   *Incorrect alignment at a different resolution*

To solve this problem, snap the control point center to a pixel center and then make all offsets relative to this location. Correctly drawing the line segment for the cross horizontal requires snapping the center point in device space, doing a relative move to the right for half of the width, and then doing a relative stroke to the left for the full width. The result is a segment that is evenly distributed on each side of the center for any screen resolution.

Example 8.1 shows the **adjust** procedure, which snaps a control point to the center of a pixel in device space. The procedure performs the snap calculation in three steps:

- Multiply the input user space coordinates by the current transformation matrix. The result is a point in device space.

- Take the floor of each coordinate of the point in device space and add 0.5 for each coordinate. This step moves the point to the center of its pixel.

- Multiply this center coordinate by the inverse of the current transformation matrix. This step gives a new point in user space, near the original point but corresponding to the center of a pixel.

Example 8.1 *Snapping a point to a pixel center in device space*

C language code:

```
static void adjust(X, Y)
  register float *X, *Y;
{
  float x, y;

  /* Convert to device space */
  x = floor(Ctm[A_COEFF] * *X + Ctm[C_COEFF] * *Y +
          Ctm[TX_CONS]);
  y = floor(Ctm[B_COEFF] * *X + Ctm[D_COEFF] * *Y +
          Ctm[TY_CONS]);

  /* Move to center of pixel */
  x += 0.5;
  y += 0.5;

  /* Convert back */
  *X = Invctm[A_COEFF] * x + Invctm[C_COEFF] * y +
      Invctm[TX_CONS];
  *Y = Invctm[B_COEFF] * x + Invctm[D_COEFF] * y +
      Invctm[TY_CONS];
} /* end adjust () */
```

Doing the calculation in the application allows a program to snap points without noticeably affecting performance. When the calculation is done in PostScript language code, drawing takes up to twice as long. Performing the calculation in PostScript language code is not even possible for combined user path and rectangle operators.

Note: *Although snapping to device space does not slow performance, it does make the program more complex. Snapping makes a big difference for small drawings, but it has a negligible effect on larger ones. It adds unnecessary complexity to applications that draw only large objects.*

8.1.2 Advanced Techniques for Device Independence

Even with the adjustment techniques discussed so far, control points may still be rendered inconsistently if their vertices fall directly on pixel boundaries. These inconsistencies are the result of floating-point calculations that are used to transform coordinates from user space into device space: the results of the floating-point calculations are rounded off to convert them to integers in device space. Round-off can make a point that should fall directly on a pixel boundary fall sometimes on one side and sometimes on the other. The resulting control points may have different shapes depending on where they are drawn on the screen—that is, rendering will be inconsistent.

To determine whether the vertices of a control point fall on pixel boundaries, compute the x and y distances, in pixels, of each vertex from the control point center. Since the center will always be snapped to the center of a pixel, a vertex falls on a pixel boundary if these distances are equal to some whole number of pixels plus one-half pixel. In mathematical terms, if the following expression is true for either the x or y coordinate of a vertex, the vertex falls on a pixel boundary:

$$\text{DistanceFromCenter } (units) \times \text{ScreenResolution} \left(\frac{pixels}{unit} \right) - 0.5 = \text{Integer } (pixels)$$

For example, the control points used in the *ControlPoint* application are four units square, placing each vertex two units from the center in both the x and y directions. Assume that the control points will be displayed on a screen with a resolution of 90 pixels per inch, and that one unit of PostScript user space is the standard 1/72 inch. The following calculation, which results in the value 2, shows that the vertices of the control points will fall on pixel boundaries when the control point center is snapped to pixel center:

$$2 \ (units) \ \times \left(90 \left(\frac{pixels}{inch} \right) \times \frac{1}{72} \left(\frac{inch}{units} \right) \right) - 0.5 = 2 \ (pixels)$$

On a screen with resolution of 126 pixels per inch, the control point vertices will also fall on pixel boundaries:

$$2 \ (units) \ \times \left(126 \left(\frac{pixels}{inch} \right) \times \frac{1}{72} \left(\frac{inch}{units} \right) \right) - 0.5 = 3 \ (pixels)$$

Figure 8.6 illustrates these two cases. The figure shows the centers and edges of a square control point that measures 4 user space units in height and width superimposed on grids representing 90-pixel-per-inch and 126-pixel-per-inch resolutions.

Figure 8.6 *Control points with vertices on pixel boundaries will be inconsistent.*

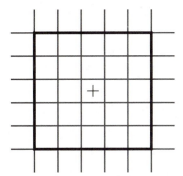

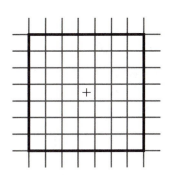

A square control point that measures 2 units from center to edge in user space measures 2.5 pixels from center to edge on a 90-pixel-per-inch screen.

The same control point measures 3.5 pixels from center to edge on a 126-pixel-per-inch screen.

When vertices fall directly on pixel boundaries you should move them slightly to make them fall consistently inside the pixel grid. Two obvious techniques to do this are to change the size of the control points by a small amount or scale the coordinate system by a small amount, effectively changing the resolution.

Example 8.2 shows how the *ControlPoint* application ensures consistent rendering of its control points. The calculations are simplified in this case because the control points have the same height and width. The procedure **adjustFigureSize** first computes the user space coordinate corresponding to (0.5, 0.5) in device space. It then finds one of the corners by subtracting half the figure size from x and y and converts this location back into device space. If the resulting point is close to a pixel boundary, the figure size is made slightly larger by adding 0.001. This small change is enough to guarantee that the corners will consistently fall on the same side of the pixel boundaries no matter where the point is drawn.

Example 8.2 *Adjusting figure size to avoid round-off errors*

C language code:

```
static void adjustFigureSize()
{
    int intX, intY;
    double floatX, floatY;
    float x, y;
```

```
                         /* Convert (0.5, 0.5) into user space */
                         x = Invctm[A_COEFF] * .5 + Invctm[C_COEFF] * .5 +
                             Invctm[TX_CONS];
                         y = Invctm[B_COEFF] * .5 + Invctm[D_COEFF] * .5 +
                             Invctm[TY_CONS];

                         /* Move to a corner */
                         x -= figureSize/2;
                         y -= figureSize/2;

                         /* Convert to device space */
                         floatX = Ctm[A_COEFF] * x + Ctm[C_COEFF] * y +
                                  Ctm[TX_CONS];
                         floatY = Ctm[B_COEFF] * x + Ctm[D_COEFF] * y +
                                  Ctm[TY_CONS];

                         /* Round to nearest integer */
                         intX = floor(floatX + 0.5);
                         intY = floor(floatY + 0.5);

                         /* If we are too close to a pixel boundary, make
                            figure larger */
                         if (ABS(floatX - (double) intX) < 0.0005 ||
                             ABS(floatY - (double) intY) < 0.0005) {
                             figureSize += 0.001;
                         }
                     }
```

Unfortunately, there is no single way to make this adjustment work for all control point shapes. The procedure **adjustFigureSize** relies on having all control point edges lie on a square centered around the control point and with each side equal to *figureSize/2*. Control point shapes that do not have this property require different adjustment code.

8.2   The ControlPoint Application

The *ControlPoint* application uses seven methods to demonstrate drawing small control point shapes. Timings enable you to measure the performance of each method. Figure 8.7 shows the *ControlPoint* window.

Figure 8.7 *ControlPoint application window*

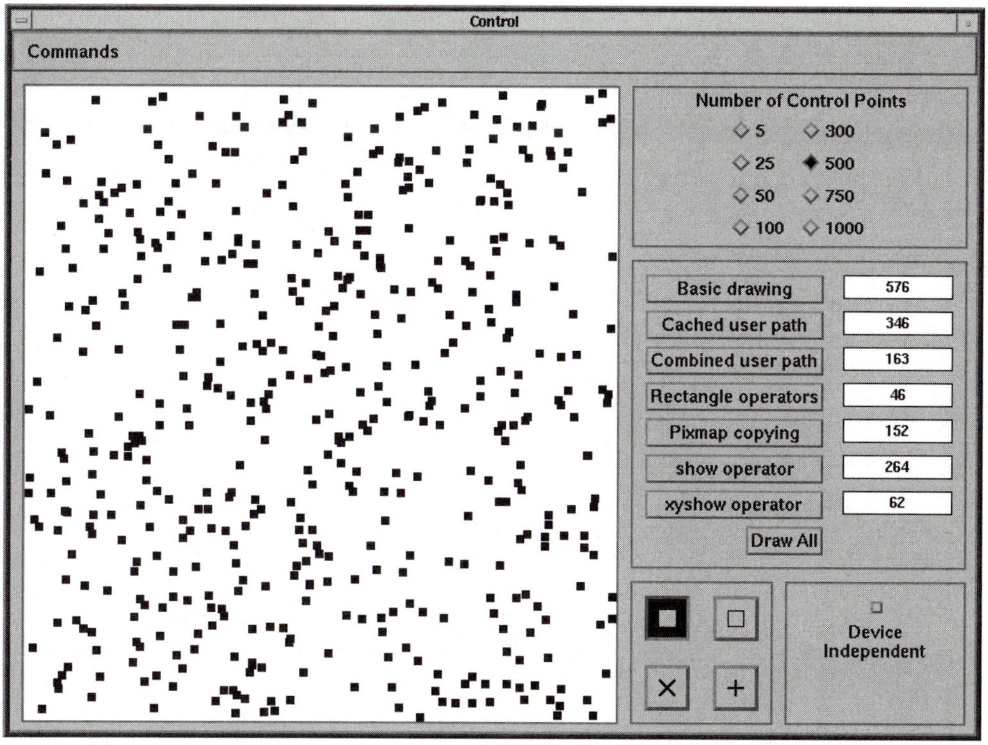

At initialization, the *ControlPoint* application creates an array containing 1,000 random locations for control points. The control settings in the user interface let the user choose 5 to 1,000 points, seven drawing methods, and four control point shapes. The user can activate or deactivate the Device Independence toggle to see the results and the performance effect of snapping the control point origins.

The application drawing methods are described below. Each section describes the implementation of the drawing method and includes a sample of the PostScript language code produced when the method is used to draw five control points. The best methods are implemented simply and produce compact PostScript traces. It is not a coincidence that the traces for the most effective approaches represent coordinates as number strings, which is the most compact and efficient representation for lists of numbers.

Example 8.11 lists some of the global data declarations for the *ControlPoint* application.

Example 8.3 *ControlPoint global data declarations*

C language code:

```
/* Master list of x/y coordinates.
 * Each consecutive pair makes one point. */
float XYPoints[MAX_ARRAY];

/* Buffers for sending user paths and xyshow characters */
PSUserPathOp OpsBuffer[MAX_UPATHOPS];
char    ShowBuffer[MAX_UPATHOPS];
float XYBuffer[MAX_UPATHPTS];
float BBox[4];

float figureSize;          /* size of control point */
float height;              /* DPS height of the X Window */
float width;               /* DPS width of the X Window */
int numPoints;             /* number of points to draw */
int index;                 /* index of points to draw */
char fontchar;             /* font character to draw */
char *basicProc;           /* basic method wrap procedure*/
char *basicOp;             /* basic method DPS operator */
float *userPtsArray;       /* user paths points array */
DPSUserPathOp *userOpsArray; /* user paths operators array */
DPSUserPathAction userOp;  /* user path action operator */
char *rectOp;              /* rectangle operator */
Boolean  devIndependent; /* state of device indep. toggle */
```

8.2.1 Basic Drawing

Basic Drawing

Display times for no adjustment and adjustment of 500 points in milliseconds

■	Filled	569	571
□	Open	463	466
+	Cross	409	408
×	X	431	432

The basic drawing method displays control points by calling a wrap for each control point. Four PostScript language procedures are used; each procedure describes a different control point. Only the procedure for the control point currently selected in the user interface is called.

Example 8.4 lists the wrap **PSWDefineControlPoints**, which defines the four PostScript language procedures **BRF**, **BRS**, **BX**, and **BC**. The procedures draw the filled-rectangle, stroked-rectangle, X, and cross control points. The wrap also defines the procedure **A**, which performs the snapping calculation shown in Example 8.1. However, here the computation is done in the PostScript language in the server instead of in the C language in the application. This procedure is used by the drawing methods, described later in the chapter, that use an application-defined font.

Example 8.4 *Definitions of control point drawing procedures*

Wrap definition:

```
defineps PSWDefineControlPoints(float size)
  /HALF size 2 div def

  % Bound rectangle fill
  /BRF {          % x y BRF -
    moveto HALF neg HALF neg rmoveto 0 size rlineto
    size 0 rlineto 0 size neg rlineto size neg 0 rlineto
    closepath fill
  } bind def

  % Bound rectangle stroked
  /BRS {          % x y BRS -
    moveto HALF neg HALF neg rmoveto 0 size rlineto
    size 0 rlineto 0 size neg rlineto size neg 0 rlineto
    closepath stroke
  } bind def

  % Bound X
  /BX {              % x y BX -
    moveto HALF neg HALF neg rmoveto size size rlineto
    0 size neg rmoveto size neg size rlineto stroke
  } bind def

  % Bound cross
  /BC {              % x y BC -
    moveto 0 HALF rmoveto 0 size neg rlineto
    HALF neg HALF rmoveto size 0 rlineto stroke
  } bind def

  % Stroke adjustment
  /A {               % x y A x' y'
    transform
    floor 0.5 add exch
    floor 0.5 add exch
    itransform
  } bind def
endps
```

Example 8.5 lists the code that displays the control points using the basic drawing method. The wrap **PSWBasic** is passed the name of one of the four procedures **BRF**, **BRS**, **BX**, and **BC**. The procedure's name comes from the global variable *basicProc*, which is set when the user selects a *ControlPoint* shape button. The variable points to a string that contains the procedure name.

Example 8.5 *Basic drawing*

Wrap definition:

```
defineps PSWBasic(float X, Y; char *Figure)
  X Y Figure
endps
```

C language code:

```
void drawBasic ()
{
  int i;
  float x, y;

  for (i = index; i < index + (numPoints * 2); i += 2) {
    x = XYPoints[i];
    y = XYPoints[i + 1];
    if (devIndependent) adjust(&x, &y);
    PSWBasic(x, y, basicProc);
  }
}
```

PostScript language trace:

```
39.540001 478.549988 BRF fill
200.600006 197.649994 BRF fill
310.220001 339.709991 BRF fill
92.360001 474.529999 BRF fill
204.139999 492.670013 BRF fill
```

If the user sets the Device Independent toggle, the **drawBasic** procedure adjusts each control point coordinate to a pixel center by calling the **adjust** procedure. As Figure 8.8 illustrates, using this method without control point adjustment leads to inconsistent pixel placement.

Figure 8.8 *Basic drawing*

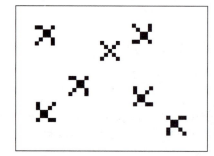
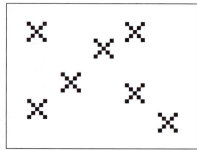

No adjustment   *Adjusted to device space*

Using conventional path construction operators like those used in the basic drawing method is not recommended for drawing control points. If you compare the performance times with those of other methods, you will see that the basic drawing method is the slowest because each wrap generates unnecessary setup, data formatting, and operator execution.

8.2.2 User Paths

Drawing control points with user paths is notably faster than the basic drawing method. However, user paths do not perform as well as some of the other control point drawing methods described later in this chapter.

The first method of drawing control points with user paths caches a single control point description in the user path cache and translates it to each location before drawing. This method, while faster than basic drawing, is still quite slow compared to the preferred methods.

Note: *For a description of a productive use of the user path cache, see Chapter 10, "Drawing and Scrolling," beginning on page PG-201.*

The second method of drawing control points with user paths places a set of user path descriptions into a large array and then draws the entire set with a single **ufile** or **ustroke** operation. This method is much faster than using cached user paths, but other methods are faster still.

User Path Descriptions

Example 8.6 lists the user path descriptions that both user path methods use to draw control points.

Example 8.6 *Control point descriptions*

C language code:

```
float ptsRectFill[ ] = {8, -2, -2, 0, 4, 4, 0, 0, -4};
DPSUserPathOp opsRectFill[ ] = {5, dps_rmoveto, dps_rlineto,
              dps_rlineto, dps_rlineto, dps_closepath};

float ptsRectStroke[ ] = {8, -2, -2, 0, 4, 4, 0, 0, -4};
DPSUserPathOp opsRectStroke[ ] = {5, dps_rmoveto,
                    dps_rlineto, dps_rlineto, dps_rlineto,
                    dps_closepath};

float ptsX[ ] = {8, -2, -2, 4, 4, 0, -4, -4, 4};
```

```
DPSUserPathOp opsX[ ] = {4, dps_rmoveto, dps_rlineto,
                         dps_rmoveto, dps_rlineto};

float ptsCross[ ] = {8, 0, 2, 0, -4, -2, 2, 4, 0};
DPSUserPathOp opsCross[ ] = {4, dps_rmoveto, dps_rlineto,
                             dps_rmoveto, dps_rlineto};
```

The first number in each array is the number of remaining entries in the array. The information from these arrays is placed into other arrays before being sent to the server, as shown in Example 8.7 and Example 8.8.

Cached User Paths

Cached User Paths		
Display times for no adjustment and adjustment of 500 points in milliseconds		
■ Filled	350	351
☐ Open	361	366
+ Cross	357	358
✕ X	354	355

The code to draw with the user path cache defines a single generic control point centered around the location (0, 0)—the origin of user space. This origin is then translated to each control point location, and the control point is drawn around that center point.

The first part of Example 8.7 puts the description of the control point into the arrays *XYBuffer*, *BBox*, and *OpsBuffer*. If device independence is set, the **adjust** procedure moves the origin of the initial control point. When the user selects a control point shape, the *ControlPoint* application sets *userPtsArray*, *userOpsArray*, and *userOp*. The variable *userPtsArray* contains the address of one of the four coordinate arrays, *userOpsArray* contains the address of one of the four operation arrays, and *userOp* contains either *dps_ufill* or *dps_ustroke*. The variable *figureSize* is the width and height of the control point (4 points, possibly modified by the **adjustFigureSize** procedure in Example 8.2).

An important step in setting up the user path is to add the *dps_ucache* operator to the constructed array. This step instructs the user-path-rendering code to cache the results of rendering the path. Subsequent uses of this path come from the user path cache.

To draw a control point, **drawUserCache** translates the origin to a specified location and draws the user path. The translation is relative to the last **translate** performed. Relative translation is faster than absolute translation encapsulated within a **gsave**/**grestore** nesting.

Example 8.7 *Drawing a cached user path*

C language code:

```c
void drawUserCache ()
{
  int i, i_op = 0, i_pt;

  /* Set the initial operator to cache the user path */
  OpsBuffer[i_op++] = dps_ucache;

  /* Set up the bounding box points */
  BBox[0] = -figureSize/2;
  BBox[1] = -figureSize/2;
  BBox[2] = figureSize/2;
  BBox[3] = figureSize/2;

  /* Start out the user path at the origin */
  XYBuffer[0] = 0;
  XYBuffer[1] = 0;
  OpsBuffer[i_op++] = dps_moveto;

  if (devIndependent) adjust(XYBuffer, XYBuffer+1);

  /* Copy the user path points and operators */
  i_pt = 2;
  for (i = 1; i <= userPtsArray[0]; i++)
          XYBuffer[i_pt++] = userPtsArray[i];
  for (i = 1; i <= userOpsArray[0]; i++)
          OpsBuffer[i_op++] = userOpsArray[i];

  /* Save the graphics state
   * for the following translations */
  PSgsave();

  /* Translate to the first point */
  PStranslate(XYPoints[index], XYPoints[index + 1]);

  for (i = index; i < index + (numPoints * 2); i += 2) {
    /* Render the control point using the cached user path */
    PSDoUserPath((DPSPointer) XYBuffer, i_pt, dps_float,
    OpsBuffer, i_op, (DPSPointer) BBox, userOp);

    /* Translate to the next point */
    PStranslate(XYPoints[i + 2] - XYPoints[i],
                XYPoints[i + 3] - XYPoints[i + 1]);
  }
```

```
                        /* Restore the graphics state */
                        PSgrestore();
                    } /* end drawUserCache ( ) */
```

PostScript language trace:

```
39.540001 478.549988 translate
[<9530000ec0800000c0800000408000004080000000000000000000000c0
000000c0000000000000000404000004040000000000000000000000c04000
00> <0b0001020404040a>] ufill
161.059998 -280.899994 translate
[<9530000ec0800000c0800000408000004080000000000000000000000c0
000000c0000000000000000404000004040000000000000000000000c04000
00> <0b0001020404040a>] ufill
109.619995 142.059998 translate
[<9530000ec0800000c0800000408000004080000000000000000000000c0
000000c0000000000000000404000004040000000000000000000000c04000
00> <0b0001020404040a>] ufill
-217.860001 134.820007 translate
[<9530000ec0800000c0800000408000004080000000000000000000000c0
000000c0000000000000000404000004040000000000000000000000c04000
00> <0b0001020404040a>] ufill
111.779999 18.140015 translate
[<9530000ec0800000c0800000408000004080000000000000000000000c0
000000c0000000000000000404000004040000000000000000000000c04000
00> <0b0001020404040a>] ufill
-65.979996 -281.380005 translate
```

In Example 8.7, the benefit of using the user path cache is negated
because a translate operation must be performed and the user path
description must be sent for each control point. Storing the user path
descriptions in the server using user objects, as discussed in Chapter 7,
does not help noticeably with simple user paths like these.

As discussed in Chapter 6, the user path machinery always adjusts the
translation portion of the current transformation matrix to an integral
pixel boundary. This adjustment guarantees that the user path renders
consistently, no matter where it appears on the screen. Coordinate
adjustment is still necessary, however, to guarantee that the shapes are
centered; otherwise the control points might be rendered consistently
but be distorted, as shown in Figure 8.9.

Figure 8.9 *Drawing consistent, distorted control points with the user path cache*

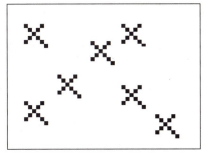

Distorted images can result when control points are not adjusted

Combined User Path

Combined User Path

Display times for no adjustment and adjustment of 500 points in milliseconds

■	Filled	160	172
□	Open	116	117
+	Cross	102	105
×	X	120	116

The combined user path method combines multiple control points into a single user path, similar to the way the *Dial* application combined graduation marks in Chapter 6. This method requires large arrays to hold the coordinates and operators. The arrays are filled alternately with a path description for each control point and a **moveto** operator. In this method, the application must transmit almost as much data to the server as in the cached user path method, but by combining rendering operations, it speeds up drawing by about three times.

The combined user path method is not as fast as the fastest methods, but it works for any control point shape, and it does not require the creation of a Type 3 font, as the **xyshow** method does. One disadvantage of this method is that it requires the application to send large amounts of data to the server, so performance degrades quickly on slow networks.

Example 8.8 lists the code for this method.

Example 8.8 *Drawing with a combined user path*

C language code:

```
void drawUserPath()
{
  int i, i_op, i_pt, j;

  /* Set up the bounding box points */
  BBox[0] = 0;
  BBox[1] = 0;
  BBox[2] = width;
```

```
                BBox[3] = height;

                i = 0; i_pt = 0; i_op = 0;
                while (i < numPoints * 2) {
                  /* Send the array to the server if
                   * the array limit has been reached */
                  if ((i_pt + userPtsArray[0] > MAX_UPATHPTS) ||
                      (i_op + (int) userOpsArray[0] > MAX_UPATHOPS)) {
                    PSDoUserPath((DPSPointer) XYBuffer, i_pt,
                                 dps_float, OpsBuffer, i_op,
                                 (DPSPointer) BBox, userOp);
                    i_pt = 0; i_op = 0;
                  }

                  /* Set the next XY coordinate point and operator */
                  XYBuffer[i_pt++] = XYPoints[index + i++];
                  XYBuffer[i_pt++] = XYPoints[index + i++];

                  if (devIndependent)
                    adjust(XYBuffer+i_pt-2, XYBuffer+i_pt-1);

                  OpsBuffer[i_op++] = dps_moveto;

                  /* Copy the user path points into the XY array */
                  for ( j = 1; j <= userPtsArray[0]; j++, i_pt++)
                    XYBuffer[i_pt] = userPtsArray[j];

                  /* Copy the operators into the operator array */
                  for ( j = 1; j <= userOpsArray[0]; j++, i_op++)
                    OpsBuffer[i_op] = userOpsArray[j];
                }

                /* Render the last control points */
                PSDoUserPath((DPSPointer) XYBuffer, i_pt, dps_float,
                             OpsBuffer, i_op, (DPSPointer) BBox, userOp);
              } /* end drawUserPath () */
```

PostScript language trace:

```
[( <220 byte string> )
<0001020404040a01020404040a01020404040a01020404040a010204040
40a>] ufill
```

This example is similar to Example 8.7, but there are some important differences. In Example 8.8, the bounding box of the user path is set to the entire drawing area, not to the size of a single control point as it was in Example 8.7. Because the combined user path method combines and draws all control points at their actual positions, the bounding box must include the entire extent of the path.

The **drawUserPath** procedure places a **moveto** operator into the user path description and follows it with the description of the control point. This process is repeated for every control point.

The **drawUserPath** procedure adjusts the new center for each control point as it adds it to the point array. This adjustment is required for consistent rendering; without it, the control points may be distorted depending on their location, just as in the basic drawing method.

A minor side effect occurs with combined user paths. When there are too many control points to fit into a single user path, they are grouped into separate user paths. Because each user path is drawn in succession, the control points appear on the screen in waves, which may be distracting to users. In the *ControlPoint* application, rendering 1,000 points requires three user paths of a few hundred points each.

Note: *Applications that produce PostScript language code suitable for emulation on Level 1 printers should limit user paths to 1,500 points, the path limit for Level 1 printers.*

8.3 Rectangle Operators

Rectangle Operators

Display times for no adjustment and adjustment of 500 points in milliseconds

■	Filled	46	54
□	Open	85	93
+	Cross	–	–
×	X	–	–

The **rectfill** and **rectstroke** operators provide the simplest method to draw small control point shapes of the seven discussed in this chapter. The drawback is that these rectangle operators can be used only for control points with rectangular shapes.

The arguments for the rectangle operators can take three forms: four numbers describing a single rectangle, an array, or an encoded number string that describes an arbitrary number of rectangles (see Example 8.9). The second and third forms are optimized versions of the first. The array or number string can contain the coordinates for multiple rectangles.

Example 8.9 *Invoking the rectfill operator*

PostScript language code:

```
x y width height    rectfill
numarray            rectfill
numstring           rectfill
```

Level 1 equivalent for the x y width height case:

```
gsave
newpath
x y moveto
width 0 rlineto
0 height rlineto
width neg 0 rlineto
closepath
fill
grestore
```

Providing an array of rectangles for rectangle operators is much faster than calling the operators many times, for the same reasons that user paths are faster than conventional drawing. Only one wrap or PostScript operator is needed to display a large number of rectangles, thereby minimizing the number of PostScript language operations executed. When the array of rectangles is replaced by individual calls to **rectfill** or **rectstroke**, the processing time increases by a factor of six. Whenever possible, combine multiple rectangles, even with different sizes, into a single operation.

Example 8.10 shows the **drawRectOp** procedure. Coordinate adjustment is required for each point to avoid inconsistent rendering. After adjustment, the origin is moved to the lower left corner of the rectangle by subtracting half the figure size.

Example 8.10 *Drawing with rectangle operators*

Wrap definition:

```
defineps PSWRectDraw(float numstring XYCoords[j]; int j;
                     char *rectOp)
  XYCoords rectOp
endps
```

C language code:

```
void drawRectOp()
{
  int i, j;

  for (i = index, j = 0; i < index + (numPoints * 2);
       i += 2, j += 4) {
    /* Draw if the array limit has been reached */
    if (j + 3 > MAX_RECTPTS) {
      PSWRectDraw(XYBuffer, j, rectOp);
      j = 0;
```

```
    }
    /* Set up XY coords and size of the next rectangle */
    XYBuffer[j] = XYPoints[i];
    XYBuffer[j + 1] = XYPoints[i + 1];
    if (devIndependent) adjust (XYBuffer+j, XYBuffer+j+1);

    XYBuffer[j] -= figureSize/2;
    XYBuffer[j + 1] -= figureSize/2;
    XYBuffer[j + 2] = figureSize;
    XYBuffer[j + 3] = figureSize;
  }
  /* Render the last control points */
  PSWRectDraw(XYBuffer, j, rectOp);
} /* end drawRectOp () */
```

PostScript language trace:

```
<95300014421828f643ee86664040000040400004347199a43442666404
0000040400000439a5c2943a91ae1404000004040000042b5b85243ec83d
74040000040400000434aa3d743f595c34040000040400000> rectfill
```

8.4 Pixmap Copying

Pixmap Copying

*Display times for no adjustment
and adjustment of 500 points
in milliseconds*

		no adj.	adj.
■	Filled	151	151
□	Open	151	151
+	Cross	151	151
×	X	151	151

This method copies a control point that has been rendered in a pixmap into each control point location. Although it is two and a half times slower than **xyshow**, copying pixmaps allows multicolored control points to be rendered without having to draw the control point multiple times. All other methods require drawing each color in the control point separately.

Because copying affects both the foreground and background, simply copying a pixmap does not produce the desired results for control points that are not solid rectangles. A simple copy changes pixels in the original drawing that should be visible through transparent sections of the control point. The pixmap copying operations should result in a composite drawing like the one shown in the upper right in Figure 8.10, in which transparent parts of the control point do not alter the original drawing. This result can be achieved by applying a logical operation to the pixmap when copying it to the screen.

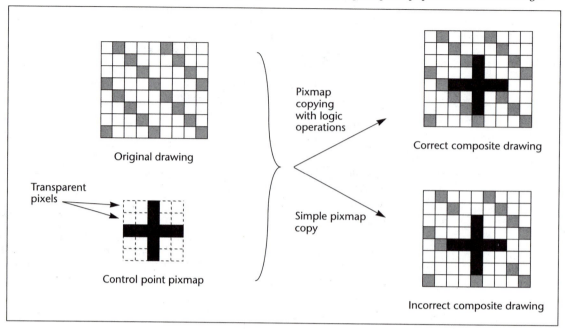

Figure 8.10 *Logic operations on control point pixmaps produce the desired image.*

The *ControlPoint* application uses the following logical operations to correctly render controls point with transparent sections:

- The control point is drawn into two pixmaps, one in which the background bits are all 0's and one in which the background bits are all 1's.

- The pixmap with the 1 background, called the bit-clearing pixmap, is logically ANDed into the existing drawing, which turns off bits that are not set in the control point. The 1 background prevents pixels that are not in the control point from being cleared.

- The pixmap with the 0 background, called the bit-setting pixmap, is logically ORed into the existing drawing, which turns on bits that are set in the control point. The 0 background prevents pixels not in the control point from being set.

Table 8.1 shows an example of these operations applied to four pixels of a composite pixmap.

Table 8.1 *Logical operations that draw a composite pixmap*

Pixmap description	Operation	Identifier	Pixel 1	Pixel 2	Pixel 3	Pixel 4
Original drawing		*A*	0011 1100	0011 1100	0011 1100	0000 0000
Control point		*B*	*undefined*	0010 1010	0010 1010	0010 1010
All 1's		*C*	1111 1111	1111 1111	1111 1111	1111 1111
Bit-clearing values	*B* AND *C* =	*D*	1111 1111	0010 1010	0010 1010	0010 1010
Intermediate result	*A* AND *D* =	*E*	0011 1100	0010 1000	0010 1000	0000 0000
All 0's		*F*	0000 0000	0000 0000	0000 0000	0000 0000
Bit-setting values	*B* OR *F* =	*G*	0000 0000	0010 1010	0010 1010	0010 1010
Composite pixmap	*E* OR *G* =	*H*	0011 1100	0010 1010	0010 1010	0010 1010

The first line in Table 8.1, identified by the label *A*, shows four pixels in the original drawing. Line *B* shows three pixels from the control point that will be overlaid on the four pixels in line *A*. Pixel 1 in line *B* is not defined as part of the control point (that is, it is transparent with respect to the original drawing). Wherever a control point pixel exists (pixels 2, 3, and 4), its value will replace the original pixel; wherever a control point pixel is not defined (pixel 1), the pixel from the original drawing will show.

Line *D* shows pixels in the bit-clearing pixmap, formed by ANDing line *B* with a pixmap that consists entirely of 1's (line *C*). The bit-clearing pixmap contains 1's wherever no control point pixel was defined (in this case, pixel 1). Line *E* is an intermediate result produced by ANDing the original drawing (line *A*) with the bit-clearing pixmap (line *D*).

Line *G* is the bit-setting pixmap formed by ORing line *B* with a pixmap composed entirely of 0's (line *F*). The bit-setting pixmap contains 0's wherever there is no control point pixel (pixel 1). The final line (labeled *H*) shows the result of ORing the intermediate pixmap *E* with the bit-setting pixmap *G*. Line *H* contains pixel 1 from the original drawing, where no control point pixel was defined, and pixels from the control point at positions 2, 3 and 4. The result of this pixmap manipulation is the desired result—an image that overlays the defined control point pixels on the existing drawing.

Note: *For solid, rectangular control points, this pixmap manipulation is not necessary. Instead, you can make the pixmap exactly the size of the control point and copy it into the original drawing at the desired location. The result is about twice as fast as the method described above because it only does one pixmap operation per control point.*

Example 8.11 shows the data declarations for the pixmap copying method.

Example 8.11 *ControlPoint global data declarations*

C language code:

```
Pixmap bitSetPixmap;        /* bit-setting pixmap ID */
GC bitSetGC;                /* bit-setting GC */
DPSGState bitSetGState;     /* gstate for setting pixmap */
Pixmap bitClearPixmap;      /* bit-clearing pixmap ID */
GC bitClearGC;              /* bit-clearing GC */
GC andGC;                   /* ANDing GC */
GC orGC;                    /* ORing GC */
DPSGState bitClearGState;   /* gstate for clearing pixmap */
unsigned pixmapHeight;      /* pixmap height */
unsigned pixmapWidth;       /* pixmap width */
```

Example 8.12 lists the code that creates two pixmaps using **XCreatePixmap**. Each pixmap has its own graphics context; the foreground and background of the bit-setting graphics context are all 1's; the foreground and background of the bit-clearing graphics context are all 0's. The width and height of the pixmaps are determined by converting the size of the control points from user space into pixel units.

Example 8.12 *Initializing pixmaps for copying*

C language code:

```
void initPixmaps()
{
    XGCValues xgc;
    float ux, uy;
    int depth;
    Display *dpy = XtDisplay(drawingArea);
```

```
/* Compute width and height for the composite
 * control points (in pixels).
 * Add one for the line width. */

ux = figureSize+1;
uy = height - figureSize - 1;
pixmapWidth = ceil(Ctm[A_COEFF] * ux + Ctm[C_COEFF] * uy
                + Ctm[TX_CONS] + XOffset) + 1;
pixmapHeight = ceil(Ctm[B_COEFF] * ux + Ctm[D_COEFF] * uy
                + Ctm[TY_CONS] + YOffset) + 1;

XtVaGetValues(drawingArea, XtNdepth, &depth, NULL);

/* Create two pixmaps into which the control point
 * will be drawn. The first is for bit-clearing; the
 * second is for bit-setting */
bitClearPixmap = XCreatePixmap(dpy, XtWindow(drawingArea),
                pixmapWidth, pixmapHeight, depth);
bitSetPixmap = XCreatePixmap(dpy, XtWindow(drawingArea),
                pixmapWidth, pixmapHeight, depth);

/* Create the GC for the bit-clearing pixmap with the
 * foreground and background pixel values all bits on */

xgc.foreground = xgc.background = ~0;
bitClearGC = XCreateGC(dpy, bitClearPixmap,
            GCForeground | GCBackground, &xgc);

/* Create the GC for the bit-setting pixmap with the
 * foreground and background pixel values all bits off */
xgc.foreground = xgc.background = 0;
bitSetGC = XCreateGC(dpy, bitSetPixmap,
            GCForeground | GCBackground, &xgc);

/* Create the ANDing and ORing GCs */
xgc.function = GXand;
andGC = XCreateGC (dpy, bitClearPixmap, GCFunction, &xgc);

xgc.function = GXor;
orGC = XCreateGC (dpy, bitSetPixmap, GCFunction, &xgc);

/* Set the DPS context window to the bit-clearing pixmap */
PSgsave();
XDPSSetContextDrawable(dpsCtxt, bitClearPixmap,
                        pixmapHeight);

XDPSCaptureContextGState(dpsCtxt, &bitSetGState);
```

```
                    /* Set the DPS context window to the bit-setting pixmap */
                    XDPSSetContextDrawable(dpsCtxt, bitSetPixmap
                                    pixmapHeight);
                    XDPSCaptureContextGState(dpsCtxt, &bitClearGState);

                    /* Reset the DPS context window to the display window */
                    PSgrestore();
                } /* end initPixmaps () */
```

Example 8.13 lists the **drawImage** procedure that draws a control point into the two pixmaps. The two pixmaps are first filled with all 1's and all 0's by means of the Xlib procedure **XFillRectangle**. After computing the center for the control point and adjusting it if necessary, **drawImage** temporarily installs the graphics state for the bit-clearing pixmap by calling **XDPSPushContextGState**. **PSWBasic**, the same wrap that the basic drawing approach used to draw into the window, now draws into the bit-clearing pixmap. **XDPSSetContextGState** replaces the bit-setting pixmap with the bit-clearing pixmap, and **PSWBasic** again draws the control point, this time into the bit-setting pixmap. The procedure **XDPSPopContextGState** restores the execution context to its original graphics state (that is, its state before **XDPSPushContextGState** was called).

Example 8.13 *Rendering the control point image pixmaps*

C language code:

```
  void drawImage ()
  {
    float x, y, x1, y1;
    Display *dpy = XtDisplay(drawingArea);
    DPSPointer pushCookie;

    XFillRectangle(dpy, bitClearPixmap, bitClearGC, 0, 0,
                    pixmapWidth, pixmapHeight);
    XFillRectangle(dpy, bitSetPixmap, bitSetGC, 0, 0,
                    pixmapWidth, pixmapHeight);

    /* Convert the center of the pixmap into a coordinate */
    x1 = ((float) pixmapWidth) / 2;
    y1 = -((float) pixmapHeight) / 2;

    x = Invctm[A_COEFF] * x1 + Invctm[C_COEFF] * y1 +
        Invctm[TX_CONS];
    y = Invctm[B_COEFF] * x1 + Invctm[D_COEFF] * y1 +
        Invctm[TY_CONS];
    if (devIndependent) adjust(&x, &y);
```

```
/* Draw into the two pixmaps */
XDPSPushContextGState(dpsCtxt, bitSetGState,
                        &pushCookie);
PSWBasic(x, y, basicProc);

XDPSSetContextGState(dpsCtxt, bitClearGState);
PSWBasic(x, y, basicProc);
XDPSPopContextGState(pushCookie);
} /* end drawImage ( ) */
```

After the control point is drawn, the only step required to display a control point is to copy the pixmaps at the control point's location. This step requires two **XCopyArea** calls.

- The first call to **XCopyArea** is with the bit-clearing pixmap; the graphics context function is set to **GXand**. This call results in the bit-clearing pixmap being logically ANDed into the drawing area and clearing only the pixels that make up the control point, leaving all other pixels untouched.

- The second call to **XCopyArea** is with the bit-setting pixmap; the graphics context function is set to **GXor**. This call results in the bit-setting pixmap image being logically ORed into the drawing area and setting only the pixels that make up the control point to the rendered pixel value, leaving all other pixels untouched.

Note: *With solid rectangular objects, the graphics context function should be set to* **GXcopy** *to copy the image pixmap into the drawing area.*

Example 8.14 lists the code that copies a pixmap of a control point. The most important procedure is the call to **DPSWaitContext** which occurs before the copy process begins. Without this call, the pixmaps could be copied before they were completely drawn.

Example 8.14 *Copying a pixmap of a control point*

C language code:

```
void drawPixmaps ()
{
   float ux, uy;
   int x, y;
   int i;
   Display *dpy = XtDisplay(drawingArea);
```

```
                          /* Render the control point to the pixmaps */
                          drawImage();

                          /* Wait to make sure the DPS image rendering has completed
                           * before any Xlib calls using the images */
                          DPSWaitContext(dpsCtxt);

                          for (i = index; i < index + (numPoints * 2); i += 2) {
                            /* Convert the user space coordinates to X coordinates */
                            ux = XYPoints [i];
                            uy = XYPoints [i + 1];
                            x = Ctm[A_COEFF] * ux + Ctm[C_COEFF] * uy +
                                Ctm[TX_CONS] + XOffset - pixmapWidth/2;
                            y = Ctm[B_COEFF] * ux + Ctm[D_COEFF] * uy +
                                Ctm[TY_CONS] + YOffset - pixmapHeight/2;

                            /* AND the bit-clearing pixmap into the display window */
                            XCopyArea(dpy, bitClearPixmap, XtWindow(drawingArea),
                                    andGC, 0, 0, pixmapWidth, pixmapHeight, x, y);
                            /* OR the bit-setting pixmap into the display window */
                            XCopyArea(dpy, bitSetPixmap, XtWindow(drawingArea),
                                    orGC, 0, 0, pixmapWidth, pixmapHeight, x, y);
                          }
                        } /* end drawComposite ( ) */
```

8.5   show Operator and xyshow Operator

The **show** and **xyshow** methods use the font machinery to cache and
display control points. In the examples in sections 8.5.1 and 8.5.2, the
character description is executed once when the character first appears.
Each subsequent display uses the description stored in the font cache.
Drawing a character that is already in the font cache can be up to 1,000
times faster than converting it by scanning from the character
description in the font.

The font cache does not retain color information; it stores the data as a
mask. As a result, the color should not be set in the character
descriptions. To draw colored characters, change the current color in
the graphics state before invoking **xyshow** or other character-rendering
operators. To draw multicolored control points, define a different
character for each different colored section and repeat **xyshow** with a
color change between each different piece, or use pixmaps as described
in Section 8.4, "Pixmap Copying."

Note: *The font description used with **show** and **xyshow** does not appear in the following code segments but is covered in section 8.6, "Creating a Type 3 Font."*

8.5.1 show Operator

show Operator

Display times for no adjustment and adjustment of 500 points in milliseconds

■	Filled	264	264
□	Open	264	264
+	Cross	264	264
×	X	264	264

The **show** operator is not recommended because each control point requires a separate wrap call to execute a **moveto** and a **show** operation (see Example 8.15). Control points do not appear simultaneously because only one character can be rendered for each **show** operator. The font caching mechanism provides some benefit, but the advantage is offset by the overhead that each wrap incurs and the processing time required for each operator.

Example 8.15 *Drawing with the show operator*

Wrap definition:

```
defineps PSWShow (float X, Y; char *Char)
   X Y moveto (Char) show
endps
```

C language code:

```
void drawShow ()
{
  char charstring[2];
  int i;

  /* Set up the control point as a single character string */
  charstring[0] = fontchar;
  charstring[1] = 0;

  /* Select and scale the font */
  PSselectfont(fontname, figureSize);

  for (i = index; i < index + ( numPoints * 2); i += 2) {
    /* Render the control point using the show operator */
    PSWShow(XYPoints[i], XYPoints[i+1], charstring);
  }
} /* end drawShow ( ) */
```

PostScript language trace:

```
39.540001 478.549988 moveto (a) show
200.600006 197.649994 moveto (a) show
310.220001 339.709991 moveto (a) show
92.360001 474.529999 moveto (a) show
204.139999 492.670013 moveto (a) show
```

Note that the **drawShow** procedure does not adjust the control point location to snap the origins into device space. The snapping is done once, in the control point definition in the cached Type 3 font, and does not need to be repeated. The font machinery guarantees consistent rendering.

8.5.2   xyshow Operator

xyshow Operator		
Display times for no adjustment and adjustment of 500 points in milliseconds		
■ Filled	62	62
☐ Open	62	62
+ Cross	62	62
✕ X	62	62

The **xyshow** operator works well for displaying control points. **xyshow** operates on a string of characters followed by an array or encoded number string of point displacements. This grouping allows all the control points to be drawn with a single wrap call.

The size of the data necessary for **xyshow** is smaller than the size of the data for either the rectangle operation or the user path methods. Only one character and two points are needed to describe the control point for **xyshow**. The rectangle operators need four points per control point and the user path description needs at least two points for each path construction operator plus an entry for the operator itself.

As shown in Example 8.16, the array passed to **xyshow** contains each character's position as an offset relative to the previously placed character, not as the absolute location of the character. The first two numbers in the array are the positions of the second character offset from the positions of the first. A current point must be established before you can execute **xyshow**. This relative positioning means that moving one control point also moves the relative positions of all the control points immediately following it.

Example 8.16 *Drawing with the xyshow operator*

Wrap definition:

```
defineps PSWXYShow(float X, Y; char *CharString;
                   float numstring XYCoords[j]; int j)
   X Y moveto (CharString) XYCoords xyshow
endps
```

C language code:

```
void drawXYShow ()
{
  int i, j;

  /* Set up the control points as a character string */
  for (i = 0; i < numPoints; i++) ShowBuffer[i] = fontchar;
  ShowBuffer[i] = 0;

  /* Select and scale the font */
  PSselectfont(fontname, figureSize);

  for (i = index + 2, j = 0; i < index + (numPoints * 2);
       i++, j++) {
    /* Calculate the deltas from the previous point */
    XYBuffer[j] = XYPoints[i] - XYPoints[i - 2];
  }
  XYBuffer[j++] = 0;
  XYBuffer[j++] = 0;

  /* Render the control points using the xyshow operator */
  PSWXYShow(XYPoints[index], XYPoints[index + 1],
            ShowBuffer, XYBuffer, j);
} /* end drawXYShow () */
```

PostScript language trace:

```
39.540001 478.549988 moveto (aaaaa)
<9530000a43210f5cc38c733342db3d70430e0f5cc359dc294306d1ec42d
f8f5c41911ec0 0000000000000000> xyshow
```

Unlike **rectfill** and **rectstroke**, **xyshow** can display different types of control points with a single operation. The different types of control points can be drawn by including different characters in the string that is passed to **xyshow**.

In both cases, the consistency between images is handled by the font machinery (see Figure 8.11). Each character is positioned at the same point within device space to ensure that the same image is produced, regardless of the user space point selected.

Figure 8.11 *Drawing with xyshow. Consistency is handled by the font machinery.*

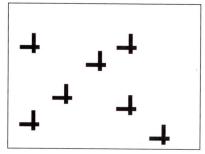 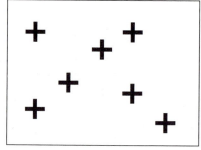

No adjustment   *Adjusted to device space*

8.6   Creating a Type 3 Font

The most significant part of the **show** and **xyshow** methods is to create a font of control points. The *PostScript Language Reference Manual, Second Edition*, and the *PostScript Language Tutorial and Cookbook* provide detailed information about how to create Type 3 fonts.

Note: *Before you define a font for your application's control points, you should check existing fonts for the shapes you need. The Symbol font and the nonalphabetic portion of other fonts contain many shapes that are suitable for use as control points. See Appendix E of the* PostScript Language Reference Manual, Second Edition, *for examples. The same techniques apply to existing fonts and application-defined fonts.*

The font program in the *ControlPoint* application employs the same snapping technique used in the other drawing methods to round the path placement to device space. However, the adjustment in this case must be performed in the PostScript language code of the character descriptions because the application cannot intervene at the appropriate point in the font creation process. While doing the adjustment in the PostScript language would be unacceptably slow for other approaches, it works well here because the adjustment occurs only once, when the character is rendered into the cache, rather than each time a control point is rendered on the screen. This approach works when simple character descriptions are employed. Applications that use more complex control points should consider using the Type 1 font format.

A font program is a dictionary containing a number of key-value pairs. Some key-value pairs are used by the font machinery and must adhere to its syntax rules, while others are optional and user definable. Each font program must have the following keys: *FontMatrix, FontType,*

FontBBox, and *Encoding*. In addition, each font program must have a procedure called **BuildChar**, which draws the character with the character code it is passed.

Note: *The **definefont** operator places an additional entry in the font dictionary. The key is **FID**, and the value is an object of type **fontID**. In Level 1, the dictionary must be made large enough to accommodate this additional entry. In Level 2, dictionaries grow automatically beyond their initial capacity, as required.*

Example 8.17 defines the Type 3 font used to display the control points. The sections that follow give a detailed description of each part of the example.

Example 8.17 *Type 3 font definition for the four control points*

Wrap definition:

```
defineps PSWDefineFont(char *fontname)
    8 dict dup begin
      /FontName /fontname def
      /FontType 3 def
      /FontMatrix [.001 0 0 .001 0 0] def
      /FontBBox [-625 -625 625 625] def

      /Encoding 256 array def
      0 1 255 {Encoding exch /.notdef put} for

      Encoding
        dup (a) 0 get /Rectfill put
        dup (b) 0 get /Rectstroke put
        dup (c) 0 get /Xstroke put
        (d) 0 get /Crossstroke put

      /CharProcs 5 dict def
      CharProcs begin
        /.notdef { } def
        /Rectfill {
          0 0 A moveto -500 -500 rmoveto 0 1000 rlineto
          1000 0 rlineto 0 -1000 rlineto closepath
          fill
        } def
        /Rectstroke {
          0 0 A moveto -500 -500 rmoveto 0 1000 rlineto
          1000 0 rlineto 0 -1000 rlineto closepath
          250 setlinewidth
          stroke
        } def
```

```
/Xstroke {
  0 0 A moveto -500 -500 rmoveto 1000 1000 rlineto
  -1000 0 rmoveto 1000 -1000 rlineto
  250 setlinewidth
  stroke
} def
/Crossstroke {
  0 0 A moveto 0 500 rmoveto 0 -1000 rlineto
  -500 500 rmoveto 1000 0 rlineto
  250 setlinewidth
  stroke
} def
end

/BuildChar {
  1000 0 -625 -625 625 625 setcachedevice
  exch begin
    true setstrokeadjust
    Encoding exch get
    CharProcs exch get
    exec
  end
} def
end

/fontname exch definefont pop
endps
```

8.6.1 Required Keys in Font Dictionary

The *FontMatrix* shown in Figure 8.12 describes the mapping of the character to the user coordinate system. Just as the current transformation matrix uses a matrix to map to device space, a font program uses a matrix to map to user space. This process eliminates the need to scale the character descriptions in order to scale the font. If you want a 10-point font, the matrix is scaled by 10. If you want a 12-point font, the matrix is scaled by 12. The font matrix is either scaled by the scalar argument passed to **scalefont** or is concatenated by the matrix argument passed to **makefont**.

Figure 8.12 *Font space to user space to device space mapping for a 12-point font*

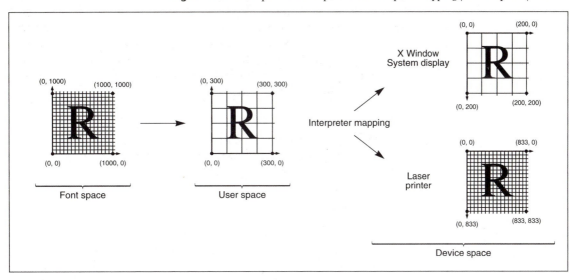

Most font programs, including the program in the *ControlPoint* application, use a *FontMatrix* of [0.001 0 0 0.001 0 0] and define the characters in terms of a 1,000-unit character coordinate system. In other words, a character is drawn so that 1,000 units in the character coordinate system will equal 10 points in a 10-point font and 20 points in a 20-point font.

In the font program for *ControlPoint*, the characters are centered at point (0, 0) and extend to the left and bottom as well as to the right and top. This positioning centers the character on the current point when the character is drawn.

Using a 1,000-unit coordinate system is partially historical and partially structural. The Type 1 font format uses a number encoding scheme to reduce the amount of space necessary to store integer values between –1,131 and +1,131. Working with a 1,000-unit coordinate system allows for a suitable drawing range while taking advantage of the compact number representation. Type 3 font programs do not use this encoding scheme, but most use the same *FontMatrix* for uniformity.

FontType indicates where the information for the character description is found and how it is represented. *FontBBox* gives the lower left and upper right coordinates for the bounding box that contains all the characters if they were drawn at the same point. The font machinery uses this array to set clipping paths and make caching decisions.

The control point characters are all 1,000 units wide. Since they are centered, they extend from –500 to +500. However, the stroke width must be taken into account. Each character has a stroke width of 250 units. When the 1,000 units in character space are mapped into 4 units of user space, the 250-unit line width maps into a 1-unit wide stroke. Half of this stroke extends on each side of the path, so the character actually extends from –625 to +625.

The *Encoding* entry is an array of 256 names that maps the character codes to the procedure names. An application or a computer system might change a font's encoding vector to match its requirements. The index into the array is the character code. The entries of the array are procedure names that draw the characters. Therefore, juggling the entries changes the encodings.

In the *ControlPoint* font program, the character codes for *a*, *b*, *c*, and *d* are the control points. The procedure names for the special predefined control points are placed in these locations of the encoding vector array as illustrated in Figure 8.13. The .notdef procedure name is placed in all the other locations. Each character name has a procedure of the same name in the *CharProcs* dictionary. The .notdef procedure is used as a placeholder for unused characters.

Figure 8.13 *Encoding array and CharProcs dictionary*

Encoding Array
(Control Point Font)

95	/.notdef
96	/.notdef
97	/Rectfill
98	/Rectstroke
99	/Xstroke
100	/Crossstroke
101	/.notdef

CharProcs Dictionary
(Control Point Font)

/.notdef	( )	
/Rectfill	(...)	→ ■
/Rectstroke	(...)	→ □
/Xstroke	(...)	→ ×
/Crossstroke	(...)	→ +

Each character procedure is similar to the basic drawing procedure for the corresponding control point. One difference is that the initial coordinate (0, 0) is adjusted by invoking the **A** procedure defined in the **PSWDefineControlPoints** wrap and shown in Example 8.18.

Example 8.18 *Adjustment procedure in PostScript language code*

PostScript language code

```
/A {            % x y A x' y'
  transform
  floor 0.5 add exch
  floor 0.5 add exch
  itransform
} bind def
```

The elements of the string rendered by **show** and **xyshow** are treated as character codes. The character codes are used as indexes into the *Encoding* array to obtain a procedure name. The procedure name is then looked up in the *CharProcs* dictionary and its value executed. The **setcachedevice** in the **BuildChar** procedure sets the dimensions of the font cache, and the **setstrokeadjust** turns on stroke adjustment. Stroke adjustment is off by default when you are building a Type 3 font character.

8.6.2 Optional Keys

Optional keys typically used in font programs are **FontName**, **PaintType**, **Metrics**, **StrokeWidth**, **FontInfo**, **UniqueID**, **CharStrings**, and **Private**. The *ControlPoint* font program uses FontName. This name is separate from the name used to define the font and is passed to the PostScript interpreter in the **definefont** operation to identify the font.

UniqueID provides a unique identifier for the system to identify characters that have already been created and cached. The font machinery uses the identifier to operate more efficiently across applications. Each font program that uses a **UniqueID** should have a different value. Font programs that have a **UniqueID** are cached across applications, while font programs that do not are cached for the immediate application.

UniqueID values that are not unique can cause incorrect characters to appear. Adobe Systems Incorporated maintains a registry of **UniqueID** numbers. The font used in the *ControlPoint* application is localized to one application and is relatively trivial, so a **UniqueID** is not used.

8.7 Printing Issues

This chapter focuses on the display of control points on the screen. The methods used here can also be used to display an arbitrary number of small objects as part of an application. Examples are displaying stars in a star map or points in a scatter plot. Objects within such an application will more than likely be printed to a printer, unlike control points in a drawing editor.

Only two methods discussed in this chapter can print on Level 1 printers without any emulation: basic drawing and the **show** operator. The PostScript language instructions produced by these methods are compatible with all PostScript language interpreters. User paths, rectangle operators, and **xyshow** require no emulation for Level 2 printers, but must be emulated for Level 1 printers. Pixmap copying is a method applicable only to displays; it is not supported by any printer.

The simplest method for an application that will be printing small objects is to define a Type 3 font, then use **xyshow** when drawing to a display and **show** when preparing output for a printer.

8.8 Comparison of Times with Adjustment

Figure 8.14 shows a comparison of display times, with adjustment (snapping the control point centers to pixel centers), for drawing a filled rectangle, open rectangle, cross, and X. The times are grouped by method, and are taken from this chapter's examples derived from the *ControlPoint* application. As the individual tables accompanying each example show, adjustment does not adversely affect the performance of any control point display method when the adjustment is performed in the application.

Of the methods shown in Figure 8.14, creating a Type 3 font and using the **xyshow** operator provides the best performance overall. The single exception is when rectangle operators are used to draw a filled rectangle. Note that this method is more than ten times faster than the basic drawing method for drawing a filled rectangle.

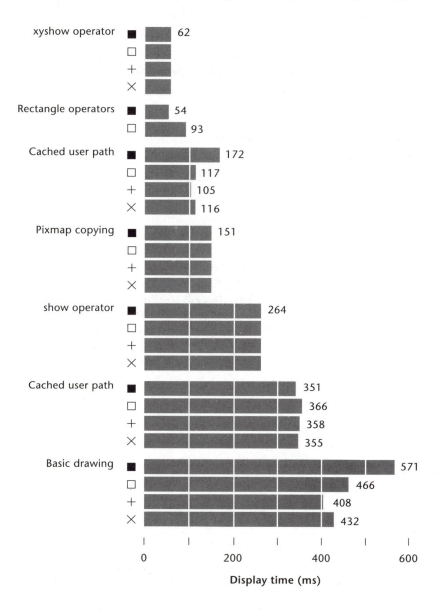

Figure 8.14 *Times for drawing 500 small objects (with adjustment) for seven methods*

8.9 Summary

- The amount of data and the number of PostScript language operators used in a drawing method have a direct correlation to its efficiency. Less data and fewer operators usually mean a more efficient method.

- Pixelization effects are much more noticeable when you are drawing small objects than large ones. Snapping into device space generates consistent, device-independent results.

- Snapping into device space should be done in the application, where it has no noticeable effect on performance. Doing the adjustment in PostScript language code is impossible for user paths and rectangles and unacceptably slow for basic drawing.

- The **rectfill**, **rectstroke**, and **rectclip** operators offer an efficient and convenient way to draw with rectangles. The performance improvement over Level 1 approaches is even more pronounced when arrays of rectangles are used with these rectangle operators.

- The combination of turning symbols into characters in a Type 3 font format and using the **xyshow** operator reduces the number of operators needed to display the symbols while at the same time taking advantage of the font cache to render the symbols quickly.

- Multicolored images require separate calls for each color when using user paths, **rectfill**, **rectstroke**, or **xyshow**. Copying pixmaps is faster when rendering multicolored images.

CHAPTER 9

Hit Detection and Buffering

This chapter and the next focus on topics that are relevant to interactive drawing applications. This chapter uses the *HitDetection* application to examine hit detection, zooming, and buffering; it also includes a brief description of Bézier curves. The next chapter focuses on the user path cache and scrolling techniques.

Unlike previous chapters, which recommend methods based on simplicity as well as performance, this chapter focuses specifically on performance. A method for redrawing a screen image is acceptable only if it can draw and redraw objects without a noticeable delay in response time.

9.1   Introduction to the HitDetection Application

An interactive drawing application must handle a number of special tasks that other applications do not. These tasks include:

- *Hit detection*—determining when a graphical object has been selected.

- *Zooming*—enlarging and reducing an object.

- *Scrolling*—moving and redrawing the visible portion of a drawing in response to mouse events.

- *Moving* selected objects and redrawing them in their new locations.

- *Redrawing* portions of a drawing that become visible when an overlying window is moved.

The *HitDetection* application, shown in Figure 9.1, handles each of these tasks.

The *HitDetection* application provides a scrollable drawing area in its main window that contains a single Bézier curve. Clicking on the curve displays the control points that define its shape. Dragging the curve moves it; dragging a control point reshapes it. Options in the Hit Options control panel window enable a grid, show the effects of selectively updating the window, change the scale of the drawing, and set the mouse sensitivity. Although the functionality is limited, the techniques illustrated by this application can be adapted to more complicated projects.

Note: *The grid in the HitDetection application provides a reference background for the curve; it does not constrain the locations of the control points.*

Figure 9.1 *HitDetection application windows*

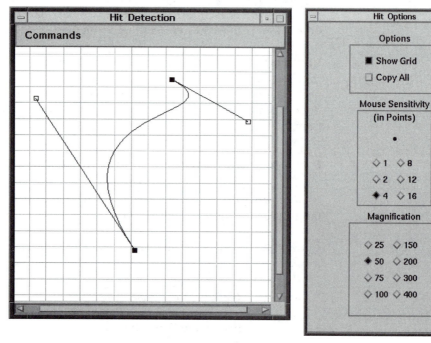

The PostScript language contains several operators that detect when a point is on, in, or near a path, or when two paths intersect. The *HitDetection* application uses the **inustroke** operator to determine when mouse clicks are near the Bézier curve. It also illustrates several ways to minimize the number of hit detection checks that are required.

The application's Bézier curve and its control points are constrained to lie within the dimensions of an 8.5 × 11- inch piece of paper. Different scale factors, chosen from the control panel, let you view the curve at different magnifications. When only part of the page is visible in the drawing window, you can select an object and drag it outside the window border; this action automatically scrolls the drawing so that the dragged object is in view in its new location.

The *HitDetection* application always draws its curve in an unscaled coordinate system. In order to display the curve at the correct magnification, the application executes the **scale** operator to change the current transformation matrix in the graphics context. This behavior is similar to the way the *Clock* application in Chapter 7 scaled its output. Here, however, the same scale factor is used in both the x and y directions so that the proportions of the curve are preserved.

Chapter 7 briefly discusses the use of offscreen buffers in the *Clock* application. The *HitDetection* application uses similar techniques to make user interaction smooth and responsive. As you move the curve or control points, the *HitDetection* window is updated without any distracting flickering or visible redrawing.

9.2 Bézier Curves

The *HitDetection* application uses a Bézier curve as an example of a user-selectable screen object. A Bézier curve is described by four points, called *control points*. Two control points define the endpoints of the curve; the two remaining control points influence the shape of the curve but do not usually lie on it. Figure 9.2 shows a sample Bézier curve. The control points (x_0, y_0) and (x_3, y_3) define the endpoints; the control points (x_1, y_1) and (x_2, y_2) influence the shape of the curve.

Figure 9.2 *Bézier curve*

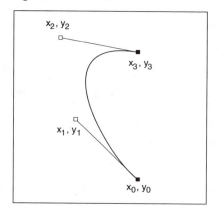

Table 9.1 shows the parametric equations that define a Bézier curve.

Table 9.1 *Parametric equation for the Bézier curve representation*

$$x(t) = (1-t)^3 x_0 + 3t(1-t)^2 x_1 + 3t^2(1-t) x_2 + t^3 x_3$$
$$y(t) = (1-t)^3 y_0 + 3t(1-t)^2 y_1 + 3t^2(1-t) y_2 + t^3 y_3$$

In the equations, the parameter t ranges from 0 to 1. At each step in the range, each point has a varying amount of influence on the resulting x and y values. At $t = 0$, the values of x and y are the coordinates of the first point. As t increases, the values are pulled first toward the second point and then toward the third until, at $t = 1$, the values are the coordinates of the last point in the description.

At the first point, (x_0, y_0), the curve is tangent to a line connecting the first point with the second point (x_1, y_1); at the fourth point, (x_3, y_3), the curve is tangent to a line connecting the fourth point and the third point (x_2, y_2). This feature allows multiple Bézier curves to be joined with no loss in continuity by forcing the common endpoint and the two adjacent control points to lie on the same line.

The **curveto** and **rcurveto** PostScript operators add a Bézier curve segment to the current path. The current point is assumed to be the first endpoint (x_0, y_0) in the Bézier description. Each operator takes six arguments, which specify the remaining three points:

x_1 y_1 x_2 y_2 x_3 y_3 **curveto**

dx_1 dy_1 dx_2 dy_2 dx_3 dy_3 **rcurveto**

The **curveto** operator interprets the arguments as absolute coordinates in user space. The **rcurveto** operator interprets the arguments as displacements in user space; each displacement is relative to the current point. That is, **rcurveto** constructs a curve from the current point (x_0, y_0) to (x_0+dx_3, y_0+dy_3), using (x_0+dx_1, y_0+dy_1) and (x_0+dx_2, y_0+dy_2) as Bézier control points.

The resulting curve lies within the convex boundary formed by the points. The *HitDetection* application takes advantage of this characteristic to improve performance by testing a potential hit against the bounding box formed by the points before continuing to a more exacting hit detection test using PostScript operators.

In the *HitDetection* application, the user can interact with the curve in three different ways:

- Selecting and dragging a curve moves the curve around on the page.

- Selecting and dragging an endpoint on the curve moves that endpoint and the adjacent control point, keeping the line between the points at their new positions parallel to the line between the points at their old positions. This operation reshapes the curve.

- Selecting and dragging an intermediate control point (that is, a control point that is not an endpoint) moves only that point. This operation also reshapes the curve.

Figure 9.3 shows these last two operations. Because the adjacent intermediate control point moves along with an endpoint, the user can change the curve while keeping its general shape. Moving an intermediate control point independently reshapes the curve. While the control point is being moved, the previous image remains in the window as a reference until the user releases the mouse button. Of course, these interaction characteristics are not the only ones possible for editing Bézier curves; others are equally valid.

Figure 9.3 *Two control point operations that reshape a Bézier curve*

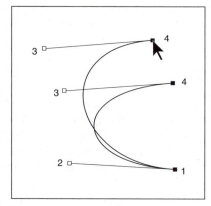 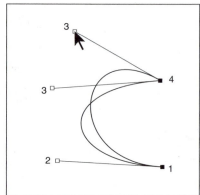

The relationship between control points 3 and 4 remains the same when control point 4 is dragged to a new location; the line between the two points in their new location is parallel to the line at the old location.

Control point 4 remains fixed when control point 3 is dragged to a new location.

9.3 Hit Detection

The Display PostScript system contains six operators for testing whether a point is on, in, or near a path. These operators are commonly referred to as hit detection operators and are shown in the following four tables.

The hit detection operators that test a point against a path are shown in Table 9.5 and Table 9.5. The three operators in the first table test a given point against the current path (as defined by parameters in the current graphics state). The three operators in the second table test the point against a user path. The operators place a boolean value on the stack: *true* if the point is in or on the path; *false* if it is not.

Table 9.2 *Operators that test a point against the current path*

Operator	Description
x y **infill** *bool*	Returns *true* if the device pixel corresponding to (*x*, *y*) in user space would be painted by **fill**. The **fill** operator paints the entire region enclosed by the current path.
x y **ineofill** *bool*	Returns *true* if the device pixel corresponding to (*x*, *y*) in user space would be painted by **eofill** when it paints the current path. The **eofill** operator is like **fill**, except that it uses a different rule (the even-odd rule) to determine insideness.
x y **instroke** *bool*	Returns *true* if the device pixel corresponding to (*x*, *y*) in user space would be painted by **stroke** when it draws the current path. The **stroke** operator draws a curve along the current path, using parameters from the current graphics state to determine line width.

Table 9.3 *Operators that test a point against a user path*

Operator	Description
x y userpath **inufill** *bool*	Returns *true* if the device pixel corresponding to (*x*, *y*) in user space would be painted by **ufill** with the path specified by *userpath*. The **ufill** operator is like **fill**, except that it fills *userpath*, not the current path.
x y userpath **inueofill** *bool*	Returns *true* if the device pixel corresponding to (*x*, *y*) in user space would be painted by **ueofill** with the path specified by *userpath*. The **ueofill** operator is like **eofill**, except that it fills *userpath*, not the current path.
x y userpath **inustroke** *bool*	Returns *true* if the device pixel corresponding to (*x*, *y*) in user space would be painted by **ustroke** when it draws the path specified by *userpath*. The **ustroke** operator is like **stroke**, except that it draws *userpath*, not the current path.

When a user path argument is substituted for the (*x*, *y*) point coordinates, the operators can be used to test for the intersection of two user paths. When these operators are used to detect mouse hits, the specified user path defines a sensitivity region, usually in the shape of a circle, around the mouse pointer. This sensitivity region is tested against the current user path to determine if any point that would be filled by the sensitivity region is on or in the current path. Because it is difficult for users to click the mouse directly on a curve, the user path forms of the hit detection operators are used more often than the point forms. These forms of the operators are shown in Table 9.5 and Table 9.5.

Table 9.4 *Operators that test a user path against the current path*

Operator	Description
userpath **infill** *bool*	Returns *true* if a point in *userpath* would be painted by **fill** when it paints the current path.
userpath **ineofill** *bool*	Returns *true* if a point in *userpath* would be painted by **eofill** when it paints the current path.
userpath **instroke** *bool*	Returns *true* if a point in *userpath* would be painted by **stroke** when it draws the current path.

Table 9.5 *Operators that test when one user path intersects another user path*

Operator	Description
userpath$_1$ *userpath$_2$* **inufill** *bool*	Returns *true* if a point in *userpath$_1$* would be painted by **ufill** when it paints *userpath$_2$*.
userpath$_1$ *userpath$_2$* **inueofill** *bool*	Returns *true* if a point in *userpath$_1$* would be painted by **ueofill** when it paints *userpath$_2$*.
userpath$_1$ *userpath$_2$* **inustroke** *bool*	Returns *true* if a point in *userpath$_1$* would be painted by **ustroke** when it draws *userpath$_2$*.

All of the operators use the parameters in the current graphics state to determine when the point or user path is in or on the current path. This determination is especially important for **instroke** and **inustroke**, as the line width combined with the path determine which pixels are used for the hit detection comparison. The line width for the hit detection check should be the same as when the line is rendered.

The *HitDetection* application uses the Display PostScript Toolkit routine **PSHitUserPath** to check if the mouse point is on the Bézier curve. This procedure takes a point, a radius, and a user path and determines if a circle around the point intersects the user path. In *HitDetection*, the user path is the description of the Bézier curve. See page TK-24 of *Display PostScript Toolkit for X* for more information on **PSHitUserPath**.

The circle being tested is centered on the mouse point, with its size determined by a set of radio buttons in the user interface. The radius of this circle determines the sensitivity region—the distance the mouse can be from the curve and still select the Bézier curve.

Example 9.1 shows a sample use of the **inustroke** operator for hit detection.

Example 9.1 *Sample inustroke operator*

PostScript language code:

```
{ % User path of the circle around the mouse point
  247 230 251 234 setbbox
  249 232 2 0 360 arc
}
{ % User path of the Bézier curve
  156 171 331 290 setbbox
  218 171 moveto
  156 209 331 290 294 189 curveto
}
inustroke % true is placed on the stack
```

Example 9.2 shows a call to **PSHitUserPath** that accomplishes this same test.

Example 9.2 *Hit detection with PSHitUserPath*

C language code:

```
result = PSHitUserPath(
  /* Point and radius */
  249.0, 232.0, 2.0,
  /* Usual user path parameters describe the curve */
  coords, numCoords, numType, ops, numOps, bbox,
  /* The test to perform */
  dps_inustroke);
```

The *HitDetection* application uses two shortcuts to avoid calling the hit detection operators unnecessarily:

- A distance computation tests against the endpoints and control points. If the distance between the mouse point and the test point is less than the mouse sensitivity or the control point size, a hit is reported on the test point.

- A bounding box test determines whether the mouse point falls inside or outside the smallest rectangle that contains the four Bézier control points, extended by the mouse sensitivity. (This rectangle encloses the convex boundary defined by the control points within which the curve itself must lie.) If the point does not lie within this rectangle, a hit on the curve itself is impossible. If the point does lie within the rectangle, **PSHitUserPath** is called to determine if the point lies near the curve (where "near" is defined by the sensitivity region). If it does, then a hit is reported on the curve.

Performing a bounding box or distance test in the application is hundreds of times faster than using a hit detection operator. The computation is performed entirely in the application, while the hit detection operator requires a round-trip to the server to find the answer and return it to the application. Testing in the application before calling **PSHitUserPath** does not noticeably speed up a simple application like *HitDetection*, but it can make an enormous difference in a real drawing program with hundreds or thousands of objects. In order to avoid client-server round-trips, perform these simple hit detection tests in your application and use bounding boxes to limit the number of objects that require PostScript operators for hit detection.

9.3.1 Hit Detection Examples

This section shows the hit detection procedures in the *HitDetection* application. The procedures **hitControl** and **hitObject** identify hits on the control points and on the Bézier curve, respectively. *HitDetection* checks against control points first and then checks against the curve only if the first test fails. Doing the tests in the other order would make it impossible to select the endpoints of the curve because these control points are also on the curve.

The *UserPath* structure holds user path parameters. It contains pointers to the coordinates and operators for the user path, a bounding box array, and counts for the coordinates and operators. Example 9.3 shows the definition of *UserPath*.

Example 9.3 *C structure for representing user paths*

C language code:

```
typedef struct {
    float            *pts;
    DPSUserPathOp    *ops;
    float            bbox[4];
    int              numPts;
    int              numOps;
} UserPath;
```

Example 9.4 shows the **hitControl** procedure. It converts the mouse point into user space coordinates and computes a hit sensitivity tolerance based on the current mouse sensitivity and the control point size. These sizes are in user space units, which may be scaled. Mouse sensitivity should not normally increase at higher magnifications and decrease at lower magnifications, so the sizes are divided by the current magnification to find a hit size in an unscaled coordinate system. If the distance between the mouse point and any of the control points is less than this scaled hit size, a hit occurs.

Example 9.4 *Hit detection on a control point*

C language code:

```
Boolean hitControl(xpoint, ptNum)
  XPoint        *xpoint;
  int           *ptNum;
{
  int           i;
  Point         center;
  float         hitSize;
  float         dx, dy;

  /* Convert mouse point into user space */
  convertToDPS(xpoint, &center);

  /*  Check for a control point hit. */
  hitSize = MAX(CtlPtSize / scale, hitSize / 2.0 / scale);

  for (i = 0; i < PTS_BEZIER * 2; i += 2) {
    dx = center.x - Curve.pts[i];
    dy = center.y - Curve.pts[i+1];
    if (sqrt(dx*dx + dy*dy) < hitSize) {
        *ptNum = i/2;
        return True;
    }
  }
  return False;
} /* end hitControl() */
```

Example 9.5 shows the **hitObject** procedure. The procedure computes the scaled hit size as before. It then extracts the bounding box information from the user path that describes the curve and extends this box by the hit size. If the mouse point is outside this box, no hit is possible, so **hitObject** returns *false*. If the point is inside the box, **PSHitUserPath** performs a more exact test.

Example 9.5 *Hit detection on a curve*

C language code:

```
Boolean    hitObject(xpoint)
  XPoint   *xpoint;
{
  Point    center;
  BBox     bounds;
  Boolean  hit = True;
  float    hitSize;

  /* Convert mouse point into user space */
  convertToDPS(xpoint, &center);

  /* Compute the hit size in scaled user space */
  hitSize = hitSize / 2.0 / scale;

  /* Check if the point is inside the bounding box. */
  bboxOfObject(&Curve, &bounds);

  if (center.x < bounds.ll.x - hitSize ||
      center.x > bounds.ur.x + hitSize ||
      center.y < bounds.ll.y - hitSize ||
      center.y > bounds.ur.y + hitSize) hit = False;

  if (hit) {
    /* We're in the bounding box,
     * so check against curve */
    hit = PSHitUserPath(center.x, center.y, hitSize,
                        Curve.pts, Curve.numPts, dps_float,
                        Curve.ops, Curve.numOps,
                        Curve.bbox, dps_inustroke);
  }
  return hit;
} /* end hitObject() */
```

PostScript language trace:

No trace. The mouse point lies outside the bounding box, so no hit detection operators are used.

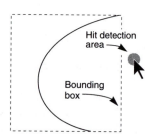

Hit detection area

Bounding box

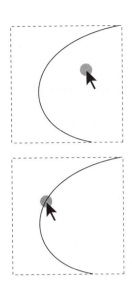

[<9530000c4335000043640000433900004368000043350004364000000000
0000408000004080000000000000000000000c0800000> <00010404040a>]
[<9530000c4080000041880000439080004388800043908000418800004080
0000432100004327000043888000435b000043878000> <000105>]
inustroke
% value returned ==> false

[<9530000c431d00004374000043210000437800000431d0000437400000000
0000408000004080000000000000000000000c0800000> <00010404040a>]
[<9530000c4080000041880000439080004388800043908000418800004080
0000432100004327000043888000435b000043878000> <000105>]
inustroke
% value returned ==> true

This example shows that the bounding box computations is quite
simple. It is always a good idea to perform a bounding box test before
invoking a hit detection operator.

9.4 Magnification

HitDetection uses a drawing area the size of an 8.5×11-inch page. A set
of radio buttons in the user interface lets the user scale the drawing
from 25% to 400%. *HitDetection* calls this scaling *magnification*; other
applications sometimes refer to it as *zooming*.

Note: *PostScript user space is, for most practical purposes, infinitely scalable.
Scaling is limited only by the application's interface and the amount of
memory it requires for offscreen buffers. The upper limit is 400% in this
application, but the Scrolling application used in Chapter 10, "Drawing
and Scrolling," allows scaling of up to 1600%. The ease of scaling in the
Display PostScript system makes it practical to let the user customize the list
of possible scale factors.*

After the user selects a scale factor, the mouse icon changes to a
magnification icon. Clicking in the drawing window changes the scale
to the new magnification. The window also scrolls so that the clicked-
on place in the drawing is at the same spot in the window after the
magnification as it was before. This interface provides the user with a
frame of reference at the new magnification.

Example 9.6 shows code from the **mouseDown** procedure, which is an event handler that is called whenever the user presses a mouse button in the drawing window. If the user has set one of the magnification buttons, the zooming flag will be *true*. In this case, **mouseDown** converts the mouse location into user space, scales the drawing area, and repositions the window to keep the user space location at the mouse location. Example 9.7 also shows the **scaleDrawingArea** procedure. The actual scaling will occur later in the **positionDrawingArea** procedure, so **scaleDrawingArea** limits its responsibility to updating the current scale factor and computing how large a window would be needed to show the entire page at the current magnification.

Example 9.6 *Magnification procedures*

C language code:

```
static void mouseDown(w, clientData, event, goOn)
    Widget      w;
    XtPointer   clientData;
    XEvent      *event;
    Boolean     *goOn;
{
    XPoint      xpoint;
    Point       point;
    XButtonPressedEvent *bp = (XButtonPressedEvent *) event;

    xpoint.x = bp->x;
    xpoint.y = bp->y;

    /* If zooming, rescale so clicked-on point remains fixed */
    if (zooming) {
      convertToDPS(&xpoint, &point);
      scaleDrawingArea();
      positionDrawingArea(point.x, point.y, xpoint.x,
                          xpoint.y);
      drawSelfAndUpdate();
      zooming = False;
    } else {
        /* Do hit detection tests... */
        ...
    }
} /* end mouseDown( ) */
```

```
void scaleDrawingArea()
{
  scale = (float) magnify / 100.0;
  /*  Compute the dimensions that would be needed
   *  to hold the entire page at the new scale factor */
  scaledWidth = PAGE_WIDTH * origXScale * scale;
  scaledHeight = PAGE_HEIGHT * origYScale * scale;
}   /* end scaleDrawingArea( ) */
```

The **positionDrawingArea** procedure is primarily concerned with manipulating Motif scroll bars, so it is not shown here. However, **positionDrawingArea** provides one important piece of Display PostScript functionality: it computes the position of the underlying drawing relative to the drawing window and stores the X Window System coordinates of the page origin in the two variables *originX* and *originY*. It then calls the **setOrigin** procedure to set the PostScript coordinate system so that the origin is at this location and the scale is as selected in the user interface. See section 10.9, "Drawing Area Limitations," on page PG-220 for more information on this technique.

Example 9.7 shows the **setOrigin** procedure. The most important thing to notice is that it does all its work in the initial, default coordinate system. The **PSWSetMatrixAndGetTransform** wrap executes **initmatrix** before translating and scaling the coordinate system. The **setOrigin** procedure uses **convertToOrigDPS** to compute the user space coordinates of the origin. This procedure uses a copy of the initial transformation matrix to do the conversion into original user space.

Example 9.7 *Setting the origin and scaling the coordinate system*

Wrap definition:

```
defineps PSWSetMatrixAndGetTransform (float tx, ty, s;
    int hx, hy | float Ctm[6], Invctm[6];
    int *XOffset, *YOffset)
  initmatrix
  tx ty translate
  s s scale
  hx hy sethalftonephase
  matrix currentmatrix dup Ctm
  matrix invertmatrix Invctm
  currentXoffset YOffset XOffset
endps
```

C language code:

```
void setOrigin()
{
  Point   pt;
  XPoint  xpt;

  xpt.x = originX;
  xpt.y = originY;
  convertToOrigDPS(&xpt, &pt);
  PSWSetMatrixAndGetTransform(pt.x, pt.y, scale,
                              originX, originY, ctm,
                              invctm, &xOffset, &yOffset);
} /* end setOrigin() */
```

Instead of using the original coordinate system, the positioning could have been done relative to the current coordinate system. Positioning relative to the current coordinate system is not recommended, however, because it would introduce round-off errors that would accumulate as the user scrolled through the picture. The accumulated round-off error would eventually cause positioning errors.

Whenever the drawing area is smaller than the window, *HitDetection* displays the page with a gray background and a drop shadow. Figure 9.4 shows the page displayed at 50% magnification.

Figure 9.4 *Drawing area at 50% scale*

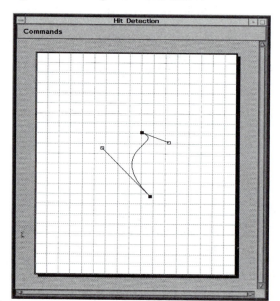

9.5 Control Points

After the user selects the curve, *HitDetection* draws in the control points and tangent lines connecting the endpoints to the internal ones. Seven methods for displaying control points are given in Chapter 8. The *HitDetection* application uses the **xyshow** operator to display the control points, mainly because of its simple interface. Because only four points need to be displayed, there is little performance difference between using **xyshow** and the other methods described in Chapter 8.

Two different control points appear: a filled square and a stroked square. Both types can be shown with one operation with the **xyshow** method. If the rectangle operators were used, both a **rectfill** and a **rectstroke** operation would be necessary. Example 9.8 shows how the four control point locations and the codes for the different points are combined into a single wrap invocation. The code that defines the font is not shown here; see Chapter 8 for this information.

Example 9.8 *Drawing control points*

Wrap definition:

```
defineps PSWDrawControlPoints (float X, Y;
    float numstring Pts[NumPts]; int NumPts;
    char *String)
  X Y moveto (String) Pts xyshow
endps
```

C language code

```
static void drawControlPoints(object)
  UserPath *object;
{
  int i, j;
  float pts[10];

  /* Set the position of the first control point */
  i = 0;
  pts[i++] = object->pts[0];
  pts[i++] = object->pts[1];

  /* Compute the positions of other points
   * relative to the previous point */
  for (j = 2; i < PTS_BEZIER * 2; j++, i++)
      pts[i] = object->pts[j] - object->pts[j - 2];
```

```
        pts[i++] = 0;
        pts[i++] = 0;
        PSWDrawControlPoints(pts[0], pts[1], &pts[2], 8, "abba");
    } /* end drawControlPoints() */
```

Example 9.9 shows the effect of changing the size of the font to reflect the scale of the page. It shows two control points for a curve at 400% magnification. In the top picture, the control point font size is 5, the same as it would be in an unscaled drawing. The resulting control points are very large. In the bottom picture, the font size (5) has been divided by the current magnification (4.0) to yield 1.25. Here the control points appear the same size as they do in an unscaled drawing.

Making the control points the same size at any magnification is a user interface design decision. Some applications may allow the size to increase, but not at the same scale as the drawing.

Example 9.9 *Control points at 400% magnification*

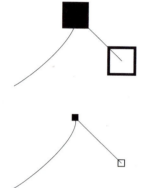

PostScript language trace:

```
% unadjusted size
/ControlPointsFont 5 selectfont
```

```
% adjusted size
/ControlPointsFont 1.25 selectfont
```

9.6 Using Offscreen Buffers

One way to improve drawing performance in any application is to draw only the objects that are visible or that change.

For example, in the *Clock* application in Chapter 7 only the items that change are drawn; the clock face remains the same. Because the clock hands are the only items that change, they are the only objects that need to be redrawn. The rendering of the clock face is kept in an offscreen buffer and copied into the main drawing window when it is needed. This method eliminates having to redraw the face for each tick of the clock. A similar technique is used in the *HitDetection* application to provide a fast, smooth response when redrawing or moving the curve.

In *HitDetection*, selecting and dragging the curve moves the curve; selecting and dragging a control point alters the shape of the curve. *HitDetection* uses two pixmaps to reduce the amount of drawing needed when either of these events occurs; one pixmap holds the original drawing and the other is a composite of the original and an intermediate feedback copy of objects in the drawing that the user is changing. The pixmaps are the same size as the drawing window and are reallocated if the window changes size (Chapter 10 discusses the trade-offs between using a pixmap the size of the window and a pixmap the size of the page).

When the user moves a drawing in a window, flickering can occur as moving objects are repeatedly drawn and erased. The same flickering can occur when objects are reshaped. Double buffering eliminates the flickering and provides visual feedback by animating the movement as the mouse drags a control point or moves an object. The double buffering in *HitDetection* works as follows:

1. The first pixmap contains the original drawing.

2. When the user selects an object and starts to move or reshape it, the application copies the first pixmap into a second one.

3. In the second pixmap, the application draws the curve as it changes. The drawing is overlaid on the original drawing to form a composite image.

4. The composite image in the second pixmap is copied onto the screen to provide feedback to the user. The second pixmap eliminates flickering of the moving feedback image.

5. After the user releases the mouse button to commit to a change, the application creates a new version of the first, original pixmap.

The Show Buffers item in the *HitDetection* Commands menu displays a window showing the two buffers. The first buffer holds the visible portion of the drawing before any change is made. In *HitDetection*, the first buffer holds the rendering of the Bézier curve; in a more sophisticated application, it would hold the rendering of all the visible objects.

Figure 9.5 shows this buffering at work. The column at the far right shows the user's view of the screen as the curve is being reshaped.

Figure 9.5 *Double buffering in the HitDetection application*

Time	Activity	Curve	Original Pixmap	Composite Pixmap	Screen
t_0	The curve rendered on screen is identical to the original pixmap.				
	The user clicks the mouse on the top control point				
t_1	The original pixmap is copied to the composite pixmap.			*Copy*	
t_2	The user drags the control point up, reshaping the curve. The curve, maintained in a temporary variable, is drawn into the composite pixmap.			*Draw*	
t_3	The composite pixmap is copied to the screen.				*Copy*
t_4	The user continues dragging the control point. Visual feedback shows reshaped curve following mouse motion.				
t_5	The original pixmap is copied to the composite pixmap.			*Copy*	
t_6	The user continues dragging the control point. The reshaped curve is drawn into the composite pixmap.			*Draw*	
t_7	The composite pixmap is copied to the screen.				*Copy*
	Steps from t_4 to t_7 repeat as long as the user drags the control point. The user sees the reshaped curve smoothly following mouse movement.		*Draw*		
t_8	The user releases the mouse. The original pixmap is cleared. The curve is drawn to the original pixmap.			*Copy*	
t_9	The original pixmap is copied to the screen.				

9.6.1 Improving Drawing Speed

The perceived responsiveness of a user interface depends not only on visual feedback but also on drawing speed. One way to improve drawing speed is to copy onto the screen only the parts of the offscreen buffer that have changed since the last copy.

Figure 9.6 shows a Bézier curve being moved. The dotted line shows the bounding box of the curve at its previous and current locations. This box, sometimes called the *dirty area* of the drawing, is the only area that needs to be copied; everything outside it remains unchanged. Normally, *HitDetection* only copies the dirty area when it updates the drawing, but the Copy All toggle button in the option panel disables this optimization. When it is set, the application always copies entire buffers instead of just the dirty area. The difference in drawing speed can be substantial, especially if the curve is much smaller than the window.

Figure 9.6 *Bounding box of the changing area*

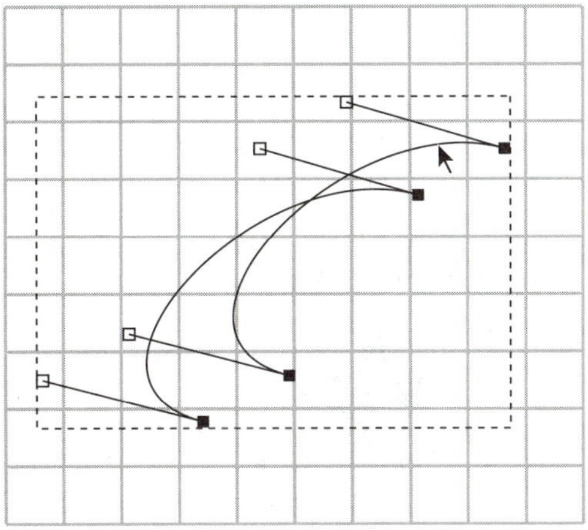

9.6.2 Providing User Feedback with Offscreen Buffers

Example 9.10 shows the **reshapeObject** procedure, which is called when the user clicks the mouse on a control point. The parameters are the coordinates of the mouse click and the number of the selected control point. *HitDetection* had earlier created gstate objects for rendering into the two pixmaps that contain the original and composite drawings. The **reshapeObject** procedure installs the composite pixmap gstate object in order to draw into the composite pixmap. The **copyCurve** procedure creates a copy of the current curve in the variable *object*; this copy—not the original—will be updated as the mouse moves. **copyOrigToComposite** copies the original pixmap into the composite pixmap. **doReshapeLoop** tracks the mouse and updates the *object* variable to reflect the mouse motion. After **doReshapeLoop** returns, the new control point positions are copied into the main curve data structure, the original pixmap's gstate object is restored, and **drawSelfAndUpdate** makes the changed curve appear in the window.

Example 9.10 *Reshaping the Bézier curve using pixmaps*

C *language code:*

```c
UserPath curve;

void reshapeObject(pt, ptNum)
  XPoint *pt;
  int ptNum;
{
  Point initPt;
  UserPath object;
  register int i;

  /* Since all our drawing is to the composite pixmap,
   * switch to that pixmap's graphics state */
  (void) XDPSSetContextGState(dpsCtxt, compGState);

  /* Convert the mouse point to user space */
  convertToDPS(pt, &initPt);

  /* Initialize the object to the existing curve */
  copyCurve(&object);

  /* Copy the original to the composite pixmap */
  copyOrigToComposite();

  /* Call reshape event dispatching loop */
  doReshapeLoop(&object, &initPt, ptNum);

  /* Done, so update stored curve from new one */
  for (i = 0; i < Curve.numPts; i++)
      Curve.pts[i] = object.pts[i];
  for (i = 0; i < 4; i++) Curve.bbox[i] = object.bbox[i];
  XtFree(object.pts);

  /* Restore drawing to original pixmap */
  (void) XDPSSetContextGState(dpsCtxt, origGState);
  drawSelfAndUpdate();
} /* end reshapeObject() */
```

Example 9.11 shows the mouse tracking loop that is used for reshaping the curve. The **getNextMouseEvent** procedure returns the next *MouseMotion* or *ButtonRelease* event in the drawing area. The loop first checks the mouse coordinates to determine if the mouse event is outside the window. If it is, **getNextMouseEvent** scrolls the window with a call to **checkScrolling**. After **getNextMouseEvent** computes the mouse motion in user space, it calls **doReshape** to draw the new shape of the curve.

Example 9.11 *The reshape mouse tracking loop*

C language code:

```
static void doReshapeLoop(object, initPt, ptNum)
  UserPath    *object;
  Point       *initPt;
  int         ptNum;
{
  Point       point, delta, lastPt;
  XEvent      event;
  XPoint      xpoint;
  Boolean     first = True, scrolled;

  lastPt = *initPt;
  do {
    /* Wait for a mouse motion or button release event */
    getNextMouseEvent(XtDisplay(drawingArea),
                      XtWindow(drawingArea), &event);

    /* See if user moved outside window, and scroll if so */
    scrolled =
          checkScrolling(event.xbutton.x,event.xbutton.y);

    /* Compute the movement of the mouse in user space */
    xpoint.x = event.xbutton.x;
    xpoint.y = event.xbutton.y;
    convertToDPS(&xpoint, &point);
    delta.x = point.x - lastPt.x;
    delta.y = point.y - lastPt.y;

    /* If the mouse moved, update */
    if (delta.x || delta.y)
      doReshape(object, &delta, &first, scrolled, ptNum);
    lastPt = point;
  } while (event.type != ButtonRelease);
} /* end doReshapeLoop() */
```

Example 9.12 shows the reshaping code. It first calls the **setPoint** procedure, which moves the selected control point of the curve by the mouse delta. If the control point is an endpoint of the curve, **setPoint** also adjusts the adjacent control point as shown in Figure 9.3. Next, **computeReshapeBBox** finds the area that needs to be updated by combining the bounding boxes of the previous and current curves. If the picture was just scrolled by dragging the control point outside the window, the dirty area is expanded to be the entire window, and the entire composite pixmap must be updated. **XCopyArea** restores the dirty area of the composite pixmap by copying from the original pixmap so that the composite pixmap is once again a copy of the original. Because the composite pixmap gstate object was installed as the current graphics state back in **reshapeObject**, the call to **drawObject** after **XCopyArea** draws the new object into the composite pixmap. A call to **DPSWaitContext** ensures that the drawing is complete, and a final call to **XCopyArea** copies the composite pixmap into the drawing area window.

Example 9.12 *Reshaping the curve*

C language code:

```
static void doReshape(object, delta, first, scrolled, ptNum)
    UserPath    *object;
    Point       *delta;
    Boolean     *first, scrolled;
    int         ptNum;
{
    static BBox   oldBBox;
    XPoint        xll, xur;
    Display       *dpy = XtDisplay(drawingArea);
    Window        win = XtWindow(drawingArea);

    /* Change the point locations of the curve */
    setPoint(ptNum, object, delta);

    /* Compute area that must be updated. If we scrolled, make
     * it everything, but we still have to compute the bbox so
     * we will have an oldBBox for next time around */
    computeReshapeBBox(object, first, &oldBBox, &xll, &xur);

    if (scrolled) {
      xll.x = xur.y = 0;
      xll.y = drawingHeight;
      xur.x = drawingWidth;
    }

    /* Copy original pixmap into composite */
```

```
    XCopyArea(dpy, original, composite, gc, xll.x, xur.y,
            xur.x - xll.x, xll.y - xur.y, xll.x, xur.y);
    /* Draw the new curve to the composite pixmap */
    drawObject(object);

    /* Sync so the drawing is complete and
     * copy into the window */
    DPSWaitContext(dpsCtxt);
    XCopyArea(dpy, composite, win, gc, xll.x, xur.y,
            xur.x - xll.x, xll.y - xur.y, xll.x, xur.y);
} /* end doReshape() */
```

Moving the curve uses pixmaps the same way reshaping it does. The only difference is that there is no need for a separate feedback curve. Instead, a translated copy of the original curve provides the feedback.

9.7 Summary

- The Bézier curve representation used in the PostScript language is compact. Bézier curves can easily be joined at their endpoints to form a single, smooth, continuous curve of arbitrarily complex shape.

- The PostScript language provides six hit detection operators to determine when a point or path lies in, on, or near another path.

- Calculating a bounding box hit test in your application is very fast. This technique can reduce the number of times you need to use the hit detection PostScript operators, which are comparatively slow because they require a round-trip to the server.

- The flexibility of the PostScript imaging model eases the task of scaling documents. In the Display PostScript system, you can scale objects by changing the mapping from user space to device space, which is easier and more efficient than recalculating a new position for each point in an object when the scale changes.

- When only some parts of a drawing change, you can speed up rendering with a pixmap. Render only the changed parts of the drawing into the pixmap, then copy the pixmap onto the screen. If you only copy those parts of the drawing that actually changed, you will improve rendering speed even more.

CHAPTER 10

Drawing and Scrolling

This chapter examines the effects that the user path cache, Display PostScript imaging techniques, and offscreen buffers have on scrolling.

Scrolling a complex image is a challenging task for several reasons: the same paths must be drawn repeatedly, the display must be synchronized with the actions of the scroll bar, and the visual feedback must be immediate. In order to meet these performance demands in a Display PostScript environment, drawing routines must be as efficient as possible.

The *Scrolling* application, shown in Figure 10.1, demonstrates a number of interrelated drawing issues. The application reads a special, highly structured subset of PostScript language files and parses them into graphical objects. The *Scrolling* application includes the code necessary to parse this type of file and to convert general PostScript language files into this special format.

Each graphical object consists of a user path, a set of graphics state parameters, a bounding box, and a path type (**fill**, **stroke**, **clip**, or **initclip**). The objects are then drawn into a Motif *XmScrolledWindow* widget using PostScript path operators, user paths, or cached user paths.

Figure 10.1 *Windows for the Scrolling application*

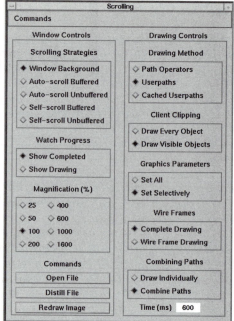

This chapter compares different drawing methods for the three drawings shown in Figure 10.2: the portrait of a nurse, a technical drawing of an engine, and an image of King Tut. The nurse is a relatively simple drawing, the engine more complex, and King Tut more complex still.

Figure 10.2 *Drawings for the Scrolling application: nurse, engine, and King Tut*

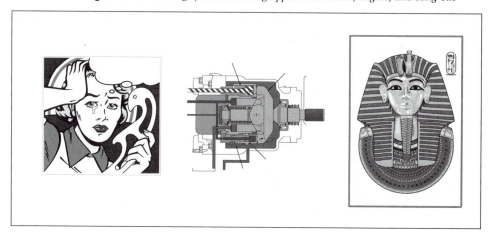

Four imaging methods can substantially improve performance in applications that perform scrolling:

- Draw only the visible or exposed portion of the image instead of drawing all objects.

- Update a graphics state parameter only when it changes instead of explicitly setting each parameter when you draw each object.

- Draw a stroked "wire frame" image instead of filling the image elements.

- Combine multiple paths into a single user path instead of drawing each path.

In addition to these topics, this chapter also discusses using the automatic and self-scrolling capabilities of the OSF/Motif *XmScrolledWindow* widget class.

10.1 Scrolling Overview

There are many ways to scroll a picture in the Display PostScript X environment. The *Scrolling* application demonstrates almost 500 combinations of Motif scrolling approaches and Display PostScript drawing options. The examples in *Scrolling* will help you decide which combination is best for your application.

The process of scrolling a graphic image in the X environment is not conceptually complex. As Figure 10.3 shows, the process can be broken down into three steps.

Figure 10.3 *Scrolling sequence*

1. A mouse event on one of the scroll bars invokes a scrolling callback procedure associated with the scroll bar widget.

2. The scrolling callback determines the new location of the image in relation to the viewing area and moves any portion of the image that will remain visible.

3. The scrolling callback computes the portion of the image newly exposed by the scrolling and redraws the contents of that area.

The scrolling process can be handled automatically by the OSF/Motif *XmScrolledWindow* widget, or it can be controlled by the application. More typically, it can be divided between toolkit event handling and application drawing. The *Scrolling* application, in its auto-scroll mode, relies entirely on the OSF/Motif widget's default functionality to refresh a buffered image. In its manual mode, *Scrolling* attaches its own callback routines to the scroll bars and the drawing area widget, and handles scrolling by relying on toolkit functions to receive and dispatch events.

10.2 User Path Cache

The PostScript interpreter can cache the results of executing user paths. Caching improves performance when the same user path is rendered more than once. The cache contains an internal representation of the user path. If a user path is found in the cache, the interpreter does not need to reconvert it to its internal representation.

The user path cache is limited in size and is a system resource, so it is shared by all applications. Although the cache is shared, it is typically monopolized by a single application for substantial periods because users typically draw in only one application at a time. You should not, however, assume that cached user paths will remain in the cache for long periods of time. Other applications may place new paths in the cache and cause your application's paths to be flushed.

Applications use the user path cache by placing **ucache** as the first operator in a user path description. **ucache** takes no arguments.

ucache tells the PostScript interpreter to look for the path in the user path cache; if the search fails, it tells the interpreter to cache the user path. The interpreter does not look for user paths in the cache if the **ucache** operator is not present. Example 10.1 shows an ASCII path description of a user path with a **ucache** operator.

Example 10.1 *Sample user path description with ucache operator*

PostScript language code:

```
{
    ucache
    0 0 100 100 setbbox
    0 0 moveto
    0 100 lineto
    100 100 lineto
    100 0 lineto
    closepath
} ufill
```

The PostScript interpreter can find user paths in the cache even when the current transformation matrix has been translated relative to its position when the path was added to the cache. However, the interpreter cannot find user paths when user spaces have been rotated or scaled. User paths drawn in a user space transformed by either rotation or scaling are reinterpreted and recached when they are first imaged with the new transformation. The transformed path is thereafter available for future cache probes.

The initial performance cost of caching and executing a user path is typically 1.3 times that of just executing the user path. Therefore, do not put user paths in the cache unless you expect to use them at least twice in a short time. However, performance can be up to 2.5 times faster once the user paths in a drawing have been cached. Tables 10.1, 10.2, and 10.3 summarize the context execution times (in seconds) for the three sample files. Each entry shows the time to draw the picture using PostScript path operators, user paths, and cached user paths. The numbers in parentheses for the cached path entries are the initial drawing times for the cached user paths: the time required to draw the paths plus the additional time needed to cache the paths.

Table 10.1 *Times for three methods of drawing the nurse portrait*

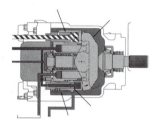

Drawing Method	Time
Display times in seconds	
PostScript path operators	0.63
User paths	0.48
User paths with cache	0.20 (0.62)*

Image: 37,075 bytes, 113 user paths cached.
*Initial setup time

Table 10.2 *Times for three methods of drawing the engine diagram*

Drawing Method	Time
Display times in seconds	
PostScript path operators	1.04
User paths	0.74
User paths with cache	0.41 (1.00)*

Image: 66,918 bytes, 494 user paths cached.
*Initial setup time

Table 10.3 *Times for three methods of drawing King Tut*

Drawing Method	Time
Display times in seconds	
PostScript path operators	7.88
User paths	6.33
User paths with cache	8.15 (8.20)*

Image: 467,761 bytes, 3191 user paths cached.
*Initial setup time

The user path cache provides the best performance with smaller files. As the number and size of the user paths increases, the benefit of the user path cache is reduced until the frequency of using the cache reaches zero. At this time, the cost of entry into the cache is incurred for each user path whenever it is drawn.

This point of diminishing returns depends on the size of the cache and the type of drawing. In the current version of the Display PostScript system, the maximum number of bytes the cache can hold is 300K, and the maximum number of paths the cache can hold is 900. The **ucachestatus** operator returns information about the current and maximum sizes of the user path cache.

The King Tut drawing contains over 3,000 paths. Because the cache limit is 900 paths, the contents of the existing cache are completely overwritten at least three times each time the image is drawn. This overwriting eliminates the chance of successfully finding a path in the cache. Therefore, drawing King Tut takes more time *with* the cache than *without* it.

The King Tut drawing is exceptionally large and complex; most drawings are much simpler. The drawings of the nurse and the engine contain fewer than 500 user paths each, and their performance with caching is very good.

To avoid completely filling the cache, limit the number of user paths drawn with the cache to some fraction of the limit of the cache. In the King Tut drawing, limiting the number of paths placed in the cache to 700 does not change initial setup time, but it eliminates the performance cost for subsequent drawings. In fact, caching user paths with this limit imposed produces 10% better performance than no caching.

Note: *Any application that uses cached user paths should obtain the maximum number of paths from* **ucachestatus** *and use a percentage of this value instead of hardwiring the number to a certain implementation. This method lets the application automatically take advantage of expanded limits and adapt to reduced limits when necessary.*

10.3   Drawing Only Visible Paths

The drawing performance of the *Scrolling* application improves significantly when it sends only the visible paths of the drawing to the server. It is tempting to rely on the server for clipping because it provides four mechanisms that you can easily program to do the job:

- Clip implicitly (to the window border)
- Clip with the **clip** PostScript operator
- Clip with the **viewclip** PostScript operator
- Clip with X graphics context clipping

While you could rely on these mechanisms to do all clipping, an application can produce significant performance gains by comparing the area being drawn with the bounding box of each path. Only paths whose bounding boxes intersect the area are sent to the server. This check, which is made by the application, greatly reduces unnecessary client-server traffic and significantly improves drawing performance. This method has the greatest impact when the region to be updated is much smaller than the entire image and the image itself is composed of a large number of relatively small, discrete elements. Three situations call for this method:

- When the image scrolls, previously hidden parts of the drawing come into view. The scrolled amount defines a rectangle that describes an area that needs to be updated.

- Windows that overlay the drawing area can be moved to expose previously hidden parts of the drawing. When part of the drawing area is exposed, the X server sends Expose events describing the newly visible area. Every Expose event contains a single rectangular area that needs to be updated. Every window exposure generates a series of these Expose events, and the application can create a list of rectangles that precisely describe the portion of the image that needs to be updated.

- When a drawing is scaled so that only a part of it is visible, the rectangle defining the window describes the area that needs to be updated.

An example of the last situation is when an image is magnified so that only a small part of the original image remains visible. In tests with the engine diagram at 100% scale, drawing all paths and drawing only visible paths took the same amount of time. Drawing only visible paths, however, was 40% faster at 400% scale and 68% faster at 1600% scale. Figure 10.4 shows the amount of drawing done at each scale and the times for drawing by both methods using noncached user paths. The Display PostScript system saves some time by not drawing invisible paths, as shown by the reduced times for drawing all paths at higher magnifications. However, the savings from never sending the invisible paths to the server at all are greater still, as shown by the figures for drawing only visible paths.

Figure 10.4 *Drawing times in seconds for all paths vs. visible paths*

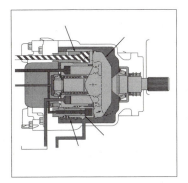 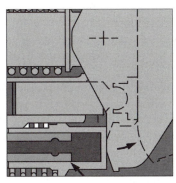 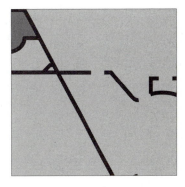

100% scale		*400% scale*		*1600% scale*			
All paths	*0.74 seconds*	*All paths*	*0.60 seconds*	*All paths*	*0.44 seconds*		
Visible paths	*0.74 seconds*	*Visible paths*	*0.36 seconds*	*Visible paths*	*0.14 seconds*		

Because paths are cached before clipping, all paths drawn are placed in the cache, whether or not they are visible. Scrolling is faster when paths in a newly exposed area come from the user path cache. However, this doesn't mean that you should draw every path in the hope of placing all the paths in the cache. The reduction in client-server requests achieved when you are drawing only the paths that are necessary outweighs any advantage that might be gained by having paths already in the cache.

Clipping paths must be treated specially when you are deciding whether to send paths to the server. A clipping path that lies entirely outside the visible area prevents any further graphics from appearing. When an application encounters a clipping path that is outside the visible area, it should skip the clipping path and all subsequent paths that would be affected by the clip.

10.4 Drawing Wire Frame Images

The *Scrolling* application displays a drawing as either a complete image or a "wire frame" image. The complete image incorporates color, line width, other line settings, and paint type (either **stroke** or **fill**). The wire frame displays the paths in outline form, with each path appearing in a line width equivalent to one pixel. The advantage of the wire frame is that it can display more quickly and show the paths more clearly.

Some applications, including Adobe Illustrator™, make extensive use of the wire frame drawing mode. The *Scrolling* application includes an option that lets you compare drawing wire frames with drawing complete images. With wire frame drawing, the color, line width, and other line settings are set at the beginning and are not changed, and then the paths are constructed and stroked.

In *Scrolling*, the wire frame color is set to black and the line width to 0. This setting optimizes line drawing speed by keeping the line width equivalent to one pixel in device space, even at 1600% scale. As shown in Figure 10.5, drawing the complete image of the nurse takes 0.48 seconds, whereas drawing the wire frame takes 0.20 seconds (both with noncached user paths). Complex images benefit even more—King Tut normally takes 6.33 seconds to draw, but the wire frame takes only 1.72 seconds.

Figure 10.5 *Drawing times for a complete image vs. a wire frame image*

Complete image: 0.48 seconds   *Wire frame image: 0.20 seconds*

10.5 Combining User Paths

Previous chapters have indicated that Display PostScript performance gains result from delaying drawing as long as possible and combining many user paths into a large set of user paths before drawing. In the *Scrolling* application, the performance improvements resulting from these methods are more dramatic.

In the PostScript language, paths are made up of a combination of disjoint subpaths. Combining paths with the same color and line width saves on the overhead that each drawing operation requires. Combining paths improves all drawing but is especially effective with wire frame images, as shown in Table 10.4.

Table 10.4 *Drawing times for the engine diagram, drawn in wire frame*

Method	PostScript Operators	User Paths	Cached User Paths
Display times in seconds			
Individual paths	0.88	0.58	0.33
Combined into paths of up to 2,000 points	0.88	0.24	0.14

By converting from PostScript operators with stroking after each path to cached user paths with combined paths, drawing time for the Engine diagram was reduced from 0.88 seconds to 0.14 seconds. This reduction in drawing time represents an 85% performance improvement.

Combined user paths can interact with the user path cache during scrolling. If you are drawing only newly visible paths, each update will probably merge a different set of paths into the combined user path. Since this combined path is different each time it is drawn, cache hits can never occur. For best performance, do not cache combined paths created during scrolling operations.

In nonscrolling situations or when drawing wire frames, combining user paths is clearly the preferred method, as shown in Table 10.4. For scrolling situations without wire frames, combining paths is unlikely to yield much improvement, so individually cached user paths should be used.

These ambiguous conclusions show that the method that best fits an application depends on the type of drawing the application performs. If images are frequently redrawn all at once, the best rendering method is usually to combine and cache user paths. If only parts of the images are drawn, a method of separately caching user paths is probably the best course. You may need to try several combinations before you arrive at the optimal approach.

Stroked paths can always be combined safely, but filled paths and clipping paths require extra care. If two filled paths or clipping paths intersect, and if they were drawn with different directions, their intersection will leave a void. Figure 10.6 illustrates this effect. Filled paths or clipping paths can be safely combined if they do not intersect or if the application can ensure that they have the same direction.

Figure 10.6 *Filling intersecting paths that have different directions produces a void.*

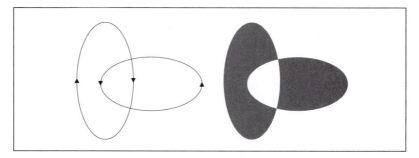

Make sure your applications only combine paths when they are in the same logical plane in the drawing, or when no path from a different plane lies between them. Combining paths from different planes can result in incorrect rendering, as shown in Figure 10.7.

Figure 10.7 *Incorrect rendering results from combining the wrong paths.*

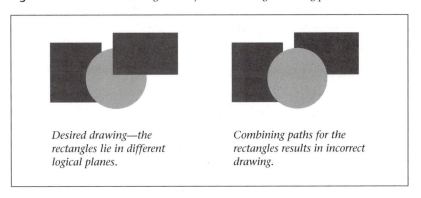

Desired drawing—the rectangles lie in different logical planes.

Combining paths for the rectangles results in incorrect drawing.

10.6 Selectively Setting Graphics State Parameters

You can improve drawing performance by changing only the graphics state parameters that differ from the current ones. In the PostScript language, most of the graphics state elements remain the same after a painting operation; the current point and path are the only ones that do not. For example, setting the current color to its current value is obviously an unnecessary operation.

In *Scrolling*, one of the option settings toggles between setting the graphics state parameters selectively (that is, setting them only when they change) and setting them explicitly for each path. In the files used for timing tests, assigning the parameter settings selectively produced a 10% to 20% improvement.

Example 10.2 and Example 10.3 show PostScript language traces for drawing the lips in the nurse drawing. In Example 10.2, the graphics state parameters are explicitly set for each path. In Example 10.3, they are set only when they change. The color changes often in the drawing, but the other line attributes, such as the line join and line cap, remain the same. Since the current graphics state (except for the path) is retained after a stroke or fill, setting these parameters explicitly is unnecessary.

Example 10.2 *Graphics state parameters set for each path*

PostScript language trace:

```
0 setlinejoin 0 setlinecap 4 setlinewidth 10 setmiterlimit
0 setgray
<path>
fill
0 setlinejoin 0 setlinecap 4 setlinewidth 10 setmiterlimit
0.322 setgray
<path>
fill
0 setlinejoin 0 setlinecap 4 setlinewidth 10 setmiterlimit
0 setgray
<path>
fill
0 setlinejoin 0 setlinecap 4 setlinewidth 10 setmiterlimit
1 setgray
<path>
fill
0 setlinejoin 0 setlinecap 4 setlinewidth 10 setmiterlimit
1 setgray
<path>
fill
0 setlinejoin 0 setlinecap 4 setlinewidth 10 setmiterlimit
1 setgray
<path>
fill
```

Example 10.3 *Graphics state parameters set only when they change*

PostScript language trace:

```
4 setlinewidth
0 setgray
<path>
fill
0.322 setgray
<path>
fill
0 setgray
<path>
fill
1 setgray
<path>
fill
```

```
<path>
fill
<path>
fill
```

Although the difference between display times for the two code
segments in these two examples is only 3 to 4 milliseconds, this
difference can become greater during the display of a complex graphic.
Drawing King Tut by explicitly setting each parameter for each path
took 7.6 seconds. Drawing the same image but setting only the
parameters that are changing took 6.3 seconds, an improvement of
17%.

The difference is even more pronounced when you are drawing wire
frames, because the graphics state parameters never change. Drawing
King Tut in wire frame took 3.1 seconds when each parameter was set
and 1.7 seconds when only those parameters that are changing were
set—an improvement of 45%.

Selectively setting the parameters is a matter of keeping a structure of
the current parameters and checking it before drawing each graphic. If
a new parameter is different from its value in the structure, you should
set it and enter the new value in the current parameter structure.

10.7   Scrolling with Pixmaps

Offscreen buffers can provide the single largest performance
improvement in Display PostScript scrolling design. In this method, the
application does not draw directly into the window; instead it draws to
a pixmap and then copies the complete drawing to the window.
Buffering requires a few extra milliseconds to copy video memory, but it
allows exposed areas of the window to be refreshed instantaneously.
Actual drawing operations are hidden from the user with this method,
which may be an advantage. However, some users may object to the
time required to display a complex image on the screen—the delay can
amount to several seconds with no visual feedback.

To use buffering, draw the image to a Display PostScript context
associated with an offscreen buffer. This action stores the rendered
image in X server memory. Once the image is in the X server, it can be
quickly accessed by **XCopyArea**, eliminating time-consuming rendering
operations in the PostScript interpreter. For relatively long-lived, static

images, the pixmap can even be made the background pixmap for a scrolled window, which allows the server to handle scrolling without involving the application.

Two limitations restrict the use of the image buffering method in X:

- The first limit is on the *size of the image* to be drawn. The X protocol permits servers to deny requests for large pixmaps. Servers that do support large pixmap sizes may not do so efficiently, and imaging performance may degrade at a very large pixmap size. Ultimately, the size of a pixmap is limited by the X protocol, which represents height and width as 16-bit values.

- The second limit results from *resource limitations* in the X server. Pixmaps consume memory, and several applications may have to contend for a limited supply of pixmaps. Limiting the number of pixmaps that an application can expect to obtain trades the memory expense of storing them for the convenience of having the drawn image resident in the server.

Images are prime candidates for buffering when they do not change after they are drawn, are moderately sized, frequently scrolled, and persist for some time. Other good candidates are images that change infrequently but are scrolled often or that can be separated into a few changeable elements that can be buffered independently. Complex images that change frequently are best handled in other ways.

10.7.1 Providing Feedback During Drawing

You can combine the speed advantage of buffering with the immediate user feedback associated with drawing directly to the window. To implement this method, the application draws to the window and when the drawing is complete uses **XCopyArea** to copy the contents of the window into a pixmap. If parts of the window were obscured, the X server generates *GraphicsExpose* events for these areas. The application uses these events to determine which parts of the buffered image need to be filled in. Usually the entire window is visible, and in this case there are no *GraphicsExpose* events and therefore no extra updating is required. Buffering this way takes about 20% longer than drawing directly to the pixmap (0.64 seconds instead of 0.48 seconds for the nurse portrait), but seeing the drawing in progress may give the impression that the updating is actually happening faster.

You can hide some of the 20% overhead by using X Toolkit work procedures. These are procedures that run in the application when the application would otherwise be blocked waiting for input. After copying the window to the pixmap, the application schedules a work procedure to do the work of updating the pixmap and stores information indicating which parts of the pixmap are incomplete. If there is no immediate user interaction, the work procedure updates the pixmap in the background. When the user scrolls or uncovers the window, the application checks to see if the part of the pixmap that is needed is complete and, if so, uses it. Only if the necessary part of the pixmap is incomplete does the user need to wait for rendering to finish.

10.8   Application Control of Scrolling

A typical Display PostScript X application needs a handler for Expose and Resize events, scroll bar callback functions, and zoom control functions.

In the following discussion, an *XmScrolledWindow* widget is used as the main graphics area widget and an *XmDrawingArea* widget is used as the actual work area. The *XmScrolledWindow* widget provides the necessary child widgets and default callback functionality. This widget consists of a container widget, horizontal and vertical scroll bar widgets, and a clip window widget through which an underlying work area widget is viewed. The work area widget is usually an *XmDrawingArea* widget. The window of the work area widget is the target of the application's graphics operations, either through direct rendering or as the destination of **XCopyArea** from a pixmap.

Most Display PostScript X applications need to request and process Expose events from the X server. These events indicate that one or more rectangular areas of the screen need to be redrawn. They can be generated on the *XmDrawingArea* window by scrolling, stacking changes, and geometry changes. If the application is using buffered drawing, it handles each Expose event by calling **XCopyArea** to copy a rectangular area of the pixmap into the window. If the application is drawing directly into the window, it starts creating a list of rectangular areas that need to be updated. By looking ahead in the event queue the application can tell if there are further Expose events for the window, and if there are it just continues event processing. If there are no further Expose events, the application takes the list of rectangular areas, converts them into PostScript user space, and uses the result as an argument to the **rectviewclip** operator. It then redraws the image, relying on the view clip to restrict the updates to the newly exposed area.

The most efficient way to restrict PostScript language rendering to part of the destination drawable is to use the view clip operators, especially **rectviewclip**. Other methods are possible—for example, setting the clipping area in the X graphics context that the PostScript execution context is using—but they are both more complex and less efficient. Using **rectviewclip** has the additional advantage that the application can use the same rectangle list to determine which paths intersect the area being updated.

10.8.1 Automatic Scrolling and Application-Controlled Scrolling

The Motif *ScrolledWindow* widget can operate in two modes: automatic and application-controlled.

In automatic scrolling, the *ScrolledWindow* widget maintains a large drawing window as a child of a clip window. When the user moves the scroll bars, the *ScrolledWindow* widget moves the drawing window around behind the clip window, and different parts of the window become visible. The application does not receive scrolling notifications, but it does receive Expose events for areas of the drawing window that become visible. The *Scrolling* application provides three variations on automatic scrolling:

- *Window Background*—creates a pixmap the size of the drawing area and renders the picture into the pixmap. When the rendering is complete, the application installs the pixmap as the background of the drawing area. The X server automatically displays the background of any newly-exposed areas, so the application ignores the resulting Expose events. Scrolling feedback is instantaneous.

- *Automatic Buffered*—is similar to window background, but the application does not install the pixmap as the window background. When an Expose event arrives, the application copies the exposed area out of the pixmap.

- *Automatic Unbuffered*—draws exposed areas directly to the window; the application does not create a pixmap.

In application-controlled scrolling, the drawing window is exactly the size it appears to be on the screen. When the user moves the scroll bars, the *ScrolledWindow* invokes application callbacks. The application is responsible for moving the contents of the window to reflect the changes in the scroll bars and for updating any newly visible areas. The *Scrolling* application provides two variations on application-controlled scrolling:

- *Self-Scrolled Buffered*—creates a pixmap the size of the window. When the user exposes undrawn parts of the window, they are copied out of the pixmap. When the user moves a scroll bar, the application shifts the image in the pixmap, fills in the newly exposed area, and copies the pixmap to the window.

- *Self-Scrolled Unbuffered*—does not use a pixmap; all drawing is directly to the window. When the user moves a scroll bar, the application shifts the image in the window and fills in the newly exposed area.

Two automatic scrolling methods yield the fastest scrolling feedback: window background and automatic buffered. The only problem is that they require a pixmap the size of the drawing. Large drawings or drawings at high magnification factors require large buffers—an 8.5 × 11-inch drawing at just 200% magnification requires over six megabytes of storage on an 8-plane, 100-dpi system. The X server may not be able to provide large buffers, and even if it does the resulting growth in the server memory requirements can slow the entire system down noticeably because of increased disk swapping. These methods are best reserved for times when the application can ensure that the drawing will never be very large. The window background method is preferred because it makes scrolling more responsive, but remember to reinstall the pixmap as the window background whenever it changes.

If the drawing can become too large for a background pixmap, the self-scrolling buffered method is recommended. This method provides immediate response to Expose events but requires redrawing in response to scroll events.

Unfortunately, it is not possible in Motif to have a *ScrolledWindow* widget change between automatic and application-controlled scrolling; the scrolling mode can be set only when the application creates the widget. An application can use window background scrolling normally and convert to self-scrolling buffered if the pixmap becomes too large, but this involves replacing the ScrolledWindow widget with a new one when the change occurs. The *Scrolling* application has a maximum pixmap size and switches from window background or automatic buffered scrolling to automatic unbuffered scrolling if a pixmap allocation failure occurs. (It also switches from self-scrolled buffered to self-scrolled unbuffered in the same circumstances, but this is unlikely because self-scrolled methods do not allocate pixmaps larger than the window.)

10.9   Drawing Area Limitations

One component of the PostScript graphics state is the clipping area. On a printer, the initial clipping area is the current paper size, but in the Display PostScript system there is no standard initial clipping area. Two different policies are used in different Display PostScript implementations.

The first policy is currently used on some Digital Equipment Corporation platforms. In it, the initial clip area starts at the origin and extends to the right and upward, taking on the size of the current drawable. If your application places the PostScript origin anywhere other than the lower left corner of the drawable, or if the drawable becomes larger than its initial size, the application must execute the **initclip** operator to make the entire drawable available for imaging.

This policy rarely presents any problems as long as you don't forget to execute the **initclip** operator. The most common symptom of neglecting to execute **initclip** is having the contents of a window that gets larger be clipped by the old window size.

The second policy is currently used on all other platforms that support the Display PostScript system. In it, the initial clip area starts at the device space origin (the offset returned by **currentXoffset**) and extends for a large, fixed distance in all four directions. The most common distance is 4,096 pixels in each direction. The clip area cannot be extended beyond this initial size.

The second policy can present problems when you draw pictures at high magnifications. The window location shows just a small part of the page, as shown in Figure 10.8. If the magnification is too large and the page origin coincides with the device space origin, the window might be outside the 4,096-pixel imageable area shown in gray in the figure.

Figure 10.8 *A drawing at high magnification*

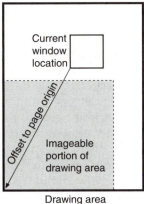

The solution when you use application-controlled scrolling techniques is to keep the device space origin fixed with respect to the window, normally in the lower left corner. Before drawing the page, the application translates the coordinate system, moving the page origin to its correct position.

The problem does not normally occur with buffered, automatic scrolling techniques because it is unlikely that the application would be able to allocate a pixmap large enough to exceed the 4,096-pixel limitation. It does occur in unbuffered automatic scrolling, however. Moving the device space origin around to keep it near the visible area is one possibility, but the code is sufficiently complex that it negates any simplicity gained from using automatic scrolling. The approach used by the *Scrolling* application is to put the origin in the center of the window and to translate to the lower left corner. On a 100-dpi screen, the resulting 8,192 pixels of imaging area are sufficient to show an 8.5×11 inch image at up to 744% magnification before clipping starts.

For maximum flexibility, your application should work with either policy. To accommodate the second policy, your application should position the device space origin with the assumption that the imaging area might be restricted. To accommodate the first policy, it should execute **initclip** whenever the window size changes or the device space origin moves.

10.10 Scrolling and Halftone Phase

Halftoning is the process by which continuous-tone colors or shades of gray are approximated by a pattern of pixels taken from a limited number of discrete colors. The halftone capabilities of the PostScript language are based on the use of a repeating pattern of halftone cells that tile the device space starting at the device space origin. This means that the halftone grid is aligned with the point (0,0) in device space regardless of the values in the current transformation matrix. The halftone patterns do not grow or shrink at different magnifications.

On a screen, the halftone mechanism must be more flexible in order to accommodate scrolling operations. Figure 10.9 shows a close-up of the bottom left corner of a window being scrolled three pixels to the right. If the image is copied to the right and then just filled in, the halftone patterns for the old and new sections do not match. The resulting effect is called a *seam* and is both noticeable and distracting. To avoid seams, the origin of the halftone pattern must be adjusted with the scrolling operation. This is called setting the halftone phase.

Figure 10.9 *Scrolling and halftone phase*

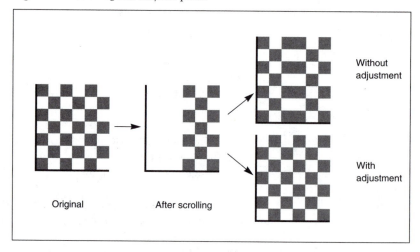

The **sethalftonephase** and **currenthalftonephase** operators allow an application to set and query the halftone phase. If a scrolling operation moves the image by (*dx, dy*) pixels, add *dx* and *dy* to the current halftone phase and set the new halftone phase to the result. See Example 9.7 on page PG-189.

10.11 Summary

- The user path cache improves performance for many types of drawing. Paths found in the cache can be rendered up to 2.5 times faster than those not in the cache. The setup cost for caching a path and rendering it the first time is 1.3 times the cost of rendering the path without caching it.

- Infrequently drawn paths and graphics that are unusually large and complex do not show any benefit when they are rendered with the user path cache. As the complexity of the drawing increases, the benefit of the cache decreases until each path incurs the setup cost every time it is drawn.

- When drawing a picture, draw only those paths that intersect the view clipping path.

- Set graphics state parameters only when they differ from the current settings.

- Whenever possible, combine paths with the same graphics state parameters into a single user path.

- Wire frame images can be rendered more quickly than complete images.

- Buffered windows provide superior scrolling performance, but they can create delays when rendering complicated drawings. Rendering to the window and copying to a pixmap lets the user see the picture being drawn but requires about 20% longer than simple buffering.

- Automatic scrolling simplifies applications, but it requires large pixmaps at high magnifications.

- You must allow for the drawing area limitations of your platform.

- Set the halftone phase when scrolling to avoid seams in the rendered image.

CHAPTER 11

Displaying Text

This chapter uses the *Text* application to examine text-management issues in the PostScript language, especially issues relevant to the display. Because text is an important part of most page descriptions, the PostScript language provides a rich set of operators to display and manage text. All text is displayed in some typeface or font, which is a set of graphical shapes that represent the characters. These graphical shapes can be manipulated through the usual PostScript operations to attain results such as scaling and rotation.

The *Text* application shown in Figure 11.1 displays two paragraphs of lines that appear in a single font, Times-Roman™, at 10, 11, or 12 points size. Although the text cannot be edited, it can be displayed using various combinations of PostScript operators, left-aligned, justified, kerned, spaced apart (tracked), and shown in screen font or outline font. The page can also be scaled, and can be imaged with or without the font cache.

The structures used in the *Text* application are not intended to provide a model for real text-handling applications. They handle only a set of static lines; the user cannot change their contents in any way. The intention of the application is to show how to display text with the PostScript language, not how to manipulate it in an application.

More information on text-handling topics is available. The book *PostScript Language Program Design* (Addison-Wesley) covers a number of text- and font-handling topics. In addition, two technical notes available from the Adobe Developers Association deal exclusively with Adobe Font Metrics (AFM) files and generic text handling: "Adobe Font Metrics File Specification" (LPS5004) and Technical Note #5118, "Overview of the Generic Text Interface."

Figure 11.1 *Text application windows*

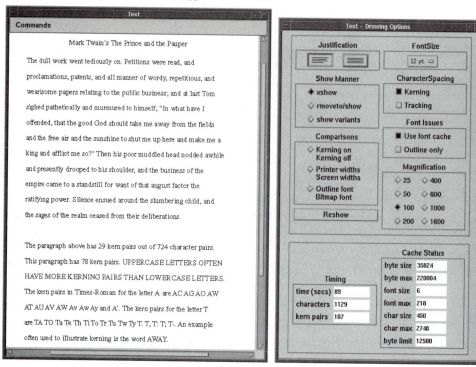

11.1 Justification, Pair Kerning, and Tracking

The simplest way to display a line of text is as a string argument to the **show** operator. This simple method is rarely sufficient to display text properly because it does not address such issues as justification, pair kerning, and tracking. Each of these operations changes the character spacings of the text. All three are important to the appearance of text.

11.1.1 Justification

Justification refers to the alignment of lines in a text block. The common types of justification are *left-aligned*, *right-aligned*, *centered*, and *justified* as illustrated in Figure 11.2. Justification is achieved by adding space between words and sometimes between characters.

Figure 11.2 *Justification styles*

This block of text is left-aligned, which means that it is aligned on the left and runs ragged on the right.	This block of text is right-aligned, which means that it is aligned on the right and runs ragged on the left.	This block of text is centered, which means that both the left and right edges run ragged.	This block of text is justified, which means that both the left and right edges are aligned.

Left-aligned   *Right-aligned*   *Centered*   *Justified*

11.1.2   Pair Kerning

The term *width*, as applied to a character in a PostScript font, is the adjustment to the current point that occurs when the character is imaged with the **show** operator. When displaying a string, **show** displays the first character at the current point, moves the current point by the first character's width, displays the second character, and so on. The width includes the default spacing between one character and the next.

Because individual characters within a font can vary in size and shape, certain combinations of letters can produce unappealing groupings when the normal spacings are used. For example, too much space may appear between the characters. This gap often results when the edges of adjacent characters recede from each other, as in the case of the letters W and A, or when the edges appear at a different height, as in the case of the letters T and e. You can modify the spacings between particular character pairs to create a more appealing separation. Modifying intercharacter spacing for specified pairs of characters is called *kerning*.

Typesetters and graphic designers go to great lengths to achieve proper positioning of characters in the material they produce and need applications that provide, at the least, kerned text. More sophisticated text-handling applications may also allow manual adjustment of character spacing or finer spacing controls.

Figure 11.3 shows the word "AWAY" displayed without and with kerning. The differences in character spacings are apparent. "AWAY" is often used to illustrate the need for kerning because the edges of the characters recede from each other and create large gaps between letters. The illustration on the right shows the characters moved more closely together (kerned) to compensate for the receding edges.

Figure 11.3 *An example of the need for kerning*

Without kerning   With kerning

Figure 11.4 shows a case where kerning adjustment is unnecessary because the combinations of character shapes do not produce noticeable gaps or spaces.

Figure 11.4 *No kerning needed*

The most common approach to kerning in a computer environment, and the one that requires the least computation, is *pair kerning*. A kerning pair is a sequence of two letters with spacing that is different from the default. In the word "AWAY," the kerning pairs are AW, WA, and AY. In the word "HERE," there are no kerning pairs.

The kerning tables for a font specify the adjustment to the position of the second character of each kerning pair. In the case of the AW pair, the kerning information for a 12-point font tells the application to move the W 0.96 points to the left of its default position.

The number of kerning pairs for a font is typically set by the font designer, although some applications let you modify the kerning tables. For most common uses, the tables supplied with the font are adequate. High-end publishers and other related industries often use custom kerning tables.

Many fonts share a common set of kerning pairs centered around key characters, including A, T, V, W, Y, and r. Kerning pairs often include punctuation symbols, numbers, and other characters besides letters. The number of kerning pairs varies among fonts. Typically, 4% to 8% of the possible character combinations are marked as kerning pairs. The Times-Roman™ font has 282 kerning pairs, Helvetica™ has 250 kerning pairs, and Adobe Garamond™ Regular has 602 kerning pairs.

11.1.3 Tracking

Tracking means adding or subtracting a uniform amount of space between the characters in a line of text. A common use of tracking is in advertising displays or letterheads where an increased amount of spacing creates an interesting effect. The word "productions" in Figure 11.5 illustrates tracking.

Figure 11.5 *Tracking applied to the word "productions"*

11.2 Adobe Font Metrics Files

Adobe Font Metrics (AFM) files are available for all Adobe Type 1 typeface software. They provide general information about the font and specific information about each character, such as width, bounding box, and kerning pairs.

The location of AFM files is system dependent, but the PostScript language resource location library, described in Appendix A of the manual *Display PostScript Toolkit for X*, can help to find the files.

An AFM file is in ASCII format. Applications read the files and place the information in arrays or other data structures that are suitable for efficient processing. The *Text* application provides routines to parse AFM files (see Example 11.3). The resulting data structures provide character widths and pair kerning information with a few table lookups.

Example 11.1 is an excerpt from the AFM file for the Times-Roman font. The initial portion, introduced with the line containing **StartFontMetrics**, contains general information about the font. The character metrics section begins with **StartCharMetrics** followed by the number of lines in the section. Subsequent lines contain the encoding number, width, name, and bounding box for a character in the font. The encoding is prefaced by the letter C, the width by WX, the name by N, and the bounding box by B. The end of the section is marked by **EndCharMetrics**.

The kerning pairs follow the character metrics. Only the pairs for the letter A appear in Example 11.1. The number on each line following the KPX and the kerning pair indicate the amount to move the second character of the pair relative to its normal position. Only a few of the two-letter combinations for A have an entry. If there is no entry, a kerning pair is not defined.

The next section, introduced by the StartComposites line, describes accented characters. These composite characters are made up of other characters in the font program.

All values, including widths, bounding boxes, and kerning adjustments, are in a 1,000-point font coordinate system—that is, the values apply to a 1,000-point version of the font. These values must be divided by 1,000 and multiplied by the font scale to derive the values appropriate for a particular instance of a scaled font.

Example 11.1 *AFM file for Times-Roman font*

```
StartFontMetrics 2.0
Comment Copyright (c) 1985, 1987, 1989, 1990
Comment Adobe Systems Incorporated. All Rights Reserved.
Comment Creation Date: Tue Mar 20 12:15:44 1990
Comment UniqueID 28416
Comment VMusage 30487 37379
FontName Times-Roman
FullName Times Roman
FamilyName Times
Weight Roman
ItalicAngle 0
IsFixedPitch false
FontBBox -168 -218 1000 898
UnderlinePosition -100
UnderlineThickness 50
Version 001.007
Notice Times is a trademark of LinotypeAG and/or its subsidiaries
EncodingScheme AdobeStandardEncoding
CapHeight 662
XHeight 450
Ascender 683
Descender -217
```

```
StartCharMetrics 228
C 32 ; WX 250 ; N space ; B 0 0 0 0 ;
C 33 ; WX 333 ; N exclam ; B 109 -14 224 676 ;
C 34 ; WX 408 ; N quotedbl ; B 70 445 337 685 ;
C 35 ; WX 500 ; N numbersign ; B 4 0 495 662 ;
...
C 65 ; WX 722 ; N A ; B 15 0 706 676 ;
C 66 ; WX 667 ; N B ; B 20 0 596 662 ;
C 67 ; WX 667 ; N C ; B 33 -14 637 676 ;
C 68 ; WX 722 ; N D ; B 20 0 689 662 ;
...
EndCharMetrics
StartKernData
StartKernPairs 113

KPX A y -92
KPX A w -92
KPX A v -74
KPX A space -55
KPX A quoteright -111
KPX A Y -92
KPX A W -80
KPX A V -129
KPX A T -111
...
EndKernPairs
EndKernData
StartComposites 56
...
CC Aacute 2 ; PCC A 0 0 ; PCC acute 194 214 ;
CC Acircumflex 2 ; PCC A 0 0 ; PCC circumflex 194 214 ;
CC Adieresis 2 ; PCC A 0 0 ; PCC dieresis 194 214 ;
CC Agrave 2 ; PCC A 0 0 ; PCC grave 194 214 ;
...
CC Atilde 2 ; PCC A 0 0 ; PCC tilde 194 214 ;
...
CC Aring 2 ; PCC A 0 0 ; PCC ring 194 214 ;
...
EndComposites
EndFontMetrics
```

11.2.1   Parsing AFM Files

The routine **AFMParseFile** provided in the *Text* application parses an
AFM file into a data structure that can be accessed by other routines.
The *AFMFontInfo* structure obtained from the font is quite complex,
containing multiple pointers to various structures of pointers to other

structures and arrays. The font metric structure *AFMFontInfo*, the set of substructures used in the *Text* application, and the calling sequence for the parsing routine **AFMParseFile** are shown in the following example. (See the file *parseAFM.h* for the definitions of the structures not used in *Text*.)

Example 11.2 *Font metric structures (defined in parseAFM.h)*

C language code:

```
/* Global Font information. */

typedef struct {
   char *afmVersion;          /* AFM file version */
   char *fontName;            /* font name */
   char *fullName;            /* full name */
   char *familyName;          /* family name */
   char *weight;              /* weight string */
   float italicAngle;         /* italic angle */
   int isFixedPitch;          /* whether font is fixed pitch */
   AFMBBox fontBBox;          /* combined bounding box */
   int underlinePosition;     /* underline position */
   int underlineThickness;    /* underline thickness */
   char *version;             /* version */
   char *notice;              /* copyright notice */
   char *encodingScheme;      /* encoding scheme */
   int capHeight;             /* capital height */
   int xHeight;               /* x-height */
   int ascender;              /* ascender */
   int descender;             /* descender */
} AFMGlobalFontInfo;

/* Per-character metric information */

typedef struct {
   int code,                  /* character code*/
      wx,                     /* width in x direction */
      wy;                     /* width in y direction */
   char *name;                /* name of character */
   AFMBBox charBBox;          /* bounding box of character */
   AFMLigature *ligs;         /* linked list of ligatures */
} AFMCharMetricInfo;

/* Pair kerning information */

typedef struct {
   char *name1;               /* first character of pair */
   char *name2;               /* second character of pair */
   int xamt,                  /* x kerning amount */
```

```
      yamt;                      /* y kerning amount */
} AFMPairKernData;

typedef struct {
  AFMGlobalFontInfo *gfi;/* global font info */
  int *cwi;                   /* 256 element array
                              * of char widths */
  int numOfChars;             /* entries in char metrics array */
  AFMCharMetricInfo *cmi;/* char metrics array */
  int numOfTracks;            /* entries in track kern array */
  AFMTrackKernData *tkd;  /* track kerning array */
  int numOfPairs;             /* entries in pair kerning array */
  AFMPairKernData *pkd;   /* pair kerning array */
  int numOfComps;             /* entries in comp char array */
  AFMCompCharData *ccd;   /* comp char array */
} AFMFontInfo;

extern int AFMParseFile ( /* FILE *fp; AFMFontInfo **fi;
                                int flags; */ );
```

The *AFMCharMetricInfo* and *AFMPairKernData* data structures are used in the *Text* application. The character metric and kerning information is copied to a local structure and is sorted for easier access. This process is done once as part of program initialization. The local data structures are shown in Example 11.3. The *kernPairs* entry of the *FontMetrics* structure contains an array of kerning pairs. The kerning pairs for a character *ch* start at *kernIndex[ch]* and have *numKernPairs[ch]* entries.

Example 11.3 *Text application font data structures*

C language code:

```
typedef struct {
  int code;                   /* second char of pair */
  float dx;                   /* adjustment */
} KernPair;

typedef struct {
  int numOfChars;             /* number of chars */
  int numOfPairs;             /* number of kern pairs */
  int maxChar;                /* maximum character code */
  int *kernIndex;             /* kern pair indices */
  int *numKernPairs;          /* kern pairs for character */
  KernPair *kernPairs;        /* kern pair structs
  float *widths;              /* character widths */
  float *bitmapWidths[NUM_SIZES]; /* bitmap width array */
```

```
} FontMetrics;

FontMetrics metrics;                 /* global font metrics */
```

Text finds the AFM file using the PostScript Language resource location
library. Example 11.4 shows the **parseAFMFile** procedure that finds and
parses the file. The call to **SetPSResourcePolicy** informs the resource
location library about the style of future library calls that the
application will be making. The set of parameters used here is
appropriate for an application that makes only a single probe into the
resource location database. **ListPSResourceFiles** searches for AFM files
for the Times-Roman font and returns in *afmFiles* a list of the AFM file
names. If there was at least one file name returned and the file could be
opened successfully, a call to **AFMParseFile** reads the file and allocates
an *AFMFontInfo* structure. The third parameter, *AFM_GMP*, tells
AFMParseFile to store the global font information, the per-character
metrics, and the pair kerning information. The **parseAFMFile** procedure
then closes the file, frees the local storage, and calls
FreePSResourceStorage to tell the resource location library to free its
internal storage.

Example 11.4 *Parsing the AFM file*

C language code:

```
static AFMFontInfo *parseAFMFile()
{
  AFMFontInfo *fi;
  FILE *AFMfp;
  char **afmNames, **afmFiles;
  int numFiles;

  SetPSResourcePolicy(PSSaveReturnValues, 0, NULL);
  numFiles = ListPSResourceFiles(NULL, ".", PSResFontAFM,
                        "Times-Roman", &afmNames, &afmFiles);

  if (numFiles == 0) {
     fprintf(stderr, "Can't locate Times-Roman AFM file\n");
     exit(1);
  }

  AFMfp = fopen (afmFiles[0], "r");
  if (AFMfp == NULL) {
```

```
            fprintf(stderr, "Can't open Times-Roman AFM file\n");
            exit(1);
    }
    AFMParseFile (AFMfp, &fi, AFM_GMP);
    fclose (AFMfp);
    free(afmFiles);
    free(afmNames);
    FreePSResourceStorage(1);

    return fi;
}
```

Example 11.5 shows the lookup that occurs for each character pair.
First, the index and number of kerning pair entries in the kerning array
are obtained from the *FontMetric* structure *kernIndex* and *numKernPairs*
entries for the first character. These values are then used to search for a
match between the second character value and the *code* field in the
kernPairs array. If a match is found, the kerning value is returned.

The parsing routine that fills the *numKernPairs* array multiplies the
kerning values in the AFM files by 0.001 before it enters them into the
array. The 0.001 factor scales the kerning values down from the 1,000-
point coordinate system. Therefore, the value in the kerning pair array
only needs to be multiplied by the point size of the font before it is
used.

Example 11.5 *Access routine for kerning information (TextMain.c)*

C language code:
```
  static float getKernValue (char1, char2)
    unsigned char char1;
    unsigned char char2;
  {
    int i, kindex, klen;

    /* Initialize the kern pair index and array length */
    kindex = metrics.kernIndex[char1];
    klen = metrics.numKernPairs[char1];
```

```
          /* Loop through the kern pair array looking for
           * the second character */
          for (i = kindex; i < kindex + klen; i++) {
            if (metrics.kernPairs[i].code == char2)
                   return metrics.kernPairs[i].dx;
          }
          return 0.0;
        } /* end getKernValue () */
```

11.2.2   Obtaining Font Metrics

Whenever AFM files are available, use the information contained in
them. For optimum processing efficiency, font metric information
should not be obtained through PostScript language operations.
Although the width of a string or character can be obtained through
stringwidth and the bounding box through **charpath pathbbox**, these
operations are not as efficient as reading the data from the AFM files.
The client-server round-trip and the number of interpreter instructions
needed to process the requests are extremely inefficient when compared
to array lookups.

There is one case, however, in which PostScript operators are necessary
to obtain font metric information. To improve legibility for a
combination of small point size and low resolution (common on
computer screens), the PostScript interpreter can substitute hand-tuned
bitmaps for outline fonts (see section 11.5, "Bitmap and Outline
Widths"). The widths of the bitmap characters differ slightly from the
scalable widths specified in the AFM file. To ensure maximum
compatibility between screen-displayed text and printed text, the
Display PostScript system by default spaces characters according to the
true, scalable widths. This spacing often results in odd character spacing
within words on screen. For situations in which maximum screen
legibility is more important than absolute printer fidelity, the Display
PostScript system allows you to select bitmap metrics for a font. The
technique is described in section 11.4, "Screen Fonts."

An application that enables bitmap spacing for a font usually needs to
know just what this spacing is, and it must obtain this information
from the PostScript interpreter. In the *Text* application, this is done
once; the character widths for the screen font are stored in arrays.
Example 11.6 shows the code that obtains the bitmap character metrics.

Example 11.6 *Fetching screen font metric information*

Wrap definition:

```
definps PSWGetStringWidth (char String[Size]; int Size |
                              float Width[Size])
  /str 1 string def
  % loop through string and return width of each character
  0 1 Size 1 sub {
    (String) exch get str 0 3 -1 roll put
    str stringwidth pop Width
  } for
  /str where pop /str undef
endps
```

C language code:

```
#define  NUM_SIZES          3
float    FontSizes[NUM_SIZES] = { 10, 11, 12 };

static void initBitmapWidths(font)
  char *font;
{
  unsigned char *buf, *ch;
  int num, c, size;

  /* Set up string of all characters */
  buf = (unsigned char *) XtMalloc(metrics.maxChar + 2);
  ch = buf;

  for (c = 1; c < metrics.maxChar+1; c++) *ch++ = c;
  *ch++ = '\0';
  size = strlen(buf);

  /* Loop through the different font sizes */
  for (num = 0; num < NUM_SIZES; num++) {
    /* Set the font size */
    PSselectfont(font, (float) FontSizes[num]);

    /* Allocate the bitmap widths array for
     * this font size */
    metrics.bitmapWidths[num] =
        (float *) XtCalloc (size, sizeof (float));
    metrics.bitmapWidths[num][0] = 0;
```

```
                    PSWGetStringWidth((char *) buf, size,
                                    &metrics.bitmapWidths[num][1]);
        }
        XtFree((XtPointer) buf);
    } /* end initBitmapWidths() */
```

Note: *The width metrics for screen fonts already contain the absolute values for the particular font size; they do not need to be scaled.*

By fetching font metrics from the server (the approach illustrated in Example 11.6), you can obtain character metrics when there is no AFM file for the font. However, the server does not have the pair kerning information found in the AFM file and so cannot provide it.

11.3 Displaying Text

The *Text* application compares the performance of three methods to display text:

- The **xshow** operator (see Example 11.7)

- The **show** operator with **rmoveto** (see Example 11.8)

- Other variants of **show**, including **ashow**, **widthshow**, and **awidthshow** (see Example 11.9)

The default character spacing for a string is the spacing that would occur if the string were displayed with the **show** operator. This default spacing corresponds to the spacing information in the AFM file (or the bitmap width spacing, for fonts for which bitmap width spacing has been selected). A Display PostScript application that changes the default character spacing should use the **xshow** operator for displaying text on the screen. Changes can result from the need for justification, kerning, or tracking. Although **show** is the fastest method to display plain text, its performance degrades significantly when the default spacing must be changed. The **xshow** operator is a more efficient and consistent way to display text.

Since **xshow** is not present in PostScript Level 1 printers, a different method is needed for printing. Some print packages provide an **xshow** emulation, but this emulation requires a separate **rmoveto** (relative **moveto**) and **show** operation for each character. A comparison of the times in Table 11.1 shows that this is not desirable—the last column of the **rmoveto, show** row shows the time required to execute an **rmoveto** and a **show** for each character.

Table 11.1 *Times for displaying text*

Method	Plain Text	Kerning	Kerning, Justification	Kerning, Justification, Tracking
Display times in milliseconds for 1,130 characters				
xshow[1]	77	85	85	83
rmoveto, show	38	101	171	596
show variants[2]	38	108	121	132

[1] *Use for display.*   [2] *Use for printing.*

A better method uses combinations of the **show, ashow, widthshow,** and **awidthshow** operators to minimize the amount of data sent and the number of operations performed. This method is not as easy as creating a PostScript language procedure to emulate **xshow** because it requires a separate code path for printing, but the performance advantage (at least 450% improvement—132 ms versus 596 ms in the last case in Table 11.1) usually makes the additional effort worthwhile.

Figure 11.6 shows the effects of kerning, justification, and tracking.

Figure 11.6 *Effects of kerning, justification, and tracking*

The dull work went tediously on. Petitions were read, and
proclamations, patents, and all manner of wordy, repetitious, and
Plain

The dull work went tediously on. Petitions were read, and
proclamations, patents, and all manner of wordy, repetitious, and
Kerning

The dull work went tediously on. Petitions were read, and
proclamations, patents, and all manner of wordy, repetitious, and
Kerning, justification

The dull work went tediously on. Petitions were read, and
proclamations, patents, and all manner of wordy, repetitious, and
Kerning, justification, tracking

11.3.1   The xshow Operator

The **xshow** operator takes a text string and either a number array or a
number string. The numbers represent the *x* displacement of each
character relative to the starting position of the preceding character, so
the width of the preceding character must be considered in the
calculation of any additional spacing. The first entry is extracted and
placed into the array after the first character has been positioned, so it
represents the displacement between the first and second characters.

Note: **yshow** *and* **xyshow,** *which are variants of* **xshow,** *allow adjustments in the y
direction instead of or in addition to the x direction. These variants are rarely
needed for displaying English text but can be useful for subscripts,
superscripts, or setting equations.*

Each line is displayed by first filling an array with the spacing
information from the AFM file (or, if bitmap widths are being used,
from the bitmap width table fetched in Example 11.6) and then calling
a wrap that does a **moveto** and an **xshow**. Example 11.7 shows the
PostScript language trace. The spacings in this example are default

values. Kerning, justification, and tracking produce values that are different from the default, but the trace that results from these adjustments is otherwise identical to the default.

Example 11.7 *PostScript trace resulting from using xshow to display text*

PostScript language trace:

```
130 620 moveto
(The dull work went tediously on. Petitions were read, and)
[ 6.45269 5.53088 5.53088 2.76544 5.53088 5.53088 2.76544
    2.76544 2.76544 8.29632 5.53088 3.68725 5.53088 2.76544
    8.29632 5.53088 5.53088 3.68725 2.76544 3.68725 5.53088
    5.53088 2.76544 5.53088 5.53088 5.53088 2.76544 5.53088
    2.76544 5.53088 5.53088 2.76544 2.76544 6.45269 5.53088
    3.68725 2.76544 3.68725 2.76544 5.53088 5.53088 5.53088
    2.76544 8.29632 5.53088 3.68725 5.53088 2.76544 3.68725
    5.53088 5.53088 5.53088 2.76544 2.76544 5.53088 5.53088
  . 5.53088 ] xshow
130 595 moveto
(proclamations, patents, and all manner of wordy,
   repetitious, and)
[ 5.53088 3.68725 5.53088 4.60907 2.76544 5.53088 8.29632
    5.53088 3.68725 2.76544 5.53088 5.53088 5.53088 2.76544
    2.76544 5.53088 5.53088 3.68725 5.53088 5.53088 3.68725
    5.53088 2.76544 2.76544 5.53088 5.53088 5.53088 2.76544
    5.53088 2.76544 2.76544 2.76544 8.29632 5.53088 5.53088
    5.53088 5.53088 3.68725 2.76544 5.53088 2.76544 2.76544
    8.29632 5.53088 3.68725 5.53088 5.53088 2.76544 2.76544
    3.68725 5.53088 5.53088 5.53088 3.68725 2.76544 3.68725
    2.76544 5.53088 5.53088 5.53088 2.76544 2.76544 5.53088
    5.53088 5.53088 ] xshow
  . . .
```

Note: *The actual wrap in the Text application sends the coordinates as an encoded number string. The trace shows an array instead, to make the functioning of the xshow operator easier to understand.*

11.3.2 The show Operator with rmoveto

The **xshow** operator is not present in PostScript Level 1 printers. The only way to emulate it is to break the string being displayed into single characters and use the **show** operator to paint them one at a time, following each **show** with an **rmoveto** operation. The *Text* application can display its text using this method, chiefly to illustrate the undesirability of such an emulation.

The **show** operator performs better than **xshow** for default character spacing. When the text is kerned but not justified or tracked, the **rmoveto, show** method appears to be a practical alternative. It does not perform quite as well as **xshow**, but the difference is not significant. Only 3% to 8% of the character pairs in text typically need kerning; the other character pairs use standard spacings. Relatively few additional operators are introduced by kerning, as the trace in Example 11.8 shows.

Example 11.8 *Kerning using rmoveto and show*

PostScript language trace:

```
130 620 moveto
(The dull work went tediously on. Petitions were read, and)
show
130 595 moveto
(proclamations, patents, and all manner of wordy) show
-0.78 0 rmoveto (, repetitious, and) show
130 570 moveto
(wearisome papers relating to the public business; and at last )
show
-0.216 0 rmoveto (T) show
-0.84 0 rmoveto (om) show
130 545 moveto
(sighed pathetically and murmured to himself, \252In what have I)
show
...
```

When kerned text is also justified, the number of additional operators increases so that, at the least, an **rmoveto, show** operator pair is needed for each word. As shown in Table 11.1, the **rmoveto, show** method is over 200% slower than the **xshow** method for kerned, justified text, and over 140% slower than the **show** variants method. A sample of the trace in Example 11.9 shows the additional data and operators needed for kerned, justified text. The arguments to **rmoveto** are the incremental displacements in the *x* and *y* directions, respectively. The *x* displacement, 7.16863, is the additional space being added between words to achieve justification.

Example 11.9 *Kerning and justification using rmoveto and show*

PostScript language trace:

```
130 620 moveto
(The ) show
7.16863 0 rmoveto (dull ) show
7.16863 0 rmoveto (work ) show
7.16863 0 rmoveto (went ) show
7.16863 0 rmoveto (tediously ) show
7.16863 0 rmoveto (on. ) show
7.16863 0 rmoveto (Petitions ) show
7.16863 0 rmoveto (were ) show
7.16863 0 rmoveto (read, ) show
7.16863 0 rmoveto (and) show
...
```

When kerned, justified text is also tracked, an **rmoveto, show** operator pair is needed for each character. The **rmoveto, show** method is over 700% slower than the **xshow** method for kerned, justified, tracked text, and over 450% slower than the **show** variants method. A small sample of the trace in Example 11.10 shows the additional data and operators needed for this worst-case scenario. This trace also highlights the disadvantage of using **rmoveto** and **show** to emulate **xshow**: the emulation results in a trace similar to Example 11.10 even when no adjustments to spacing are being made.

Example 11.10 *Kerning, justification, and tracking using rmoveto and show*

PostScript language trace:

```
130 620 moveto
(T) show                              ⌐
2 0 rmoveto (h) show
2 0 rmoveto (e) show
2 0 rmoveto ( ) show
11.1686 0 rmoveto (d) show
2 0 rmoveto (u) show
2 0 rmoveto (l) show
2 0 rmoveto (l) show
2 0 rmoveto ( ) show
11.1686 0 rmoveto (w) show
2 0 rmoveto (o) show
2 0 rmoveto (r) show
2 0 rmoveto (k) show
2 0 rmoveto ( ) show
11.1686 0 rmoveto (w) show
```

```
2 0 rmoveto (e) show
2 0 rmoveto (n) show
2 0 rmoveto (t) show
2 0 rmoveto ( ) show
...
```

Because the **rmoveto, show** method is so slow for all but plain text, it is not a good general choice for either display or printing.

11.3.3   Variants of the show Operator

The PostScript language includes several variations of the **show** operator. Among these are **ashow**, **widthshow**, and **awidthshow**. Used separately or intermixed, they can adequately handle the demands made by kerning, justification, and tracking.

- **ashow** adds a uniform amount of spacing between each character in the string.

- **widthshow** adds spacing after a specific character (usually the space character).

- **awidthshow** does both; it adds uniform spacing and additional spacing after a specific character.

The *Text* application uses a subset of the Generic Text Interface framework described in the technical note "Overview of the Generic Text Interface." The Generic Text Interface provides a series of low-level routines that fit between the line-breaking and editing algorithms and the printing machinery. It assumes that the actual layout of the text has already taken place. It defines a structure for data that describes the layout of each line and determines which display approaches are appropriate for the data.

In the *Text* application, line breaks cannot be changed by the user, but other characteristics such as kerning, justification, and tracking can be turned on or off. When the user changes these characteristics, the Generic Text Interface routines generate a description of the text in PostScript language:

- Routines examine each line and fill up the required structure with a description of the lines.

- A text display routine steps through the structure, sending the data and the appropriate **show** variation to the server.

The following examples show the output of this method for four cases:

- Plain text
- Kerned text
- Kerned and justified text
- Kerned, justified, and tracked text

Example 11.11 *Plain text—no spacing adjustments*

PostScript language trace:

```
130 620 moveto
(The dull work went tediously on. Petitions were read, and)
show
130 595 moveto
(proclamations, patents, and all manner of wordy, repetitious,
and) show
...
```

Example 11.12 *Kerning using show variants (same as Example 11.8)*

PostScript language trace:

```
130 620 moveto
(The dull work went tediously on. Petitions were read, and)
show
130 595 moveto
(proclamations, patents, and all manner of wordy) show
-0.78 0 rmoveto
(, repetitious, and) show
130 570 moveto
(wearisome papers relating to the public business; and at last )
show
-0.216 0 rmoveto
(T) show
-0.84 0 rmoveto
(om) show
130 545 moveto
(sighed pathetically and murmured to himself, \252In what have I)
show
...
```

Example 11.13 *Kerning and justification using show variants*

PostScript language trace:

```
130 620 moveto
7.16863 0 32 (The dull work went tediously on. Petitions were
read, and) widthshow
130 595 moveto
4.12927 0 32 (proclamations, patents, and all manner of wordy)
widthshow
-0.78 0 rmoveto
4.12927 0 32 (, repetitious, and) widthshow
130 570 moveto
2.77793 0 32 (wearisome papers relating to the public business;
and at last ) widthshow
-0.216 0 rmoveto
2.77793 0 32 (T) widthshow
-0.84 0 rmoveto
2.77793 0 32 (om) widthshow
130 545 moveto
5.42742 0 32 (sighed pathetically and murmured to himself,
\252In what have I) widthshow
...
```

Example 11.14 *Kerning, justification, and tracking using show variants*

PostScript language trace:

```
130 620 moveto
9.16862 0 32 2 0 (The dull work went tediously on. Petitions
were read, and) awidthshow
130 595 moveto
4.37926 0 32 2 0 (proclamations, patents, and all manner of
wordy) awidthshow
-0.78 0 rmoveto
4.37926 0 32 2 0 (, repetitious, and) awidthshow
130 570 moveto
2.97792 0 32 2 0 (wearisome papers relating to the public
business; and at last ) awidthshow
-0.216 0 rmoveto
2.97792 0 32 2 0 (T) awidthshow
-0.84 0 rmoveto
2.97792 0 32 2 0 (om) awidthshow
130 545 moveto
6.76075 0 32 2 0 (sighed pathetically and murmured to himself,
\252In what have I) awidthshow
...
```

11.3.4   Choosing a Text Display Method

The PostScript traces in the previous examples help explain the timing figures shown in Table 11.1: the more operators sent to the server, the slower the display time.

The **xshow** method is simple and efficient. It sends the server a moderate amount of data but a minimum number of operators. Further, the **xshow** method is a simple and general way to set text, no matter how the spacing is adjusted. It is the method of choice whenever spacing adjustments might be required. The **xshow** operator cannot be used, however, for printing to a Level 1 printer. An emulation may be available, but it requires an **rmoveto** and **show** operator pair *for each character*.

Because the **rmoveto, show** method is so slow for all but plain or kerned text, it is not a good general choice for either display or printing.

Use a method that employs variants of the **show** operator whenever a significant amount of text must be sent to a printer. Even though it is more complex than an **xshow** emulation, the gains in performance outweigh the loss in simplicity.

11.4   Screen Fonts

A screen font is a collection of hand-tuned character bitmaps at a given point size. Outline fonts have a number of advantages over screen fonts. Outline fonts are infinitely scalable, making a continuous range of point sizes available—even fractional sizes. They also take up less disk space. Unlike screen fonts, which require different bitmaps for each size, only one outline font description is needed for all sizes. The PostScript font machinery scales the outline to fit the point size you want.

At small point sizes and low screen resolutions, outline fonts can sometimes present legibility problems. Even though the algorithms for displaying type at small point sizes have improved greatly, hand-tuned bitmaps still provide the best visual representation for small point sizes. Screen fonts can be used in the Display PostScript system. They are sometimes provided by an OEM along with system software; at other times they are delivered with outline fonts by a font manufacturer.

Four entries in the top level of the dictionary for each font specify the screen font substitution behavior: *BitmapWidths, ExactSize, InBetweenSize,* and *TransformedChar.* Refer to Section 7.4 of the *PostScript Language Reference Manual, Second Edition* for more information on these entries and their values. When an application requests a font, the Display PostScript system by default responds as follows:

- If a screen font the exact size of the requested font is available it is used. If the exact size is not available, the closest match, within limits, is used instead. The system adapts screen fonts that are near the requested size by adjusting their spacing.

- When the coordinate system is skewed or rotated, the outline font is used instead of a screen font.

- When the coordinate system is uniformly scaled, a screen font is used, if possible. For example, when 50-point text is displayed at one-quarter size, the 12-point screen font is substituted.

In a typical case, a 12-point screen font is used when a 12-point font is requested, and a 10-point screen font is used when a 10-point font is requested. For an 11-point font, the system substitutes character glyphs from a 10-point screen font but uses 11-point character width and spacing, taken from the outline font metrics (unless *BitmapWidths* has been set to *true*).

The *Text* application can override the default behavior and use the outline font at all times. It does this by creating a copy of the font and setting the font dictionary to turn off any screen font substitution. The *Text* application can also override the default behavior to demonstrate two other synthesized fonts: a screen font that uses bitmap widths instead of outline widths and a printer font that uses bitmap widths. The wrap and C language code in Example 11.15 show how this is done. The name of the font to copy, the name of the new font, and values for *BitmapWidths, ExactSize, InBetweenSize,* and *TransformedChar* are passed as arguments. The wrap copies the font, omitting any **FID** entry during the copy. There is an option to not copy the **UniqueID** entry. This is used by *Text* to create a font that is never cached, but this would not normally be done by real applications. After setting the specified entries, the wrap defines the font under the new name. The resulting font can be set with **selectfont** like any resident font.

Example 11.15 *Redefining a font to override default behavior*

Wrap definition:

```
defineps PSWCopyFont(char *F1, *F2;
                     boolean BMWValue, CopyUniqueID;
                     int ESValue, IBSValue, TCValue)
    /F1 findfont
    dup length 4 add dict begin
        {
            1 index /FID eq 2 index /UniqueID eq
                CopyUniqueID not and or
            { pop pop } { def } ifelse
        } forall
        /BitmapWidths BMWValue def
        /ExactSize ESValue def
        /InBetweenSize IBSValue def
        /TransformedChar TCValue def
        /F2 currentdict
    end
    definefont pop
endps
```

C language code:

```
...
/* Screen font uses bitmap font with bitmap widths */
PSWCopyFont(FONT_BASE, FONT_SCREEN, True, True, 1, 1, 0);

/* Printer font uses bitmap font with outline widths */
PSWCopyFont(FONT_BASE, FONT_PRINTER, False, True, 1, 1, 0);

/* Outline font uses outline characters and widths */
PSWCopyFont(FONT_BASE, FONT_OUTLINE, False, True, 0, 0, 0);
...
```

Figure 11.7 shows 10-, 11-, and 12-point Times-Roman type represented with screen fonts. (The actual bitmaps may differ on various systems because of different bitmap resolutions and font versions.)

Figure 11.7 *Screen font screen capture (enlarged 200%)*

> 10 pt **Petitions were read,**
>
> 11 pt **Petitions were read,**
>
> 12 pt **Petitions were read,**

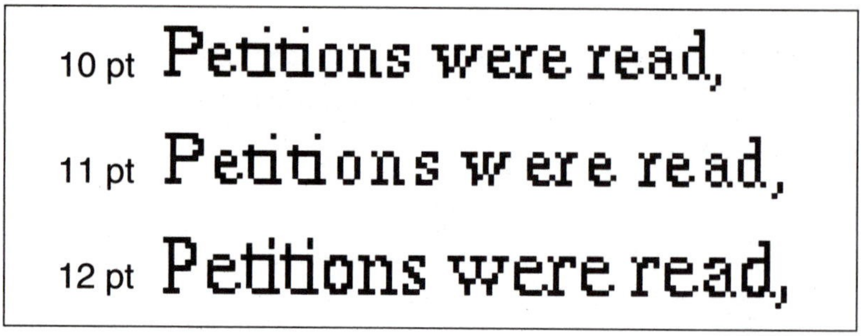

Figure 11.8 shows the screen captures of the fonts in Figure 11.7 displayed with an outline font instead of a screen font.

Figure 11.8 *Outline font screen capture (enlarged 200%)*

> 10 pt Petitions were read,
>
> 11 pt Petitions were read,
>
> 12 pt Petitions were read,

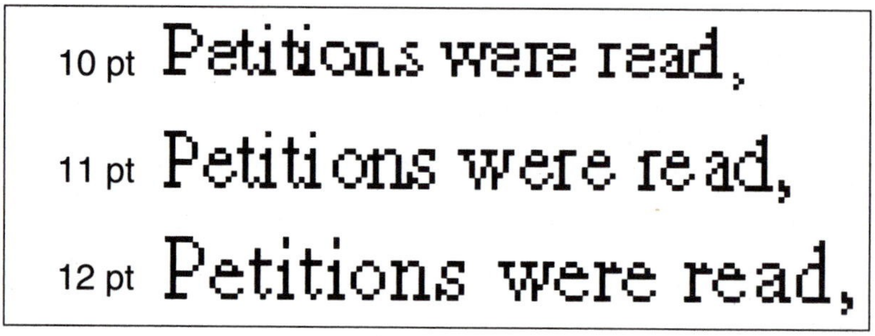

The screen captures for the outline font show that they are legible even at small point sizes. This indicates the level of sophistication that font-rendering algorithms have achieved. At the same time, ambiguities and inconsistent weights appear (most noticeably in serif fonts). These irregularities are magnified when fonts are viewed on a screen showing a large number of characters. Screen fonts, because they are hand-tuned, can often provide a more consistent and readable image. Until screen resolution improves, screen fonts are likely to be an important part of text display.

Note: *The text in Figure 11.7 and Figure 11.8 looks much more jagged on the printed page than it does onscreen. Each pixel onscreen is represented by a round phosphor dot with indistinct edges, but each printed pixel is represented by a high-contrast square.*

11.5 Bitmap and Outline Widths

Besides reduced legibility, another concern is inconsistent character widths when outline fonts are displayed at small point sizes. Differences in character placement can have a significant impact on the appearance of a word. In some cases, low screen resolution produces annoying character placement artifacts: one word can appear as two, or two words as one. Although the word or words will print correctly, reading or editing text on screen is difficult.

For a concrete example, consider the character "x". Assume that the outline width of the character at a particular font and size corresponds to 6.25 pixels on the screen. The rendered character, however, cannot be 6.25 pixels wide—its width must be some whole number of pixels, probably 6. Now consider displaying "xxxxxxxx" at the same font size. The eight characters should ideally take up 50 pixels (8×6.25), but when displayed as 6-pixel-wide characters, they occupy fewer than 50 pixels. Intercharacter spacing cannot be uniform on the screen when outline widths are used for this "word." The use of bitmap widths reduces the amount of variation between letters, resulting in a more readable display. Using bitmap widths, the eight characters would be 48 pixels wide (8×6) on screen instead of 50. The intercharacter spacing would be uniform, but the overall width of the word would be different from its printed version. The extra two pixels would be accounted for by additional interword spacing on screen.

Bitmap widths, like screen fonts, are tuned for the screen. The *BitmapWidths* key in a font dictionary controls how the Display PostScript system spaces the text; the default is *false*, which directs the system to use outline widths and ensures that line lengths will appear the same on the screen as on a printer.

Users rightly expect line breaks in onscreen text to match line breaks in printed text. When screen fonts are used on screen, the application should display characters with bitmap widths but use outline widths for calculating the line breaks in order to ensure WYSIWYG line lengths and page layout. Left-aligned, justified, and right-aligned text require separate treatment for best results:

- *Left-aligned* text is most legible on screen when you allow the total line width to equal the sum of the screen widths of the individual characters. The resulting line widths will often be slightly different from printer output, but this rarely presents a problem.

- *Justified* text requires a different technique, since the difference in line widths between onscreen and printed text would result in a ragged right margin. The best approach here is to start each word at the position calculated from the scalable widths, effectively distributing the spacing difference between words.

- *Right-aligned* text should be displayed with a smooth right margin, so base the position of each word on its end rather than its beginning.

Figure 11.9 shows a sentence from the *Text* application. The top line uses the bitmap widths, and the bottom line uses the outline widths. Look closely at the words "tediously" and "read." The bitmap widths provide more legibility, avoiding the crowded look and overlapping characters that occur with the outline widths. If the bitmap widths were used when printing, however, the result would be the irregular spacing evident in the top line of Figure 11.10.

Figure 11.9 *Screen capture using bitmap and outline widths*

| Bitmap | The dull work went tediously on. Petitions were read, and |
| Outline | The dull work went tediously on. Petitions were read, and |

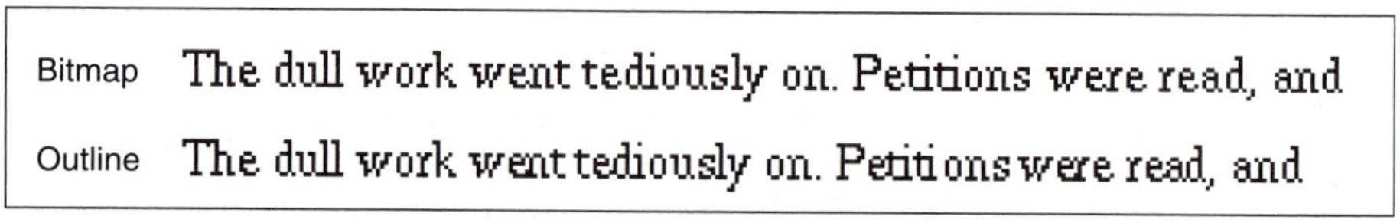

Figure 11.10 *Printed sample using bitmap and outline widths*

| Bitmap | The dull work went tedious ly on. Petitions were read, and |
| Outline | The dull work went tediously on. Petitions were read, and |

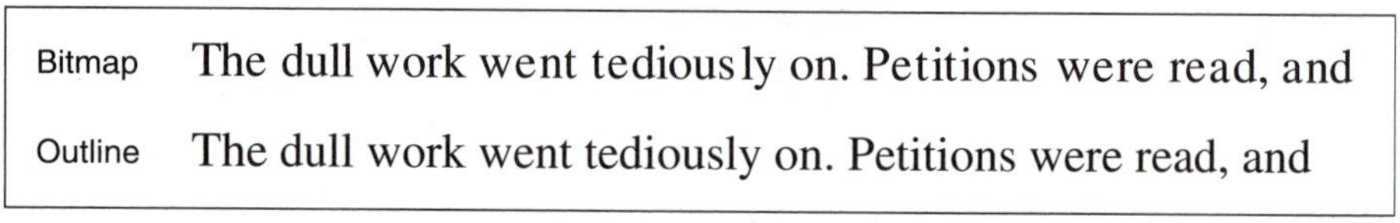

Maximum screen legibility is usually more important than absolute printer fidelity. There are times, however, when fidelity is more important. An example would be when a user draws a box to exactly contain a line of text. In this case, the user needs to know exactly where the text line will end in the printed output. To accommodate these situations, sophisticated applications should provide a mode in which text is displayed using the outline widths that are used during printing.

11.6   Font Cache

The font cache is a Display PostScript system resource that stores character descriptions as masks. When a character is requested, the cache is checked; if a matching mask is found, it is used instead of rendering a new character. The time it takes to display a set of characters with the cache can be up to 1,000 times faster than without the cache. See Table 11.2 for a font cache performance comparison.

The font cache should not be disabled in real applications; the *Text* application disables the font cache only to illustrate its benefit. For the most part, the settings of the font cache should not be changed.

Note: *The font cache is a global, persistent server resource. Characters in the cache are shared among contexts and remain in the cache even after the caching context terminates. Resetting the server is normally the only event that completely flushes the cache.*

Table 11.2 *Performance with cached and uncached fonts*

Method	Time
Display times in milliseconds for 1,130 characters	
With font cache	77
Without font cache	5,468

11.7 Summary

- The **xshow** operator is the fastest and most general way to show text on the screen whenever there are adjustments to the default character spacing. Use **show** variants when creating PostScript language code destined for a Level 1 printer.

- Justification, pair kerning, and tracking are three cases in which you must override the default character spacing in order to display text properly.

- The most common approach to kerning in a computer environment is to use kerning pairs provided with the font or created by an application. These pairs indicate where and by how much the space between characters should change.

- Adobe Font Metrics (AFM) files provide general information about a font and specific information about each character, such as widths, bounding boxes, and kerning pairs. The **AFMParseFile** routine used in the *Text* application parses an AFM file and places the information into a structure that can be accessed quickly.

- The Display PostScript system supports several screen font substitution strategies. By default, it substitutes a screen font when the screen font size and the requested size match exactly or are a close approximation. This behavior can be modified.

- Using bitmap widths improves legibility on the screen, but outline widths should still be used for layout computations.

CHAPTER 12

Encapsulated PostScript Files

This chapter describes how to handle Encapsulated PostScript (EPS) files in Display PostScript applications. EPS files are a standard way to exchange single-page illustrations between applications.

EPS files let you import an illustration produced by one application into another application. The application that produces the EPS file is called the *exporter*, and the application that includes the EPS file is called the *importer*. An EPS file contains a PostScript language description of an illustration and, optionally, a bitmapped preview image. The preview image is used to display EPS graphics in environments without the Display PostScript system.

The ability to exchange illustrations between applications simplifies many tasks. For example, a user can prepare a chart in a spreadsheet program and incorporate it into a newsletter prepared with a page layout program; a designer can create a logo in one graphic illustration program and place it within an illustration drawn with another illustration program. Most of the illustrations in this book are EPS files created with drawing programs or screen capture utilities.

Without the Display PostScript system, an application that imports an EPS file must rely on the preview image to present the illustration to the user. The preview image has several drawbacks:

- If the illustration is scaled or rotated, or the resolution of the user's screen does not match the resolution of the preview, the quality of the displayed image suffers.

- The preview lacks any color information that may be present in the illustration.

- The preview image is optional. If it is not present, the application may have to display a gray box in place of the illustration.

A Display PostScript application can execute the PostScript language code in the EPS file to produce high-quality color images at any scale, rotation, or resolution. Further, the Display PostScript system makes it easy for applications that generate EPS files to generate preview images for display in non–Display PostScript systems.

Figure 12.1 shows the main window for the *Import* application. *Import* lets the user import EPS files, position them in the window, and create a new EPS file with the combined images.

Figure 12.1 *Main drawing window for the Import application*

The remainder of this chapter discusses significant EPS file-handling issues, summarized in the following paragraphs:

- *Placing an imported file in a window.* To place an EPS file in a window, first translate, rotate, and scale the file as required, then translate the origin and set the clipping mask.

- *Storing the position of an imported file.* Applications can use various data structures to represent the position of an EPS file. The *Import* application represents an imported file as the original bounding box of the illustration, the translation, the rotation, and the scale.

- *Error response and recovery for imported EPS files.* EPS files should not be executed in the application's main PostScript execution context. A separate context should be created to protect the application's main context from possible errors in the imported file. When the application's main context is used for executing an EPS file, errors in the file can cause a fatal application error.

- *Offscreen buffering of EPS files.* Applications usually render a newly imported EPS file into an offscreen buffer so that when the user repositions the image the application can copy the buffer to the new position without executing the file again.

- *Parsing EPS files.* EPS files contain information about the size of the image and the resource requirements of the file. Applications that import EPS files must parse the files to find this information.

- *Resource handling.* An importing application must resolve the resource requirements of the EPS file. If the file uses any resources that are not resident in the system, the application must locate the resources and load them into the server. One common resource requirement is a font that is not included in the file.

- *Saving an EPS file with a preview image.* The Encapsulated PostScript File Format specification lists several options for incorporating a preview image along with the PostScript code. The complete EPS file format is described in Appendix H of the *PostScript Language Reference Manual, Second Edition*. Applications should support, at a minimum, the Encapsulated PostScript Interchange (EPSI) preview format.

- *Exchanging illustrations between live applications.* The EPS file format provides an ideal way to exchange pictures between concurrently executing applications through the X selection mechanism.

The *Import* application addresses these issues and introduces several user interface techniques for interacting with imported files. The techniques include several ways to manipulate the imported image:

- Move, scale, and rotate the image

- Constrain the image to original size and aspect ratio

- Position the image by clicking and dragging the mouse

These are not the only possible interaction techniques, nor are they meant to establish a standard interface for imported files. They are provided as examples of basic capabilities that are possible when importing files into an application.

12.1 EPS File Format

An EPS file is a PostScript language program that describes a single-page illustration. An EPS file is the same as any other PostScript language page description, with a few restrictions that allow the file to be imported into an application and still behave in a predictable and expected manner. The format is limited to one page in order to avoid the difficult problems that would result from attempting to import one multipage document into another. The single-page constraint allows EPS files to be independent of page size and output device.

Every EPS file must contain two PostScript language comments. One comment identifies the file as an EPS file and the other describes the bounding box of the file. The bounding box provides an importing application with the information it needs to place the EPS file.

Other comments and components are optional but are often included to provide additional capabilities. One of the more common components is a preview image. Although the preview image is not required by the EPS specification, it is encouraged in environments that do not have access to the Display PostScript system and cannot image the files on screen. A preview image is not necessary in a Display PostScript environment because the file itself can be rendered on the screen.

Other optional comments identify the fonts used in or needed by the file, the colors used in the file, the names of included component files, and a number of other items.

Example 12.1 shows a simple EPS file that draws a black box. It contains no preview image and uses no fonts.

Example 12.1 *A simple EPS file*

PostScript language code:

```
%!PS-Adobe-3.0 EPSF-3.0
%%BoundingBox: 100 100 200 200
%%EndComments

newpath
100 100 moveto 200 100 lineto 200 200 lineto 200 100 lineto
closepath 0 setgray
fill
%%EOF
```

Example 12.2 shows a more complex file that illustrates how EPS files can contain other EPS files as subparts. It includes the file from Example 12.1 as part of the file.

Example 12.2 *An EPS file that contains another EPS file*

PostScript language code:

```
%!PS-Adobe-3.0 EPSF-3.0
%%BoundingBox: 0 0 500 500
%%EndComments

    ...The first part of the outer EPS file goes here...

%%BeginDocument: EmbeddedFile.eps
%!PS-Adobe-3.0 EPSF-3.0
%%BoundingBox: 100 100 200 200
%%EndComments

newpath
100 100 moveto 200 100 lineto 200 200 lineto 200 100 lineto
closepath 0 setgray
fill

%%EOF
%%EndDocument

    ...The rest of the outer EPS file goes here...

%%EOF
```

12.2 Placing an Imported Image in a Page

The steps required to place an imported EPS file in a page description are straightforward. However, before the EPS file can be rendered, the application must determine the image's position, scale, and rotation. Implementing an interface that allows the user to specify these values can be a complex programming task. The *Import* application is one example of such an interface.

The bounds of an EPS file are represented by the lower left and upper right corners of its bounding box. For example, a file with the comment

```
%%BoundingBox: 20 20 80 80
```

specifies the lower left corner of the graphic at (20, 20) and the upper right corner of the graphic at (80, 80). The width of the bounding box is the difference between the x values; height is the difference in y values.

Since the lower left corner of the bounding box is not necessarily at (0, 0), placing the image on the page requires a translation to compensate for the distance of the bounding box from the origin. Otherwise, an imported image would be out of position by the distance between (0, 0) and the lower left corner of the bounding box.

Positioning an EPS file involves five steps, as illustrated in Figure 12.2:

1. Translate to where the lower left corner of the bounding box will appear.

2. Rotate the image the desired number of degrees.

3. Scale the coordinate system to the desired image size.

4. Translate the coordinate space in the opposite direction of step 1 in order to counteract the offset from the origin. (For this calculation, use the negative of the values that designate the lower left corner of the original image bounding box.)

5. Place a clipping rectangle around the imported image using the dimensions from the bounding box as the frame for the clip. The clipping rectangle prevents any marks drawn by the EPS file from appearing outside the bounding box of the file.

The clipping rectangle would not be necessary if all EPS files were truthful about their bounding boxes. However, there is no guarantee that the bounding box specified by the exporting application is correct. Setting a clipping path protects the rest of the page from stray marks generated by incorrect EPS files.

Figure 12.2 *Placing an imported file within a page description*

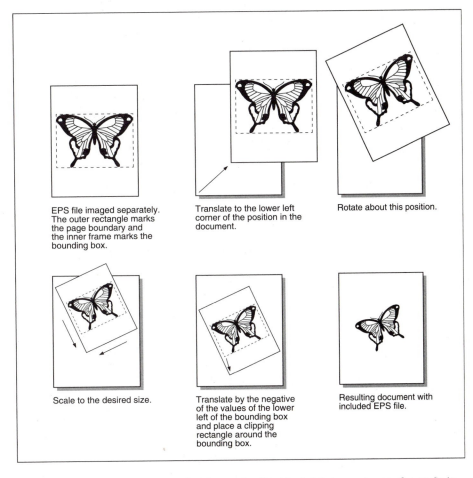

EPS file imaged separately. The outer rectangle marks the page boundary and the inner frame marks the bounding box.

Translate to the lower left corner of the position in the document.

Rotate about this position.

Scale to the desired size.

Translate by the negative of the values of the lower left of the bounding box and place a clipping rectangle around the bounding box.

Resulting document with included EPS file.

EPS files are supposed to leave the PostScript interpreter in the state it was in before the file was executed. Unfortunately, not all EPS files do this correctly. In particular, it is necessary to protect the state of the operand and dictionary stacks and to initialize the graphics state for the EPS file before importing the file.

• Returning the operand and dictionary stacks to the states they were in before the file was imported is important. Items left on these stacks by an EPS file can cause problems for subsequent operations that rely on stack values or dictionaries.

- Initializing the graphics state is important because you cannot rely on imported files to do it. For example, if an application leaves the current color white and imports a file that assumes the current color to be black, then part or all of the file might incorrectly appear white.

Example 12.3 shows the wraps *Import* uses when it prepares to render an EPS file and to position it in the document. The last line of the **PSWBeginEPSF** wrap loads the ExecPS procedure, and the first line of the **PSWEndEPSF** wrap tests the success of the included code. Both are described in section 12.5, "Error Response and Recovery for EPS Files." The **PSWTransformBeforeEPSF** wrap implements the coordinate transformations described in Figure 12.2.

Example 12.3 *Wraps used to prepare an EPS file for imaging*

Wrap definitions:

```
defineps PSWBeginEPSF(DPSContext ctxt)
  /EPSFsave save def
  count /OpStackSize exch def
  /DictStackSize countdictstack def
  /showpage {} def
  0 setgray 0 setlinecap
  1 setlinewidth 0 setlinejoin
  10 setmiterlimit [] 0 setdash newpath
  /languagelevel where {
      pop languagelevel 1 ne {
          false setstrokeadjust false setoverprint
      } if
  } if
  /ExecPS load
endps


defineps PSWEndEPSF(DPSContext ctxt | boolean *err)
  execSuccess not err
  count OpStackSize sub
  dup 0 lt {neg {pop} repeat} {pop} ifelse
  countdictstack DictStackSize sub
  dup 0 lt {neg {end} repeat} {pop} ifelse
endps


defineps PSWTransformBeforeEPSF(DPSContext ctxt; float tx,
                                ty, sx, sy, r, ox, oy)
  initgraphics tx ty translate r rotate
  sx sy scale ox oy translate
endps
```

Appendix H in the *PostScript Language Reference Manual, Second Edition,* provides full details of the positioning and preparation steps for importing EPS files.

12.3 Representing the Position of an Imported Image

The position of an imported image within a page can be represented in several ways. The approach taken in the *Import* application uses variables to store the image's position and orientation: its bounding box, translation, rotation, and scale. Example 12.4 shows the data structure that *Import* maintains for each imported EPS file.

Example 12.4 *Data structure for an imported EPS file*

C language code:

```
typedef struct _Element {
    char            *filename; /* Name of file. */
    unsigned long   length;    /* Size in bytes of file */
    FILE            *f;         /* Open file pointer */
    BBox            origBBox;   /* Element's bounding box */
    float           tx, ty;     /* Current translation */
    float           sx, sy;     /* Current scale */
    float           rotation;   /* Current rotation */
    Pixmap          image;      /* Rendered image */
    Pixmap          mask;       /* Image rendered as mask */
    XRect           xBBox;      /* X bounding box of image */
    XRect           sizeBox;    /* Unrotated size of image */
    ResourceType    *resources; /* Resources for this file*/
    struct _Element *next, *prev;/* Links of elements */
} Element;
```

The *filename* field holds the full path name of the imported file, and the *length* field holds the file size in bytes. If the file is currently open, its file pointer is in *f*.

The *origBBox* field holds the original bounding box information from the file. The translation in *tx* and *ty*, the scale in *sx* and *sy*, and the rotation in *rotation* describe the position of the file on the page. The rotation is stored in degrees, which is how angles are specified in the PostScript language. Any C library calculations involving the rotation require conversion into radians.

The *image* and *mask* fields are the pixmaps holding the rendered image and its mask as described in section 12.6, "Pixmaps for Imaged Files."

xBBox describes a rectangular bounding box that holds the dimensions of the imported image in X coordinates. This bounding box is aligned with the *x* and *y* axes, with its origin is in the upper left corner. It completely frames the imported image, even if the image has been rotated or scaled. It describes the area covered by the *image* pixmap and simplifies hit detection.

sizeBox describes another rectangular bounding box. *sizeBox* holds the dimensions of the imported image in X coordinates, but it does not take rotation into consideration. It is not necessarily aligned with the *x* and *y* axes, and its origin coincides with the lower left corner of the imported image.

The *resources* field points to a data structure describing the resource needs of the imported file. Resources are described in section 12.7, "Parsing an EPS File."

Figure 12.3 illustrates the difference between the *xBBox* and *sizeBox* rectangles. The *xBBox* rectangle follows standard X convention by having its origin in the upper left corner and positive height extending downward. In contrast, the origin of the *sizeBox* rectangle is at the lower left corner of the image, and height is negative, extending upwards. If the image is scaled, the *sizeBox* rectangle changes to represent the scaled size. The *sizeBox* rectangle and the current rotation define the location, size, and orientation of the image on the screen.

Figure 12.3 *The xBBox and sizeBox rectangles*

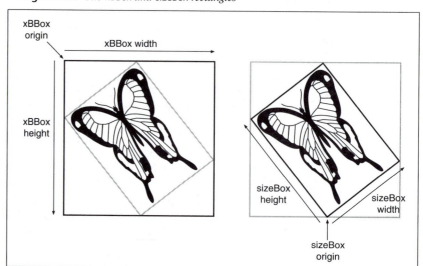

12.4 Importing EPS Files

The Display PostScript Toolkit contains a set of procedures for importing EPS files. Two procedures handle all the required EPS setup and error recovery activities:

- **XDPSCreatePixmapForEPSF** finds the %%BoundingBox comment and creates a pixmap large enough to hold the results of imaging the file.

- **XDPSImageFileIntoDrawable** executes an EPS file and leaves the results in a pixmap or window.

These two procedures are discussed in *Display PostScript Toolkit for X*— see pages TK-32 and TK-35 for basic descriptions.

These procedures provide basic capabilities for importing EPS files. Unfortunately, they can render images only in an unrotated, evenly scaled coordinate system, and they cannot resolve the resource requirements of imported EPS files. The *Import* application contains enhanced procedures that address these two shortcomings.

The first step in importing a file is to parse the document comments, which is done in *Import* by the **parseFileHeader** procedure. This procedure reads the file and fills in the bounding box and resource fields of an *Element* structure. *Import* calls **parseFileHeader** immediately after it opens a file, since the user interaction techniques used to position the image in the window require the file's bounding box. Section 12.7 on page PG-275 discusses parsing EPS files in some detail.

After the user has selected a position and scale for the file, *Import* allocates pixmaps for the imported image and calls **imageToPixmap**, shown in Example 12.5. The **imageToPixmap** procedure works as follows:

- The call to **setDrawingParameters** sets the imaging context to the image pixmap—the pixmap into which the file's image will be rendered.

- The **PSWTransformBeforeEPSF** wrap implements the coordinate transformation described on page PG-260. The wrap is shown in Example 12.3.

- The **imageFile** procedure actually executes the file and places its image into the image pixmap. This procedure is shown in Example 12.7.

- If the execution is successful, the process is repeated again for the mask pixmap—the pixmap that allows the page background to show through transparent parts of the image. The **imageFile** procedure that is used for the image pixmap is also used for the mask pixmap. However, because the context is set for the mask pixmap, the results end up there. See section 12.6, "Pixmaps for Imaged Files," for more information on the mask and for the implementation of **setMaskParameters**. Note that it is possible to chain two contexts together and render the file into both pixmaps simultaneously, but this actually takes longer—the overhead in the interpreter generated by switching between the two contexts outweighs the communication cost of transferring the file contents twice.

Example 12.5 *The imageToPixmap procedure*

C language code:

```
static Boolean imageToPixmap(e)
  Element *e;
{
  XPoint xpt;
  Point pt;

  /* Compute the user space coordinates of the origin
   * of the pixmap. This must be subtracted from the
   * translation of the element to obtain the translation
   * within the pixmap */
  xpt.x = e->xBBox.x + originX;
  xpt.y = e->xBBox.y + e->xBBox.height - scaledHeight +
          originY;
  convertToDPS(&xpt, &pt);

  setDrawingParameters(e->image, e->xBBox.height);
  PSWTransformBeforeEPSF(imageCtxt, e->tx - pt.x,
                  e->ty - pt.y, e->sx, e->sy, e->rotation,
                  -e->origBBox.ll.x, -e->origBBox.ll.y);
  DPSerasepage(imageCtxt);

  /* Execute the file using the current settings. imageFile
   * will return whether there was an error. If there was
   * no error, proceed to the mask rendering */
  if (!imageFile(e)) {
    DPSgsave(imageCtxt);
```

```
      setMaskParameters(e->mask, e->xBBox.height);
      PSWTransformBeforeEPSF(imageCtxt, e->tx - pt.x,
                             e->ty - pt.y, e->sx, e->sy,
                             e->rotation, -e->origBBox.ll.x,
                             -e->origBBox.ll.y);

      /* We need to make sure the mask starts out with 0's */
      XFillRectangle(XtDisplay(drawingArea), e->mask,
                     bitmapgc, 0, 0, e->xBBox.width,
                     e->xBBox.height);
      (void) imageFile(e);
      DPSgrestore(imageCtxt);
      return False;
   } else return True;
}
```

Example 12.6 shows the **setDrawingParameters** procedure. It calls the Display PostScript Toolkit procedure **XDPSSetContextParameters** to set the context for rendering into the pixmap. Since the context that does the rendering frequently shifts among different drawables with different depths, it is necessary to set all of the drawing parameters, including screen, depth, and colormaps.

The final parameter to **XDPSSetContextParameters** indicates what to set—in this case, everything. The two *XDPSStandardColormap* parameters are *NULL*; this is a special case that tells **XDPSSetContextParameters** to use the default color cube and gray ramp for the screen.

Example 12.6 *Setting the drawing parameters*

C language code:

```
#define XDPSContextAll (XDPSContextScreenDepth |
                XDPSContextDrawable | XDPSContextGrayMap |
                XDPSContextRGBMap)

static void setDrawingParameters(d, height)
   Drawable d;
   int height;
{
   (void) XDPSSetContextParameters(imageCtxt,
              XtScreen(drawingArea), depth, d, height,
              (XDPSStandardColormap *) NULL,
              (XDPSStandardColormap *) NULL, XDPSContextAll);
}
```

12.5 Error Response and Recovery for EPS Files

Because an application has no control over the contents of an imported EPS file, it cannot ensure that executing the file won't produce errors. In a non–Display PostScript environment, errors in imported EPS files are not catastrophic. An EPS file error might keep a document from printing or cause it to print incorrectly, but it won't affect the operation of the user's application.

In a Display PostScript environment, however, the situation is more serious. PostScript language errors can cause unpredictable side effects within a context. If the application executes the imported file in its main context, the application itself is at risk. To avoid this risk, the application must protect its main context from errors in EPS files. Both the Display PostScript Toolkit procedure **XDPSImageFileIntoDrawable** and the *Import* application take considerable pains to isolate errors and recover gracefully from them. Still, it is impossible to anticipate every type of error that may occur. The best approach is to execute EPS files in a separate context reserved just for this purpose to protect the application's main context from unforeseen problems.

Note: *The rest of this section contains advanced information and requires a good understanding of the PostScript language. If you have access to the Import application, you can copy its import procedures into your own program without worrying about exactly how they perform error detection. If you do not have the Import application, read on to learn how to implement the functionality.*

To detect errors, execute the imported PostScript language code within a **stopped** clause. That way, control transfers to the instruction immediately following the **stopped** operator when an error occurs. However, only a small amount of code can be protected this way because all protected code must fit on the execution stack. Example 12.7 shows a way around this limitation.

Example 12.7 *Catching errors in EPS files*

PostScript language code:

```
/ExecPS {
  /execSuccess false def
  (%stdin) (r) file
  cvx stopped
  pop                      % always true
  % Flush until you get the magic line
```

```
        {
            {currentfile 256 string readline} stopped
            pop                 % don't care stopped result
            pop                 % don't care readline bool result
            (Special marker line) eq
            {exit} if
        } loop
    } bind def
```

C language code:

```
Boolean imageFile(e)
  Element *e;
{
#define BUFSIZE 256
  char buf[BUFSIZE];
  static char eobuf[] = "/execSuccess true def\n\stop\n\
                         Special marker line\n";
  static char restorebuf[] = "\nEPSFsave restore\n";
  int err;

  /* Reset to beginning of file */
  rewind(e->f);

  /* Prepare to execute PostScript code */
  PSWBeginEPSF(imageCtxt);
  DPSWritePostScript(imageCtxt, "\nexec\n", 6);

  /* Copy file to context */
  while (fgets(buf, BUFSIZE, e->f) != NULL) {
    DPSWritePostScript(imageCtxt, buf, strlen(buf));
  }

  /* Mark the end of the data stream */
  DPSWritePostScript(imageCtxt, eobuf, strlen(eobuf));

  /* Check the results of the imaging:
   * Get the error status and restore the context */
  PSWEndEPSF(imageCtxt, &err);

  /* Can't do this as a wrap because of restore semantics */
  DPSWritePostScript(imageCtxt, restorebuf,
                        strlen(restorebuf));
  return err;
#undef BUFSIZE
}
```

PostScript language trace:

```
/EPSFsave save def

    ...The rest of the PSWBeginEPSF() operations...

/ExecPS load
exec
%!PS-Adobe-3.0 EPSF-3.0

    ...contents of EPS file...

/execSuccess true def stop
Special marker line

    ...PSWEndEPSF() operations to restore state...

EPSFsave restore
```

The ExecPS procedure converts the %stdin file into an executable object. This causes the PostScript interpreter to read and execute the lines that follow the invocation of ExecPS. If there is an error in the EPS file, the reading of lines stops and execution continues after the **stopped** operator in the ExecPS procedure. If there is no error in the file, the line following the EPS code sets execSuccess to *true* and then executes the **stop** operator. Executing **stop** has the same effect as an error; it makes execution continue after the **stopped** operator.

If the EPS file contains an error, the remainder of the file must be flushed in order to return the interpreter to a consistent state. ExecPS does this by reading and discarding lines until it finds one that matches a special marker line. The actual line used is not "Special marker line," as shown in the example, but is instead a long string of characters that contains many PostScript language syntax errors. It is extremely unlikely than any real EPS file would contain such a string.

After ExecPS has detected the special marker line, the application can check execSuccess to determine whether the file contained errors. If there was no error, the line
```
/execSuccess true def stop
```
was executed, changing execSuccess to *true*. If there was an error, this line was flushed with all the other code that followed the error, leaving execSuccess in its initial state, *false*.

This error recovery technique is quite robust and leaves the context in the same state as it was before the EPS file was executed. Nevertheless, we recommend executing the EPS file in a separate context to avoid unforeseen problems.

12.6 Pixmaps for Imaged Files

EPS files can be of any length or complexity. Some execute almost instantly, while others may take many seconds. The *Import* application uses pixmaps to reduce the number of times a file must be executed. By copying these pixmaps into the window when needed, the application can provide quick user feedback when imported images are moved in the window.

Import renders a file's image into a pixmap when the file is first imported, when the image size is changed, or when the rotation is changed. When the user changes the image size or rotation, only a rectangular border appears on the screen while the mouse is being moved. When the user releases the mouse button, the imported image is rendered in a pixmap to fit the rectangle, then copied to the screen.

Because the imported image cannot be seen on screen while it is being rendered into the pixmap, the *Import* application sets a wait cursor during the rendering to provide visual feedback. When the image is complete, the pixmap is copied into the window.

The *Import* application sets the maximum pixmap size at 1.5 times the screen size. If you do not set an upper limit on buffer size, disk thrashing can result when the size of an imported file exceeds the available RAM size.

The user interface provides a toggle to turn on or off the rendering of imported images. When this option is set to turn off rendering, a gray box appears in place of the image. This option is helpful for users editing documents that have many imported files because it speeds up rendering of the document. The gray boxes can be rotated and resized, and the effect will be seen on the images when full imaging is turned back on. Figure 12.4 shows a rotated image displayed as a gray box.

Figure 12.4 *Example of imaging turned off*

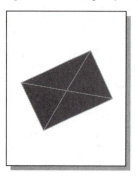

Instead of displaying only the rectangular border of an imported image when the user resizes or rotates it, the application could show the actual image. However, to do so the application must reexecute the EPS file at each increment of resizing or rotation as the mouse moves. The resulting user feedback is sluggish when compared to displaying only a rectangular outline. The option would be valuable, though, for times when a user needs to see these intermediate views to arrive at the right size and position for the image.

If you decide to present these intermediate views in your application, you should render the EPS file directly to the final pixmap instead of to an intermediate one. During resizing or rotation, the chance that the exact same image will be needed more than once is extremely small, so saving the image in an intermediate pixmap at each increment of mouse motion serves no purpose.

When images are moved, as opposed to resized or rotated, saving them in an intermediate pixmap is useful. As the user drags an image with the mouse, the image in the pixmap does not change; to provide responsive user feedback, the application can copy the pixmap to a different location each time the mouse moves.

Unfortunately, when you copy a pixmap to the screen, the entire rectangular area of the pixmap is copied, including portions that should not block background images. This problem is most obvious in a rotated image like the one shown in Figure 12.5. The triangular areas in each corner of the pixmap are not part of the rotated image, and should be treated as transparent. Even unrotated images can have holes or unimaged areas around the edges that should not block the background.

Figure 12.5 *A rotated image in a pixmap*

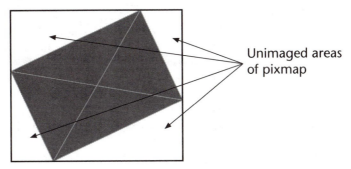

Unimaged areas
of pixmap

When the pixmap is copied to the screen, some logical manipulations are required to allow background images to show through transparent parts of the pixmap. A method similar to the one used in section 8.4, "Pixmap Copying," could be used here, but for large images a different solution works better. The solution involves executing the EPS file twice, once into a pixmap and once into a bitmap (a pixmap that is only one bit deep), which is used as a mask for the image. For the mask execution, the transfer functions in the graphics state are altered so that all imaged areas come out black. The result is a mask exactly the shape of the illustration. Figure 12.6 shows a simple illustration and the resulting mask.

Figure 12.6 *An illustration and its mask*

Original picture   *Picture converted into a mask*

Example 12.8 shows how to set up a context to produce a mask. The **PSWSetMaskTransfer** wrap sets the transfer function so that any input color comes out as black. The **setMaskParameters** procedure creates a gray ramp with pixel value 1 as black and pixel value 0 as white. The result is a bitmap with a 1 value in every pixel where imaging has occurred.

Example 12.8 *Setting the graphics parameters to produce a mask*

Wrap definition:

```
defineps PSWSetMaskTransfer(DPSContext ctxt)
  {pop 0} settransfer
endps
```

C language code:

```
static void setMaskParameters(d, height)
  Drawable d;
  int height;
{
  XDPSStandardColormap maskMap;
  XDPSStandardColormap rgbMap;

  /* Set up gray ramp with 0 = white, 1 = black */
  maskMap.colormap = None;
  maskMap.red_max = 1;
  maskMap.red_mult = -1;
  maskMap.base_pixel = 1;

  /* Set up an empty color cube */
  rgbMap.colormap = None;
  rgbMap.red_max = rgbMap.green_max = rgbMap.blue_max =
        rgbMap.red_mult = rgbMap.green_mult =
        rgbMap.blue_mult = rgbMap.base_pixel = 0;

  (void) XDPSSetContextParameters(imageCtxt,
                    XtScreen(drawingArea), 1, d, height,
                    &rgbMap, &maskMap, XDPSContextAll);
  PSWSetMaskTransfer(imageCtxt);
}
```

The resulting bitmap can be used in an X graphics context as a clip mask, as shown in Example 12.9. When **XCopyArea** copies the image to the screen, the copy only affects areas that are set in the mask.

Example 12.9 *Copying with a mask*

C language code:

```
XSetClipOrigin(dpy, gc, rect->x, rect->y);
XSetClipMask(dpy, gc, adding->mask);
XCopyArea(dpy, adding->image, original, gc,
        0, 0, rect->width, rect->height, rect->x, rect->y);
XSetClipMask(dpy, gc, None);
```

12.7 Parsing an EPS File

An application that imports an EPS file must parse it in order to validate the file as a legal EPS file and to obtain the bounding box of the image.

The first line in a valid EPS file is the comment
  %!PS-Adobe-*N.N* EPSF-*n.n*
N.N corresponds to the version of the Document Structuring Conventions (DSC), and *n.n* corresponds to the version of the Encapsulated PostScript File Format specification. The parsing routines in the *Import* application look for this line to determine whether a file is valid EPS.

The version numbers provide information about the types of document structuring comments and capabilities you can expect in the file, but they are not important to an importing application like *Import*. They are of more interest to applications such as print managers and color separators.

The bounding box comment can appear at the beginning or end of an EPS file. If the comment is not present, the importing application should issue an error message and terminate the import. The format of the comment is
  %%BoundingBox: *llx lly urx ury*
where *llx, lly* are the coordinates of the lower left of the image and *urx, ury* are the coordinates of the upper right of the image. (These dimensions are in user space; they are not the same as the origin and size dimensions in the *XRectangle* structure.)

Note: *The specification for EPS files requires the numbers in a bounding box comment to be integers. Many applications break this rule and put floating point numbers in the EPS files they generate. For robustness, your application should accept files with floating point numbers. For correctness, it should place only integers in EPS files it creates.*

12.7.1 Handling Resource Requirements

Applications must handle comments that describe the resource requirements of the imported file. Resources are objects like fonts, character encodings, and procedure sets (sets of PostScript language procedures) that might be used by but are not included in the EPS file. The application must ensure that all required resources are available.

Resources in Imported Files

If an imported file contains resource comments, the application must ensure that the resources are present before executing the file. There are several ways this can be done.

- The resource may be included in the file. In this case there will be another comment indicating that the resource is present.

- The resource may be resident in PostScript interpreter memory. For example, most implementations provide the Times-Roman font.

- The resource may be downloadable to the interpreter. For example, if a file uses the Adobe Garamond font and if the font is not already resident in PostScript interpreter memory, the application can download the font before executing the file.

Resources in Exported Files

Resources must also be considered when exporting an EPS file. When an application writes a PostScript language file, it must specify the resources that the application uses directly and the resources that are used by included files. If more than one included file has the same included resources, it is highly recommended (but not mandatory) that the application remove duplicate copies in order to reduce file size.

Note: *Removing multiple copies of procedure set definitions is possible once the importing application knows the procedure sets and where they lie. For example, importing two Adobe Illustrator files brings in two separate copies of the procedure sets. Propagating the procedure sets to the beginning of the document and eliminating multiple sets reduces the size of the document. The savings increase with each subsequent inclusion of an Illustrator file. Imported procedure sets are not handled in this way in the* Import *application, but programmers of applications that make extensive use of imported files should consider this.*

Section G.6 of the *PostScript Language Reference Manual, Second Edition,* describes in detail the comments that define a file's resource requirements.

Example 12.10 shows an excerpt from an EPS file. It uses two font resources, *Times-Roman* and *Caslon,* and two procedure set resources, *Adobe_packedarray* and *Adobe_cmykcolor.* Note how the font resource *Times-Roman,* used by the embedded document, has been propagated to the outer *%%DocumentFonts* and *%%DocumentNeededFonts* comments.

Example 12.10 *Sample EPS File*

PostScript language code:

```
%!PS-Adobe-2.0 EPSF-1.2
%%Creator: Adobe Illustrator 88(TM) 1.9.3
%%For: (Joe Green) (Adobe Systems Incorporated)
%%Title: (SampleFile.eps)
%%CreationDate: (5/18/90) (15:13)
%%DocumentFonts: Times-Roman Caslon
%%DocumentNeededFonts: Times-Roman Caslon
%%DocumentProcSets: Adobe_packedarray 1 0
%%+ Adobe_cmykcolor 2 0
%%DocumentSuppliedProcSets: Adobe_packedarray 1 0
%%+ Adobe_cmykcolor 2 0
%%BoundingBox:117 54 436 675
%%DocumentPreview: None
%%EndComments

    ...The rest of the prolog and the procedure set
       definitions go here...

%%EndProlog

    ...The first part of the document goes here...

%%BeginDocument: EmbeddedFile.eps
%!PS-Adobe-2.0 EPSF-1.2
%%DocumentFonts: Times-Roman
%%DocumentNeededFonts: Times-Roman
%%BoundingBox:0 0 612 792
%%EndComments
%%EndProlog

    ...The embedded file goes here...

%%EndDocument
```

...The rest of the document goes here...

```
%%Trailer
%%EOF
```

Whenever the parsing routines encounter a comment that specifies a resource, they add the resource to the resource list for the EPS file. Example 12.11 shows the data structures used to maintain the resource list. Each type of resource has a *ResourceType* structure, and each resource instance has a *Resource* structure.

Example 12.11 *Data structures holding resource requirements*

C language code:

```
typedef struct _Resource {
   String          name;
   String          version, revision; /* For procsets only */
   Boolean         included;
   struct _Resource *next;
} Resource;

typedef struct _ResourceType {
   String              name;
   Resource            *list;
   struct _ResourceType   *next;
} ResourceType;
```

After all the resources in the file have been identified, *Import* verifies that all the required resources are available. Example 12.12 shows the wrap that verifies whether a font is resident in the interpreter. The font is resident if it is defined in the **SharedFontDirectory** or **FontDirectory** dictionaries or if the file name (%font%*name*) is known to the interpreter.

Example 12.12 *Verifying the presence of a font*

Wrap definition:

```
defineps PSWCheckFontResident(DPSContext ctxt; char *name; |
                                 boolean *resident)
   SharedFontDirectory /name known {
      true resident

   } {
```

```
      FontDirectory /name known {
            true resident
      } {
        /buf (name) length 6 add string def
        buf 0 (%font%) putinterval
        buf 6 (name) putinterval
        false buf {pop pop true} buf filenameforall resident
        } ifelse
    } ifelse
endps
```

If the resource is not present in PostScript VM, *Import* uses the
PostScript language resource location library to locate a copy of the
resource (described in Appendix A of *Display PostScript Toolkit for X*).
Example 12.13 shows the **downloadResource** procedure, which locates
and downloads a resource. The call to **ListPSResourceFiles** identifies files
on the system that contain a definition of the desired resource. If a
matching file cannot be found, **ListPSResourceFiles** returns 0. The
downloadResource procedure switches to shared memory allocation
mode, writes the contents of the file to shared VM, and restores the
previous memory allocation mode. By thus defining the resource, it will
be available to any future files that also use it. Finally,
downloadResource calls **markResident** so that *Import* knows that the
resource is now resident in the interpreter's memory.

Example 12.13 *Locating and downloading a resource*

C language code:

```
static Boolean downloadResource(type, name) char *type,
                                   *name;
{
    int numFiles;
    char **fontNames, **files;
    FILE *f;
#define BUFLEN 256
    char buf[BUFLEN];

    /* Try to find a file that defines this resource */
    numFiles = ListPSResourceFiles(NULL, ".", type, name,
                                   &fontNames, &files);

    if (numFiles == 0) return False;


    f = fopen(files[0], "r");
```

```
    if (f == NULL) {
      free(names);
      free(files);
      return False;
    }

    /* Switch to shared VM and write file to the server */
    DPSPrintf(imageCtxt, "\ncurrentshared true setshared\n");
    while (fgets(buf, BUFLEN, f) != NULL) {
      DPSWritePostScript(imageCtxt, buf, strlen(buf));
    }
    DPSPrintf(imageCtxt, "\nsetshared\n");
    fclose(f);
    free(fontNames);
    free(files);

    /* Mark the resource as resident for future tests */
    markResident(type, name);
    return True;
#undef BUFLEN
}
```

12.8 Exporting an EPS File

The *Import* application can write an EPS file that combines all the
images displayed in its window. Writing such a file is straightforward.
The header for the combined file contains a %%BoundingBox comment
that describes the combined bounding box for all the images. It also
contains resource requirement comments that merge the requirements
of all included files.

The exporting step of *Import* does not require Display PostScript
capabilities. It simply writes a global header, then inserts a short file
header before each imported file. Example 12.14 shows an example of
an output file from *Import*. The BeginEPSF and EndEPSF procedures
correspond to the **PSWBeginEPSF** and **PSWEndEPSF** wraps of Example
12.3.

Example 12.14 *Sample exported file*

PostScript language code:

```
%!PS-Adobe-3.0 EPSF-3.0
%%BoundingBox: 237 305 259 349
%%Pages: 1
%%DocumentFonts: StoneSans-Bold StoneSans-Semibold
```

```
%%EndComments
%%BeginProlog
/BeginEPSF {
  /EPSFsave save def
  count /OpStackSize exch def
  /DictStackSize countdictstack def
  /showpage {} def
  0 setgray 0 setlinecap
  1 setlinewidth 0 setlinejoin
  10 setmiterlimit [] 0 setdash newpath
  /languagelevel where
  {pop languagelevel 1 ne
      {false setstrokeadjust false setoverprint} if
  } if
} bind def

/EndEPSF {
  count OpStackSize sub
  dup 0 lt {neg {pop} repeat} {pop} ifelse
  countdictstack DictStackSize sub
  dup 0 lt {neg {end} repeat} {pop} ifelse
  EPSFsave restore
} bind def
%%EndProlog

%%Page: 1 1
/pagesave save def

BeginEPSF
237.105 305.843 translate 0.212121 0.210384 scale 0 rotate
-99 -99 translate
99 99 moveto 201 99 lineto 201 301 lineto 99 301 lineto
closepath clip newpath

%%BeginDocument: /user/green/art1.eps

    ...First included file...

%%EndDocument
EndEPSF

BeginEPSF
102.57 258.987 translate 1.44 1.342 scale 32.67 rotate
200 -200 translate
200 200 moveto 400 200 lineto 400 400 lineto 200 400 lineto
closepath clip newpath

%%BeginDocument: /user/green/art2.eps
...Second included file...
```

```
%%EndDocument
EndEPSF

pagesave restore showpage
%%EOF
```

Import is a simple application in that its data consists solely of imported EPS files. Applications that draw in other ways can produce output files using the text context facility provided by the Display PostScript Client Library. A text context can be drawn to just like a regular execution context (using wraps, single-ops, or any other method), but it produces a text log of the Display PostScript code instead of executing the code.

12.9 Including Preview Data in Exported EPS Files

Display PostScript applications can directly execute EPS files and display the images they describe. However, applications that don't use the Display PostScript system as their imaging model cannot execute the PostScript code in EPS files. These applications must rely on a preview image in the EPS file for rendering on the screen.

The *Import* application exports one type of preview image: the EPSI format described in Section H.6 of the *PostScript Language Reference Manual, Second Edition*. This format consists of an EPS file with a hexadecimal preview image appearing as comments in the header. The hexadecimal data is enclosed within a %%BeginPreview and %%EndPreview comment nesting. Example 12.15 shows an example of the EPSI format.

Example 12.15 *EPS file with preview image*

PostScript language code:

```
%!PS-Adobe-2.0 EPSF-1.2
%%Title: simple.eps
%%BoundingBox: 102 536 126 559
%%EndComments
%%BeginPreview: 28 23 1 23
% 00000000
% 00000700
% 0000ff00
% 001fc000
% 0fe30000
% 0c0c0000
```

```
% 00080000
% 00100000
% 00200000
% 00400000
% 00400000
% 00400000
% 00800000
% 00400000
% 00400000
% 00200000
% 00200000
% 00200000
% 00300000
% 07080000
% 00ff0000
% 0003e000
% 00000000
%%EndPreview

%%EndProlog
...

%%Trailer
...
```

Preview images are defined as raster images without color information, so *Import* creates a new pixmap to hold a black and white or gray scale rendering of the page. After rendering the file to the pixmap, *Import* converts the pixmap into an *XImage* with a call to **XGetImage**. The pixels are then read and written as hexadecimal comments sandwiched between %%BeginPreview and %%EndPreview comments.

Import can write either 1-bit- or 8-bit-deep preview images. Example 12.16 shows the two procedures that set the context for EPSI rendering. The two procedures are similar but set up different gray ramps. For a 1-bit preview image, the gray ramp is set up with pixel 0 as white and pixel 1 as black. For an 8-bit preview image, the gray ramp is set up with pixel 0 as white and pixel 255 as black, with 254 shades of gray in between.

Example 12.16 *Setting a context for EPSI rendering*

C language code:

```
static void setEPSIBitmapParameters(d, height)
  Drawable d;
  int height;
```

```
{
    XDPSStandardColormap grayMap;
    XDPSStandardColormap rgbMap;

    /* Set up gray ramp with 0 = white, 1 = black */
    grayMap.colormap = None;
    grayMap.red_max = 1;
    grayMap.red_mult = -1;
    grayMap.base_pixel = 1;

    /* Set up empty color cube */
    rgbMap.colormap = None;
    rgbMap.red_max = rgbMap.green_max = rgbMap.blue_max =
      rgbMap.red_mult = rgbMap.green_mult = rgbMap.blue_mult =
      rgbMap.base_pixel = 0;

    (void) XDPSSetContextParameters(imageCtxt,
                        XtScreen(drawingArea), 1, d, height,
                        &rgbMap, &grayMap, XDPSContextAll);
}

static void setEPSIPixmapParameters(d, height)
    Drawable d;
    int height;
{
    XDPSStandardColormap grayMap;
    XDPSStandardColormap rgbMap;

    /* Set up gray ramp with 0 = white, 255 = black,
     * and 254 values in between */
    grayMap.colormap = None;
    grayMap.red_max = 255;
    grayMap.red_mult = -1;
    grayMap.base_pixel = 255;

    /* Set up an empty color cube */
    rgbMap.colormap = None;
    rgbMap.red_max = rgbMap.green_max = rgbMap.blue_max =
      rgbMap.red_mult = rgbMap.green_mult = rgbMap.blue_mult =
      rgbMap.base_pixel = 0;

    (void) XDPSSetContextParameters(imageCtxt,
                        XtScreen(drawingArea), 8, d, height,
                        &rgbMap, &grayMap, XDPSContextAll);
}
```

After setting the parameters using one of the above procedures, *Import* executes the EPS file and renders its image into a pixmap. When the execution is complete, a call to **XGetImage** retrieves the rendered image. Example 12.17 shows how to write the hexadecimal preview data to the output file from the X image data. The *writeFunc* parameter is a passed-in procedure that either writes its data to a file for output or copies it into a string for use as the selection value.

Example 12.17 *Writing a preview image*

C language code:

```
static void writePreview(im, writeFunc, data)
  XImage *im;
  void (*writeFunc)();
  char *data;
{
  int size;
  int lines = 1;
  register int i, j;
  int chars;
  int pixel;
  int accum;
  char buf[257];

  /* Compute characters per line of preview */
  if (im->depth == 1) size = (im->width + 7) / 8 * 2;
  else size = im->width * 2;

  lines = (size + 249) / 250;

  sprintf(buf, "%%%%BeginPreview: %d %d %d %d", im->width,
          im->height, im->depth, lines * im->height);
  (*writeFunc)(buf, data);

  /* If depth is 8, write 2 hex digits per pixel */
  if (im->depth == 8) {
    for (i = 0; i < im->height; i++) {
      (*writeFunc)("\n%", data);
      chars = 0;

      /* Go through pixels in line,
       * making sure output line doesn't get too long */
      for (j = 0; j < im->width; j++) {
        if (chars > 250) {
          (*writeFunc)("\n%", data);
          chars = 0;
        }
```

```
              pixel = XGetPixel(im, j, i);
              sprintf(buf, "%02x", pixel);
              (*writeFunc)(buf, data);
              chars += 2;
              }
        }

      /* If depth is 1, write 2 hex digits per 8 pixels */
      } else {
        for (i = 0; i < im->height; i++) {
          (*writeFunc)("\n%", data);
          chars = 0;
          accum = 0;
          for (j = 0; j < im->width; j++) {
            if (chars > 250) {
              (*writeFunc)("\n%", data);
              chars = 0;
            }
            pixel = XGetPixel(im, j, i);
            accum = (accum << 1) + pixel;
            if (((j + 1) % 8) == 0) {
              sprintf(buf, "%02x", accum);
              (*writeFunc)(buf, data);
              chars += 2;
              accum = 0;
            }
          }

          /* If there are leftover pixels,
           * shift left and write */
          if ((im->width % 8) != 0) {
            accum = accum << 8 - (im->width % 8);
            if (chars > 250) (*writeFunc)("\n", data);
            sprintf(buf, "%02x", accum);
            (*writeFunc)(buf, data);
          }
        }
      }
  (*writeFunc)("\n%%EndPreview\n", data);
  XDestroyImage(im);
  }
```

Two variations on EPS files include the preview image as binary data.
These variations are used primarily in Macintosh® and MS-DOS®
environments, and their formats are described in Appendix H of the

PostScript Language Reference Manual, Second Edition. Import cannot import or export these formats, but a real application that shares files across platforms should be designed to handle them.

12.10 Exchanging EPS Data Through Selections

The X Window System defines a selection mechanism to exchange data between active applications. When the Display PostScript extension is available, the selection mechanism can pass high-quality images in the form of EPS files. The selection mechanism is conceptually quite simple:

- An application notifies the X server that it has taken ownership of a selection.

- Another application requests the value of the selection from the X server.

- The X server tells the first application to send the selection value to the second application.

The details of the selection mechanism are quite complex and are beyond the scope of this book. This section outlines how the *Import* application uses selections; the same techniques can be used to provide live exchange of EPS data in other applications.

The *Import* application takes ownership of the clipboard selection when the user selects an object on screen and chooses the Cut or Copy menu items. Example 12.18 shows the callback procedure for the Copy menu item. The call to **XtOwnSelection** informs the X Toolkit that *Import* is taking ownership of the clipboard selection. It also informs the X Toolkit that if another application requests the selection, then the **convertSelection** procedure should be called to provide the value. The procedure for the Cut menu item is similar, but it also removes the currently selected object from the screen and moves it to a special "pending cut" area.

Example 12.18 *Taking ownership of the selection*

C language code:

```
static void copyProc(w, clientData, callData)
    Widget w;
    XtPointer clientData, callData;
{
```

```
        (void) XtOwnSelection(drawingArea, XA_CLIPBOARD,
                XtLastTimestampProcessed(XtDisplay(w)),
                convertSelection, loseSelection, NULL);
    } /* end copyProc() */
```

The **convertSelection** procedure, shown in Example 12.19, does the
actual work of providing the selection value. A requesting application
can ask for the selection in various formats; the *target* parameter
indicates the format desired. The special value TARGETS is a request for a
list of all the formats that are available. The **convertSelection** procedure
replies with a list that includes EPS format, EPSI format, the name of the
file that generated the selected image, and the pixmap that holds the
rendered file.

If the requested type is ADOBE_EPS or ADOBE_EPSI format,
convertSelection calls **convertToEPS**. This procedure prepares an output
file as described in sections 12.8, "Exporting an EPS File," and 12.9,
"Including Preview Data in Exported EPS Files," but in this case the file
contains only the selected element. If its second parameter is *true*,
convertToEPS includes an EPSI preview image in the output. The
returned buffer holds the contents of the output file.

If the requested type is FILENAME, **convertSelection** supplies the name
of the file that holds the picture. If the requested type is PIXMAP,
convertSelection returns the identifier for the pixmap that holds the
rendered image.

Example 12.19 *The selection conversion procedure*

C language code:

```
    static Boolean convertSelection(w, selection, target, type,
                                    value, length, format)
        Widget w;
        Atom *selection, *target, *type;
        XtPointer *value;
        unsigned long *length;
        int *format;
    {
        Element *e;
        char *buf;

        /* Return supported types */
        if (*target == XA_TARGETS) {
            Atom *targets = (Atom *) XtMalloc(4 * sizeof(Atom));
            targets[0] = XA_ADOBE_EPS;
```

```
                targets[1] = XA_ADOBE_EPSI;
                targets[2] = XA_FILE_NAME;
                targets[3] = XA_PIXMAP;
                *value = (XtPointer) targets;
                *type = XA_ATOM;
                *length = 4;
                *format = 32;
                return TRUE;
            }

            /* If there is a pending cut, deliver it;
             * otherwise deliver selected element */
            if (pendingCut != NULL) e = pendingCut;
            else if (selected != NULL) e = selected;
            else return FALSE;

            /* Return data in EPS format with or without preview */
            if (*target == XA_ADOBE_EPS || *target == XA_ADOBE_EPSI) {
                buf = convertToEPS(e, (*target == XA_ADOBE_EPSI));
                *value = (XtPointer) buf;
                *length = strlen(buf) + 1;
                *type = XA_STRING;
                *format = 8;
                return TRUE;
            }

            /* Return name of file */
            if (*target == XA_FILE_NAME) {
                char *name = XtNewString(e->filename);
                *value = (XtPointer) name;
                *length = strlen(name) + 1;
                *type = XA_STRING;
                *format = 8;
                return TRUE;
            }

            /* Return pixmap */
            if (*target == XA_PIXMAP) {
                Pixmap *p = XtNew(Pixmap);
                *p = e->image;
                *value = (XtPointer) p;
                *length = 1;
                *type = XA_DRAWABLE;
                *format = 32;
                return TRUE;
            }
```

```
                            /* Unrecognized type */
                            return FALSE;
                     }
```

Example 12.20 shows the other half of the selection transaction: what happens when the user selects the Paste menu item. The call to **XtGetSelectionValue** requests the value of the clipboard selection in Adobe EPS format and tells the X Toolkit to call the **gotSelection** procedure when the selection value arrives.

Example 12.20 *Requesting the selection*

C language code:

```
    static void pasteProc(w, clientData, callData)
       Widget w;
       XtPointer clientData, callData;
    {
       XtGetSelectionValue(drawingArea, XA_CLIPBOARD,
                        XA_ADOBE_EPS, gotSelection, NULL,
                        XtLastTimestampProcessed(XtDisplay(w)));
    } /* end pasteProc() */
```

Example 12.21 shows the **gotSelection** procedure. It checks to make sure that the selection arrived in the expected format, then calls **pasteEPS** to add the selection to the onscreen image. The **pasteEPS** procedure is not shown here. It creates a temporary file, writes the selection value to the file, and then reopens the file and adds it to the onscreen image just like any other file.

Example 12.21 *Getting the selection value*

C language code:

```
    static void gotSelection(w, data, selection, type, value,
                                   length, format)
       Widget w;
       XtPointer data;
       Atom *selection, *type;
       XtPointer value;
       unsigned long *length;
       int *format;
    {
       if (*selection != XA_CLIPBOARD || *type != XA_STRING ||
       *format != 8 || value == NULL) return;
```

```
    pasteEPS((char *) value, *length);
}
```

Most X applications are able to cut and paste text selections. The Display PostScript system makes it possible to transfer high-quality images just as easily as text by supporting EPS as a standard transfer format.

12.11 User Interface Features

This section describes some basic interface techniques for manipulating imported files. The items addressed include rotation, constraining to original aspect, click-to-drop and click-and-drag placement interfaces, and Original Size and Original Ratio menu options. The examples presented here illustrate basic techniques; they are not meant to establish a user interface standard for importing EPS files.

12.11.1 Rotating an Imported File

Rotating an imported image is not as common as translating or scaling, but it is just as easy to perform in the PostScript language. The image should be translated first, then rotated, and finally scaled. (When scaling is not proportional, scaling before rotating skews the axes.)

A procedure in the *Import* application takes a rectangle rotated about a point at a given angle and calculates the enclosing frame. Figure 12.7 illustrates the concept. The solid rectangle is the rotated rectangle, and the dotted rectangle is its bounding box in nonrotated space.

Figure 12.7 *Frame enclosing rotated rectangle*

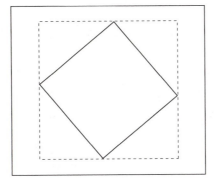

12.11.2   Constraining to Original Aspect Ratio

The ability to preserve or restore the original ratio between width and height can be provided when resizing imported files. Although distorting the image by scaling its width and height differently can produce interesting special effects, users may want to return to the original proportions (see the next section, "Original Ratio Menu Command").

In the *Import* application, the file is constrained to the original proportions when the user imports a file. The user selects a file to import, clicks the mouse at the desired location of the image, and drags to create a rectangle. If this rectangle does not have the same aspect ratio as the imported image, *Import* places the largest possible image, at its original aspect ratio, into the area bounded by the user-defined rectangle. Subsequent resizing can change this aspect ratio.

12.11.3   Original Ratio Menu Command

Import also provides the Original Ratio menu command to restore a drawing to its original aspect ratio. This is useful after the user has changed the proportions of the imported image (see Figure 12.8). The resizing uses the smaller of the *x* and *y* scale factors to calculate the scale of the restored image. This action fits the newly proportioned file into the previous bounding box.

Figure 12.8 *Returning an image to its original aspect ratio*

 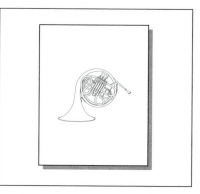

EPS file scaled nonproportionally   *After original ratio command is applied*

12.11.4 Original Size Menu Command

The Original Size menu command is similar to the Original Ratio menu command. It returns the imported file to its original width and height. The lower left corner of the new location remains in the same spot as the previous location.

12.11.5 Placing Imported Files

The problem of how initially to position an imported file within a document arises in any application that imports files. The user begins by selecting the file name from a selection panel. After this, many interface options are possible. Four of the most common are the following:

- *Original dimensions rendering* renders the file at the image's original dimensions and places the image either in the center of the document or within a selected mask or frame. The user can then move and scale the image.

- *Click-to-drop* changes the cursor shape to notify the user that the application is waiting for a mouse click to identify the desired location of the image. When the user clicks the mouse in the document, the file is rendered at its original width and height, with the center or a corner of the image positioned at the mouse-down point. The user can then scale the drawing.

- *Click-and-drag* also changes the cursor shape and waits for a mouse-down event from the user. However, instead of acting immediately, the interface marks the mouse-down location and tracks the mouse until a mouse-up event occurs. While the user drags the mouse, the application draws a rectangle between the mouse-down location and the current mouse position. When the user releases the mouse, the file is rendered into the rectangle. This type of interface allows a user to resize the image and position it before the file is actually rendered.

- *Click-to-drop plus click-and-drag* combines features of the previous two interfaces. If the user clicks the mouse in the document, the application places the image at the click location with its original width and height. If the user presses the mouse button and drags, the application uses the size of the user-defined rectangle for the image. This is the interface style used in the *Import* application.

12.12 Summary

- An EPS file contains a PostScript language program that describes a single-page illustration.

- Display PostScript applications can execute EPS files and show their contents on the screen. For environments that do not support the Display PostScript system, the EPS format allows an optional preview image to be included in the file.

- To ensure robust error recovery from incorrect EPS files, execute imported EPS files in a context separate from your application's main context.

- Rendering an EPS file into a pixmap allows for a more responsive interface when users reposition images.

- When an application imports an EPS file, it must parse the file to obtain bounding box dimensions and resource requirements.

- Exporting an EPS file involves generating the correct comments for the image's bounding box, preview image, and resource requirements. The Display PostScript system makes it easy to generate preview images.

- The EPS format makes it easy to exchange pictures between active applications by means of the X selection mechanism.

POSTSCRIPT™
Software From Adobe

The Display PostScript System

Adobe Systems Incorporated

Client Library Reference Manual

CL

Client Library
Reference Manual

1 About This Manual

This *Client Library Reference Manual* describes Client Library procedures and conventions, which form the programming interface to the Display PostScript system.

Section 2, "About the Client Library," introduces the Client Library and provides a diagram of its relationship to the Display PostScript system.

Section 3, "Overview of the Client Library," gives a brief overview of the Client Library, describes the phases of an application program's interaction with the Display PostScript system, introduces the C header files that represent the Client Library interface, and discusses the use of wrapped procedures.

Section 4, "Basic Client Library Facilities," explains the basic concepts an application programmer needs to know before writing a simple application for the Display PostScript system.

Section 5, "Handling Output from the Context," discusses callback procedures of various kinds, including text and error handlers.

Section 6, "Additional Client Library Facilities," explains advanced Client Library concepts including context chaining, encoding and translation, buffering, application/context synchronization, and forked contexts.

Section 7, "Programming Tips," provides programming tips and summarizes notes and warnings.

Section 8, "Example Application Program," lists and documents an application program that illustrates how to communicate with the Display PostScript system using the Client Library.

Section 9, "dpsclient.h Header File," documents the basic Client Library data structures and procedures found in *dpsclient.h*.

Section 10, "Single-Operator Procedures," describes the single-operator procedures that implement PostScript™ operators and contains a listing of the *dpsops.h* header file in which they are declared.

Section 11, "Runtime Support for Wrapped Procedures," explains the *dpsfriends.h* header file and its support of C-callable procedures produced by the *pswrap* translator.

Appendix A provides an example error handler for the X Window System™ implementation of the Display PostScript system.

Appendix B explains how an application can recover from PostScript language errors and provides an example of an exception handler.

2 About the Client Library

The Client Library is your link to the Display PostScript system, which makes the imaging power of the PostScript interpreter available for displays as well as for printing devices. An application program can display text and images on the screen by calling Client Library procedures. These procedures are written with a C language interface. They generate PostScript language code and send it to the PostScript interpreter in the window system for execution. This process is illustrated in Figure 1.

Figure 1 *The Client Library link to the PostScript interpreter*

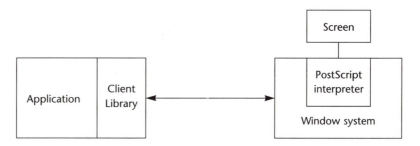

You can customize and optimize applications by writing PostScript language programs. The *pswrap* translator produces application-defined PostScript language programs with C-callable interfaces.

Note: *The terms "input" and "output" apply to the execution context in the PostScript interpreter, not to the application. An application "sends input" to a context and "receives output" from a context. This usage prevents ambiguity that might exist since input with respect to the context is output with respect to the application; and vice versa.*

3 Overview of the Client Library

The Client Library is a collection of procedures that provide an application program with access to the PostScript interpreter. It includes procedures for creating, communicating with, and destroying PostScript execution contexts. A context consists of all the information (or state) needed by the PostScript interpreter to execute a PostScript language program. In the Client Library interface, each context is represented by a *DPSContextRec* data structure pointed to by a *DPSContext* handle. PostScript execution contexts are described in section 7.1, "Multiple Execution Contexts," of *PostScript Language Reference Manual, Second Edition.*

It might appear that Client Library procedures directly produce graphical output on the display. In fact, these procedures generate PostScript language statements and transmit them to the PostScript interpreter for execution. The PostScript interpreter then produces graphical output that is displayed by device-specific procedures in the Display PostScript system. In this way, the Client Library makes the full power of the PostScript interpreter and imaging model available to a C language program.

The recommended way to send PostScript language code to the interpreter is to call wrapped procedures generated by the *pswrap* translator. For simple operations, you can send PostScript language fragments to the interpreter by calling single-operator procedures, or *single-ops*, each the equivalent of a single PostScript operator.

3.1 Phases of an Application

The following describes a typical application program, written in C, using the Client Library in the different phases of its operation:

- *Initialization.* The application establishes communication with the Display PostScript system. It then calls Client Library procedures to create a context for executing PostScript language programs. It also performs other window-system-specific initialization. Higher-level facilities, such as toolkits, perform initialization automatically.

- *Execution.* Once an application is initialized, it displays text and graphics by sending PostScript language programs to the interpreter. These programs can be of any complexity from a single-operator procedure to a program that previews full-color illustrations. The Client Library sends the programs to the PostScript interpreter and handles the results received from the interpreter.

- *Termination.* When the application is ready to terminate, it calls Client Library procedures to destroy its contexts, free their resources, and end the communications session.

3.2 Header Files

The Client Library procedures that an application can call are defined in C header files, also called *include* or *interface* files. The Client Library interface represented by these header files can be extended in an implementation, and the extensions are compatible with the definitions given in this appendix. There are four Client Library–defined header files and one or more system-specific header files.

- *dpsclient.h* provides support for managing contexts and sending PostScript language programs to the interpreter. It supports applications as well as application toolkits. It is always present.

- *dpsfriends.h* provides support for wrapped procedures created by *pswrap*, as well as data representations, conversions, and other low-level support for context structures. It is always present.

- *dpsops.h* provides single-operator procedures that require an explicit context parameter. It is optional.

- *psops.h* provides the single-operator procedures that implicitly derive their context parameter from the current context. It is optional.

- One or more system-specific header files provide support for context creation. These header files can also provide system-specific extensions to the Client Library, such as additional error codes.

3.3 Wrapped Procedures

The most efficient way for an application program to send PostScript language code to the interpreter is to use the *pswrap* translator to produce *wrapped procedures*, that is, PostScript language programs that are callable as C procedures. A wrapped procedure (*wrap* for short) consists of a C language procedure declaration enclosing a PostScript language body. There are several advantages to using wraps:

- Complex PostScript programs can be invoked by a single procedure call, avoiding the overhead of a series of calls to single-operator procedures.

- You can insert C arguments into the PostScript language code at runtime instead of having to push the C arguments onto the PostScript operand stack in separate steps.

- Wrapped procedures can efficiently produce custom graphical output by combining operators and other elements of the PostScript language in a variety of ways.

- The PostScript language code sent by a wrapped procedure is interpreted faster than ASCII text.

You prepare a PostScript language program for inclusion in the application by writing a wrap and passing it through the *pswrap* translator. The output of *pswrap* is a procedure written entirely in the C language. It contains the PostScript language body as data. This has been compiled into a binary object sequence (an efficient binary encoding), with placeholders for arguments to be inserted at execution. The translated wraps can then be compiled and linked into the application program.

When a wrapped procedure is called by the application, the procedure's arguments are substituted for the placeholders in the PostScript language body of the wrap. A wrap that draws a black box is defined in Example 1.

Example 1 *Wrap that draws a black box*

Wrap definition:

```
defineps PSWBlackBox(float x, y)
  gsave
    0 0 0 setrgbcolor
    x y 72 72 rectfill
  grestore
endps
```

pswrap produces a procedure that can be called from a C language program as follows (the values shown are only examples):

```
PSWBlackBox(12.32, -56.78);
```

This procedure replaces the *x* and *y* operands of **rectfill** with the corresponding procedure arguments, producing executable PostScript language code:

```
gsave
   0 0 0 setrgbcolor
   12.32 -56.78 72 72 rectfill
grestore
```

All wrapped procedures work the same way as Example 1. The arguments of the C language procedure must correspond in number and type to the operands expected by the PostScript operators in the body of the wrap. For instance, a procedure argument declared to be of type *float* corresponds to a PostScript real object; an argument of type *char ** corresponds to a PostScript string object; and so on.

The nominal outcome of calling a wrapped procedure is the transmission of PostScript language code to the interpreter for execution, normally resulting in display output. The Client Library can also provide the means, on a system-specific basis, to divert transmission to another destination, such as a printer or a text file.

4 Basic Client Library Facilities

This section introduces the concepts you need to write a simple application program for the Display PostScript system, including: creating a context, sending code and data to a context, and destroying a context.

4.1 Contexts and Context Data Structures

An application creates, manages, and destroys one or more contexts. A typical application creates a single context in a single private VM (space). It then sends PostScript language code to the context to display text, graphics, and scanned images on the screen.

The context is represented by a record of type *DPSContextRec*. A handle to this record (a pointer of type *DPSContext*) is passed explicitly or implicitly with every Client Library procedure call. In essence, the *DPSContext* handle is the context.

A context can be thought of as a destination to which PostScript language code is sent. The destination is set when the context is created. In most cases, the code draws graphics in a window or specifies how a page is printed. Other destinations include a file (for execution at a later time) or the standard output; multiple destinations are allowed. The execution by the interpreter of PostScript language code sent to a context can be immediate or deferred, depending on the context creation procedure called and on the setting of *DPSContextRec* variables.

4.2 System-Specific Context Creation

The system-specific interface contains, at minimum, procedures for creating the *DPSContextRec* record for the implementation of the Client Library. It also provides support for extensions to the Client Library interface such as additional error codes. The system-specific interface is described in a system-specific header file. In the X Window System, this file is *<DPS/dpsXclient.h>*.

Every context is associated with a system-specific object such as a window or a file. The context is created by calling a procedure in the system-specific interface. Once the context has been created, however, a set of standard Client Library operations can be applied to it. These operations, including context destruction, are defined in the standard header file *dpsclient.h*. (See section 9, "dpsclient.h Header File," for more information.)

4.3 Example of Context Creation

Context creation facilities are system-specific because they often need data objects that represent system-specific entities, such as windows and files. However, most context creation facilities share a number of common attributes. In this section, procedure parameters common to most systems are described in detail, while system-specific parameters are listed without further discussion.

The procedures described in this section were designed for the X Window System. They provide an example of an actual system implementation while at the same time demonstrating basic functions that all window systems must provide for context creation.

The creation of a *DPSContextRec* data structure is usually part of application initialization. Contexts persist until they are destroyed. The following example is a context creation for the X Window System.

Example 2 *Context creation for the X Window System*

C language code:

```
DPSContext XDPSCreateSimpleContext(dpy, drawable,
                gc, x, y, textProc, errorProc, space)
   Display *dpy;
   Drawable drawable;
   GC gc;
   int x, y;
   DPSTextProc textProc;
   DPSErrorProc errorProc;
   DPSSpace space;

typedef void (*DPSTextProc)( /* DPSContext ctxt,
   char *buf,
   long unsigned int count */ );

typedef void (*DPSErrorProc)( /* DPSContext ctxt,
   DPSErrorCode errorCode,
   long unsigned int arg1, arg2 */ );
```

XDPSCreateSimpleContext is a system-specific procedure that creates an execution context in the PostScript interpreter. The arguments *dpy*, *gc*, *x*, and *y* have specific uses in the X Window System; detailed discussion of these uses is beyond the scope of this manual. The *drawable* argument associates the *DPSContextRec* data structure with a system-specific imaging object. In this case, it is an X drawable object, which can be a window or a pixmap. **DPSTextProc** and **DPSErrorProc** are standard procedure types declared in *dpsclient.h*; their type definitions are included here for ease of reading.

The *space* argument identifies the private PostScript VM in which the new context executes. If *space* is *NULL*, a new space is created for the context; otherwise, it shares the specified space with contexts previously created in the *space*. An application that creates one space and one context can pass *NULL* for the *space* argument.

The *textProc* and *errorProc* arguments point to facilities that can be customized for handling text and errors sent by the interpreter. Passing *NULL* for these arguments is allowed but means that text and errors are ignored. For simple applications, you specify the system-specific default text procedure (**DPSDefaultTextBackstop** in the X Window System implementation) and **DPSDefaultErrorProc**. You can use **DPSGetCurrentTextBackstop** to get the current default text procedure.

XDPSCreateSimpleContext creates a context for which the PostScript interpreter is the destination of code and data sent to the context. It is sometimes useful to send the code and data elsewhere, such as to a file, terminal (UNIX *stdout*), or printer. The following example shows how to do this.

```
DPSContext DPSCreateTextContext(textProc, errorProc)
    DPSTextProc textProc;
    DPSErrorProc errorProc;
```

DPSCreateTextContext creates a context whose input is converted to ASCII encoding (text that is easily transmitted and easily read by humans). The ASCII-encoded text is passed to the *textProc* procedure rather than to the PostScript interpreter. Since the application provides the implementation of *textProc*, it determines where the ASCII text goes from there. The text can be sent to a file, a terminal, or a printer's communication port.

The *errorProc* procedure associated with a context handles errors that arise when a wrap or Client Library procedure is called with that context. The *textProc* argument calls *errorProc* to handle an error only when an appropriate error code has been defined.

4.4 The Current Context

The current context is the one that was specified by the last call to **DPSSetContext**. If the application has only one context, call **DPSSetContext** at the time the application is initialized. If the application manages more than one context, it must set the current context when necessary.

Many Client Library procedures do not require the application to specify a context; they assume the current context. This is true of all single-operator procedures defined in *psops.h* as well as any wrapped procedures that were defined to use the current context implicitly.

An application can find out which is the current context by calling **DPSGetCurrentContext**.

4.5 Sending Code and Data to a Context

Once the context has been created, the application can send PostScript language code to it by calling procedures such as:

- Wraps (custom wrapped procedures) developed for the application

- Single-operator procedures defined in *dpsops.h* and *psops.h*

- The **DPSPrintf**, **DPSWritePostScript**, and **DPSWriteData** Client Library procedures provided for writing to a context

A wrapped procedure is a PostScript language program encoded as a binary object sequence. These are described in section 3.12.2, "Binary Object Sequences," of the *PostScript Language Reference Manual, Second Edition*. Creating wrapped procedures is discussed in the *pswrap Reference Manual*.

Once the PostScript language program has been embedded in the body of a wrap by using the *pswrap* translator, it can be called like any other C procedure. Wraps are the most efficient way to specify any PostScript language program as a C-callable procedure.

The following list contains six examples of sending code and data to a context.

- Consider a wrap that draws a small colored circle around the point where the mouse was clicked, given an RGB color and the *x, y* coordinate returned by a mouse-click event. The exact PostScript language implementation is left for you as an exercise, but the C declaration of the wrap might look like this:

```
extern void PSWDrawSmallCircle(/*
    DPSContext ctxt; int x, y; float r, g, b*/);
```

An application might call this procedure as part of the code that handles mouse clicks. Suppose the struct *event* contains the *x, y* coordinate. To draw a bright green circle around the spot, call the wrapped procedure with the following arguments:

```
PSWDrawSmallCircle(ctxt, event.x, event.y, 0.0, 1.0, 0.0);
```

- If a wrap returns values, the procedure that calls it must pass pointers to the variables into which the values will be stored. Consider a wrap that, given a font name, tells whether the font is in the **SharedFontDirectory**. Define the wrap as follows:

```
defineps PSWFontLoaded(
   DPSContext ctxt; char *fontName| boolean *found)
```

The corresponding C declaration is

```
extern void PSWFontLoaded( /* DPSContext ctxt;
      char *fontName; int *found*/);
```

Note that Booleans are of the C type *int*. Call the wrapped procedure by providing a pointer to a variable of type *int* as follows:

```
int fontFound;
PSWFontLoaded(ctxt, "Helvetica", &fontFound);
```

Wraps are the most efficient way to specify any PostScript language program as a C-callable procedure.

- Occasionally, a small PostScript language program (one operator) is needed. In this case, a single-operator procedure is appropriate. For example, to get the current gray level, provide a pointer to a *float*, and call the single-operator procedure equivalent of the PostScript **currentgray** operator, use the following lines:

```
float gray;
DPScurrentgray(ctxt, &gray);
```

See section 10.4, "dpsops.h Procedure Declarations," for a complete
list of single-operator procedure declarations.

- **DPSPrintf** is one of the Client Library facilities provided for writing
  PostScript language code directly to a context. **DPSPrintf** is similar to
  the standard C library routine **printf**. It formats arguments into
  ASCII text and writes this text to the context. Small PostScript
  language programs or text data can be sent this way. The following
  example sends formatted text to the **show** operator to represent an
  author's byline:

```
struct {
    int x, y;                    /* location on page for byline */
    char *titleString;           /* title of document */
    char *authorsName;           /* name of author */
} byline;

DPSPrintf(ctxt, "%d %d moveto (%s by %s) show\n",
    byline.x,
    byline.y,
    byline.titleString,
    byline.authorsName);
```

The *x, y* coordinate is formatted in place of the two %d field specifiers,
the title replaces the first %s, followed by the word by. The author's
name replaces the second %s.

Caution: *When you use **DPSPrintf**, leave white space (newline with \n, or just a
space) at the end of the format string if the string ends with an operator.
PostScript language code written to a context appears as a continuous
stream. Thus, consecutive calls to **DPSPrintf** appear as if all the text were
sent at once. For example, suppose the following calls were made:*

```
DPSPrintf(ctxt, "gsave");
DPSPrintf(ctxt, "stroke");
DPSPrintf(ctxt, "grestore");
```

The context receives a single string "gsavestrokegrestore", with all
the operators run together. Of course, this might be useful for
constructing a long string that isn't part of a program, but when
sending operators to be executed, add white space to the end of each
format string. For example:

```
    DPSPrintf(ctxt, "gsave\n");
```

- The **DPSWritePostScript** procedure is provided for writing PostScript language code of any encoding to a context. If **DPSChangeEncoding** is provided by the system-specific interface, use **DPSWritePostScript** to convert a binary-encoded PostScript language program into another binary form (for instance, binary object sequences to binary-encoded tokens) or into ASCII text. Send code for immediate execution by the interpreter as binary object sequences. Send code that's intended to be read by a human as ASCII text.

Note: *Although PostScript language of any encoding can be written to a context, unexpected results can occur when intermixing code of different encodings. This is particularly important when ASCII encoding is mixed with binary encoding. (See section 3.12, "Binary Encoding Details," of the PostScript Language Reference Manual, Second Edition for a discussion of encodings.)*

The following code, which looks correct, might fail with a syntax error in the interpreter, depending on the contents of the buffer:

```
while (/* more buffers to send */) {
   count = GetBuffer(file, buffer);
   DPSWritePostScript(ctxt, buffer, count);
   MyWrap(ctxt);
}
```

GetBuffer reads a PostScript language program in the ASCII encoding from a file. The call to **MyWrap** generates a binary object sequence. If the program in the buffer passed to **DPSWritePostScript** is complete, with no partial tokens, **MyWrap** works correctly. If, however, the end of the buffer contains a partial token, "mov", and the next buffer starts with "eto", the binary object sequence representing **MyWrap** is inserted immediately after the partial token, resulting in a syntax error.

This applies to all procedures that send code or data to a context, including the Client Library procedures **DPSPrintf**, **DPSWritePostScript**, and **DPSWriteData**.

- To send any type of data to a context (such as hexadecimal image data) or to avoid the automatic conversion behavior built into **DPSWritePostScript**, use **DPSWriteData**.

The following example reads hexadecimal image data line by line from a file and sends the data to a context:

Example 3 *Reading hexadecimal image data from a file and sending it to a context*

```
while (!feof(fp)) {
  fgets(buf, BUFSIZE, fp);
  DPSWriteData(ctxt, buf, strlen(buf));
}
```

4.6 Spaces

A context is created in a space. The space is either shared with a previously created context or is created when a new context is created. Multiple contexts in the same space share all data. Coordination is required to ensure that they don't interfere with each other. Contexts in different spaces can operate more or less independently and still share data by using shared VM. See the discussion of VM and spaces in *PostScript Language Reference Manual, Second Edition.*

Destroying a space automatically destroys all of the contexts within it. **DPSDestroySpace** calls **DPSDestroyContext** for each context in the space.

The parameters that define a space are contained in a record of type *DPSSpaceRec.*

4.7 Interrupts

An application might need to interrupt a PostScript language program running in the PostScript interpreter. Call **DPSInterruptContext** for this. (Although this procedure returns immediately, an indeterminate amount of time can pass before execution is actually interrupted.)

An interrupt request causes the context to execute an **interrupt** error. Since the implementation of this error can be changed by the application, the results of requesting an interrupt cannot be defined here. The default behavior is that the **stop** operator executes.

4.8 Destroying Contexts

An application should destroy all the contexts it creates when they are no longer needed by calling **DPSDestroyContext** or **DPSDestroySpace**. Destroying a context does not destroy the space it occupies, but destroying a space destroys all of its contexts.

Caution: *A common error in Display PostScript programming is neglecting to destroy a context's space when you destroy a context. This leads to memory leaks. Unless you plan to create a new context that uses the destroyed context's space, you should destroy a context by calling* **DPSDestroySpace** *on its space.*

The PostScript interpreter detects when an application terminates abnormally and destroys any spaces and contexts that the application has created.

5 Handling Output from the Context

Output is information returned from the PostScript interpreter to the application. In the Display PostScript system, three kinds of output are possible:

- Output parameters (results) from wrapped procedures

- ASCII text written by the context (for example, by the **print** operator)

- Errors

Each kind of output is handled by a separate mechanism in the Client Library. Handling text and errors is discussed in the remainder of this section.

Note: *You may not get text and error output when you expect it.*

For example, a wrap that generates text to be sent to the application (for instance, with the **print** operator) might return before the application receives the text. Unless the application and the interpreter are synchronized, the text might not appear until some other Client Library procedure or wrap is called. This is due to delays in the communications channel or in scheduling execution of the context in the PostScript interpreter.

These delays are an important consideration for handling errors, since notification of the error can be received by the application long after the code that caused the error was sent.

5.1 Callback Procedures

You must specify callback procedures to handle text and errors. A callback procedure is code provided by an application and called by a system function.

A text handler is a callback procedure that handles text output from the context. It is specified in the *textProc* field of the *DPSContextRec*. A system-specific default text handler might be provided.

An error handler is a callback procedure that handles errors arising when the context is passed as a parameter to any Client Library procedure or wrap. It is specified in the *errorProc* field of the *DPSContextRec*. **DPSDefaultErrorProc** is the default error handler provided with every Client Library implementation.

Text and error handlers are associated with a context when the context is created, but the **DPSSetTextProc** and **DPSSetErrorProc** procedures give the application the flexibility to change these handlers at any time.

Using a callback procedure reverses the normal flow of control, which is as follows:

1. An application that is active calls the system to provide services, for example, to get memory or open a file.

2. The application gives up control until the system has provided the service.

3. The system procedure returns control to the application, passing the result of the service that was requested.

In the case of callback procedures, the application wants a custom service provided at a time when it is not in control. It does this as follows:

1. The application notifies the system, often at initialization, of the address of the callback procedure to be invoked when the system recognizes a condition (for example, an error condition).

2. When the error is raised, the system gets control.

3. The system passes control to the error handler specified by the application, thus "calling back" the application.

4. The error handler does processing on behalf of the application.

5. When the error handler completes, it returns to the system.

In the Display PostScript system, the text and error handlers in the Client Library interface are designed to be used this way.

Note: *To protect the application against unintended recursion, Client Library procedures and wraps normally should not be called from within a callback procedure. However, there may be system-specific circumstances in which such calls are safe. See the system-specific documentation for more information.*

5.2 Text Handlers

A context generates text output with operators such as **print**, **writestring**, and ==. The application handles text output with a text handler, which is specified in the *textProc* field of the *DPSContextRec*. The text handler is passed a buffer of text and a count of the number of characters in the buffer; what is done with this buffer is up to the application. The text handler might be called several times to handle large amounts of text.

Note that the Client Library just gets buffers; it doesn't provide any logical structure for the text and it doesn't indicate (or know) where the text ends.

The text handler can be called as a side effect of calling a wrap, a single-operator procedure, or a Client Library procedure that takes a context. You can't predict when the text handler for a context will be called unless the application is synchronized with the interpreter.

Caution: *Never generate text output that contains non-ASCII characters (characters with the high bit set). Doing so can cause unpredictable and often fatal errors in the Client Library.*

5.3 Text Handler Example

Consider an application that normally displays a log window to which it appends plain text or error messages received from the interpreter. The handlers were associated with the context when it was created.

Occasionally, the application calls a wrapped procedure that generates a block of text intended for a file. Before calling the text-generating procedure, the application must install a temporary text handler for its output. The temporary text handler stores the text it receives in a file instead of in the log window. When the text-generating procedure completes, the application restores the original text handler.

The following example shows such an application, written for the X Window System.

Example 4 *Text handler*

Wrap definition:

/* wrapped procedure that generates text */

```
defineps WrapThatGeneratesText(DPSContext ctxt
            | boolean *done)
   % send a text representation of the contents of mydict
   mydict {== ==} forall
   % returning a value flushes output as a side effect
   true done
endps
```

/* normal text proc appends to a log window */

```
void LogTextProc(ctxt, buf, count)
   DPSContext ctxt;
   char *buf;
   long unsigned int count;
{
   /* ... code that appends text to a log window... */
}
```

/* special text proc stores text to a file */

```
void StoreTextProc(ctxt, buf, count)
   DPSContext ctxt:
   char *buf;
   long unsigned int count;
{
   /* ... code that appends text to a file ... */
}
```

/* application initialization */

```
ctxt = XDPSCreateSimpleContext(dpy, drawable, gc, x, y,
      LogTextProc, DPSDefaultErrorProc, NULL);
(void) XDPSSetEventDelivery(dpy, dps_event_pass_through);
```

/* main loop for application */

```
while (1) {
   /* get an input event */
   XNextEvent(dpy, &event);
   if (DPSDispatchEvent(&event)) continue;
   /* any text that comes from processing
      EVENT_A or EVENT_B is logged */
```

```
      switch (event.type) {
    /* react to event */
      case EVENT_A: ...
      case EVENT_B: ...
      /* but EVENT_C means store the text in a file */
      case EVENT_C: {
        int done;
        DPSTextProc tmp = ctxt->textProc;

        /* make sure interpreter is ready */
        DPSWaitContext(ctxt);
        /* temporarily install the other text proc */
        DPSSetTextProc(ctxt, StoreTextProc);
        /* call the wrapped procedure */
        WrapThatGeneratesText(ctxt, &done);
        /* since wrap returned a value, we know the
            interpreter is ready when we get here;
            restore original textProc */
        DPSSetTextProc(ctxt, tmp);
        /* close file by calling textProc with count = 0 */
        StoreTextProc(ctxt, NULL, 0);
        break;
    }
  }
}
```

5.4 Error Handlers

The *errorProc* field in the *DPSContextRec* contains the address of a
callback procedure for handling errors. The error callback procedure is
called when there is a PostScript language error or when an error internal
to the Client Library, such as use of an invalid context identifier, is
encountered.

When the interpreter detects a PostScript language error, it invokes the
standard **handleerror** procedure to report the error, then forces the
context to terminate. The error callback procedure specified in the
DPSContextRec is called with the *dps_err_ps* error code.

After a PostScript language error, the context becomes invalid; further
use causes another error. See Appendix A for a sample error handler.

5.5 Error Recovery Requirements

For many applications, error recovery might not be an issue because an unanticipated PostScript language error or Client Library error represents a bug in the program that will be fixed during development. However, since applications sometimes go into production with undiscovered bugs, provide an error handler that allows the application to exit gracefully.

There are a small number of applications that require error recovery more sophisticated than simply exiting. If an application falls into one of the following categories, it is likely that some form of error recovery will be needed:

- Applications that read and execute PostScript language programs generated by other sources (for example, a previewer application for PostScript language documents generated by a word-processing program). Since the externally provided PostScript language program might have errors, the application must provide error recovery.

- Applications that allow you to enter PostScript language programs. This category is a subset of the previous category.

- Applications that generate PostScript language programs dynamically in response to user requests (for example, a graphics art program that generates an arbitrarily long path description of a graphical object). Since there are system-specific resource limitations on the interpreter, such as memory and disk space, the application should be able to back away from an error caused by exhausting a resource and attempt to acquire new or reclaim used resources.

Error recovery is complicated because both the Client Library and the context can be left in unknown states. For example, the operand stack might have unused objects on it.

In general, if an application needs to intercept and recover from PostScript language errors, keep it simple. For some applications, the best strategy when an error occurs is either to destroy the space and construct a new one with a new context or to restart the application.

A given implementation of the Client Library might provide more sophisticated error recovery facilities. Consult your system-specific documentation. Your system might provide the general-purpose exception handling facilities described in Appendix B, which can be used in conjunction with **DPSDefaultErrorProc**.

5.6   Backstop Handlers

Backstop handlers handle output when there is no other appropriate handler. The Client Library automatically installs backstop handlers.

Call **DPSGetCurrentTextBackstop** to get a pointer to the current backstop text handler. Call **DPSSetTextBackstop** to install a new backstop text handler. The text backstop can be used as a default text handler implementation. The definition of what the default text handler does is system specific. For instance, for UNIX systems, it writes the text to *stdout*.

Call **DPSGetCurrentErrorBackstop** to get a pointer to the current backstop error handler. Call **DPSSetErrorBackstop** to install a new backstop error handler. The backstop error handler processes errors internal to the Client Library, such as a lost server connection. These errors have no specific *DPSContext* handle associated with them and therefore have no error handler.

CL

6 Additional Client Library Facilities

The Client Library includes a number of utilities and support functions for applications. This section describes:

- Sending the same code and data to a group of contexts by chaining them

- Encoding and translating PostScript language code

- Buffering and flushing the buffer

- Synchronizing an application with a context

- Communicating with a forked context

6.1 Chained Contexts

Occasionally it is useful to send the same PostScript language program to several contexts. This is accomplished by chaining the contexts together and sending input to one context in the chain; for example, by calling a wrap with that context.

Two Client Library procedures are provided for managing context chaining:

- **DPSChainContext** links a context to a chain.

- **DPSUnchainContext** removes a child context from its parent's chain.

One context in the chain is specified as the parent context, the other as the child context. The child context is added to the parent's chain. Subsequently, any input sent to the parent is sent to its child, and the child of the child, and so on. Input sent to a child is not passed to its parent.

A context can appear on only one chain. If the context is already a child on a chain, **DPSChainContext** returns a nonzero error code. However, you can chain a child to a context that already has a child.

Note: *A parent context always passes its input to its child context. However, for a chain of more than two contexts, the order in which the contexts on the chain receive the input is not defined. Therefore, an application should not rely on* **DPSChainContext** *to create a chain whose contexts process input in a particular order.*

For chained contexts, output is handled differently from input, and text and errors are handled differently from results. If a context on a chain generates text or error output, the output is handled by that context only. Such output is not passed to its child. When a wrap that returns results is called, all of the contexts on the chain get the wrap code (the input), but only the context with which the wrap was called receives the results.

The best way to build a chain is to identify one context as the parent. Call **DPSChainContext** to make each additional context the child of that parent. For example, to chain contexts *A*, *B*, *C*, and *D*, choose *A* as the parent and make the following calls to **DPSChainContext**:

```
DPSChainContext(A,B);
DPSChainContext(A,C);
DPSChainContext(A,D);
```

Once the chain is built, send input only to the designated parent, *A*.

The most common use of chained contexts is in debugging. A log of PostScript operators executed can be kept by a child context whose purpose is to convert PostScript language programs to ASCII text and write the text to a file. This child is chained to a parent context that sends normal application requests to the interpreter. The parent's calls to wrapped procedures are logged in human-readable form by the child as a debugging audit trail.

Chained contexts can also be used for duplicate displays. An application might want several windows or several different display screens to show the same graphics without having to explicitly call the wrapped procedure in a loop for all of the contexts.

6.2 Encoding and Translation

PostScript language code can be sent to a context in three ways:

- As a binary object sequence typically used for immediate execution on behalf of a context.

- As binary-encoded tokens typically used for deferred execution from a file.

- As ASCII text typically used for debugging, display, or deferred execution from a file.

See section 3.12, "Binary Encoding Details," of the *PostScript Language Reference Manual, Second Edition* for the binary encoding formats' complete specifications.

Since the application and the PostScript interpreter can be on different machines, the Client Library automatically ensures that the binary representation of numeric values, including byte order and floating-point format, are correctly interpreted.

6.2.1 Encoding PostScript Language Code

On a system-specific basis, the Client Library supports a variety of conversions to and from the encodings and formats defined for the PostScript language. These are:

- Binary object sequence to binary object sequence, for expanding user name indexes back to their printable names.

- Binary object sequence to ASCII encoding, for backward compatibility with printers, interchange, and debugging.

- Binary object sequence to binary-encoded tokens, for long-term storage.

- Binary-encoded tokens to ASCII, for backward compatibility and interchange.

DPSProgramEncoding defines the three encodings available to PostScript language programs. *DPSNameEncoding* defines the two encodings for user names in PostScript language programs.

6.2.2 Translation

Translation is the conversion of program encoding or name encoding from one form to another. Any code sent to the context is converted according to the setting of the encoding fields. For a context created with the system-specific routine **DPSCreateTextContext**, code is automatically converted to ASCII encoding.

An application sometimes exchanges binary object sequences with another application. Since binary object sequences have user name indexes by default, the sending application must provide name-mapping information to the receiving application which can be lengthy.

Instead, some implementations allow the application to translate name indices back into user names by changing the *nameEncoding* field to *dps_strings*. In many implementations, **DPSChangeEncoding** performs this function.

6.3 Buffering

For optimal performance, programs and data sent to a context might be buffered by the Client Library. For the most part, you don't need to be concerned with this. Flushing of the buffer happens automatically as required, such as just before waiting for input events.

However, in certain situations, the application can explicitly flush a buffer. **DPSFlushContext** allows the application to force any buffered code or data to be sent to the context. Using **DPSFlushContext** is usually not necessary. Flushing does not guarantee that code is executed by the context, only that any buffered code is sent to the context.

Unnecessary flushing is inefficient. It is unusual for the application to flush the buffer explicitly. Cases where the buffer might need to be flushed include the following:

- When there is nothing to send to the interpreter for a long time (for example, "going to sleep" or doing a long computation).

- When there is nothing expected from the interpreter for a long time. (Note that getting input automatically flushes the output buffers.)

When the client and the server are separate processes and the buffered code doesn't need to be executed immediately, the application can flush the buffers with **flush** rather than synchronizing with the context.

6.4 Synchronizing Application and Context

The PostScript interpreter can run as a separate operating system process (or task) from the application; it can even run on a separate machine. When the processes are separate, you must take into account the communication between the application and the PostScript interpreter. This is important when time-critical actions must be performed based on the current appearance of the display. Also, errors arising from the execution of a wrapped procedure can be reported long after the procedure returns.

The application and the context are synchronized when all code sent to the context has been executed, and it is waiting to execute more code. When the two are not synchronized, the status of code previously sent to the context is unknown to the application. Synchronization can be effected in two ways: as a side effect of calling wraps that return values, or explicitly, by calling the **DPSWaitContext** procedure.

A wrapped procedure that has no result values returns as soon as the wrap body is sent to the context. The data buffer is not necessarily flushed in this case. Sometimes, however, the application's next action depends on the completed execution of the wrap body by the PostScript interpreter. The following describes the kind of problem that can occur when the assumption is made that a wrap's code has been executed by the time it returns.

For example, an application calls a wrapped procedure to draw a large, complex picture into an offscreen buffer (such as an X11 pixmap). The wrapped procedure has no return value, so it returns immediately, although the context might not have finished executing the code. The application then calls procedures to copy the screen buffer to a window for display. If the context has not finished drawing the picture in the buffer, only part of the image appears on the screen. This is not what the application programmer intended.

Wrapped procedures that return results flush any code waiting to be sent to the context and then wait until all results have been received. They automatically synchronize the context with the application. The wrapped procedure won't return until the interpreter indicates that all results have been sent. In this case, the application knows that the context is ready to execute more code as soon as the wrapped procedure returns, but the wrapped procedure might return prematurely if an error occurs, depending on how the error handler works.

The preceding discussion describes the side effect of calling a wrap that returns a value, but it is not always convenient or correct to use this method of implementation. Forcing the application to wait for a return result for every wrap is inefficient and might degrade performance.

If an application has a few critical points where synchronization must occur, and a wrap that returns results is not needed, **DPSWaitContext** can be used to synchronize the application with the context. It flushes any buffered code, and then waits until the context finishes executing all code that has been sent to it so far. This forces the context to finish before the application continues.

Like wraps that return results, use **DPSWaitContext** only when necessary. Performance can be degraded by excessive synchronization.

6.5 Forked Contexts

When the **fork** operator is executed in the PostScript interpreter, a new execution context is created. In order to communicate with a forked context, the application must create a *DPSContextRec* for it. For example, **DPSContextFromContextID** is an X Window System procedure that creates a *DPSContextRec* for a forked context.

```
DPSContext DPSContextFromContextID(ctxt, cid, textProc,
        errorProc)
    DPSContext ctxt;
    long int cid,
    DPSTextProc textProc,
    DPSErrorProc errorProc;
```

ctxt is the context that executed the **fork** operator.

cid is the integer value of the new context's identifier. *NULL* is returned if *cid* is invalid.

If *textProc* or *errorProc* are *NULL*, **DPSContextFromContextID** copies the corresponding procedure pointer from *ctxt* to the new *DPSContext*; otherwise the new context gets the specified *textProc* and *errorProc*.

All other fields of the new context are initialized with values from *ctxt*, including the *space* field.

7 Programming Tips

This section contains tips for avoiding common mistakes made when using the Client Library interface.

- Don't guess the arguments to a single-operator procedure call; look them up in the listing in section 10, "Single-Operator Procedures."

- Variables passed to wrapped procedures and single-operator procedures must be of the correct C type. A common mistake is to pass a pointer to a *short int* (only 16 bits) to a procedure that returns a boolean. A boolean is defined as an *int*, which can be 32 bits on some systems.

- Make sure that PostScript language code is properly separated by white space when using **DPSPrintf**. Variables passed to **DPSPrintf** must be of the right type. Passing type *float* to a format string of "%d" will yield unpredictable results.

- There are two ways of synchronizing the application with the context: Either call **DPSWaitContext**, which causes the application to wait until the interpreter has executed all the code sent to the execution context, or call a wrap that returns a result, which causes synchronization as a side effect. If synchronization is not required, use a wrap that returns results only when results are needed. Unnecessary synchronization by either method degrades performance.

- Use of **DPSFlushContext** is usually not necessary.

- Don't read from the file returned by the operator **currentfile** from within a wrap. In general, don't read directly from the context's standard input stream *%stdin* from within a wrap. Since a binary object sequence is a single token, the behavior of the code is different from what it would be in another encoding, such as ASCII. This will lead to unpredictable results. See Appendix B on page CL-85 and the *PostScript Language Reference Manual, Second Edition*.

- If the context is an execution context for a display, do not write PostScript language programs (particularly in wraps) that depend on reading the end-of-file (EOF) indicator. Support for EOF on the communications channel is system specific and should not be relied on. However, PostScript language programs that will be written to a file or spooled to a printer can make use of EOF indicators.

- Be careful when sending intermixed encoding types to a context. In particular, it's best to avoid mixing ASCII encoding with binary encoding. See the following tip on **DPSWaitContext** .

- Before calling **DPSWaitContext**, make sure that code that has already been sent to the context is syntactically complete, such as a wrap or a correctly terminated PostScript operator or composite object.

- Use of the **fork** operator requires understanding of a given system's support for handling errors from the forked context. A common error while developing multiple context applications is to fail to handle errors arising from forked contexts.

- To avoid unintended recursions, don't call Client Library procedures or wraps from within a callback procedure.

- To avoid confusion about which context on a chain will handle output, don't send input to a context that's been made the child of another context; send input only to the parent. (This doesn't apply to text contexts, since they never get input.)

- Program wraps carefully. Copying the entire prolog from a PostScript printer driver into a wrap without change probably won't result in efficient code.

- Avoid doing all your programming in the PostScript language. Because the PostScript language is interpreted, not compiled, the application can generally do arithmetic computation and data manipulation (such as sorting) more efficiently in C. Reserve the PostScript language for what it does best: displaying text and graphics.

- To avoid memory leaks, destroy a context's space instead of destroying the context itself (see section 4.8 on page 17 for details).

7.1 Using the Imaging Model

A thorough understanding of the imaging model is essential to writing efficient Display PostScript system applications.

The imaging model helps make your application device independent and resolution independent. Device independence ensures that your application will work and look as you intended on any display or print media.

Resolution independence lets you use the power of the PostScript language to scale, rotate, and transform your graphical display without loss of quality. Use of the imaging model automatically gives you the best possible rendering for any device.

Design your application with the imaging model in mind. Consider issues like converting coordinate systems, representing paths and graphics states with data structures, rendering colors and patterns, setting text, and accessing fonts (to name just a few).

Specific tips are:

- Coordinates sent to the PostScript interpreter should be in the user coordinate system (user space). It might be more convenient to express coordinates in the window coordinate system, but this makes your code resolution-dependent. When you need to convert window-system coordinates into user space, do the conversion in your program in C code rather than letting the interpreter do it. For example, if you need to draw something at the point where the user clicked the mouse, convert the mouse coordinates into user space in your application rather than sending them to the interpreter unconverted.

- Think in terms of color. Avoid programming to the lowest common denominator (low-resolution monochrome). The imaging model always gives the best rendering possible for a device, so use colors even if your application might be run on monochrome or gray-scale devices. Avoid using **setgray** unless you want a black, white, or gray level. Use **setrgbcolor** for all other cases. The imaging model will use a gray level or halftone pattern if the device does not support color, so objects of different colors will be distinguishable from one another.

- Don't use **setlinewidth** with a width of zero to get thin lines. On high-resolution devices the lines are practically invisible. To get lines narrower than one point, use fractions such as 0.3 or 0.25.

8 Example Application Program

This section provides an example of how to use the Display PostScript system through the Client Library. The example

- Establishes communication with an X11 server

- Creates a window and a context

- Draws an ochre rectangle in the window

- Waits for a mouse click

- Terminates when the button is pressed

To use the PostScript imaging model, an application must describe its graphical operations in the PostScript language. Therefore, an application using the Display PostScript system is a combination of C code and PostScript language code.

The *pswrap* program generates a C code file and a C header file that defines the interface to the procedures in the code file. The application source code and the *pswrap* output file are compiled and linked together with the program libraries of the Client Library to form the executable application program. Figure 2 illustrates the complete process.

Figure 2 *Creating an application*

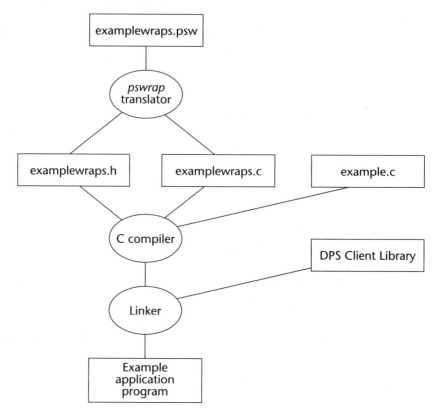

8.1 Example C Code

The code in the following example is used in conjunction with the wrap in the next section.

Example 5 *Simple X Window System application*

C language code:

```
/* example.c - simple X Window System application.
   Uses the Display PostScript extension to draw
   an ochre box and uses X primitives to
   wait for a mouse click before terminating. */
```

```c
#include <stdio.h>                  /* Standard C library I/O
                                       routines */

#include <X11/Intrinsic.h>          /* X Toolkit definitions */
#include <DPS/psops.h>              /* Interface to single operator
                                       procedures */

#include <DPS/dpsXclient.h>         /* DPS/X Client Library */
#include "examplewraps.h"           /* Generated from
                                       examplewraps.psw */


/* Window geometry definitions */
#define XWINDOW_X_ORIGIN     100
#define XWINDOW_Y_ORIGIN     100
#define XWINDOW_WIDTH        500
#define XWINDOW_HEIGHT       500

XtAppContext appContext;

void main(argc, argv)
   int argc;
   char **argv;
{
   Display *dpy;                    /* X display structure */
   int screen;                      /* screen on display */
   DPSContext ctxt;                 /* DPS drawing context */
   DPSContext txtCtxt;              /* DPS text context for
                                       debugging */

   Window xWindow;                  /* window where drawing
                                       occurs */

   int blackPixel, whitePixel;
   int debug = False;
   GC gc;
   XSetWindowAttributes attributes;
   float x, y, width, height;

   /* Connect to the window server by opening the display.
      Most of command line is parsed by XtOpenDisplay,
      leaving any options not recognized by the X toolkit:
      look for local -debug switch */

   XtToolkitInitialize();
   appContext = XtCreateApplicationContext();
   dpy = XtOpenDisplay(appContext, (String) NULL,
        "example", "example",
        (XrmOptionDescRec *) NULL, 0, &argc, argv);
   screen = DefaultScreen(dpy);
```

```
                    if (argc == 2)
                      if (strcmp(argv[1], "-debug") == 0) debug = TRUE;
                      else {
                        printf("Usage: example [-display xx:0] [-sync]
                          [-debug]\n");
                        exit (1);
                      }

                    /* Create a window to draw in; register interest in mouse
                       button and exposure events */

                    blackPixel = BlackPixel(dpy, screen);
                    whitePixel = WhitePixel(dpy, screen);
                    attributes.background_pixel = whitePixel;
                    attributes.border_pixel = blackPixel;
                    attributes.bit_gravity = SouthWestGravity;
                    attributes.event_mask = ButtonPressMask | ButtonReleaseMask
                              | ExposureMask;

                    xWindow = XCreateWindow(dpy, DefaultRootWindow(dpy),
                        XWINDOW_X_ORIGIN, XWINDOW_Y_ORIGIN, XWINDOW_WIDTH,
                        XWINDOW_HEIGHT, 1, CopyFromParent, InputOutput,
                        CopyFromParent, CWBackPixel | CWBorderPixel
                        | CWBitGravity | CWEventMask, &attributes);

                    XMapWindow(dpy, xWindow);

                    gc = XCreateGC(dpy, RootWindow(dpy, screen), 0, NULL);

                    /* Create a DPS context to draw in the window just created.
                       If the user asked for debugging, create a text context
                       chained to the drawing context */

                    ctxt = XDPSCreateSimpleContext(dpy, xWindow, gc, 0,
                        XWINDOW_HEIGHT, DPSDefaultTextBackstop,
                        PSDefaultErrorProc, NULL);
                    if (ctxt == NULL) {
                      fprintf (stderr,
                            "Error attempting to create DPS context.\n");
                      exit(1);
                    }

                    DPSSetContext(ctxt);
                    (void) XDPSSetEventDelivery(dpy, dps_event_pass_through);
```

```
    if (debug) {
      txtCtxt = DPSCreateTextContext(DPSDefaultTextBackstop,
               DPSDefaultErrorProc);
      DPSChainContext(ctxt, txtCtxt);
    }

    /* Wait for Expose event */

    while (NextEvent() != Expose);

    /* Convert the X Window System coordinates at the lower
       right corner of the window to get the width and height
       in user space */

    PSitransform ((float) XWINDOW_WIDTH, (float) XWINDOW_HEIGHT,
                  &width, &height);

    /* Locate the box in the middle of the window */

    x = width/4.0;
    y = height/4.0;
    PSWDrawBox(0.77, 0.58, 0.02, x, y, width/2.0, height/2.0);

    /* Wait for a mouse click on any button then terminate */

    while (NextEvent() != ButtonPress);
    while (NextEvent() != ButtonRelease);
    DPSDestroySpace(DPSSpaceFromContext(ctxt));
    exit(0);
}

int NextEvent()
{
    XEvent event;

    /* Wait for X event, dispatching DPS events */

    do {
      XtAppNextEvent(appContext, &event);
    } while (XDPSDispatchEvent(&event));
    return(event.type);
}
```

8.2 Wrap Example

The following wrap provides the PostScript language routine used by the example application. It appears as *examplewraps.psw* in Figure 2.

Example 6 *PSWDrawBox wrap for example application*

Wrap definition:

```
defineps PSWDrawBox(float r, g, b, x, y, width, height)
  gsave
  r g b setrgbcolor
  x y width height rectfill
  grestore
endps
```

8.3 Description of the Example Application

The example application demonstrates the use of Client Library functions and custom wraps in the X11 environment. The application draws a rectangle in the middle of a window, waits for a mouse click in the window, and terminates.

The program starts by initializing the toolkit and connecting to the display device. Command-line options can include all options recognized by the X Intrinsics resource manager plus a local *–debug* option, which demonstrates the use of a chained text context for debugging.

The program creates a window that contains the drawing produced by the PostScript operators. The window's attributes are set to indicate interest in mouse button and exposure events in that window.

The program creates a context with *xWindow* as its *drawable*. The system-specific default handlers **DPSDefaultTextBackstop** and **DPSDefaultErrorProc** are specified in the **XDPSCreateSimpleContext** call. These handlers are adequate for this application.

The program calls **XDPSSetEventDelivery** to specify that it will dispatch Display PostScript events itself.

If the *–debug* option is selected, the program creates a context that converts binary-encoded PostScript language programs into readable text. The text is passed to **PrintProc**. This context is then chained to the drawing context. The result is that any code sent to the drawing context will be also sent to the text context and displayed on *stdout*. This is a common technique for debugging wrapped procedures.

The program waits for an *Expose* event to arrive. This event indicates that the window has appeared on the screen and can be safely drawn to.

Once the application is completely initialized, PostScript language code can be executed to draw a rectangle into the window. This is done by using both a single-operator procedure and a customized wrapped procedure.

The single-operator procedure **PSitransform** determines the bounds of the window in terms of PostScript user space; this allows the program to scale the size of the rectangle appropriately.

The wrap procedure **PSWDrawBox** takes red, green, and blue levels to specify the color of the rectangle. It also takes *x* and *y* coordinates for the bottom left corner of the rectangle, and it takes the rectangle's width and height. Simple arithmetic computation is most efficiently done in C code by the application, rather than in PostScript language code by the interpreter.

PSWDrawBox is called to draw a colored square. If the display supports color, you'll see a square painted in ochre (a dark shade of orange). The values 0.77 for red, 0.58 for green, and 0.02 for blue approximate the color ochre. If the display supports only gray scale or monochrome, you'll see a square painted in some shade of gray.

The program now waits for events. Since the only events registered in this window are mouse-button events, events such as window movement and resizing are not directed to the application. When a button-press event is followed by a button-release event, the program destroys the space used by the drawing context. This destroys the context and its chained text context as well. The program then terminates normally.

The **NextEvent** procedure returns the next X event. It dispatches any Display PostScript events that it receives by calling **XDPSDispatchEvent**. This function returns *true* if the event passed to it is a Display PostScript event and *false* otherwise.

9 dpsclient.h Header File

The procedures in *dpsclient.h* constitute the core of the Client Library and are system independent. The contents of the header file are described in the following sections.

9.1 Procedure Types

The following procedure types are defined with typedef statements.

DPSErrorProc
```
typedef void (*DPSErrorProc)(/*
    DPSContext ctxt;
    DPSErrorCode errorCode;
    long unsigned int arg1, arg2;*/);
```

DPSErrorProc handles errors caused by the context. These can be PostScript language errors reported by the interpreter or errors that occur when the Client Library is called with a context. *errorCode* is one of the predefined codes that specify the type of error encountered. *errorCode* determines the interpretation of PostScript language errors *arg1* and *arg2*.

The following list shows how *arg1* and *arg2* are handled for each *errorCode*:

dps_err_ps	*arg1* is the address of the binary object sequence sent by **handleerror** to report the error. The sequence has one object, which is an array of four objects. *arg2* is the number of bytes in the entire binary object sequence.
dps_err_nameTooLong	Error in wrap argument. The PostScript user name and its length are passed as *arg1* and *arg2*. A name of more than 128 characters causes an error.
dps_err_resultTagCheck	Error in formulation of wrap. The pointer to the binary object sequence and its length are passed as *arg1* and *arg2*. There is one object in the sequence.
dps_err_resultTypeCheck	Incompatible result types. A pointer to the binary object is passed as *arg1*; *arg2* is unused.

dps_err_invalidContext   Stale context handle (probably terminated).
arg1 is a context identifier; *arg2* is unused.

DPSTextProc

```
typedef void (*DPSTextProc)(/*
    DPSContext ctxt;
    char *buf;
    long unsigned int count; */);
```

DPSTextProc handles text emitted from the interpreter, for example, by the == operator. *buf* is a pointer to *count* characters.

9.2   dpsclient.h Data Structures

The context record *DPSContextRec* is shared by the application and the PostScript interpreter. Except for the *priv* field, this data structure should not be altered directly. The *dpsclient.h* header file provides procedures to alter it.

When calling Client Library procedures, refer to the context record by its handle, *DPSContext*.

DPSContext

```
/* handle for context record */
```

See *DPSContextRec*.

DPSContextRec

```
typedef struct_t_DPSContextRec {
        char *priv;
        DPSSpace space;
        DPSProgramEncoding programEncoding;
        DPSNameEncoding nameEncoding;
        DPSProcs procs;
        void (*textProc)( );
        void (*errorProc)( );
        DPSResults resultTable;
        unsigned int resultTableLength;
        struct_t_DPSContextRec *chainParent, *chainChild;
} DPSContextRec, *DPSContext;
```

DPSContextRec defines the data structure pointed to by *DPSContext*.

Note that this record is used by *dpsclient.h* procedures but is actually defined in the *dpsfriends.h* header file.

priv is used by application code. It is initialized to *NULL* and is not touched thereafter by the Client Library implementation.

Note: *Although it is possible to read all fields of DPSContextRec directly, do not modify them directly except for priv. Data structures internal to the Client Library depend on the values in these fields and must be notified when they change. Call the procedures provided for this purpose, such as* **DPSSetTextProc**.

space identifies the space in which the context executes.

programEncoding and *nameEncoding* describe the encoding of the PostScript language that is sent to the interpreter. The values in these fields are established when the context is created. Whether or not the encoding fields can be changed after creation is system specific.

procs points to a *struct* containing procedures that implement the basic context operations, including writing, flushing, interrupting, and so on.

The Client Library calls the *textProc* and *errorProc* procedures to handle interpreter-generated ASCII text and errors.

resultTableLength and *resultTable* define the number, type, and location of results expected by a wrap. They are set up by the wrap procedure before any values are returned.

chainParent and *chainChild* are used for chaining contexts. *chainChild* is a pointer to the context that automatically receives code and data sent to the context represented by this *DPSContextRec*. *chainParent* is a pointer to the context that automatically sends code and data to the context represented by this *DPSContextRec*.

DPSErrorCode   `typedef int DPSErrorCode;`

DPSErrorCode defines the type of error code used by the Client Library. The following are the standard error codes:

• *dps_err_ps* identifies standard PostScript interpreter errors.

- *dps_err_nameTooLong* flags user names that are too long. 128 characters is the maximum length for PostScript language names.

- *dps_err_resultTagCheck* flags erroneous result tags; these are most likely due to erroneous explicit use of **printobject**.

- *dps_err_resultTypeCheck* flags incompatible result types.

- *dps_err_invalidContext* flags an invalid *DPSContext* argument. An attempt to send PostScript language code to a context that has terminated is probably the cause of this error.

9.3   dpsclient.h Procedures

This section contains descriptions of the procedures in the Client Library header file *dpsclient.h*, listed alphabetically.

DPSChainContext

```
int DPSChainContext(parent, child)
    DPSContext parent, child;
```

DPSChainContext links *child* onto the context chain of *parent*. This is the chain of contexts that automatically receive a copy of any code or data sent to *parent*. A context appears on only one such chain.

DPSChainContext returns zero if it successfully chains *child* to *parent*. It fails if *child* is on another context's chain; in that case, it returns –1.

DPSDefaultErrorProc

```
void DPSDefaultErrorProc(ctxt, errorCode, arg1, arg2)
    DPSContext ctxt;
    DPSErrorCode errorCode;
    long unsigned int arg1, arg2;
```

DPSDefaultErrorProc is a sample **DPSErrorProc** for handling errors from the PostScript interpreter.

The meaning of *arg1* and *arg2* depend on *errorCode*. See **DPSErrorProc**.

DPSDestroyContext
```
void DPSDestroyContext(ctxt)
    DPSContext ctxt;
```

DPSDestroyContext destroys the context represented by *ctxt*. The context is first unchained if it is on a chain.

What happens to buffered input and output when a context is destroyed is system specific.

Destroying a context does not destroy its space; see **DPSDestroySpace**.

DPSDestroySpace
```
void DPSDestroySpace(spc)
    DPSSpace spc;
```

DPSDestroySpace destroys the space represented by *spc*. This is necessary for application termination and cleanup. It also destroys all contexts within *spc*.

DPSFlushContext
```
void DPSFlushContext(ctxt)
    DPSContext ctxt;
```

DPSFlushContext forces any buffered code or data to be sent to *ctxt*. Some Client Library implementations use buffering to optimize performance.

DPSGetCurrentErrorBackstop
```
DPSErrorProc DPSGetCurrentErrorBackstop( );
```

DPSGetCurrentErrorBackstop returns the *errorProc* passed most recently to **DPSSetErrorBackstop**, or *NULL* if none was set.

DPSGetCurrentTextBackstop
```
DPSTextProc DPSGetCurrentTextBackstop( );
```

DPSGetCurrentErrorBackstop returns the *textProc* passed most recently to **DPSSetTextBackstop**, or *NULL* if none was set.

DPSInterruptContext

```
void DPSInterruptContext(ctxt)
    DPSContext ctxt;
```

DPSInterruptContext notifies the interpreter to interrupt the execution of the context, resulting in the PostScript language **interrupt** error. The procedure returns immediately after sending the notification.

DPSPrintf

```
void DPSPrintf(ctxt, fmt, [, arg ...]);
    DPSContext ctxt;
    char *fmt;
```

DPSPrintf sends string *fmt* to *ctxt* with the optional arguments converted, formatted, and logically inserted into the string in a manner identical to the standard C library routine **printf**. It is useful for sending formatted data or a short PostScript language program to a context.

DPSResetContext

```
void DPSResetContext(ctxt)
    DPSContext ctxt;
```

DPSResetContext resets the context after an error occurs. It ensures that any buffered I/O is discarded and that the context is ready to read and execute more input. **DPSResetContext** works in conjunction with **resynchandleerror**.

DPSSetErrorBackstop

```
void DPSSetErrorBackstop(errorProc)
    DPSErrorProc errorProc;
```

DPSSetErrorBackstop establishes *errorProc* as a pointer to the backstop error handler. This error handler handles errors that are not handled by any other error handler. *NULL* will be passed as the *ctxt* argument to the backstop error handler.

DPSSetErrorProc

```
void DPSSetErrorProc(ctxt, errorProc)
    DPSContext ctxt;
    DPSErrorProc errorProc;
```

DPSSetErrorProc changes the context's error handler.

DPSSetTextBackstop

```
void DPSSetTextBackstop(textProc)
    DPSTextProc textProc;
```

DPSSetTextBackstop establishes the procedure pointed to by *textProc* as the handler for text output for which there is no other handler. The text handler acts as a backstop for text output.

DPSSetTextProc

```
void DPSSetTextProc(ctxt, textProc)
    DPSContext ctxt;
    DPSTextProc textProc;
```

DPSSetTextProc changes the context's text handler.

DPSSpaceFromContext

```
DPSSpace DPSSpaceFromContext(ctxt)
    DPSContext ctxt;
```

DPSSpaceFromContext returns the space handle for the specified context. It returns *NULL* if *ctxt* does not represent a valid execution context.

DPSUnchainContext

```
void DPSUnchainContext(ctxt)
    DPSContext ctxt;
```

DPSUnchainContext removes *ctxt* from the chain that it is on, if any. The parent and child pointers of the unchained context are set to *NULL*.

DPSWaitContext

```
void DPSWaitContext(ctxt)
    DPSContext ctxt;
```

DPSWaitContext flushes output buffers belonging to *ctxt* and then waits until the interpreter is ready for more input to *ctxt*. It is not necessary to call **DPSWaitContext** after calling a wrapped procedure that returns a value.

Before calling **DPSWaitContext**, ensure that the last code sent to the context is syntactically complete, such as a wrap or a correctly terminated PostScript operator or composite object.

DPSWriteData   void DPSWriteData(ctxt, buf, count)
                        DPSContext ctxt;
                        char *buf;
                        unsigned int count;

DPSWriteData sends *count* bytes of data from *buf* to *ctxt. ctxt* specifies the destination context. *buf* points to a buffer that contains *count* bytes. The contents of the buffer will not be converted according to the context's encoding parameters.

DPSWritePostScript   void DPSWritePostScript(ctxt, buf, count)
                            DPSContext ctxt;
                            char *buf;
                            unsigned int count;

DPSWritePostScript sends PostScript language to a context in any of the three language encodings. *ctxt* specifies the destination context. *buf* points to a buffer that contains *count* bytes of PostScript language code. The code in the buffer will be converted according to the context's encoding parameters as needed; refer to the system-specific documentation for a list of supported conversions.

10 Single-Operator Procedures

For each operator defined in the PostScript language, the Client Library provides a procedure to invoke the most common usage of the operator. These are called the single-operator procedures, or *single-ops*. If the predefined usage is not the one you need, you can write wraps for variant forms of the operators.

There are two Client Library header files for single-ops: *dpsops.h* and *psops.h*. The name of the Client Library single-op is the name of the PostScript operator preceded by either DPS or PS:

DPS prefix   Used when the context is explicitly specified; for example, **DPSgsave**. The first argument must be of type *DPSContext*. These single-ops are defined in *dpsops.h.*

PS prefix   Used when the context is assumed to be the current context; for example, **PSgsave**. These single-ops are defined in *psops.h*. The procedure **DPSSetContext**, defined in *dpsclient.h*, sets the current context.

For example, to execute the PostScript operator **translate**, the application can call

```
DPStranslate(ctxt, 1.23, 43.56)
```

where *ctxt* is a variable of type *DPSContext*, the handle that represents a PostScript execution context.

Note: *Most PostScript operator names are lowercase, but some contain uppercase letters; for example* **FontDirectory***. In either case, the name of the corresponding single-op is formed by using PS or DPS as a preface.*

The **DPStranslate** procedure sends the binary encoding of

```
1.23 43.56 translate
```

to execute in *ctxt*.

10.1 Setting the Current Context

The single-ops in *psops.h* assume the current context. The **DPSSetContext** procedure, defined in *dpsclient.h*, sets the current context. When the application deals with only one context it is convenient to use the procedures in *psops.h* rather than those in *dpsops.h*. In this case, the application would set the current context during its initialization phase:

```
DPSSetContext(ctxt);
```

In subsequent calls on the procedures in *psops.h*, *ctxt* is used implicitly. For example:

```
PStranslate(1.23, 43.56);
```

has the same effect as

```
DPStranslate(ctxt, 1.23, 43.56);
```

The explicit method is preferred for situations that require intermingling of calls to multiple contexts. It is also useful in subroutine libraries that should not disturb the application's current context.

Note: *It is important to pass the correct C types to the single-ops. In general, if a PostScript operator takes operands of arbitrary numeric type, the corresponding single-op takes parameters of type float. Coordinates are always type float. Passing an integer literal to a procedure that expects a floating-point literal is a common error:*

incorrect: PSlineto(72, 72);

correct: PSlineto(72.0, 72.0);

Procedures that appear to have no input arguments might actually take their operands from the operand stack, for example, **PSdef** and **DPSdef**.

10.2 Types in Single-Operator Procedures

When using single-operator procedures, inspect the calling protocol (that is, order and types of formal parameters) for every procedure to be called.

Note: *Throughout this section, references to single-ops with a DPS prefix are applicable to the equivalent procedures with a PS prefix.*

10.3 Guidelines for Associating Data Types with Single-Operator Procedures

There is no completely consistent system for associating data types with particular single-ops. In general, look up the definition in the header file. However, there are a few rules that can be applied. All these rules have exceptions.

- Coordinates are specified as type *float*. For example, all of the standard path construction operators (**moveto**, **lineto**, **curveto**, and so on) take type *float*.

- Booleans are specified as type *int*. The comment
    ```
    /* int *b */
    ```
  or
    ```
    /* int *it */
    ```
  in the header file means that the procedure returns a boolean.

- If the operator takes either integer or floating-point numbers, the corresponding procedure takes type *float*. If the operator specifies a number type (such as **rand** and **vmreclaim**), the procedure takes arguments of that type (typically type *int*).

- Operators that return values must always be specified with a pointer to the appropriate data type. For example, **currentgray** returns the current gray value of the graphics state. You must pass **DPScurrentgray** a pointer to a variable of type *float*.

- If an operator takes a data type that does not have a directly analogous C type, such as dictionaries, graphics states, and executable arrays, the single-op takes no arguments. It is assumed that you will arrange for the appropriate data to be on the operand stack before calling the procedure; see **DPSsendchararray** and **DPSsendfloat**, among others.

- If a single-op takes or returns a matrix, the matrix is specified as
    ```
    float m[ ]
    ```
  which is an array of six floating-point numbers.

- In general, the integer parameter *size* is used to specify the length of a variable-length array; see, for example, **DPSxshow**. For single-ops that take two variable-length arrays as parameters, the length of the first array is specified by the integer *n*; the length of the second array is specified by the integer *l*; see, for example, **DPSustroke**.

The following operators are worth noting for unusual order and types of arguments, or for other irregularities. After reading these descriptions, inspect the declarations in the listing or in the header file.

- **DPSdefineuserobject** takes no arguments. One would expect it to take at least the index argument, but because of the requirement to have the arbitrary object on the top of the stack, it is better to send the index down separately, perhaps with **DPSsendint**.

- **DPSgetchararray** and other get array operators specify the length of the array first, followed by the array. (Mnemonic: get the array last.)

- **DPSsendchararray**, **DPSsendfloatarray**, and other send array operators specify the array first, followed by the length of the array. (Mnemonic: send the array first.)

- **DPSinfill**, **DPSinstroke**, and **DPSinufill** support only the *x, y* coordinate version of the operator. The optional second userpath argument is not supported.

- **DPSinueofill**, **DPSinufill**, **DPSinustroke**, **DPSuappend**, **DPSueofill**, **DPSufill**, **DPSustroke**, and **DPSustrokepath** take a userpath in the form of an encoded number string and operator string. The lengths of the strings follow the strings themselves as argument.

- **DPSsetdash** takes an array of numbers of type *float* for the dash pattern.

- **DPSselectfont** takes type *float* for the font scale parameter.

- **DPSsetgray** takes type *float*. (DPSsetgray(1) is wrong.)

- **DPSxshow**, **DPSxyshow**, and **DPSyshow** take an array of numbers of type *float* for specifying the coordinates of each character.

- **DPSequals** is the procedure equivalent to the = operator.

- **DPSequalsequals** is the procedure equivalent to the == operator.

- **DPSversion** returns the version number in a character array *buf[ ]* whose length is specified by *bufsize*.

10.3.1 Special Cases

A few of the single-operator procedures have been optimized to take user objects for arguments, since they are most commonly used in this way. In the list in section 10.4, these user object arguments are specified as type *int*, which is the correct type of a user object.

- **DPScurrentgstate** takes a user object that represents the gstate object into which the current graphics state should be stored. The gstate object is left on the stack.

- **DPSsetfont** takes a user object that represents the font dictionary.

- **DPSsetgstate** takes a user object that represents the gstate object that the current graphics state should be set to.

10.4 dpsops.h Procedure Declarations

The procedures in *dpsops.h* and *psops.h* are identical except for the first argument. *dpsops.h* procedures require the *ctxt* argument; *psops.h* procedures do not. The procedure name is the lowercase PostScript language operator name preceded by *DPS* or *PS* as appropriate. Only the *dpsops.h* procedures are listed here.

Note: **DPSSetContext** *must have been called before calling any procedure in psops.h.*

```
extern void DPSFontDirectory( /* DPSContext ctxt */ );
extern void DPSISOLatin1Encoding( /* DPSContext ctxt */ );
extern void DPSSharedFontDirectory( /* DPSContext ctxt */ );
extern void DPSStandardEncoding( /* DPSContext ctxt */ );
extern void DPSUserObjects( /* DPSContext ctxt */ );
extern void DPSabs( /* DPSContext ctxt */ );
extern void DPSadd( /* DPSContext ctxt */ );
extern void DPSaload( /* DPSContext ctxt */ );
extern void DPSanchorsearch( /* DPSContext ctxt;
            int *truth */ );
extern void DPSand( /* DPSContext ctxt */ );
extern void DPSarc( /* DPSContext ctxt;
            float x, y, r, angle1, angle2 */ );
extern void DPSarcn( /* DPSContext ctxt;
            float x, y, r, angle1, angle2 */ );
extern void DPSarct( /* DPSContext ctxt;
            float x1, y1, x2, y2, r */ );
```

```
extern void DPSarcto( /* DPSContext ctxt;
            float x1, y1, x2, y2, r;
            float *xt1, *yt1, *xt2, *yt2 */ );
extern void DPSarray( /* DPSContext ctxt; int len */ );
extern void DPSashow( /* DPSContext ctxt;
            float x, y; char *s */ );
extern void DPSastore( /* DPSContext ctxt */ );
extern void DPSatan( /* DPSContext ctxt */ );
extern void DPSawidthshow( /* DPSContext ctxt; float cx, cy;
            int c; float ax, ay; char *s */ );
extern void DPSbanddevice( /* DPSContext ctxt */ );
extern void DPSbegin( /* DPSContext ctxt */ );
extern void DPSbind( /* DPSContext ctxt */ );
extern void DPSbitshift( /* DPSContext ctxt; int shift */ );
extern void DPSbytesavailable( /* DPSContext ctxt; int *n */ );
extern void DPScachestatus( /* DPSContext ctxt */ );
extern void DPSceiling( /* DPSContext ctxt */ );
extern void DPScharpath( /* DPSContext ctxt;
            char *s; int b */ );
extern void DPSclear( /* DPSContext ctxt */ );
extern void DPScleardictstack( /* DPSContext ctxt */ );
extern void DPScleartomark( /* DPSContext ctxt */ );
extern void DPSclip( /* DPSContext ctxt */ );
extern void DPSclippath( /* DPSContext ctxt */ );
extern void DPSclosefile( /* DPSContext ctxt */ );
extern void DPSclosepath( /* DPSContext ctxt */ );
extern void DPScolorimage( /* DPSContext ctxt */ );
extern void DPSconcat( /* DPSContext ctxt; float m */ );
extern void DPSconcatmatrix( /* DPSContext ctxt */ );
extern void DPScondition( /* DPSContext ctxt */ );
extern void DPScopy( /* DPSContext ctxt; int n */ );
extern void DPScopypage( /* DPSContext ctxt */ );
extern void DPScos( /* DPSContext ctxt */ );
extern void DPScount( /* DPSContext ctxt; int *n */ );
extern void DPScountdictstack( /* DPSContext ctxt; int *n */ );
extern void DPScountexecstack( /* DPSContext ctxt; int *n */ );
extern void DPScounttomark( /* DPSContext ctxt; int *n */ );
extern void DPScurrentblackgeneration( /* DPSContext ctxt */ );
extern void DPScurrentcacheparams( /* DPSContext ctxt */ );
extern void DPScurrentcmykcolor( /* DPSContext ctxt;
            float *c, *m, *y, *k */ );
extern void DPScurrentcolorscreen( /* DPSContext ctxt */ );
extern void DPScurrentcolortransfer( /* DPSContext ctxt */ );
extern void DPScurrentcontext( /* DPSContext ctxt;
            int *cid */ );
extern void DPScurrentdash( /* DPSContext ctxt */ );
extern void DPScurrentdict( /* DPSContext ctxt */ );
extern void DPScurrentfile( /* DPSContext ctxt */ );
```

```
extern void DPScurrentflat( /* DPSContext ctxt;
            float *flatness */ );
extern void DPScurrentfont( /* DPSContext ctxt */ );
extern void DPScurrentgray( /* DPSContext ctxt;
            float *gray */ );
extern void DPScurrentgstate( /* DPSContext ctxt; int gst */ );
extern void DPScurrenthalftone( /* DPSContext ctxt */ );
extern void DPScurrenthalftonephase( /* DPSContext ctxt;
            float *x, *y */ );
extern void DPScurrenthsbcolor( /* DPSContext ctxt;
            float *h, *s, *b */ );
extern void DPScurrentlinecap( /* DPSContext ctxt;
            int *linecap */ );
extern void DPScurrentlinejoin( /* DPSContext ctxt;
            int *linejoin */ );
extern void DPScurrentlinewidth( /* DPSContext ctxt;
            float *width */ );
extern void DPScurrentmatrix( /* DPSContext ctxt */ );
extern void DPScurrentmiterlimit( /* DPSContext ctxt;
            float *limit */ );
extern void DPScurrentobjectformat( /* DPSContext ctxt;
            int *code */ );
extern void DPScurrentpacking( /* DPSContext ctxt; int *b */ );
extern void DPScurrentpoint( /* DPSContext ctxt;
            float *x, *y */ );
extern void DPScurrentrgbcolor( /* DPSContext ctxt;
            float *r, *g, *b */ );
extern void DPScurrentscreen( /* DPSContext ctxt */ );
extern void DPScurrentshared( /* DPSContext ctxt; int *b */ );
extern void DPScurrentstrokeadjust( /* DPSContext ctxt;
            int *b */ );
extern void DPScurrenttransfer( /* DPSContext ctxt */ );
extern void DPScurrentundercolorremoval( /*
            DPSContext ctxt */ );
extern void DPScurveto( /* DPSContext ctxt;
            float x1, y1, x2, y2, x3, y3 */ );
extern void DPScvi( /* DPSContext ctxt */ );
extern void DPScvlit( /* DPSContext ctxt */ );
extern void DPScvn( /* DPSContext ctxt */ );
extern void DPScvr( /* DPSContext ctxt */ );
extern void DPScvrs( /* DPSContext ctxt */ );
extern void DPScvs( /* DPSContext ctxt */ );
extern void DPScvx( /* DPSContext ctxt */ );
extern void DPSdef( /* DPSContext ctxt */ );
extern void DPSdefaultmatrix( /* DPSContext ctxt */ );
extern void DPSdefinefont( /* DPSContext ctxt */ );
extern void DPSdefineusername( /* DPSContext ctxt;
            int i; char *username */ );
extern void DPSdefineuserobject( /* DPSContext ctxt */ );
```

```
extern void DPSdeletefile( /* DPSContext ctxt;
            char *filename */ );
extern void DPSdetach( /* DPSContext ctxt */ );
extern void DPSdeviceinfo( /* DPSContext ctxt */ );
extern void DPSdict( /* DPSContext ctxt; int len */ );
extern void DPSdictstack( /* DPSContext ctxt */ );
extern void DPSdiv( /* DPSContext ctxt */ );
extern void DPSdtransform( /* DPSContext ctxt;
            float x1, y1; float *x2, *y2 */ );
extern void DPSdup( /* DPSContext ctxt */ );
extern void DPSecho( /* DPSContext ctxt; int b */ );
extern void DPSend( /* DPSContext ctxt */ );
extern void DPSeoclip( /* DPSContext ctxt */ );
extern void DPSeofill( /* DPSContext ctxt */ );
extern void DPSeoviewclip( /* DPSContext ctxt */ );
extern void DPSeq( /* DPSContext ctxt */ );
extern void DPSequals( /* DPSContext ctxt */ );
extern void DPSequalsequals( /* DPSContext ctxt */ );
extern void DPSerasepage( /* DPSContext ctxt */ );
extern void DPSerrordict( /* DPSContext ctxt */ );
extern void DPSexch( /* DPSContext ctxt */ );
extern void DPSexec( /* DPSContext ctxt */ );
extern void DPSexecstack( /* DPSContext ctxt */ );
extern void DPSexecuserobject( /* DPSContext ctxt;
            int userObjIndex */ );
extern void DPSexecuteonly( /* DPSContext ctxt */ );
extern void DPSexit( /* DPSContext ctxt */ );
extern void DPSexp( /* DPSContext ctxt */ );
extern void DPSfalse( /* DPSContext ctxt */ );
extern void DPSfile( /* DPSContext ctxt;
            char *name, *access */ );
extern void DPSfilenameforall( /* DPSContext ctxt */ );
extern void DPSfileposition( /* DPSContext ctxt; int *pos */ );
extern void DPSfill( /* DPSContext ctxt */ );
extern void DPSfindfont( /* DPSContext ctxt; char *name */ );
extern void DPSflattenpath( /* DPSContext ctxt */ );
extern void DPSfloor( /* DPSContext ctxt */ );
extern void DPSflush( /* DPSContext ctxt */ );
extern void DPSflushfile( /* DPSContext ctxt */ );
extern void DPSfor( /* DPSContext ctxt */ );
extern void DPSforall( /* DPSContext ctxt */ );
extern void DPSfork( /* DPSContext ctxt */ );
extern void DPSframedevice( /* DPSContext ctxt */ );
extern void DPSge( /* DPSContext ctxt */ );
extern void DPSget( /* DPSContext ctxt */ );
extern void DPSgetboolean( /* DPSContext ctxt; int *it */ );
extern void DPSgetchararray( /* DPSContext ctxt;
            int size; char s */ );
extern void DPSgetfloat( /* DPSContext ctxt; float *it */ );
```

CL

```
extern void DPSgetfloatarray( /* DPSContext ctxt;
          int size; float a */ );
extern void DPSgetint( /* DPSContext ctxt; int *it */ );
extern void DPSgetintarray( /* DPSContext ctxt;
          int size; int a */ );
extern void DPSgetinterval( /* DPSContext ctxt */ );
extern void DPSgetstring( /* DPSContext ctxt; char *s */ );
extern void DPSgrestore( /* DPSContext ctxt */ );
extern void DPSgrestoreall( /* DPSContext ctxt */ );
extern void DPSgsave( /* DPSContext ctxt */ );
extern void DPSgstate( /* DPSContext ctxt */ );
extern void DPSgt( /* DPSContext ctxt */ );
extern void DPSidentmatrix( /* DPSContext ctxt */ );
extern void DPSidiv( /* DPSContext ctxt */ );
extern void DPSidtransform( /* DPSContext ctxt;
          float x1, y1; float *x2, *y2 */ );
extern void DPSif( /* DPSContext ctxt */ );
extern void DPSifelse( /* DPSContext ctxt */ );
extern void DPSimage( /* DPSContext ctxt */ );
extern void DPSimagemask( /* DPSContext ctxt */ );
extern void DPSindex( /* DPSContext ctxt; int i */ );
extern void DPSineofill( /* DPSContext ctxt;
          float x, y; int *b */ );
extern void DPSinfill( /* DPSContext ctxt;
          float x, y; int *b */ );
extern void DPSinitclip( /* DPSContext ctxt */ );
extern void DPSinitgraphics( /* DPSContext ctxt */ );
extern void DPSinitmatrix( /* DPSContext ctxt */ );
extern void DPSinitviewclip( /* DPSContext ctxt */ );
extern void DPSinstroke( /* DPSContext ctxt;
          float x, y; int *b */ );
extern void DPSinueofill( /* DPSContext ctxt;
          float x, y; char nums[]; int n;
          char ops[]; int l; int *b */ );
extern void DPSinufill( /* DPSContext ctxt; float x, y;
          char nums[]; int n; char ops[];
          int l; int *b */ );
extern void DPSinustroke( /* DPSContext ctxt; float x, y;
          char nums[]; int n; char ops[];
          int l; int *b */ );
extern void DPSinvertmatrix( /* DPSContext ctxt */ );
extern void DPSitransform( /* DPSContext ctxt; float x1, y1;
          float *x2, *y2 */ );
extern void DPSjoin( /* DPSContext ctxt */ );
extern void DPSknown( /* DPSContext ctxt; int *b */ );
extern void DPSkshow( /* DPSContext ctxt; char *s */ );
extern void DPSle( /* DPSContext ctxt */ );
extern void DPSlength( /* DPSContext ctxt; int *len */ );
extern void DPSlineto( /* DPSContext ctxt; float x, y */ );
```

```
extern void DPSln( /* DPSContext ctxt */ );
extern void DPSload( /* DPSContext ctxt */ );
extern void DPSlock( /* DPSContext ctxt */ );
extern void DPSlog( /* DPSContext ctxt */ );
extern void DPSloop( /* DPSContext ctxt */ );
extern void DPSlt( /* DPSContext ctxt */ );
extern void DPSmakefont( /* DPSContext ctxt */ );
extern void DPSmark( /* DPSContext ctxt */ );
extern void DPSmatrix( /* DPSContext ctxt */ );
extern void DPSmaxlength( /* DPSContext ctxt; int *len */ );
extern void DPSmod( /* DPSContext ctxt */ );
extern void DPSmonitor( /* DPSContext ctxt */ );
extern void DPSmoveto( /* DPSContext ctxt; float x, y */ );
extern void DPSmul( /* DPSContext ctxt */ );
extern void DPSne( /* DPSContext ctxt */ );
extern void DPSneg( /* DPSContext ctxt */ );
extern void DPSnewpath( /* DPSContext ctxt */ );
extern void DPSnoaccess( /* DPSContext ctxt */ );
extern void DPSnot( /* DPSContext ctxt */ );
extern void DPSnotify( /* DPSContext ctxt */ );
extern void DPSnull( /* DPSContext ctxt */ );
extern void DPSnulldevice( /* DPSContext ctxt */ );
extern void DPSor( /* DPSContext ctxt */ );
extern void DPSpackedarray( /* DPSContext ctxt */ );
extern void DPSpathbbox( /* DPSContext ctxt;
                float *llx, *lly, *urx, *ury */ );
extern void DPSpathforall( /* DPSContext ctxt */ );
extern void DPSpop( /* DPSContext ctxt */ );
extern void DPSprint( /* DPSContext ctxt */ );
extern void DPSprintobject( /* DPSContext ctxt; int tag */ );
extern void DPSprompt( /* DPSContext ctxt */ );
extern void DPSpstack( /* DPSContext ctxt */ );
extern void DPSput( /* DPSContext ctxt */ );
extern void DPSputinterval( /* DPSContext ctxt */ );
extern void DPSquit( /* DPSContext ctxt */ );
extern void DPSrand( /* DPSContext ctxt */ );
extern void DPSrcheck( /* DPSContext ctxt; int *b */ );
extern void DPSrcurveto( /* DPSContext ctxt;
                float x1, y1, x2, y2, x3, y3 */ );
extern void DPSread( /* DPSContext ctxt; int *b */ );
extern void DPSreadhexstring( /* DPSContext ctxt; int *b */ );
extern void DPSreadline( /* DPSContext ctxt; int *b */ );
extern void DPSreadonly( /* DPSContext ctxt */ );
extern void DPSreadstring( /* DPSContext ctxt; int *b */ );
extern void DPSrealtime( /* DPSContext ctxt; int *i */ );
extern void DPSrectclip( /* DPSContext ctxt;
                float x, y, w, h */ );
extern void DPSrectfill( /* DPSContext ctxt;
                float x, y, w, h */ );
```

CL

```
extern void DPSrectstroke( /* DPSContext ctxt;
            float x, y, w, h */ );
extern void DPSrectviewclip( /* DPSContext ctxt;
            float x, y, w, h */ );
extern void DPSrenamefile( /* DPSContext ctxt;
            char *old, *new */ );
extern void DPSrenderbands( /* DPSContext ctxt */ );
extern void DPSrepeat( /* DPSContext ctxt */ );
extern void DPSresetfile( /* DPSContext ctxt */ );
extern void DPSrestore( /* DPSContext ctxt */ );
extern void DPSreversepath( /* DPSContext ctxt */ );
extern void DPSrlineto( /* DPSContext ctxt; float x, y */ );
extern void DPSrmoveto( /* DPSContext ctxt; float x, y */ );
extern void DPSroll( /* DPSContext ctxt; int n, j */ );
extern void DPSrotate( /* DPSContext ctxt; float angle */ );
extern void DPSround( /* DPSContext ctxt */ );
extern void DPSrrand( /* DPSContext ctxt */ );
extern void DPSrun( /* DPSContext ctxt; char *filename */ );
extern void DPSsave( /* DPSContext ctxt */ );
extern void DPSscale( /* DPSContext ctxt; float x, y */ );
extern void DPSscalefont( /* DPSContext ctxt; float size */ );
extern void DPSscheck( /* DPSContext ctxt; int *b */ );
extern void DPSsearch( /* DPSContext ctxt; int *b */ );
extern void DPSselectfont( /* DPSContext ctxt;
            char *name; float scale */ );
extern void DPSsendboolean( /* DPSContext ctxt; int it */ );
extern void DPSsendchararray( /* DPSContext ctxt; char s[];
            int size */ );
extern void DPSsendfloat( /* DPSContext ctxt; float it */ );
extern void DPSsendfloatarray( /* DPSContext ctxt; float a[];
            int size */ );
extern void DPSsendint( /* DPSContext ctxt; int it */ );
extern void DPSsendintarray( /* DPSContext ctxt; int a[];
            int size */ );
extern void DPSsendstring( /* DPSContext ctxt; char *s */ );
extern void DPSsetbbox( /* DPSContext ctxt;
            float llx, lly, urx, ury */ );
extern void DPSsetblackgeneration( /* DPSContext ctxt */ );
extern void DPSsetcachedevice( /* DPSContext ctxt;
            float wx, wy, llx, lly, urx, ury */ );
extern void DPSsetcachelimit( /* DPSContext ctxt; float n */ );
extern void DPSsetcacheparams( /* DPSContext ctxt */ );
extern void DPSsetcharwidth( /* DPSContext ctxt;
            float wx, wy */ );
extern void DPSsetcmykcolor( /* DPSContext ctxt;
            float c, m, y, k */ );
extern void DPSsetcolorscreen( /* DPSContext ctxt */ );
extern void DPSsetcolortransfer( /* DPSContext ctxt */ );
extern void DPSsetdash( /* DPSContext ctxt; float pat[];
```

```
                           int size; float offset */ );
        extern void DPSsetfileposition( /* DPSContext ctxt;
                           int pos */ );
        extern void DPSsetflat( /* DPSContext ctxt;
                           float flatness */ );
        extern void DPSsetfont( /* DPSContext ctxt; int f */ );
        extern void DPSsetgray( /* DPSContext ctxt; float gray */ );
        extern void DPSsetgstate( /* DPSContext ctxt; int gst */ );
        extern void DPSsethalftone( /* DPSContext ctxt */ );
        extern void DPSsethalftonephase( /* DPSContext ctxt;
                           float x, y */ );
        extern void DPSsethsbcolor( /* DPSContext ctxt;
                           float h, s, b */ );
        extern void DPSsetlinecap( /* DPSContext ctxt; int
                           linecap */ );
        extern void DPSsetlinejoin( /* DPSContext ctxt;
                           int linejoin */ );
        extern void DPSsetlinewidth( /* DPSContext ctxt;
                           float width */ );
        extern void DPSsetmatrix( /* DPSContext ctxt */ );
        extern void DPSsetmiterlimit( /* DPSContext ctxt;
                           float limit */ );
        extern void DPSsetobjectformat( /* DPSContext ctxt;
                           int code */ );
        extern void DPSsetpacking( /* DPSContext ctxt; int b */ );
        extern void DPSsetrgbcolor( /* DPSContext ctxt;
                           float r, g, b */ );
        extern void DPSsetscreen( /* DPSContext ctxt */ );
        extern void DPSsetshared( /* DPSContext ctxt; int b */ );
        extern void DPSsetstrokeadjust( /* DPSContext ctxt; int b */ );
        extern void DPSsettransfer( /* DPSContext ctxt */ );
        extern void DPSsetucacheparams( /* DPSContext ctxt */ );
        extern void DPSsetundercolorremoval( /* DPSContext ctxt */ );
        extern void DPSsetvmthreshold( /* DPSContext ctxt; int i */ );
        extern void DPSshareddict( /* DPSContext ctxt */ );
        extern void DPSshow( /* DPSContext ctxt; char *s */ );
        extern void DPSshowpage( /* DPSContext ctxt */ );
        extern void DPSsin( /* DPSContext ctxt */ );
        extern void DPSsqrt( /* DPSContext ctxt */ );
        extern void DPSsrand( /* DPSContext ctxt */ );
        extern void DPSstack( /* DPSContext ctxt */ );
        extern void DPSstart( /* DPSContext ctxt */ );
        extern void DPSstatus( /* DPSContext ctxt; int *b */ );
        extern void DPSstatusdict( /* DPSContext ctxt */ );
        extern void DPSstop( /* DPSContext ctxt */ );
        extern void DPSstopped( /* DPSContext ctxt */ );
        extern void DPSstore( /* DPSContext ctxt */ );
        extern void DPSstring( /* DPSContext ctxt; int len */ );
        extern void DPSstringwidth( /* DPSContext ctxt;
```

```
                                char *s; float *xp, *yp */ );
extern void DPSstroke( /* DPSContext ctxt */ );
extern void DPSstrokepath( /* DPSContext ctxt */ );
extern void DPSsub( /* DPSContext ctxt */ );
extern void DPSsystemdict( /* DPSContext ctxt */ );
extern void DPStoken( /* DPSContext ctxt; int *b */ );
extern void DPStransform( /* DPSContext ctxt;
                float x1, y1; float *x2, *y2 */ );
extern void DPStranslate( /* DPSContext ctxt; float x, y */ );
extern void DPStrue( /* DPSContext ctxt */ );
extern void DPStruncate( /* DPSContext ctxt */ );
extern void DPStype( /* DPSContext ctxt */ );
extern void DPSuappend( /* DPSContext ctxt; char nums[]; int n;
                char ops[]; int l */ );
extern void DPSucache( /* DPSContext ctxt */ );
extern void DPSucachestatus( /* DPSContext ctxt */ );
extern void DPSueofill( /* DPSContext ctxt;
                char nums[]; int n; char ops[];
                int l */ );
extern void DPSufill( /* DPSContext ctxt; char nums[];
                int n; char ops[]; int l */ );
extern void DPSundef( /* DPSContext ctxt; char *name */ );
extern void DPSundefinefont( /* DPSContext ctxt;
                char *name */ );
extern void DPSundefineuserobject( /* DPSContext ctxt;
                int userObjIndex */ );
extern void DPSupath( /* DPSContext ctxt; int b */ );
extern void DPSuserdict( /* DPSContext ctxt */ );
extern void DPSusertime( /* DPSContext ctxt;
                int *milliseconds */ );
extern void DPSustroke( /* DPSContext ctxt; char nums[];
                int n; char ops[]; int l */ );
extern void DPSustrokepath( /* DPSContext ctxt; char nums[];
                int n; char ops[]; int l */ );
extern void DPSversion( /* DPSContext ctxt;
                int bufsize; char buf */ );
extern void DPSviewclip( /* DPSContext ctxt */ );
extern void DPSviewclippath( /* DPSContext ctxt */ );
extern void DPSvmreclaim( /* DPSContext ctxt; int code */ );
extern void DPSvmstatus( /* DPSContext ctxt;
                int *level, *used, *maximum */ );
extern void DPSwait( /* DPSContext ctxt */ );
extern void DPSwcheck( /* DPSContext ctxt; int *b */ );
extern void DPSwhere( /* DPSContext ctxt; int *b */ );
extern void DPSwidthshow( /* DPSContext ctxt; float x, y;
                int c; char *s */ );
extern void DPSwrite( /* DPSContext ctxt */ );
extern void DPSwritehexstring( /* DPSContext ctxt */ );
extern void DPSwriteobject( /* DPSContext ctxt; int tag */ );
```

```
extern void DPSwritestring( /* DPSContext ctxt */ );
extern void DPSwtranslation( /* DPSContext ctxt;
            float *x, *y */ );
extern void DPSxcheck( /* DPSContext ctxt; int *b */ );
extern void DPSxor( /* DPSContext ctxt */ );
extern void DPSxshow( /* DPSContext ctxt; char *s;
            float numarray[]; int size */ );
extern void DPSxyshow( /* DPSContext ctxt; char *s;
            float numarray[]; int size */ );
extern void DPSyield( /* DPSContext ctxt */ );
extern void DPSyshow( /* DPSContext ctxt; char *s;
            float numarray[]; int size */ );
```

CL

11 Runtime Support for Wrapped Procedures

This section describes the procedures in the *dpsfriends.h* header file that are called by wrapped procedures: the C-callable procedures that are output by the *pswrap* translator. This information is not normally required by the application programmer.

A description of *dpsfriends.h* is provided for those who need finer control over the following areas:

- Transmission of code for execution

- Handling of result values

- Mapping of user names to user name indexes

11.1 Sending Code for Execution

One of the primary purposes of the Client Library is to provide runtime support for the code generated by *pswrap*. Each wrapped procedure builds a binary object sequence that represents the PostScript language code to be executed. Since a binary object sequence is structured, the procedures for sending a binary object sequence are designed to take advantage of this structure.

The following procedures efficiently process binary object sequences generated by wrapped procedures:

- **DPSBinObjSeqWrite** sends the beginning of a new binary object sequence. This part includes, at minimum, the header and the top-level sequence of objects. It can also include subsidiary array elements and/or string characters if those arrays and strings are static (lengths are known at compile time and there are no intervening arrays or strings of varying length). **DPSBinObjSeqWrite** can convert the binary object sequence to another encoding, depending on the *DPSContextRec* encoding variables. For a particular wrapped procedure, **DPSBinObjSeqWrite** is called once.

- **DPSWriteTypedObjectArray** sends arrays (excluding strings) that were specified as input arguments to a wrapped procedure. It writes PostScript language code specified by the context's format and encoding variables, performing appropriate conversions as needed. For a particular wrapped procedure, **DPSWriteTypedObjectArray** is called zero or more times, once for each input array specified.

- **DPSWriteStringChars** sends the text of strings or names. It appends characters to the current binary object sequence. For a particular wrapped procedure, **DPSWriteStringChars** is called zero or more times to send the text of names and strings.

The length of arrays and strings sent by **DPSWriteTypedObjectArray** and **DPSWriteStringChars** must be consistent with the length information specified in the binary object sequence header sent by **DPSBinObjSeqWrite**. In particular, don't rely on **sizeof** to return the correct size value of the binary object sequence.

11.2   Receiving Results

Each wrapped procedure with output arguments constructs an array containing elements of type *DPSResultsRec*. This array is called the result table. The index position of each element corresponds to the ordinal position of each output argument as defined in the wrapped procedure: The first table entry (index 0) corresponds to the first output argument, the second table entry (index 1) corresponds to the second argument, and so on.

Each entry defines one of the output arguments of a wrapped procedure by specifying a data type, a count, and a pointer to the storage for the value. **DPSSetResultTable** registers the result table with the context.

The interpreter sends return values to the application as binary object sequences. Wrapped procedures that have output arguments use the **printobject** operator to tag and send each return value. The tag corresponds to the index of the output argument in the result table. After the wrapped procedure finishes sending the PostScript language program, it calls **DPSAwaitReturnValues** to wait for all of the results to come back.

As the Client Library receives results from the interpreter, it places each result into the output argument specified by the result table. The tag of each result object in the sequence is used as an index into the result table. When the Client Library receives a tag that is greater than the last defined tag number, **DPSAwaitReturnValues** returns. This final tag is called the termination tag.

Certain conventions must be followed to handle return values for wrapped procedures properly:

- The tag associated with the return value is the ordinal of the output parameter, as listed in the definition of the wrapped procedure, starting from 0 and counting from left to right (see the following example).

- If the *count* field of the *DPSResultsRec* is –1, the expected result is a single element, or scalar. Return values with the same tag overwrite previous values. Otherwise, the *count* indicates the number of array elements that remain to be received. In this case, a series of return values with the same tag are stored in successive elements of the array. If the value of *count* is zero, further array elements of the same tag value are ignored.

- **DPSAwaitReturnValues** returns when it notices that the *resultTable* pointer in the *DPSContextRec* data object is *NULL*. The code that handles return values should note the reception of the termination tag by setting *resultTable* to *NULL* to indicate that there are no more return values to receive for this wrapped procedure.

Example 7 shows a wrap with return values. Resulting PostScript language code is shown in the trace that follows the wrap definition.

Example 7 *Implementation of wrap return values*

Wrap definition:

```
defineps Example(| int *x, *y, *z)
    10 20 30 x y z
endps
```

PostScript language trace:

```
10 20 30
0 printobject
  % pop integer 30 off the operand stack,
  % use tag = 0 (result table index = 0,
  %             first parameter 'x')
  % write binary object sequence
1 printobject
  % pop integer 20 off the operand stack,
  % use tag = 1 (result table index = 1,
  %             second parameter 'y')
  % write binary object sequence
2 printobject
  % pop integer 10 off the operand stack,
  % use tag = 2 (result table index = 2,
  %             third parameter 'z')
  % write binary object sequence
```

```
0 3 printobject
   % push dummy value 0 on operand stack
   % pop integer 0 off operand stack,
   % use tag = 3 (termination tag)
   % write binary object sequence
flush
   % make sure all data is sent back to the application
```

11.3   Managing User Names

Name indexes are the most efficient way to specify names in a binary
object sequence. The Client Library manages the mapping of user
names to indexes. Wrapped procedures map user names automatically.
The first time a wrapped procedure is called, it calls **DPSMapNames** to
map all user names specified in the wrapped procedure into indexes.
The application can also call **DPSMapNames** directly to obtain name
mappings.

A name map is stored in a space. All contexts associated with that space
have the same name map. The name mapping for the context is
automatically kept up-to-date by the Client Library in the following
way:

- Every wrapped procedure calls **DPSBinObjSeqWrite**, which, in
  addition to sending the binary object sequence, checks to see if the
  user name map is up-to-date.

- **DPSBinObjSeqWrite** calls **DPSUpdateNameMap** if the name map of
  the space does not agree with the Client Library's name map.
  DPSUpdateNameMap can send a series of **defineusername** operators
  to the PostScript interpreter.

DPSNameFromIndex returns the text for the user name with the given
index. The string returned is owned by the Client Library; treat it as a
read-only string.

11.4   Binary Object Sequences

Syntactically, a binary object sequence is a single token. The structure is
described in section 3.12.1, "Binary Tokens," of the *PostScript Language
Reference Manual, Second Edition*. The definitions in this section
correspond to the components of a binary object sequence.

```
#define DPS_HEADER_SIZE   4
```

```
#define DPS_HI_IEEE        128
#define DPS_LO_IEEE        129
#define DPS_HI_NATIVE      130
#define DPS_LO_NATIVE      131

#ifndef DPS_DEF_TOKENTYPE
#define DPS_DEF_TOKENTYPE DPS_HI_IEEE
#endif DPS_DEF_TOKENTYPE

typedef struct {
   unsigned char tokenType;
   unsigned char nTopElements;
   unsigned short length;
   DPSBinObjRec objects[1];
} DPSBinObjSeqRec, *DPSBinObjSeq;
```

A binary object sequence begins with a 4-byte header. The first byte indicates the token type. A binary object is defined by one of the four token type codes listed. *DPS_DEF_TOKENTYPE* defines the default token type for binary object sequences generated by a particular implementation of the Client Library. It must be consistent with the machine architecture upon which the Client Library is implemented.

The *nTopElements* byte indicates the number of top-level objects in the sequence. A binary object sequence can have from 1 to 255 top-level objects. If more top-level objects are required, use an extended binary object sequence.

The next two bytes form a nonzero 16-bit integer that is the total byte length of the binary object sequence.

The header is followed by a sequence of objects:

```
#define DPS_NULL          0
#define DPS_INT           1
#define DPS_REAL          2
#define DPS_NAME          3
#define DPS_BOOL          4
#define DPS_STRING        5
#define DPS_IMMEDIATE     6
#define DPS_ARRAY         9
#define DPS_MARK          10
```

The first byte of an object describes its attributes and type. The types listed here correspond to the PostScript language objects that *pswrap* generates.

```
#define DPS_LITERAL        0
#define DPS_EXEC           0x080
```

The high-order bit indicates whether the object has the literal (0) or executable (1) attribute. The next byte is the tag byte, which must be zero for objects sent to the interpreter. Result values sent back from the interpreter use the tag field.

The next two bytes form a 16-bit integer that is the length of the object. The unit value of the length field depends on the type of the object. For arrays, the length indicates the number of elements in the array. For strings, the length indicates the number of characters.

The last four bytes of the object form the value field. The interpretation of this field depends on the type of the object.

```
typedef struct {
   unsigned char attributedType;
   unsigned char tag;
   short length;
   long int val;
} DPSBinObjGeneric;     /* Boolean, int, string,
                           name and array */


typedef struct {
   unsigned char attributedType;
   unsigned char tag;
   short length;
   float realVal;
} DPSBinObjReal;        /* float */
```

DPSBinObjGeneric and *DPSBinObjReal* are defined for the use of wraps. They make it easier to initialize the static portions of the binary object sequence.

```
typedef struct {
   unsigned char attributedType;
   unsigned char tag;
   short length;
   union {
      long int integerVal;
      float realVal;
      long int nameVal;  /* offset or index */
      long int booleanVal;
      long int stringVal;/* offset */
```

```
                long int arrayVal; /* offset */
            } val;
        } DPSBinObjRec;
```

DPSBinObjRec is a general-purpose variant record for interpreting an object in a binary object sequence.

11.5   Extended Binary Object Sequences

An *extended binary object sequence* is required if there are more than 255 top-level objects in the sequence. The extended binary object sequence is represented by *DPSExtendedBinObjSeqRec*, as follows:

Byte 0   Same as for a normal binary object sequence; it represents the token type.

Byte 1   Set to zero; indicates that this is an extended binary object sequence. (In a normal binary object sequence, this byte represents the number of top-level objects.)

Bytes 2-3   A 16-bit value representing the number of top-level elements.

Bytes 4-7   A 32-bit value representing the overall length of the extended binary object sequence.

The bytes are ordered in numeric fields according to the number representation specified by the token type. The layout of the remainder of the extended binary object sequence is identical to that of a normal binary object sequence.

11.6   dpsfriends.h Data Structures

This section describes the data structures used by *pswrap* as part of its support for wrapped procedures.

Note: *The DPSContextRec data structure and its handle, DPSContext, are part of the dpsfriends.h header file. They are documented in section 9.2 because they are also used by dpsclient.h procedures.*

DPSBinObjGeneric

```
typedef struct {
    unsigned char attributedType;
    unsigned char tag;
    unsigned short length;
    long int val;
} DPSBinObjGeneric; /* boolean, int, string, name and array */
```

DPSBinObjGeneric is defined for the use of wraps. It is used to initialize the static portions of the binary object sequence. See *DPSBinObjReal* for type *real*.

DPSBinObjReal

```
typedef struct {
    unsigned char attributedType;
    unsigned char tag;
    unsigned short length;
    float realVal;
} DPSBinObjReal;              /* float */
```

DPSBinObjReal is similar to *DPSBinObjGeneric* but represents a real number.

DPSBinObjRec

```
typedef struct {
    unsigned char attributedType;
    unsigned char tag;
    unsigned short length;
    union {
        long int integerVal;
        float realVal;
        long int nameVal;      /* offset or index */
        long int booleanVal;
        long int stringVal;    /* offset */
        long int arrayVal;     /* offset */
    } val;
} DPSBinObjRec;
```

DPSBinObjRec is a general-purpose variant record for interpreting an object in a binary object sequence.

DPSBinObjSeqRec
```
typedef struct {
    unsigned char token Type;
    unsigned char nTopElements;
    unsigned short length;
    DPSBinObjRec objects[1];
} DPSBinObjSeqRec, *DPSBinObjSeq;
```

DPSBinObjSeqRec is provided as a convenience for accessing a binary object sequence copied from an I/O buffer.

DPSDefinedType
```
typedef enum {
    dps_tBoolean,
    dps_tChar, dps_tUChar,
    dps_tFloat, dps_tDouble,
    dps_tShort, dps_tUShort,
    dps_tInt, dps_tUInt,
    dps_tLong, dps_tULong
} DPSDefinedType;
```

DPSDefinedType enumerates the C data types used to describe wrap arguments.

DPSExtendedBinObjSeqRec
```
typedef struct {
    unsigned char tokenType;
    unsigned char escape; /* zero if this is an ext. sequence */
    unsigned short nTopElements;
    unsigned long length;
    DPSBinObjRec objects[1];
} DPSExtendedBinObjSeqRec, *DPSExtendedBinObjSeq;
```

DPSExtendedBinObjSeqRec has a purpose similar to *DPSBinObjSeqRec* but it is used for extended binary object sequences.

DPSNameEncoding
```
typedef enum {
    dps_indexed, dps_strings
} DPSNameEncoding;
```

DPSNameEncoding defines the two possible encodings for user names in the *dps_binObjSeq* and *dps_encodedTokens* forms of PostScript language programs.

DPSProcs   /* pointer to procedures record */

See *DPSProcsRec.*

DPSProcsRec

```
typedef struct {
    void (*BinObjSeqWrite)( /* DPSContext ctxt; char *buf;
        unsigned int count */ );
    void (*WriteTypedObjectArray)( /* DPSContext ctxt;
        DPSDefinedType type; char *array;
        unsigned int length */ );
    void (*WriteStringChars)( /* DPSContext ctxt;
        char *buf; unsigned int count; */ );
    void (*WriteData)( /* DPSContext ctxt; char *buf;
        unsigned int count */ );
    void (*WritePostScript)( /* DPSContext ctxt; char *buf;
        unsigned int count */ );
    void (*FlushContext)( /* DPSContext ctxt */ );
    void (*ResetContext)( /* DPSContext ctxt */ );
    void (*UpdateNameMap)( /* DPSContext ctxt */ );
    void (*AwaitReturnValues)( /* DPSContext ctxt */ );
    void (*Interrupt)( /* DPSContext ctxt */ );
    void (*DestroyContext)( /* DPSContext ctxt */ );
    void (*WaitContext)( /* DPSContext ctxt */ );
} DPSProcsRec, *DPSProcs;
```

DPSProcsRec defines the data structure pointed to by *DPSProcs.*

This record contains pointers to procedures that implement all the operations that can be performed on a context. These procedures are analogous to the instance methods of an object in an object-oriented language.

Note: *You do not need to be concerned with the contents of this data structure. Do not change the DPSProcs pointer or the contents of DPSProcsRec.*

DPSProgramEncoding

```
typedef enum {
    dps_ascii, dps_binObjSeq, dps_encodedTokens
} DPSProgramEncoding;
```

DPSProgramEncoding defines the three possible encodings of PostScript language programs: ASCII encoding, binary object sequence encoding, and binary token encoding.

DPSResultsRec

```
typedef struct {
DPSDefinedType type;
int count;
char *value;
} DPSResultsRec, *DPSResults;
```

Each wrapped procedure constructs an array called the *result table*, which consists of elements of type *DPSResultsRec*. The index position of each element corresponds to the ordinal position of each output parameter as defined in the wrapped procedure; for example, index 0 (the first table entry) corresponds to the first output parameter, index 1 corresponds to the second output parameter, and so on.

type specifies the format type of the return value. *count* specifies the number of values expected; this supports array formats. *value* points to the location of the first value; the storage beginning must have room for *count* values of type *type*. If *count* is –1, *value* points to a scalar (single) result argument. If *count* is zero, any subsequent return values are ignored.

DPSSpace

```
/* handle for space record */
```

See *DPSSpaceRec*.

DPSSpaceProcsRec

```
typedef struct {
   void (*DestroySpace)(/* DPSSpace space */ );
} DPSSpaceProcsRec, *DPSSpaceProcs;
```

See **DPSDestroySpace** in *dpsclient.h*.

DPSSpaceRec

```
typedef struct {
   DPSSpaceProcs procs;
} DPSSpaceRec, *DPSSpace;
```

DPSSpaceRec provides a representation of a space. See also **DPSDestroySpace**.

11.7 dpsfriends.h Procedures

The following is an alphabetical listing of the procedures in the Client Library header file *dpsfriends.h*. These procedures are for experts only; most application developers don't need them. The *pswrap* translator inserts calls to these procedures when it creates the C-callable wrapped procedures you specify.

DPSAwaitReturnValues

```
void DPSAwaitReturnValues(ctxt)
    DPSContext ctxt;
```

DPSAwaitReturnValues waits for all results described by the result table; see *DPSResultRec*. It uses the tag of each object in the sequence to find the corresponding entry in the result table. When **DPSAwaitReturnValues** receives a tag that is greater than the last defined tag number, there are no more return values to be received and the procedure returns. This final tag is called the termination tag. **DPSSetResultTable** must be caged to set the result table before any calls to **DPSBinObjSeqWrite**.

DPSAwaitReturnValues can call the context's error procedure with *dps_err_resultTagCheck* or *dps_err_resultTypeCheck*. It returns prematurely if it encounters a *dps_err_ps* error.

DPSBinObjSeqWrite

```
void DPSBinObjSeqWrite(ctxt, buf, count)
    DPSContext ctxt;
    char *buf;
    unsigned int count;
```

DPSBinObjSeqWrite sends the beginning of a binary object sequence generated by a wrap. *buf* points to a buffer containing *count* bytes of a binary object sequence. *buf* must point to the beginning of a sequence, which includes at least the header and the entire top-level sequence of objects.

DPSBinObjSeqWrite can also include subsidiary array elements and/or strings. It writes PostScript language as specified by the format and encoding variables of *ctxt*, doing appropriate conversions as needed. If the buffer does not contain the entire binary object sequence, one or more calls to **DPSWriteTypedObjectArray** and/or **DPSWriteStringChars**

must follow immediately; *buf* and its contents must remain valid until the entire binary object sequence has been written. **DPSBinObjSeqWrite** ensures that the user name map is up-to-date.

`DPSContext DPSGetCurrentContext( );`

DPSGetCurrentContext returns the current context.

```
void DPSMapNames(ctxt, nNames, names, indices)
    DPSContext ctxt;
    unsigned int nNames;
    char **names;
    long int **indices;
```

DPSMapNames maps all specified names into user name indices, sending new **defineusername** definitions as needed. *names* is an array of strings whose elements are the user names. *nNames* is the number of elements in the array. *indices* is an array of pointers to *(long int*)* integers, which are the storage locations for the indexes.

DPSMapNames is normally called automatically from within wraps. The application can also call this procedure directly to obtain name mappings. **DPSMapNames** calls the context's error procedure with *dps_err_nameTooLong*.

Note that the caller must ensure that the string pointers remain valid after the procedure returns. The Client Library becomes the owner of all strings passed to it with **DPSMapNames**.

The same name can be used several times in a wrap. To reduce string storage, duplicates can be eliminated by using an optimization recognized by **DPSMapNames**. If the pointer to the string in the array *names* is null, that is *(char *)0*, **DPSMapNames** uses the nearest non null name that precedes the *(char *)0* entry in the array. The first element of *names* must be non null. This optimization works best if you sort the names so that duplicate occurrences are adjacent.

For example, **DPSMapNames** treats the following arrays as equivalent, but the one on the right saves storage.

```
{                       {
"boxes",                "boxes",
"drawMe",               "drawMe",
"drawMe",               (char *)0,
"init",                 "init",
"makeAPath",            "makeAPath",
"returnAClip",          "returnAClip",
"returnAClip",          (char *)0,
"returnAClip"           (char *)0
}                       }
```

DPSNameFromIndex

```
char *DPSNameFromIndex(index)
    long int index;
```

DPSNameFromIndex returns the text for the user name with the given index. The string returned must be treated as read-only. *NULL* is returned if *index* is invalid.

DPSSetContext

```
void DPSSetContext(ctxt)
    DPSContext ctxt;
```

DPSSetContext sets the current context. Call **DPSSetContext** before calling any procedures defined in *psops.h*.

DPSSetResultTable

```
void DPSSetResultTable(ctxt, tbl, len)
    DPSContext ctxt;
    DPSResults tbl;
    unsigned int len;
```

DPSSetResultTable sets the result table and its length in *ctxt*. This operation must be performed before a wrap body that can return a value is sent to the interpreter.

DPSUpdateNameMap

```
void DPSUpdateNameMap(ctxt)
    DPSContext ctxt;
```

DPSUpdateNameMap sends a series of **defineusername** commands to the interpreter. This procedure is called if the name map of the context's space is not synchronized with the Client Library name map.

DPSWriteStringChars
```
void DPSWriteStringChars(ctxt, buf, count);
    DPSContext ctxt;
    char *buf;
    unsigned int count;
```

DPSWriteStringChars appends strings to the current binary object sequence. *buf* contains *count* characters that form the body of one or more strings in a binary object sequence. *buf* and its contents must remain valid until the entire binary object sequence has been sent.

DPSWriteTypedObjectArray
```
void DPSWriteTypedObjectArray(ctxt, type, array, length)
    DPSContext ctxt;
    DPSDefinedType type;
    char *array;
    unsigned int length;
```

DPSWriteTypedObjectArray writes PostScript language code as specified by the format and encoding variables of *ctxt,* doing appropriate conversions as needed. *array* points to an array of *length* elements of type *type*. *array* contains the element values for the body of a subsidiary array that was passed as an input argument to *pswrap*. *array* and its contents must remain valid until the entire binary object sequence has been sent.

Example Error Handler

An error handler must deal with all errors defined in *dpsclient.h* as well as any additional errors defined in system-specific header files.

A.1 Error Handler Implementation

An example implementation of an error handler, **DPSDefaultErrorProc**, follows. The code is followed by explanatory text.

Example A.1 *Error handler implementation*

```
#include "dpsclient.h"

void DPSDefaultErrorProc(ctxt, errorCode, arg1, arg2)
  DPSContext ctxt;
  DPSErrorCode errorCode;
  long unsigned int arg1, arg2;

  DPSTextProc textProc = DPSGetCurrentTextBackstop( );

  char *prefix = "%%[ Error: ";
  char *suffix = "]%%\n";

  char *infix = "; OffendingCommand: ";
  char *nameinfix = "User name too long; Name: ";
  char *contextinfix = "Invalid context: ";
  char *taginfix = "Unexpected wrap result tag: ";
  char *typeinfix = "Unexpected wrap result type; tag: ";

  switch (errorCode) {
    case dps_err_ps: {
      char *buf = (char *)arg1;
      DPSBinObj ary = (DPSBinObj) (buf+DPS_HEADER_SIZE);
      DPSBinObj elements;
      char *error, *errorName;
```

```
                    integer errorCount, errorNameCount;
                    boolean resyncFlg;

                    Assert((ary->attributedType & 0x7f) == DPS_ARRAY);
                    Assert(ary->Iength == 4);

                    elements = (DPSBinObj)(((char *) ary) +
                                ary->val.arrayVal);
                    errorName = (char *)(((char *) ary) +
                                elements[1].val.nameVal);
                    errorNameCount = elements[1].length;

                    error = (char *)(((char *) ary) +
                                elements[2].val.nameVal);
                    errorCount = elements[2].Iength;

                    resyncFlg = elements[3].val.booleanVal;

                    if (textProc != NIL) {
                      (*textProc)(ctxt, prefix, strlen(prefix));
                      (*textProc)(ctxt, errorName, errorNameCount);
                      (*textProc)(ctxt, infix, strlen(infix));
                      (*textProc)(ctxt, error, errorCount);
                      (*textProc)(ctxt, suffix, strlen(suffix));
                    }
                    if (resyncFlg && (ctxt != dummyCtx)) {
                      RAISE(dps_err_ps, ctxt);
                      CantHappen( );
                    }
                    break;
                }
                case dps_err_nameTooLong:
                    if (textProc != NIL) {
                      char *buf = (char *)arg1;
                      (*textProc)(ctxt, prefix, strlen(prefix));
                      (*textProc)(ctxt, nameinfix, strlen(nameinfix));
                      (*textProc)(ctxt, buf, arg2);
                      (*textProc)(ctxt, suffix, strlen(suffix));
                    }
                    break;
                case dps_err_invalidContext:
                    if (textProc != NIL) {
                      char m[100];
                      (void) sprintf(m, "%s%s%d%s", prefix,
                                contextinfix, arg1, suffix);
                      (*textProc)(ctxt, m, strlen(m));
                    }
                    break;
                case dps_err_resuItTagCheck:
```

```
        case dps_err_resultTypeCheck:
            if (textProc != NIL) {
                char m[100];
                unsigned char tag = *((unsigned char *) arg1 +1);
                (void) sprintf(m, "%s%s%d%s", prefix, typeinfix, tag,
                        suffix);
                (*textProc)(ctxt, m, strlen(m));
            }
            break;
        case dps_err_invalidAccess:
            if (textProc != NIL) {
                char m[100];
                (void) sprintf (m, "%sInvalid context access.%s",
                        prefix, suffix);
                (*textProc) (ctxt, m, strlen (m));
            }
            break;
        case dps_err_encodingCheck:
            if (textProc != NIL) {
                char m[100];
                (void) sprintf (m,
                        "%sInvalid name/program encoding: %d/%d.%s",
                        prefix, (int) arg1, (int) arg2, suffix);
                (*textProc) (ctxt, m, strlen (m));
            }
            break;
        case dps_err_closedDisplay:
            if (textProc != NIL) {
                char m[100];
                (void) sprintf (m,
                        "%sBroken display connection %d.%s",
                        prefix, (int) arg1, suffix);
                (*textProc) (ctxt, m, strlen (m));
            }
            break;
        case dps_err_deadContext:
            if (textProc != NIL) {
                char m[100];
                (void) sprintf (m, "%sDead context 0x0%x.%s", prefix,
                        (int) arg1, suffix);
                (*textProc) (ctxt, m, strlen (m));
            }
            break;
        default:;
    }
} /* DPSDefaultErrorProc */
```

A.2 Description of the Error Handler

DPSDefaultErrorProc handles errors that arise when a wrap or Client Library procedure is called for the context. The error code indicates which error occurred. Interpretation of the *arg1* and *arg2* values is based on the error code.

The error handler initializes itself by getting the current backstop text handler and assigning string constants that will be used to formulate and report a text message. The section of the program that deals with the various error codes begins with the switch statement. Each error code can be handled differently.

If a *textProc* was specified, the error handler calls the text handler to formulate an error message, passing it the name of the error, the object that caused the error, and the string constants used to format a standard error message. For example, a **typecheck** error reported by the **cvn** operator is reported as a *dps_err_ps* error code and printed as follows:

```
%%[ Error: typecheck; OffendingCommand: cvn ]%%
```

The following error codes are common to all Client Library implementations:

dps_err_ps	represents all PostScript language errors reported by the interpreter, that is, the errors listed under each operator in *PostScript Language Reference Manual, Second Edition*.
dps_err_nameTooLong	arises if a binary object sequence or encoded token has a name whose length exceeds 128 characters. *arg1* is the PostScript user name; *arg2* is its length.
dps_err_invalidcontext	arises if a Client Library routine was called with an invalid context. This can happen if the client is unaware that the execution context in the interpreter has terminated. *arg1* is a context identifier; *arg2* is unused.
dps_err_resultTagCheck	occurs when an invalid tag is received for a result value. There is one object in the sequence. *arg1* is a pointer to the binary object sequence; *arg2* is the length of the binary object sequence.

dps_err_resultTypeCheck occurs when the value returned is of a type incompatible with the output parameter (for example, a string returned to an integer output parameter). *arg1* is a pointer to the binary object (the result with the wrong type); *arg2* is unused.

A.3 Handling PostScript Language Errors

The following discussion applies only to the *dps_err_ps* error code. This error code represents all possible PostScript operator errors. Because the interpreter provides a binary object sequence containing detailed information about the error, more options are available to the error handler than for other client errors.

arg1 points to a binary object sequence that describes the error. The binary object sequence is a four-element array consisting of the name *Error*, the name that identifies the specific error, the object that was executed when the error occurred, and a Boolean indicating whether the context expects to be resynchronized.

The type and length of the array are checked with assertions. The body of the array is pointed to by the *elements* variable. Each element of the array is extracted and placed in a variable.

Section B.1, "Recovering from PostScript Language Errors," describes a strategy for recovering from PostScript language errors. The strategy uses the **resynchstart** operator and the **resynchandleerror** handler. **DPSDefaultErrorProc** raises an exception only if the context uses this resynchronization method. The *resyncFlag* variable contains the value of the fourth element of the binary object sequence array, the Boolean that indicates whether resynchronization is needed. *resyncFlag* will be *false* if **handleerror** handled the error. It will be *true* if **resynchandleerror** handled the error.

If *resyncFlag* is *true* and the context handling the error is a context created by the application, the error handler raises the exception by calling *RAISE*. This call never returns.

Exception Handing

CL

This appendix describes a general-purpose exception-handling facility. It provides help for a narrowly defined problem area handling PostScript language errors. Most application programmers need not be concerned with exception handling. These facilities can be used in conjunction with PostScript language code and a sophisticated error handler such as **DPSDefaultErrorProc** to provide a certain amount of error recovery capability. Consult the system-specific documentation for alternative means of error recovery.

Note: *Certain systems may restrict the use of this exception-handling facility. The X Window System implementation, for example, limits exception handling to a few narrowly defined situations. Consult the system-specific documentation for more information.*

An *exception* is an unexpected condition such as a PostScript language error that prevents a procedure from running to normal completion. The procedure could simply return when an exception occurs, but this technique might leave data structures in an inconsistent state and produce incorrect returned values.

Instead of returning, the procedure can raise the exception, passing a code that indicates what has happened. The exception is intercepted by some caller of the procedure that raised the exception (any number of procedure calls deep); execution then resumes at the point of interception. As a result, the procedure that raised the exception is terminated, as are any intervening procedures between it and the procedure that intercepted the exception, an action called "unwinding the call stack."

The Client Library provides a general-purpose exception-handling mechanism in *dpsexcept.h*. This header file provides facilities for placing exception handlers in application subroutines to respond cleanly to exceptional conditions.

Note: *Application programs might need to contain the following statement:*

```
#include "dpsexcept.h"
```

As an exception propagates up the call stack, each procedure encountered can deal with the exception in one of three ways:

- It ignores the exception, in which case the exception continues on to the caller of the procedure.

- It intercepts the exception and handles it, in which case all procedure calls below the handler are unwound and discarded.

- It intercepts, handles, and then raises the exception, allowing handlers higher in the stack to notice and react to the exception.

The body of a procedure that intercepts exceptions is written as follows:

```
DURING
  statement1;
  statement2;
   . . .
HANDLER
  statement3
  statement4;
   . . .
END_HANDLER
```

The statements between *HANDLER* and *END_HANDLER* make up the exception handler for exceptions occurring between *DURING* and *HANDLER*. The procedure body works as follows:

- Normally, the statements between *DURING* and *HANDLER* are executed.

- If no exception occurs, the statements between *HANDLER* and *END_HANDLER* are bypassed; execution resumes at the statement after *END_HANDLER*.

- If an exception is raised while executing the statements between *DURING* and *HANDLER* (including any procedure called from those statements), execution of those statements is aborted and control passes to the statements between *HANDLER* and *END_HANDLER*.

In terms of C syntax, treat these macros as if they were C code brackets, as shown in Table B.1.

Table B.1 *C equivalents for exception macros*

Macro	C Equivalent
DURING	{{
HANDLER	}{
END_HANDLER	}}

In general, exception-handling macros either should entirely enclose a code block (the preferred method, Example B.1) or should be entirely within the block (Example B.2).

Example B.1 *Exception handling macros—enclosing a code block*

```
DURING
    while ( /* Example 1 */ ) {
        ...
    }
HANDLER
    ...
END_HANDLER
```

Example B.2 *Exception handling macros—within a code block*

```
while ( /* Example 2 */ ) {
    DURING
    ...
    HANDLER
    ...
    END_HANDLER
}
```

When a procedure detects an exceptional condition, it can raise an exception by calling *RAISE*. *RAISE* takes two arguments. The first is an error code (for example, one of the values of **DPSErrorCode**). The second is a pointer, *char **, which can point to any kind of data structure, such as a string of ASCII text or a binary object sequence.

The exception handler has two local variables: *Exception.Code* and *Exception.Message*. When the handler is entered, the first argument that was passed to *RAISE* gets assigned to *Exception.Code* and the second argument gets assigned to *Exception.Message*. These variables have valid contents only between *HANDLER* and *END_HANDLER*.

If the exception handler executes *END_HANDLER* or returns, propagation of the exception ceases. However, if the exception handler calls *RERAISE*, the exception, along with *Exception.Code* and *Exception.Message*, is propagated to the next outer dynamically enclosing occurrence of *DURING...HANDLER*.

A procedure can choose not to handle an exception, in which case one of its callers must handle it. There are two common reasons for wanting to handle exceptions:

- To deallocate dynamically allocated storage and clean up any other local state, then allow the exception to propagate further. In this case, the handler should perform its cleanup, then call *RERAISE*.

- To recover from certain exceptions that might occur, then continue normal execution. In this case, the handler should compare *Exception.Code* with the set of exceptions it can handle. If it can handle the exception, it should perform the recovery and execute the statement that follows *END_HANDLER*; if not, it should call *RERAISE* to propagate the exception to a higher-level handler.

Note: *It is illegal to execute a statement between DURING and HANDLER that would transfer control outside of those statements. In particular, return is illegal: an unspecified error will occur. This restriction does not apply to the statements between HANDLER and END_HANDLER. To return from the exception handler, call E_RETURN_VOID; to perform return(x), call E_RETURN(x).*

B.1   Recovering from PostScript Language Errors

The example **DPSDefaultErrorProc** procedure can be used with the PostScript operator **resyncstart** to recover from PostScript language errors. If you use this strategy, an exception can be raised by any of the Client Library procedures that write code or data to the context: any wrap, any single-operator procedure, **DPSWritePostScript**, and so on. The strategy is as follows:

1. Send **resyncstart** to the context immediately after it is created. **resyncstart** is a simple, read-evaluate-print loop enclosed in a *stopped* clause which, on error, executes **resynchandleerror**.

   resynchandleerror reports PostScript errors back to the client in the form of a binary object sequence of a single object: an array of four elements as described in section 3.12.2 of *PostScript Language Reference Manual, Second Edition*. The fourth element of the binary object sequence, a Boolean, is set to *true* to indicate that **resynchandleerror** is executing. The *stopped* clause itself executes within an outer loop.

2. When a PostScript language error is detected, **resynchandleerror** writes the binary object sequence describing the error, flushes the output stream %stdout, then reads and discards any data on the input stream %stdin until *EOF* (an end-of-file marker) is received. This effectively clears out any pending code and data, and makes the context do nothing until the client handles the error.

3. The binary object sequence sent by **resynchandleerror** is received by the client and passed to the context's error handler. The error handler formulates a text message from the binary object sequence and displays it, for example, by calling the backstop text handler.

   It then inspects the binary object sequence and notices that the fourth element of the array, a Boolean, is *true*. This means **resynchandleerror** is executing and waiting for the client to recover from the error. The error handler can then raise an exception by calling *RAISE* with *dps_err_ps* and the *DPSContext* pointer in order to allow an exception handler to perform error recovery.

4. The *dps_err_ps* exception is caught by one of the handlers in the application program. This causes the C stack to be unwound, and the handler body to be executed. To handle the exception, the application can reset the context that reported the error, discarding any waiting code.

5. The handler body calls **DPSResetContext**, which resets the context after an error occurs. This procedure guarantees that any buffered I/O is discarded and that the context is ready to read and execute more input. Specifically, **DPSResetContext** causes *EOF* to be put on the context's input stream.

6. We have come full circle now. *EOF* is received by **resynchandleerror**, which causes it to terminate. The outer loop of **resyncstart** then reopens the context's input stream %stdin, which clears the end-of-file indication and resumes execution at the top of the loop. The context is now ready to read new code.

Although this strategy works well for some applications, it leaves the context and the contents of its private VM in an unknown state. For example, the dictionary and operand stacks might be cluttered, free-running forked contexts might have been created, or the contents of **userdict** might have been changed. Clearing the state of such a context can be very complicated.

You might not get PostScript language error exceptions when you expect them. Because of delays related to buffering and scheduling, a PostScript language error can be reported long after the C procedure responsible for the error has returned. This makes it difficult to write an exception handler for a given section of code. If this code can cause a PostScript language error and therefore cause **DPSDefaultErrorProc** to raise an exception, you can ensure that you get the exception in a timely manner by using synchronization.

Note: *In multicontext applications that require error recovery, the code to recover from PostScript errors can get complicated. An exception reporting a PostScript error caused by one context can be raised by any call on the Client Library, even one on behalf of some other context, including calls made from wraps. Although* **DPSDefaultErrorProc** *passes the context that caused the error as an argument to RAISE, it is difficult in general to deal with an exception from one context that arises while the application is working with another.*

When the **handleerror** procedure is called to report an error, no recovery is possible except to display an error message and destroy the context.

B.2   Example Exception Handler

A typical application might have the following main loop. Assume that a context has already been created with **DPSDefaultErrorProc** as its error procedure, and that **resyncstart** has been executed by the context.

Example B.3 *Exception handler*

C language code:

```
#include <dpsexcept.h>

    while (/* the user hasn't quit */) {
        /* get an input event */
        event = GetEventFromQueue( );
        /* react to event */
        DURING
          switch (event) {
            case EVENT_A:
               UserWrapA(context, ...);
               break;
            case EVENT_B:
```

```
                    UserWrapB(context, ...);
                    break;
                case EVENT_C:
                    ProcThatCallsSeveralWraps(context);
                    break;
            /* ... */
                default:;
        }
    HANDLER
        /*  the context's error proc has already posted an
            error for this exception, so just reset.
            Make sure the context we're using is the
            one that caused the error! */
        if (Exception.Code == dps_err_ps)
            DPSResetContext((DPSContext)Exception.Message);
    END_HANDLER
}
```

Most of the calls in the *switch* statement are either direct calls to wrapped procedures or indirect calls (that is, calls to procedures that make direct calls to wrapped procedures or to the Client Library). All of the procedure calls between *DURING* and *HANDLER* can potentially raise an exception. The code between *HANDLER* and *END_HANDLER* is executed only if an exception is raised by the code between *DURING* and *HANDLER*. Otherwise, the handler code is skipped.

Suppose **ProcThatCallsSeveralWraps** is defined as follows:

Example B.4 *Propagating exceptions with RERAISE*

```
void ProcThatCallsSeveralWraps(context)
    DPSContext context;
{
    char *s = ProcThatAllocsAString (...);
    int n;

    DURING
        UserWrapC1 (context, ...);
        UserWrapC2(context, &n); /* user wrap returns value */
        /* client lib proc */
        DPSPrintf(context, "/%s %d def\n", s, n);
    HANDLER
        if ((DPSContext)Exception.Message == context)
        {
        /* clean up the allocated string */
        free(s);
```

```
                s = NULL;
            }
        /* let the caller handle resetting the context */
            RERAISE;
        END_HANDLER

        /* clean up, if we haven't already */
        if (s != NULL) free(s);
    }
```

This procedure unconditionally allocates storage, then calls procedures that might raise an exception. If no handlers are here and the exception is propagated to the main loop, the storage allocated for the string would never be reclaimed. The solution is to define a handler that frees the storage and then calls *RERAISE* to allow another handler to do the final processing of the exception.

POSTSCRIPT™
Software From Adobe

The Display PostScript System

Adobe Systems Incorporated

Client Library Supplement for X

CLX

Client Library Supplement for X

1 About this Manual

Client Library Supplement for X contains information about the Client
Library interface to the Display PostScript system implemented as an
extension to the X Window System. The Display PostScript extension is
the application programmer's means of displaying text and graphics on
a screen using the PostScript language.

The system-independent interface for Display PostScript is documented
in *Client Library Reference Manual*. Only extensions to the interface are
discussed in *Client Library Supplement for X*. The header file
<DPS/dpsXclient.h> includes both system-independent and X system-
specific procedures.

1.1 What this Manual Contains

Section 2, "About the Display PostScript Extension to X," briefly
introduces the Display PostScript system extension to the X Window
System.

Section 3, "Basic Facilities," introduces concepts that will enable you to
write a simple application, including connecting to the X server;
creating and terminating a context; differences in coordinate systems;
issues of rendering in X versus PostScript language; clipping, repainting,
and resizing; error codes; user object indices; and status events.

Section 4, "Additional Facilities," describes advanced concepts that not
all applications need, including client and server identifiers, encodings,
synchronization, shared resources, and multiple servers.

Section 5, "Programming Tips," contains tips for the application programmer on files, fonts, coordinate conversions, and other issues that require special attention.

Section 6, "X-Specific Data and Procedures," describes the X-specific data and procedures found in the *<DPS/dpsXclient.h>* header file.

Section 7, "X-Specific Custom PostScript Operators," describes the X-specific PostScript operators provided for the Display PostScript extension to X.

2 About the Display PostScript Extension to X

In order to understand the relationship of the Display PostScript system to the development of X applications, you should be familiar with the following concepts:

- *The PostScript imaging model*, which allows the application developer to express graphical displays at a higher level of abstraction than is possible with Xlib. This improves device independence and portability. The integration of the imaging model with X requires consideration of several issues, including coordinate system conversions (see "Coordinate Systems" in section 3.3, "Execution"), event handling (see section 3.4, "Status Events"), and resource management (see section 4.7, "Sharing Resources").

- *The PostScript interpreter*, which allows an application to execute PostScript language code.

- *Wrapped procedures*, which allow PostScript language programs to be embedded in an application as C-callable procedures.

CLX

3 Basic Facilities

Client Library Reference Manual introduces the facilities needed to write a simple application program for the Display PostScript system. This manual discusses Display PostScript system issues of particular concern in the X Window System environment, in the following categories:

- Initialization

- Creating a context

- Execution of PostScript language code

- Termination

3.1 Initialization

Before performing any Display PostScript operations, the application must establish a connection to the X server. You can connect to the server by using Xlib's **XOpenDisplay** routine or a standard toolkit's initialization process. Regardless of how the connection is established, an X *Display* record will be defined for the connection. Subsequent Display PostScript system operations will use this *Display* record to identify the server. Once the *Display* record is obtained, the application must create a *drawable* (window or pixmap) for Display PostScript imaging operations, and an X *GC* out of which certain fields are used by Display PostScript. There are a number of facilities in Xlib for creating new windows and *GC*s, such as **XCreateSimpleWindow** and **XCreateGC**.

3.2 Creating a Context

In Display PostScript, a context (as described in *Client Library Reference Manual*) is a resource in the server that represents all of the execution state needed by the PostScript interpreter to run PostScript language programs.

DPSContextRec is a data structure on the client side that represents all of the state needed by the Client Library to communicate with a context. A pointer of type *DPSContext* is a handle to this data structure. When the application creates a context in the interpreter, a *DPSContextRec* structure is automatically created for use by the client (except for forked contexts; see section 4.5, "Forked Contexts"). The *DPSContextRec* contains pointers to procedures that implement all of the basic operations that a context can perform.

There are two procedures that create both a context in the server and a *DPSContextRec* for the client. The first, **XDPSCreateSimpleContext**, uses the default colormap, and is adequate for most applications. The second, **XDPSCreateContext**, is a more general function that allows you to specify colormap information. Other procedures for creating just the *DPSContextRec*—for contexts that already exist in the server—are covered in section 4, "Additional Facilities."

3.2.1 Using XDPSCreateSimpleContext

To create a context using the default colormap, call **XDPSCreateSimpleContext**:

XDPSCreateSimpleContext
```
DPSContext XDPSCreateSimpleContext(dpy, drawable, gc, x, y,
        textProc, errorProc, space)
    Display *dpy;
    Drawable drawable;
    GC gc;
    int x;
    int y;
    DPSTextProc textProc;
    DPSErrorProc errorProc;
    DPSSpace space;
```

Client Library Reference Manual contains a general discussion of **XDPSCreateSimpleContext**, but does not discuss the details that are relevant to X. These details are covered here.

A context is created on the specified *Display* and is associated with a *Drawable* and *GC* on that *Display*. The context uses the following fields in the *GC* to render text and graphics on the *Drawable*:

- plane_mask

- subwindow_mode

- clip_x_origin

- clip_y_origin

- clip_mask

If the *Drawable* or *GC* is not specified (that is, passed as *None*), the context will execute programs correctly but will not render any text or graphics (it renders to the null device). A valid *Drawable* and *GC* may be associated with such a context at a later time using the **setXgcdrawable** operator, documented in section 7, "X-Specific Custom PostScript Operators."

The arguments *x* and *y* are offsets that specify where the device space origin is relative to the window origin. To place the device space origin (and thus the user space origin) in the standard lower-left corner, pass zero for *x* and the height of the window in pixels for *y*. See the discussion of coordinate systems in section 3.3, "Execution."

The other arguments to **XDPSCreateSimpleContext** are described fully in *Client Library Reference Manual*. To summarize: *textProc* is a callback procedure that handles text output from the context, *errorProc* is a callback procedure that handles errors reported by the context, and *space* is the private VM that the context uses for storage. If the space is passed as *NULL*, a new space is created.

If all of the arguments are valid and the context is successfully created in the server, a *DPSContext* handle is returned. Otherwise, *NULL* is returned.

XDPSCreateSimpleContext uses the default colormap. A device-specific number of grays is reserved in the default colormap, which represents a gray ramp. If the device supports color, an RGB color cube is also reserved. If a requested RGB color is found in the color cube or gray ramp, the associated pixel value is used. Otherwise, the color is approximated by dithering pixel values from the colormap to give the best possible rendering of the color.

XDPSCreateSimpleContext may allocate a substantial number of cells in the default colormap. For example, a typical allocation for an 8-plane PseudoColor device is 64 cells for the color cube, representing a 4x4x4 RGB cube. The gray ramp typically uses nine cells. **XDPSCreateSimpleContext** checks the root window for the *RGB_DEFAULT_MAP* and *RGB_GRAY_RAMP* properties. If the properties exists, the color cells they specify are used for the context's color cube and gray ramp. If the properties do not exist, color cells are allocated and the properties are defined. The allocated cells are typically treated as "read-only retained" so that other Display PostScript clients may share the allocated colors.

The Display PostScript system uses entries from the default X colormap to display colors and grey values. You can configure this usage. Giving the Display PostScript system more colormap entries improves the quality of its rendering, but leaves fewer entries available to other applications since the default colormap is shared.

Resources in your *.Xdefaults* file control the colormap usage. Each resource entry should be of the form

DPSColorCube.*visualType.depth.color: size*

where

visualType is one of GrayScale, PseudoColor, or DirectColor.

depth is 1, 2, 4, 8, 12, or 24 and should be the largest depth equal to or less than the default depth.

color is one of the strings "reds", "greens", "blues", or "grays".

size is the number of values of that color to allocate .

These resources are not used for the static visual types *StaticGray*, *StaticColor*, or *TrueColor*.

Specifying 0 for reds directs the Client Library to use only a gray ramp. This specification is particularly useful for gray-scale systems that incorrectly use *PseudoColor* as the default visual.

For example, to configure a 5x5x4 color cube and a 17-element gray ramp for an 8-bit *PseudoColor* screen, specify these resources:

DPSColorCube.PseudoColor.8.reds: 5
DPSColorCube.PseudoColor.8.greens: 5
DPSColorCube.PseudoColor.8.blues: 4
DPSColorCube.PseudoColor.8.grays: 17

These resources use 117 colormap entries, 100 for the color cube and 17 for the gray ramp. For the best rendering results, specify an odd number for the gray ramp.

Resources that are not specified take these default values:

DPSColorCube.GrayScale.4.grays: 9
DPSColorCube.GrayScale.8.grays: 17

```
DPSColorCube.PseudoColor.4.reds: 2
DPSColorCube.PseudoColor.4.greens: 2
DPSColorCube.PseudoColor.4.blues: 2
DPSColorCube.PseudoColor.4.grays: 2
DPSColorCube.PseudoColor.8.reds: 4
DPSColorCube.PseudoColor.8.greens: 4
DPSColorCube.PseudoColor.8.blues: 4
DPSColorCube.PseudoColor.8.grays: 9
DPSColorCube.PseudoColor.12.reds: 6
DPSColorCube.PseudoColor.12.greens: 6
DPSColorCube.PseudoColor.12.blues: 5
DPSColorCube.PseudoColor.12.grays: 17

DPSColorCube.DirectColor.12.reds: 6
DPSColorCube.DirectColor.12.greens: 6
DPSColorCube.DirectColor.12.blues: 6
DPSColorCube.DirectColor.12.grays: 6
DPSColorCube.DirectColor.24.reds: 7
DPSColorCube.DirectColor.24.greens: 7
DPSColorCube.DirectColor.24.blues: 7
DPSColorCube.DirectColor.24.grays: 7
```

If none of the above defaults apply to the display, the Client Library uses no color cube and a 2-element gray ramp; that is, black and white.

The advantage of using the color allocation facilities provided by **XDPSCreateSimpleContext** is that the application has available a wide range of colors (many more than the number of cells), each with a reasonable rendering, without having to provide for the possibility that colormap allocations may fail. The disadvantage is that a large number of color cells may be allocated from the default colormap.

3.2.2   Using XDPSCreateContext

To create a context with specific color information, call **XDPSCreateContext**:

XDPSCreateContext

```
DPSContext XDPSCreateContext(dpy, drawable, gc, x, y,
        eventmask, grayramp, ccube, actual,
        textProc, errorProc, space)
    Display *dpy;
    Drawable drawable;
    GC gc;
    int x;
    int y;
    unsigned int eventmask;
    XStandardColormap *grayramp;
    XStandardColormap *ccube;
    int actual;
    DPSTextProc textProc;
    DPSErrorProc errorProc;
    DPSSpace space;
```

The *dpy*, *drawable*, *gc*, *x*, *y*, *textProc*, *errorProc*, and *space* arguments for **XDPSCreateContext** are the same as for **XDPSCreateSimpleContext**. The *eventmask* is currently not implemented and should be passed as zero.

The *grayramp* and *ccube* arguments are pointers to *XStandardColormap* data structures (defined in the *<X11/Xutil.h>* header file). An *XStandardColormap* specifies a colormap, a base pixel value, and multipliers and limits for red (or gray), green, and blue ramps. A valid gray ramp is required; *ccube* is optional (may be passed as *NULL*). If a color cube is present and is specified by *ccube*, *grayramp* may use pixel values in the color cube in order to conserve colormap entries. The X colormap resource specified in the *ccube* and *grayramp* arguments must be identical. The application must ensure that the specified colormap is installed—for example, by using **XSetWindowColormap** to set the colormap as an attribute of the window.

The application provides a colormap with a uniform distribution of colors. The colormap must provide a uniform distribution of grays (colors where red, green, and blue are equal in intensity), which is described by *grayramp*. However, the *grayramp* may be as simple as two levels: black and white. The colormap may also contain a uniform distribution of RGB colors arranged as a color cube, which is described by *ccube*. See X Window System reference documents for details about the *XStandardColormap* data structure.

The argument *actual* can be used to conserve colormap entries as well as to display pure (nondithered) colors. If the application has been informed which colors it will use, or if the number of colors to be used is relatively few (fewer than the default allocation that

XDPSCreateSimpleContext would use for the device), the *actual* argument can be used. *actual* is a hint about the number of colors the context is going to request. It is considered a hint because the server cannot guarantee that the specified number of colors will be available. The server will reserve the number of cells specified by *actual* or the number of cells available in the specified colormap, whichever is smaller. As the context makes color requests, colormap entries are defined on a "first come, first served" basis. For example, suppose *actual* is given the value 3 and there are at least three cells available. The first time the context executes the **setrgbcolor** operator, the requested color will be stored in the colormap, leaving two more cells reserved by *actual*. When the context executes **setrgbcolor** for a different color, the second cell reserved by *actual* is used, and so on. The colors requested by the PostScript language program executed by the context will be rendered without dithering.

Note: *Supporting actual is an optional part of a Display PostScript system. Some implementations ignore actual, so portable applications should not count on its effects.*

Consider the characteristics of your application when deciding whether to use **XDPSCreateSimpleContext**, with its default allocation of colors, or **XDPSCreateContext**, with *actual*. An application may allow the end user to define a variety of colors. Such an application—a graphics editor, for example—could use **XDPSCreateSimpleContext**.

On the other hand, an application that uses only a few colors—the foreground and background colors of a performance meter, for example—could use **XDPSCreateContext**, specify a small color cube, and set *actual* to the number of colors used. Since *actual* is just a hint, the small cube is necessary as a fallback strategy; it ensures that the application will display correctly regardless of the environment.

If all the arguments are valid and the context is successfully created in the server, a *DPSContext* handle is returned. Otherwise, *NULL* is returned.

3.3   Execution

This section discusses the following Display PostScript issues: coordinate systems, rendering, clipping, repainting, resizing a window, user object indices, and errors.

3.3.1 Coordinate Systems

The application must specify user space coordinates when communicating with the PostScript interpreter and X coordinates when communicating with other parts of the X Window System. Therefore coordinate conversions may be necessary. This section explains:

- How to specify the device space origin for the window at context creation time

- How to convert user space coordinates to X coordinates

- How to convert X coordinates to user space coordinates

PostScript Language Reference Manual, Second Edition, describes the coordinate system used by the PostScript imaging model. To summarize: coordinates are specified in a user-defined space and are automatically converted to the output device space. The default user space unit is 1/72 of an inch. The default origin is in the lower left corner of the page, with x increasing to the right and y increasing to the top (upwards).

Figure 1 shows a linear transformation from user space to device space by means of the current transformation matrix (CTM). Note that this transformation is one-way only.

Figure 1 *User space and device space*

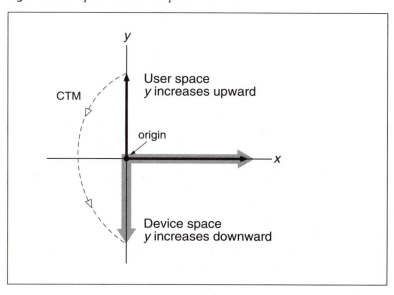

In PostScript language terminology, the window is the output device. In Display PostScript, the window is treated as a page, with the conventional location of the origin in the lower left corner. The device space is equivalent to the X coordinate system for the window, except for the following:

- The device space origin is offset from the window origin.

- Device space is a real-number space, whereas the X coordinate system is an integer space.

As described in *PostScript Language Reference Manual, Second Edition*, pixel boundaries fall on integer coordinates in device space. A pixel is a half-open region, meaning that it includes half its boundary points. For any point (x, y) in device space, let $i = \text{floor}(x)$ and $j = \text{floor}(y)$, where x and y are real numbers and i and j are integers. The pixel that contains this point is the one identified as (i, j), which is equivalent to the X coordinate for that pixel.

To convert user space coordinates to X coordinates:

1. Convert the user space coordinates to device space coordinates by computing a linear transformation using the current transformation matrix (CTM).

2. Compute the X coordinates by applying an additional translation to the device space coordinates derived in Step 1 to account for the offset of the device space origin from the window origin.

Similarly, to convert X coordinates to user space coordinates:

1. Translate the X coordinates to device space coordinates by applying the offset of the device space origin to the X coordinates.

2. Convert the device space coordinates to user space coordinates by using the inverse of the current transformation matrix.

See section 5.5, "Coordinate Conversions," for examples of coordinate conversions.

Figure 2 illustrates how the device space origin is located in the window as an offset from the window origin. The x and y offset values are established at context creation time (see section 3.2, "Creating a Context"); they can be changed by X-specific PostScript operators such as **setXoffset**.

Figure 2 *Window origin and device space origin*

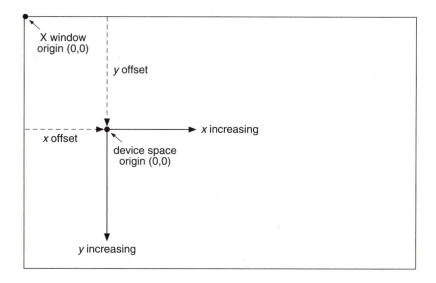

The device origin is offset in order to support the method of scrolling that involves copying areas of the window (as opposed to shifting a child window under an ancestor). You can put the device space origin anywhere in the window. Then, as you scroll the contents of the window, you can offset the origin from its original position to make coordinate conversions easier. The default location for the device space origin is in the lower left corner of the window.

Coordinate conversions are required under the following conditions:

- If you use the PostScript imaging model to render graphics using coordinates received from X events, the X coordinates must first be converted into user space coordinates. For instance, if you allow the user to select a line of text in a text editor, coordinate conversions are required.

- If X rendering is to be done in the same window as PostScript language rendering, it may be necessary to convert user space coordinates to X coordinates—for example, call **XCopyArea** to move a graphical object that was rendered by the PostScript interpreter.

Coordinate conversions are not required under the following conditions:

- If you use the PostScript imaging model for output only (rendering text and graphics without user interaction in the display area), no coordinate conversions are required. Simply express coordinates in user space.

  For example, assuming the default user space, the letter *A* shown at coordinate *(x=72, y=72)* will appear upright 1 inch to the right and 1 inch above the bottom left corner of the window.

- If the only rendering you do in response to X events is with X primitives, you don't have to perform coordinate conversions unless you are altering pixels that were rendered by the PostScript interpreter.

Resizing the window may have an effect on the device space origin, and thus the offsets to that origin, depending upon the bit gravity of the window. See the section titled "Resizing the Window" on page PG-19.

3.3.2   Mixing Display PostScript and X Rendering

X drawing requests and PostScript language code can be sent to the same drawable. For example, X primitives such as **XCopyArea** can be used to move, copy, and change pixels that have been painted with PostScript language programs.

Interactive feedback, such as selection highlighting and control points, can be accomplished with X drawing requests. For example, control points on a graphics object in a graphics editor application can be displayed with X primitives as follows:

- Copy the pixels that were painted by a PostScript language program to a pixmap with several **XCopyArea** calls. These pixels will temporarily be obscured by the control points, so they must be preserved.

- Call **XFillRectangle** to paint the control points, which may be grabbed and stretched, rotated, moved, and so on.

Now suppose a control point is moved. Handle a series of subsequent mouse events as follows:

- Copy the pixels underlying the control point back from the pixmap, effectively erasing the control point at the original location.

- Compute the new position of the control point from the mouse event.

- Copy the pixels at the new location to the pixmap. Call **XFillRectangle** to display the control point at the new location.

Here are some considerations to keep in mind when mixing X and Display PostScript system imaging:

- Their coordinate systems are different. See the section titled "Coordinate Systems" on page PG-13 for more information.

- PostScript language programs run asynchronously with respect to other X requests. A PostScript language rendering request is not guaranteed to be complete before a subsequent X request is executed, unless synchronized. See section 4.8, "Synchronization," for more information.

- X tends to be pixel and plane oriented; graphic operations that manipulate pixels and planes are necessarily device dependent. The PostScript imaging model deals with abstract graphical representations (paths) and abstract colors. The PostScript interpreter tries to give the best rendering possible for the device. If device independence is important for your application, use X primitives sparingly, preserving device independence as much as possible.

3.3.3   Clipping and Repainting

Text and graphics rendered with the PostScript interpreter are subject to all of the X clipping rules as well as the clipping defined by the PostScript imaging model.

The default clipping region is the window. When clipping other than to the default, the following recommendations apply:

- If you're drawing with PostScript language code only, use the clipping mechanism provided by the PostScript imaging model. This is sufficient for nearly all applications.

- If you're also using X primitives and want to clip them as well as draw using PostScript language code, use the clipping specified by the X GC.

Expose events may be handled with a variety of strategies:

- Repainting all graphics for the window

- Repainting all graphics through composite view clip

- Repainting selected graphics through composite view clip

Repainting the entire window is the simplest strategy to implement and is suitable for simple applications. To do so:

- Ignore exposure events with counts greater than zero.

- For exposure events with counts equal to zero, clear the window and then redisplay all of the text and graphics objects by executing the PostScript language programs that describe them.

Though simple to implement, this strategy makes the window flash or flicker every time it is repainted, which can be distracting to the end user.

A somewhat more sophisticated strategy involves making a list of the rectangles specified in a series of exposure events until a zero count is detected, as follows:

- Create a view clip (see *PostScript Language Reference Manual, Second Edition*) by converting the coordinates of the list of exposure rectangles to user space coordinates and executing **rectviewclip** with this list.

- Then redisplay all the text and graphics objects by executing the PostScript language programs that describe them. Only those areas within the view clip will actually be repainted.

This strategy reduces annoying window flicker, but may do more work than is necessary since programs describing graphics objects that are completely clipped are executed anyway.

The most sophisticated technique, perhaps the optimal strategy, is similar to the one just described:

- Use a list of rectangles from the exposure events to create a view clip.

- Then, instead of running all of the PostScript language programs, redraw only those graphics objects whose bounding boxes intersect the view clip.

This strategy requires that the application keep track of the bounding boxes and locations of each graphical object, but this task is usually necessary anyway, particularly for interactive applications that allow selection and manipulation of objects. User paths are handy for this purpose (see *PostScript Language Reference Manual, Second Edition*), since they are compact data structures that contain their own bounding box information. The list of rectangles obtained from the exposure events can be enumerated and intersected with the bounding box of each user path. Bounding box intersection may still result in some code being executed unnecessarily, but it is a good compromise between time spent deciding which graphical objects to redraw and time spent drawing the objects.

3.3.4   Resizing the Window

When the window is resized, the X server moves the window bits according to the bit gravity of the window. If the window is being used for imaging with the PostScript language, the origin of the device space is also moved according to the bit gravity of the window; see the section titled "Coordinate Systems" on page PG-13" for a discussion of coordinate systems. The result of this automatic movement is that the x and y offsets that were specified when the context was created (or that were last changed with the **setXoffset** operator) are changed. The application may need to keep track of these changes.

Table 1 shows the changes to the x and y offsets for each bit gravity type.

Table 1 *How bit gravity affects offsets*

Symbol	Meaning
oldX	Original x offset
oldY	Original y offset
wc	Change in window size along the x axis (width)
hc	Change in window size along the y axis (height)

Bit Gravity	New x offset	New y offset
NorthWest	oldX	oldY
North	oldX + wc/2	oldY
NorthEast	oldX + wc	oldY
West	oldX	oldY + hc/2
Center	oldX + wc/2	oldY + hc/2
East	oldX + wc	oldY + hc/2
SouthWest	oldX	oldY + hc
South	oldX + wc/2	oldY + hc
SouthEast	oldX + wc	oldY + hc

ForgetGravity	*No change*	*No change—appears as if NorthWest*
Static	oldX + wc	oldY + hc

To get the current *x* and *y* offsets, use **currentXoffset**.

3.3.5   User Object Indices

The Client Library provides a convenient and efficient way to refer to PostScript language objects. This section presents one set of utilities available for working with these objects. An alternate set of utilities is available in the Display PostScript Toolkit and documented in section 4 of the *Display PostScript Toolkit for X*.

Some types of composite or structured objects, such as dictionaries, gstates, and user paths, are not visible as data outside the PostScript interpreter; that is, they cannot be represented directly in any encoding of the language, not even in binary object sequence encoding. Instead, an application must refer to such objects by means of surrogate objects whose values can be encoded and communicated easily.

The surrogate objects provided by the Client Library are called user objects. A user object is simply an identifier (typically an integer of type *long int*) that represents an actual object (of any type) in the interpreter. To define a new user object, the application must first obtain a user object index from the Client Library. The **DPSNewUserObjectIndex** procedure returns a new user object index. The Client Library is the sole allocator of new user object indices in order to guarantee that indices are unique. User object indices are dynamic and should not be used as arithmetic values (for example, don't add 1 to get the next available index). Also, do not store user object indices in a file or other long-term storage.

After obtaining a user object index, the application must associate this index with an actual object. You first execute a PostScript language program to create the object, then execute the **defineuserobject** operator.

Once a user object has been defined, the application may call wrapped procedures to manipulate it. User objects may be passed as input arguments to a wrapped procedure.

User objects are typically employed under the following circumstances:

- *When graphical objects or other application objects are created dynamically,* such as the user path a graphics editor builds as the user draws an illustration.

- *When a user name should not be employed.* A user object is a convenient and efficient substitute for a dynamically defined user name, which must be passed to a wrap as a string.

See *PostScript Language Reference Manual, Second Edition,* and *pswrap Reference Manual* for further discussion of user objects.

Note that it is the responsibility of the application and any runtime facilities or support software (such as toolkits) to keep track of user object definitions. A user object must be defined before it is used. Unlike user name indices (which are defined automatically by the Client Library), user objects must be defined explicitly. To assist in keeping track of user object definitions, the last user object index assigned can be read from *DPSLastUserObjectIndex*, which should be treated as read-only.

In the following code example, a hypothetical toolkit implements a user interface that displays icons for files and programs. The user interface allows the end user to customize the label of the icon by changing the text and to specify the font of the label text. The icon is represented as a PostScript language dictionary.

Example 1 *Implementing a user interface to display icons*

Wrap definitions:

```
defineps New_Icon(long iconIndex; int x,y; long progIndex;
              char *font, *text)
    % Input Arguments:
    % iconIndex
    %     user object index provided by application
    % x,y
    %     coordinates of lower left corner of icon
    % progIndex
    %     user object index which represents a PostScript
    %     language program for drawing the icon
    % font
    %     string to be used as a font name
    % text
    %     label for icon
```

```
                5 dict dup          % Create the icon dict.
                iconIndex exch defineuserobject
                                    % Define the user object for the dict.

                begin               % Begin the icon dict.
                /icon_x x def       % Assign x coordinate.
                /icon_y y def       % Assign y coordinate.
                /icon_prog
                   UserObjects progIndex get
                                    % Get and def icon drawing procedure
                   def              % (assumes userdict is on dict stack)
                /icon_font /font def    % Assign label font name.
                /icon_label (text) def  % Assign label text.
                end                     % End icon dictionary.
            endps

            /* a wrapped procedure to draw an arbitrary icon */

            defineps Draw_Icon(userobject icon)
                % Input Arguments:
                % icon
                %       user object representing an icon dictionary.
                %       Note: since we are going to execute the object,
                %       we can declare it asuserobject to pswrap.

                icon begin      % Gets and execs the user object
                                % which is a dictionary, begins it.
                                % Note that there is an implicit
                                % execuserobject here since icon
                                % was declared 'userobject'.

                gsave
                icon_x icon_y translate     % Put origin at specified
                                            % coordinates.

                gsave
                icon_prog               % Draw icon.
                grestore

                1 setgray
                icon_font 10 selectfont  % Scale and set icon label font.
                0 0 moveto
                icon_label show          % Show label.
                grestore
                end

            endps
```

C language code:

```
void MakeNewIcon(x, y, prog, label)
  int x, y;
  long prog;   /* user object defined by application code */
  char *label;
{
  /* get a new user object index */
  long icon = DPSNewUserObjectIndex( );
  char *defaultFontName = GetDefaultFontName( );

  /* Icon is a user object index: define icon user object */
  NewIcon(icon, x, y, prog, defaultFontName, label);
  /* Icon is now a user object: draw it */
  DrawIcon(icon);
  /* The following procedure call is not defined
   * in this example. It saves the user object created for
   * the new icon so that the application can use the user
   * object to refer to the icon. */
  SaveNewIconObject(icon);
}
```

3.3.6 Errors and Error Codes

Two classes of errors can occur while using Display PostScript: protocol errors and context errors.

Protocol errors are generated when invalid requests are sent to the server. The result of receiving a protocol error is that lower-level facilities in Xlib handle the error and perhaps print a message, while the higher-level facilities simply return *NULL* or do nothing. The default protocol error handler prints an error message and causes the application to exit. The application can substitute its own error handler for protocol errors, but results are undefined if the handler returns rather than exiting. (Generally, an attempt to continue processing after a protocol error results in incorrect operation of procedures further up in the call stack.)

Context errors can arise whenever a *DPSContext* handle is passed to a Display PostScript procedure or wrap. X-specific error codes are discussed in "Extended Error Codes" in section 6.1, "Data Structures." See *Client Library Reference Manual* for a discussion of the standard Display PostScript error codes.

Because of various delays related to buffering and scheduling, a PostScript language error may be reported long after the C procedure responsible for the error has returned. Consider the following example:

```
DPSPrintf(ctxt, "%d %d %s\n", x, y, operatorName);
MyWrap1(ctxt);
MyWrap2(ctxt, &result);
```

Suppose the string pointed to by *operatorName* does not contain a valid operator and therefore generates an **undefined** error. The error may not be received when **DPSPrintf** returns. It may not be received even when **MyWrap1** returns. **MyWrap2** returns a result, thereby forcing synchronization, so any errors caused by the call to **DPSPrintf** or **MyWrap1** will finally be received.

If **MyWrap2** is called several statements after **MyWrap1**, it may be difficult to figure out where the error originated. However, you can determine where errors are likely to collect, such as places where the application and context will be forced into synchronization, and work backward from there. If you make a list of synchronization points in your code, say, A, B, C, D, and so on, an error received at point C must have been generated by code somewhere between B and C. This will help narrow down your debugging search.

A debugging alternative is to have the application check for an error by forcing synchronization. (The synchronization should be removed in the final version of the software because of its negative impact on performance.) For the details of implementing synchronization, see section 6.4 in *Client Library Reference Manual*.

The code in Example 2 has been simplified to make the principle clear; in an actual application, you would probably want to choose a less verbose means of including the debugging procedures. Every procedure call that sends PostScript language code is followed by a call to *DEBUG_SYNC*. If the macro *DEBUGGING* is *true*, *DEBUG_SYNC* will force the context to be synchronized; if there are any errors, they will be reported. If *DEBUGGING* is *false*, *DEBUG_SYNC* will do nothing. Note that although a call to *DEBUG_SYNC* after the call to **MyWrap2** would be harmless, it is not needed because **MyWrap2** returns a value and is therefore automatically synchronized.

Example 2 *Debugging by forcing synchronization*

C language code:

```
#ifdef DEBUGGING
#define DEBUG_SYNC(c) DPSWaitContext((c))
#else
#define DEBUG_SYNC(c)
#endif
```

```
      ...
    DPSPrintf(ctxt, "%d %d %s\n", x, y, operatorName);
    DEBUG_SYNC(ctxt);
    MyWrap1(ctxt);
    DEBUG_SYNC(ctxt);
    MyWrap2(ctxt, &result);
```

3.3.7 Termination

When an application exits normally, all resources allocated on its
behalf, including contexts and spaces, are automatically freed. (This
actually depends upon the "close-down mode" of the server.) This is the
most typical and convenient method of releasing resources. However,
any storage allocated in shared VM (such as fonts loaded by the
application) remains allocated even after the application exits.

DPSDestroyContext and **DPSDestroySpace** are provided to allow an
application to release these resources without exiting. This might be
needed if, for example, the context and space must be destroyed and
recreated from scratch to recover from a PostScript language error.
These procedures are described in detail in *Client Library Reference
Manual*. To summarize, **DPSDestroyContext** destroys the context
resource in the server and the *DPSContextRec* in the client.
DPSDestroySpace destroys the space resource in the server and the
DPSSpaceRec in the client as well as all contexts within the space,
including their *DPSContextRec* records.

Note that closing the display—with **XCloseDisplay**, for example—
destroys all context and space resources associated with that display, but
does not destroy the corresponding client data structures
(*DPSContextRec* or *DPSSpaceRec*).

3.4 Status Events

At any given time, a context has a specific execution status. Status
events are provided for low level monitoring of context status. Most
simple applications won't need this facility.

Status events can be used to perform the following tasks:

- Sending code, using flow control, from the application to a context.

- Controlling the suspension and resumption of execution.

- Synchronizing PostScript interpreter execution with X rendering requests.

- Monitoring a context to determine whether it is runaway, "wedged" (stuck), or zombie.

A status event is generated whenever a context changes from one state to another. Status events can be masked in the server so that uninteresting events are not sent to the client (see **XDPSSetStatusMask**). Furthermore, the application will not see any status events unless it registers a status event handler by calling **XDPSRegisterStatusProc**. The default is to have no status events enabled and no status event handler registered.

The procedure **XDPSGetContextStatus** returns the current status of a context (as a synchronous reply to a request, not as an asynchronous event). The status of a context may be one of the following states:

- *PSSTATUSERROR*. The context is in a state that is not described by the other four status values. For example, a context that has been created but has never been scheduled to execute will return *PSSTATUSERROR* to **XDPSGetContextStatus**. No asynchronous status event will have this value.

- *PSRUNNING*. The context has been running, has code to execute, or is capable of being run. Fine point: No context is running while the server processes requests or generates events, so this value really means that the context is runnable.

- *PSNEEDSINPUT*. The context is waiting for code to execute, a condition commonly known as being "blocked on input."

- *PSFROZEN*. The execution of the context has been suspended by the **clientsync** operator. A frozen context may be killed with **DPSDestroyContext**, interrupted with **DPSInterruptContext**, or reactivated with **XDPSUnfreezeContext**.

- *PSZOMBIE*. The context is dead. The resource data allocated for the context still exists in the server, but the PostScript interpreter no longer recognizes the context.

Except for *PSSTATUSERROR*, these status events can be disabled (see below).

If an application requires information about one or more types of status events, a handler of type *XDPSStatusProc* must be defined. Two arguments will be passed to the callback procedure: the *DPSContext* handle for the context that generated the status event and a code specifying the status event type. The **XDPSRegisterStatusProc** procedure associates a status event handler with a particular *DPSContext*. Each context may have a different handler.

Once a status event handler is established for the context, the application should set the status event masks for the context by calling **XDPSSetStatusMask**. The symbols for the mask values are

- *PSRUNNINGMASK*

- *PSNEEDSINPUTMASK*

- *PSZOMBIEMASK*

- *PSFROZENMASK*

A mask is constructed by applying a logical OR of the mask values to the appropriate mask; for example,

```
enableMask = PSRUNNINGMASK | PSNEEDSINPUTMASK;
```

sets the bits that indicate interest in the *PSRUNNING* and *PSNEEDSINPUT* status event types. A 1-bit means interest in that type; a 0-bit means "no change" or "don't care."

The context can handle a given status event type in one of three ways:

- If the application wants to be notified of the event every time it occurs, the event should be enabled.

- If the application wants never to be notified of the event, the event should be disabled.

- If the application wants to be notified of only the next occurrence of the event, the event should be set to *next*.

Caution: *Because the Display PostScript extension executes asynchronously from the application, careful synchronization must take place when requesting the next occurrence of an event or future occurrences of the event. Without this synchronization, the event that the application is looking for may have already occurred and been discarded.*

The application defines the method of handling each status event type by setting bits in three masks: *enableMask*, *disableMask*, and *nextMask*.

Call **XDPSSetStatusMask** to set the masks. Note that a particular bit may be set in only one mask. Bits set in the *nextMask* enable the events of that type. When the context changes state, an event is generated. If its type is specified in the *nextMask*, the application is notified of the event and all subsequent events of that type are automatically disabled.

In Example 3, an application currently has *PSNEEDSINPUT* and *PSRUNNING* enabled and all other types disabled. It now asks to be notified of every transition to *PSFROZEN* and *PSZOMBIE* and only the next transition to *PSNEEDSINPUT*. The masks would be constructed as follows:

Example 3 *Constructing masks*

C language code:

```
enableMask = PSFROZENMASK | PSZOMBIEMASK;
disableMask = PSRUNNINGMASK;
nextMask = PSNEEDSINPUTMASK;

XDPSSetStatusMask(ctxt, enableMask, disableMask, nextMask);
```

Even though the previous setting for *PSNEEDSINPUT* was enabled, *PSNEEDSINPUT* need not be disabled in order to change the treatment of this event to "next only."

See section 4.8, "Synchronization," for details on how the *PSFROZEN* status event can be used.

3.4.1 Event Dispatching

The Client Library is responsible for handling events from the Display PostScript X extension. In addition to the status events described in the previous section, the library handles output events that send wrap return values and PostScript language output back to the application.

The Client Library usually dispatches events from the Display PostScript extension in a wire-to-event converter (a procedure that Xlib calls to format event data from the X server). The events do not appear in the normal X event stream. This can cause problems with certain software libraries—for example, the R4 Xt library—that assume that **XNextEvent** will not block if its connection has data available to be read. If you use one of these libraries and the library calls **XNextEvent**, that call does not return until there is an actual X event to dispatch. Since the events the

Display PostScript extension sends do not appear on the normal X event stream, your application may hang until the user does something to generate an event.

Further, event handlers that are invoked using this internal dispatching scheme (described in the previous paragraph) cannot call X or Display PostScript procedures, since Xlib is not reentrant at this level. In that case, the event handler must either queue a task to be done outside the handler or must set a flag. The resulting program logic is often complex.

An alternative to internal event dispatching is pass-through event dispatching. Here, the Client Library causes the events to appear in the normal X event stream. The application is then responsible for dispatching the events by calling **XDPSDispatchEvent**.

To change or query how the Client Library delivers events, an application can call **XDPSSetEventDelivery**. **XDPSSetEventDelivery** allows an application to choose between the default, internal event dispatching, and pass-through event dispatching.

Applications that use pass-through event delivery can call **XDPSIsDPSEvent**, **XDPSIsStatusEvent**, and **XDPSIsOutputEvent** to identify events from the Display PostScript extension. Alternatively, they can pass all events to **XDPSDispatchEvent** and let **XDPSDispatchEvent** identify the extension events.

Pass-through event dispatching is strongly recommended for the following types of applications:

- Applications that use the X Toolkit (Including OSF/Motif applications)

- Applications that handle status events

- Applications that handle text messages from the Display PostScript extension by displaying them in a window

When using pass-through event delivery, you *must* pass all output events to **XDPSDispatchEvent**. Status events may be passed to **XDPSDispatchEvent**, or they may be handled in place. **XDPSDispatchEvent** passes any status events to the status event handler for the event's context. If the application wants to handle events in place, it can call **XDPSIsStatusEvent**, which identifies an event as a status event and extracts the status information from it. The application can then process the information directly.

Applications that use pass-through event delivery must not use **XtAppProcessEvent** to handle X events; **XtAppProcessEvent** ignores the extension events. It is safe to call **XtAppProcessEvent** with a mask of *XtIMTimer* or *XtIMAlternateInput*, but it is unsafe to call it with a mask of *XtIMXEvent* or *XtIMAll*.

Always call **XDPSDispatchEvent** before calling **XtDispatchEvent**. In the MIT release of the X Window System, a bug in the implementation of **XtDispatchEvent** may cause a core dump when an extension event is passed. The Xt main loop for this case is shown in Example 4.

Example 4 *Calling XtDispatchEvent*

C language code:

```
while (1) {
   XEvent event;
   XtAppNextEvent(app, &event);
   if (!XDPSDispatchEvent(&event) &&
         !XtDispatchEvent(&event)) {
     /* Handle undispatched event */
   }
}
```

The call

```
XDPSIsDPSEvent(&event)
```

is equivalent to

```
(XDPSIsStatusEvent(&event, NULL, NULL) ||
     XDPSIsOutputEvent (&event))
```

The call

```
XDPSDispatchEvent(&event)
```

is equivalent to

```
if (XDPSIsStatusEvent(&event, NULL, NULL)) {
   <Call status event handler>
   return True;
} else if (XDPSIsOutputEvent(&event)) {
   <call output event handler>
   return True;
} else return False;
```

3.4.2 Wrap Considerations

When an application calls a wrap that returns a value, the Client Library must wait for the results. During this wait, the Client Library dispatches any status and output events to the appropriate event handler as they arrive, using the current event dispatching mode.

If pass-through event dispatching is used, status event handlers and text procedures are allowed to call wraps that do not return values, Xlib procedures, and Display PostScript procedures other than **DPSWaitContext**. They are not allowed to call **DPSWaitContext** or wraps that return a value; if they do, a *dps_err_recursiveWait* error can occur.

If a status event handler or text procedure is invoked with internal event dispatching, it may not call wraps or any X or Client Library procedures.

If a *dps_err_recursiveWait* error occurs, wraps usually return incorrect values, and further errors may be triggered. Applications that handle their own errors should treat *dps_err_recursiveWait* as a fatal error.

Note: *To avoid occurrences of dps_err_recursiveWait errors, status event handlers and text procedures must not call* **DPSWaitContext** *or wraps that return values.*

4 Additional Facilities

This section describes advanced features of the Display PostScript extension to the X Window System.

4.1 Identifiers

Display PostScript defines two new server resource types: one for contexts and another for spaces. A context or space resource in the server is defined by an X resource ID (XID).

The client has its own representation of contexts and spaces. *DPSContext* is a handle (a pointer) to a *DPSContextRec* allocated in the client's memory. *DPSSpace* is a handle to a *DPSSpaceRec* allocated in the client's memory.

Applications need not use X resource IDs to refer to contexts or spaces. Instead, they can pass the appropriate handle to Client Library procedures.

However, if the resource ID of a context or space is required, there are routines available for translating back and forth between handles and IDs.

- **XDPSXIDFromContext** returns an X resource ID for a given *DPSContext* handle.

- **XDPSXIDFromSpace** returns an X resource ID for a given *DPSSpace* handle.

- **XDPSContextFromXID** returns a *DPSContext* handle, given its X resource ID.

- **XDPSSpaceFromXID** returns a *DPSSpace* handle, given its X resource ID.

The PostScript interpreter uses a unique integer, the *context identifier*, to identify a context. The context identifier is defined by the PostScript language and is completely independent of X resource IDs. The **currentcontext** operator returns the context identifier for the current PostScript context.

Note: *A context created by an existing context with the* **fork** *operator has no identity other than the context identifier returned by the* **fork** *operator; the forked context has neither an X resource ID nor a DPSContext handle. See section 4.5, "Forked Contexts" for more information on forked contexts.*

To get the *DPSContext* handle associated with a particular context identifier, call **XDPSFindContext**. If the client knows about the specified context, a valid *DPSContext* handle is returned; otherwise *NULL* is returned.

There is no direct translation between the PostScript context identifier and the X resource ID.

If a PostScript context terminates (either by request or as the result of an error), the resource allocated for it lingers in the server. The X resource ID for the context is still valid, but the context identifier is not. Such a context is called a zombie. See section 4.2, "Zombie Contexts," for more information.

4.2 Zombie Contexts

A context can die in a number of ways, most commonly as the result of a PostScript language error, such as operand stack underflow or use of an undefined name.

If a context is killed, or dies from an error, its server resource lingers. An X server resource that represents a terminated context is known as a *zombie context*. Requests made to a zombie context will fail. The resource associated with a zombie context can be freed with the **DPSDestroyContext** procedure. Alternatively, the resources will be freed when the *Display* is closed, typically at application exit.

Any request made to a zombie context will generate a status event of type *PSZOMBIE*. See section 3.4, "Status Events," for more information.

4.3 Buffers

As discussed in *Client Library Reference Manual*, buffering is often used to enhance throughput. For the most part, an application need not be concerned with buffering of requests to a context or output from a context. However, facilities are provided to flush buffers if needed.

All Display PostScript requests sent to the server are buffered by Xlib, like any other X requests. **DPSFlushContext** will flush any code or data pending for a context, as well as any X requests that have been buffered. For portability and performance enhancement, use **DPSFlushContext** rather than **XFlush** if the application has sent code or data to a context since the last flush.

Streams created by the PostScript interpreter are buffered, including the input and output streams associated with a PostScript execution context. Buffers are automatically flushed as needed. The automatic flushing is usually sufficient. However, should the application need to flush output from a context, the **flush** operator can be used. Note that wrapped procedures that return results include a **flush** operator at the end of the wrap code.

4.4 Encodings

Client Library Reference Manual discusses the general concept of encodings and conversions. A wrapped procedure always generates a binary object sequence, which is passed to the context for further processing. Typically, the binary object sequence is simply passed to the lowest level of the Client Library to be packaged into a request, without any change to its contents. However, by setting the encoding parameters of the *DPSContextRec* with the **DPSChangeEncoding** procedure, you can convert the binary object sequence to some other encoding before it is sent or written.

Display PostScript supports the conversions shown in Table 2:

Table 2 *Encoding conversions*

Conversion	Description
Binary object sequence to ASCII	This conversion makes a binary object sequence readable by humans. It allows the output of wrapped procedures to be inspected and analyzed. It is also useful for generating page descriptions to be printed. This is the default setting for text contexts. Execution contexts can also be made to convert binary object sequences to ASCII, but there is little purpose in doing so.
Binary object sequence to binary-encoded tokens	Binary-encoded token encoding is the most compact encoding for the PostScript language. This conversion is useful for storing code permanently or for exchanging code with another application. Either a text context or an execution context can perform this conversion, but it is mainly used for text contexts.

Binary object sequence with user name indices to binary object sequence with user name strings

This conversion is necessary if the binary object sequence is going to be stored permanently (for example, on a file) or if the binary object sequence is to be used by another client or with a shared context (see section 4.7, "Sharing Resources"). User name indices are created dynamically and are unique only within a single "instance" of the Client Library—for example, in the application's process address space. In this case, user names must be represented by strings if they are to be used outside the application's process address space.

Binary-encoded tokens to ASCII This conversion allows binary-encoded tokens read from an external data source such as a file to be converted to ASCII for human inspection, sent to an interpreter, or stored in a page description for printing. After the context's encoding has been set using **DPSChangeEncoding**, buffers of binary-encoded tokens can be read and passed to **DPSWritePostScript** for conversion. Either a text context or an execution context can perform this conversion, but it is used mainly for text contexts.

For example, the procedure call below causes a text context to generate binary-encoded tokens:

```
DPSChangeEncoding(textContext, dps_encodedTokens,
    textContext->nameEncoding);
```

The next example causes an execution context to convert user name indices to user name strings:

```
DPSChangeEncoding(context, context->programEncoding,
    dps_strings);
```

4.5 Forked Contexts

The PostScript language allows an existing context to create another context by means of the **fork** operator. However, when a forked context is created, it has no *DPSContext* handle or X resource ID associated with it (see section 4.1, "Identifiers"). This is fine if the application does not need to communicate with the forked context. A context that was forked to do some simple task in the background may terminate without generating any output. If the application does need to communicate with a forked context, both a *DPSContext* handle and an X resource ID must be created for the context.

To create a resource ID and *DPSContext* handle for a forked context, call **DPSContextFromContextID**:

```
DPSContext DPSContextFromContextID(ctxt, cid, textProc,
                                                    errorProc)
    DPSContext ctxt;
    ContextPSID cid;
    DPSTextProc textProc;
    DPSErrorProc errorProc;
```

ctxt specifies the context that created the forked context. In other words, *ctxt* is the context that executed the **fork** operator. *cid* is a *long int* that specifies the PostScript context identifier (not the X resource ID) of the forked context.

textProc and *errorProc* are the usual context output handlers. If *textProc* is *NULL*, the text handler from *ctxt* is used. If *errorProc* is *NULL*, the error handler from *ctxt* is used.

DPSContextFromContextID returns a *DPSContext* handle if *ctxt* and *cid* are valid, otherwise it returns *NULL*.

Note: *Implementation limitations should be kept in mind when using the **fork** operator. A context can consume a significant amount of memory. Furthermore, the total number of contexts that can be created in a server is relatively small—on the order of 50 to 100.*

Caution: *When using forked contexts, plan to use **DPSContextFromContextID** to hook up with them for debugging, even if the eventual use of the forked context does not require that the application communicate with it. If a forked context generates a PostScript language error but there is no resource ID or DPSContext handle associated with it, the application will never see the error.*

Contexts created by **fork** exist until they are killed or joined (using the **join** operator). A context terminated by the **detach** operator, however, goes away as soon as it finishes executing.

4.6   Multiple Servers

An application may create contexts simultaneously on several display devices, each with its own server, at the same time. In these cases, the application must process events from each server to which it is connected.

In order to support access to multiple servers, Display PostScript procedures take a pointer to *Display* records where appropriate.

4.7 Sharing Resources

Execution contexts and spaces can be identified by their X resource identifiers. These identifiers can be passed to other clients to enable sharing of resources.

Caution: *There is no support in the Client Library for maintaining the consistency of shared resources. In general, applications should not share resources because of the complexity of managing them.*

*If an application needs to share execution context information with other clients, the shared VM facility and the mutual exclusion operators provided by the PostScript language (**lock**, **monitor**, and so on) may be adequate for that purpose. See PostScript Language Reference Manual, Second Edition.*

If these facilities are not adequate, the procedures described in this section can be used.

XDPSContextFromSharedID and **XDPSSpaceFromSharedID** are provided to allow a client to communicate with resources created by a different client.

For the most part, a *DPSContext* handle created for a shared resource can be used like any other handle. However, there are some restrictions. The following list, though not exhaustive, presents some of the issues related to sharing resources:

- User names in binary encodings of the PostScript language must be sent as strings. This is because the mapping of user name indices is not guaranteed to be unique across clients. The default *DPSNameEncoding* of the *DPSContextRec* created for a shared context is *dps_string*. It cannot be changed to *dps_indexed*.

- Output from the context, including wrap result values, text, and errors, is sent only to the context's original creator, not to any clients sharing the context. Status events, however, are sent to all clients sharing the context, as specified by the status event mask (see section 3.4, "Status Events").

- When **DPSDestroyContext** or **DPSDestroySpace** is applied to a shared context or space, only the client-side data structures are destroyed. The execution context, the space, and the resources associated with these objects can be destroyed only by the creator.

- If the creator destroys resources, any reference to a destroyed resource will result in a protocol error, which is sent to the client sharing the resource.

It is up to the application that allows resource identifiers to be shared, and the clients sharing those resources, to cooperate and maintain consistency.

4.8 Synchronization

As discussed in "Mixing Display PostScript and X Rendering" in section 3.3, "Execution," X rendering primitives and PostScript language execution may, in most cases, be intermixed freely. However, in some situations PostScript language execution needs to be synchronized with X.

See *Client Library Reference Manual* for a discussion of the general requirements for synchronization. To summarize, you can synchronize either by calling wraps that return results or by calling **DPSWaitContext**. Enforced synchronization is expensive and should be used only when absolutely necessary.

Note: *Synchronizing with the Display PostScript extension also synchronizes with the X server; there is no need to call* **XSync** *explicitly. The reverse is not true; calling* **XSync** *does not synchronize with the Display PostScript extension.*

Flushing, however, works both ways: flushing an X connection flushes all contexts on that connection, and flushing a context flushes the X connection of that context.

For example, suppose a previewer application displays a page of text and graphics that is represented by a PostScript language page description in a file. The user interface of the application may require the entire page to be imaged to a pixmap before it is realized on the physical display. The application reads the ASCII-encoded PostScript language code from the file and sends it to the server with the **DPSWritePostScript** procedure. The context executes the code as it is received, and renders to the pixmap.

If the file contains only one page, and the page description is simple, the application knows that the pixmap is complete when it has read to the end of the input file and called **DPSWaitContext**. It may now call **XCopyArea** to copy the pixmap to the application display window.

However, if the file contains more than one page, the application cannot know when the rendering to the pixmap is complete. If it calls **XCopyArea** too soon, the context may not have finished drawing. As a result, an incomplete image will be displayed on the screen.

There are two main strategies for handling situations such as the one described above: waiting and freezing. The first is applicable if the application has sufficient knowledge of the content of the PostScript language code to know where the beginning and the end are located. The second is used only if the application has no reliable knowledge of the code content.

4.8.1   Waiting

Causing the context to wait is appropriate when the PostScript language code to be executed has a known structure. This is true in either of the following circumstances:

- The application has complete control of the code to be executed. That is, it uses wrapped procedures, single-operator procedures, or dynamically generated code fragments such as user path descriptions. No code comes from external sources such as end-user input.

- The application reads external files with a known structure that can be parsed and understood, such as PostScript language page descriptions that are compliant with Adobe's Document Structuring Conventions.

Most applications that require synchronization fall into one of the two categories described above. In both cases, the application knows exactly how much PostScript language code needs to be sent for a complete display. In these cases, the application sends the code and then forces all code to be executed, either with **DPSWaitContext** or as a side effect of calling a wrap that returns a value. When either of these procedures returns, the application knows that all rendering is done and that other X requests can now be sent.

4.8.2   Freezing

Freezing a context is appropriate if the application cannot determine the completeness of the PostScript language code to be executed. This can happen if an end user is allowed to enter arbitrary PostScript language programs (for instance, in an interactive interpreter executive) or if an input file lacks a well-defined structure.

In this case, the input must contain an executable name that the application has defined. For example, the **showpage** operator terminates each page in a page description file. The application can take advantage of this by defining **showpage** to execute an operator that will notify the application that the page is done. The **clientsync** operator fulfils this function:

```
/old_showpage /showpage load def
/showpage {old_showpage clientsync} bind def
```

When **clientsync** is executed, the context is put into the *PSFROZEN* state, and a *PSFROZEN* event is generated. The application must have enabled the *PSFROZEN* event and registered a handler for that context; see section 3.4, "Status Events" for more information on status events. The handler may then set a flag indicating that the image in the pixmap is complete. The next time the application goes around its main loop, it can test the flag and call **XCopyArea**.

A frozen context can still receive interrupts. **DPSInterruptContext** will interrupt a context whether it is frozen or not.

5 Programming Tips

This section contains tips to help you program applications that use the Display PostScript system extension to the X Window System.

5.1 Avoid XIfEvent

If your application uses internal event dispatching as described in section 3.4, it should not use **XIfEvent**. This routine will cause events that were generated and queued by an execution context to be processed repeatedly (once for each call to **XIfEvent**) without being dequeued. This may result in wrap results or text output being erroneously duplicated or may cause false status events to be reported. Use **XCheckIfEvent** instead.

This restriction does not apply to applications using pass-through event dispatching and may not apply to future implementations of Xlib.

Caution: *If your toolkit uses **XIfEvent**, you may see the erroneous effects described above even though your application does not use **XIfEvent** directly.*

5.2 Include Files

Include the *<DPS/dpsXclient.h>* header file when compiling Display PostScript applications. This header file includes the required header files (*dpsclient.h* and *dpsfriends.h*) described in sections 9 and 11 of *Client Library Reference Manual*.

Include *<DPS/dpsops.h>* if your application uses single-operator procedures with explicit contexts.

Include *<DPS/psops.h>* if your application uses single-operator procedures with implicit contexts.

Include *<DPS/dpsexcept.h>* if your application uses exception handling as defined in *Client Library Reference Manual*.

5.3 Use Pass-Through Event Dispatching

Use **XDPSSetEventDelivery** as described in section 3.4 to set pass-through event dispatching for your application's contexts. Pass-through event dispatching has many advantages:

- Your application can make X and Display PostScript calls in its text and status event handlers. For example, writing a text handler that displays the text in a window is easy. In contrast, internal event dispatching would require the text handler to queue up the display task and leave its execution to the main application.

- Your application avoids potential delays from toolkits that do not expect events to be dispatched internally.

- Your application can handle status events directly rather than having a status event handler that sets flags for the main application to test.

Note: *Here are two important things to remember when using pass-through event dispatching in X Toolkit applications:*

- Always call **XDPSDispatchEvent** before calling **XtDispatchEvent**.

- Never use **XtAppProcessEvent** to handle X events.

5.4 Be Careful With Exception Handling

The exception handling facilities described in Appendix B of *Client Library Reference Manual* can be used in X programs, but you must be very careful not to jump through any Xlib or X Toolkit procedures. The internal state of the libraries may become corrupted. Here are some examples of uses that *not* safe:

- Do not raise an exception in any X Toolkit callback procedure.

- Do not raise an exception in the predicate procedure to **XIfEvent** or any of the related event handling procedures.

- Do not raise an exception in an event handler or text procedure unless you are using pass-through event dispatching.

- Do not raise an exception in an error handler.

5.5 Coordinate Conversions

The code examples in this section demonstrate an efficient method of doing coordinate conversions. (For an introduction to coordinate system issues, see "Coordinate Systems" in section 3.3, "Execution.")

At initialization, and immediately after any user space transformation has been performed (for example, after **scale**, **rotate**, or **setmatrix**), the application should execute PostScript language code to get the CTM (current transformation matrix), the inverse of the CTM, and the current origin offset. The wrap shown in Example 5 will return these values:

Example 5 *Getting CTM, inverse CTM, and current origin offset*

Wrap definition:
```
defineps PSWGetTransform(DPSContext ctxt | float ctm[6],
                         invctm[6]; int *xOffset, *yOffset)
   matrix currentmatrix dup ctm
   matrix invertmatrix invctm
   currentXoffset yOffset xOffset
endps
```

Call the **PSWGetTransform** wrap as necessary, saving the return values in storage associated with the window:

Example 6 *Calling PSWGetTransform*

C language code:
```
DPSContext ctxt;
float ctm[6], invctm[6];
int xOffset, yOffset;

PSWGetTransform(ctxt, ctm, invctm, &xOffset, &yOffset);
```

To convert an X coordinate into a user space coordinate, perform the calculations shown in Example 7.

Example 7 *Converting an X coordinate to user space*

C language code:
```
#define A_COEFF 0
#define B_COEFF 1
#define C_COEFF 2
#define D_COEFF 3
#define TX_CONS 4
#define TY_CONS 5

int x, y;               /* X coordinate */
float ux, uy;           /* user space coordinate */

x -= xOffset;
```

```
y -= yOffset;
ux = invctm[A_COEFF] * x + invctm[C_COEFF] * y +
                                    invctm[TX_CONS];
uy = invctm[B_COEFF] * x + invctm[D_COEFF] * y +
                                    invctm[TY_CONS];
```

To convert a user space coordinate into an X coordinate, perform the calculations shown in Example 8.

Example 8 *Converting a user space coordinate to an X coordinate*

C language code:

```
x = ctm[A_COEFF] * ux + ctm[C_COEFF] * uy + ctm[TX_CONS] +
                                    xOffset;

y = ctm[B_COEFF] * ux + ctm[D_COEFF] * uy + ctm[TY_CONS] +
                                    yOffset;
```

The equations listed above have the following limitations:

- X coordinates must be positive. Otherwise, use the **floor** function to avoid the implicit truncation that happens when floating-point values are assigned to integers.

- Beware of round-off errors. Incorrect coordinates may be computed in either direction.

5.6 Fonts

The **filenameforall** operator can be used to obtain a list of the fonts available to the server. See *PostScript Language Reference Manual, Second Edition*, for a description of **filenameforall**. Use the pattern
   (%font%*)
to generate a list of fonts. The font file names may be sent back as ASCII text and processed with a customized text handler, or they may be stored in an array and then accessed one at a time by calling a wrapped procedure.

Outline fonts are resources. As with any other resource, there's no guarantee that a given font will be present on any particular server. The application must be written to deal with a **findfont** or **selectfont** operator that fails because it can't find the font. It is possible to redefine

findfont and **selectfont** so that they substitute some default font when the requested font is not available. Indeed, the default definition of **findfont** in a given environment may already do this.

5.7 Portability Issues

The Display PostScript extension enhances the portability of X applications by providing flexibility with respect to color, resolution, and fonts.

5.7.1 Color

Use PostScript operators such as **setrgbcolor** rather than X primitives to draw with color. The PostScript interpreter will provide the best rendering possible for the device. The Display PostScript system can produce a variety of halftone patterns representing gray values or colors, so that one color can be seen against the background of another color even on a monochrome device. Contrast this with the rendering facilities of the X Window System, where a request for any color other than white on a monochrome device will give you black.

Display PostScript color rendering is device independent. Here's how Display PostScript handles color requests:

- On a monochrome device, you'll get a dithered (halftone) pattern of black and white pixels. For example, if you ask for red by specifying *1 0 0 setrgbcolor* you'll get some halftone gray pattern composed of black and white pixels; this pattern will be distinct from other "colors."

- On a grayscale device, you'll get a halftone pattern using gray levels; this offers greater distinction among "colors."

- On a color device (4-plane, 8-plane, and so on), you'll get the requested color if it's one of those predefined for the context; otherwise you'll get a dithered pattern of RGB pixels that approximates the color.

- If you've allocated solid colors beyond those predefined for the context, you'll get a nondithered color just as you would with X (subject to the same restrictions).

- A color request will never simply fail.

X Window System color rendering, on the other hand, is device dependent:

- On a monochrome device, a request for any color will give you black. There's no way to differentiate between "pink" and "olive green," as there is with PostScript language color rendering.

- On a color device, you'll get the color you requested only if there's space in the colormap or the device is a TrueColor device.

- A color request can fail, and there's no recourse except to try requesting a different color.

5.7.2 Resolution

The Display PostScript extension offers you device independence with respect to resolution.

In Display PostScript, positions and extents are specified with resolution-independent units such as points. An inch is always an inch. Window elements will always have the same absolute size, regardless of the device.

In the X Window System, positions and extents are specified in units of pixels. The size of a pixel depends on the device. One inch may be 75 pixels on one display and 100 pixels on another display. This causes strange distortions of size when creating windows on various display devices.

5.7.3 Fonts

In the X Window System, you can't rely on the availability of a given point size/typeface combination. If you request 9-point Helvetica*, for example, and that point size is not available, you must make another request.

The Display PostScript extension gives you added flexibility with respect to fonts:

- You can have any point size as long as the typeface is present. If you request a size that's not available, Display PostScript generates it for you.

- The typeface can be rendered in any rotation or two-dimensional transformation.

5.8 Using Custom Operators

After the execution of a **setXgcdrawable**, **setXgcdrawablecolor**, or **setXoffset** operator, the following graphics state parameters are left in an indeterminate state:

- The current transformation matrix

- The clipping path

- The transfer function

Each of the parameters will either keep its previous value or be restored to its initial value, but it is not always possible to predict which. To return the parameters to a known state, follow one of the following techniques:

- Reset the parameters to their initial values after executing **setXgcdrawable**, **setXgcdrawablecolor**, or **setXoffset** by executing the following PostScript language code:

Example 9 *Resetting clipping path, transfer function, and CTM*

PostScript language code:

```
initmatrix
initclip
gsave initgraphics currenttransfer grestore settransfer
```

- Retain the previous values of the parameters by surrounding the use of **setXgcdrawable**, **setXgcdrawablecolor**, or **setXoffset** with the following PostScript language code:

Example 10 *Retaining previous values of clipping path, transfer function, and CTM*

PostScript language code:

```
matrix currentmatrix
clippath
currenttransfer
%
% use of setXgcdrawable,
% setXgcdrawablecolor, or setXoffset
%
settransfer
initclip clip
setmatrix
```

Note that the second method changes the current path; maintaining both the current path and the clipping path is complex and rarely necessary. Retaining the graphics state parameter values may lead to unexpected results when the application switches among drawables on different screens or different visuals, and is not recommended in this case.

You may mix the two techniques for different graphics state parameters. For example, to reset the clipping path and transfer function but keep the current transformation matrix, execute the following PostScript language code:

Example 11 *Resetting clipping path and transfer function while keeping CTM*

PostScript language code:

```
matrix currentmatrix
%
% use of setXgcdrawable, setXgcdrawablecolor, or setXoffset
%
setmatrix
initclip
gsave initgraphics currenttransfer grestore settransfer
```

If you know that one of the parameters has not been changed from its initial value, you can safely ignore that parameter. For example, if you do not change the transfer function, it will be left in its initial state after you execute **setXgcdrawable**, **setXgcdrawablecolor**, or **setXoffset**— either because the initial value has been reestablished, or because it has been inherited.

For performance reasons, you should execute **setXgcdrawable**, **setXgcdrawablecolor**, and **setXoffset** as infrequently as possible. It is more efficient to capture a particular graphics state configuration as a gstate object and use **setgstate** to return to it than to use **setXgcdrawable**, **setXgcdrawablecolor**, or **setXoffset** to reestablish the configuration each time you need it. In addition, the graphics state indeterminacies described above do not occur when using gstate objects.

5.9 Changing Fields in Graphics Contexts

If you change any fields in a graphics context (GC) that is being used by an execution context, you must ensure correct synchronization with the extension by performing the following steps:

1. Call **DPSWaitContext** for each execution context that is using the GC. This guarantees that all PostScript language code that should execute with the old GC values has completed. You can omit this step if the contexts are already synchronized with the application.

2. Use Xlib calls to change the values in the GC.

3. Call **XFlushGC** for the GC. **XFlushGC** was added to Xlib in X11 Release 5 and is not available in libraries conforming to earlier releases. If necessary, you can define it in your program as shown in Example 12.

Example 12 *Defining XFlushGC*

C language code:

```
#ifndef XlibSpecificationRelease          /* New to X11/R5 */
#include <X11/Xlibint.h>

void    XFlushGC(dpy, gc)
        Display *dpy;
        GC gc;
{
        FlushGC(dpy, gc);
}
#endif /* XlibSpecificationRelease */
```

4. Further PostScript language code now executes with the new values of the GC.

6 X-Specific Data and Procedures

This section describes the system-specific data types and procedures for the Display PostScript extension to X.

6.1 Data Structures

Data structures defined in the *<DPS/dpsXclient.h>* header file are described below.

6.1.1 Extended Error Codes

The following error codes for the X Window System are in addition to those described under *DPSErrorCode* in *Client Library Reference Manual*:

dps_err_invalidAccess   An attempt was made to receive output from a context created by another client. Contexts send their output only to the original creator. If the application tries to get output from a context created by another client—for example, by calling a wrap that returns a result—this error is reported.

dps_err_encodingCheck   An attempt was made to change name or program encoding to unacceptable values. This error can occur when changing name encoding for a context created by another client or a context created in a space that was created by another client. Such contexts must have string name encoding (*dps_strings*).

dps_err_closedDisplay   An attempt was made to send PostScript language code to a context whose display is closed.

dps_err_deadContext   An attempt was made to get output from a zombie context (a context that has died in the server but still has its X resources active).

dps_err_recursiveWait   An event handler called **DPSWaitContext** or a wrap that returns a value; see "Wrap Considerations" on page CLX-25 for more information

6.1.2 Status Event Masks

The status event types supported in Display PostScript are shown in Table 3. The first column shows the status event type that is reported by the server. The second column shows the associated single-bit status mask values that can be combined with logical OR to set a context's status mask. The third column describes the status event.

Table 3 *Status events*

Status Event	Mask ValueStatus	Description
PSRUNNING	PSRUNNINGMASK	Context is runnable.
PSNEEDSINPUT	PSNEEDSINPUTMASK	Context needs input to continue running.
PSZOMBIE	PSZOMBIEMASK	Context is dead, but its X resources remain.
PSFROZEN	PSFROZENMASK	Context was frozen by PostScript language program.
PSSTATUSERROR	—	Could not reply to status request.

For more information on status events, see section 3.4 on page CLX-25.

6.1.3 Types and Global Variables

DPSEventDelivery

```
typedef enum {
    dps_event_pass_through,
    dps_event_internal_dispatch,
    dps_event_query
} DPSEventDelivery;
```

DPSEventDelivery provides the possible options for **XDPSSetEventDelivery**.

This enumeration is not available in early versions of the Client Library.

DPSLastUserObjectIndex

```
long int DPSLastUserObjectIndex;
```

DPSLastUserObjectIndex is a global variable containing the last user object index assigned for this application. This variable should be treated as read-only. For more information about user object indices, see **DPSNewUserObjectIndex** on page CLX-54 and "User Object Indices" on page CLX-12.

XDPSStatusProc

```
typedef void (*XDPSStatusProc)(/*
   DPSContext ctxt,
   int code */);
```

This is a procedure type for defining the callback procedure that handles status events for the client. The procedure will be called with two parameters: the context it was registered with and the status code derived from the event. For more information about status events, see **XDPSRegisterStatusProc** on page CLX-59 and "Status Event Masks" on page CLX-50.

6.2 Procedures

This section contains descriptions of the system-specific procedures in the <*DPS/dpsXclient.h*> header file, listed alphabetically.

DPSChangeEncoding

```
void DPSChangeEncoding(ctxt, newProgEncoding, newNameEncoding)
   DPSContext ctxt;
   DPSProgramEncoding newProgEncoding;
   DPSNameEncoding newNameEncoding;
```

DPSChangeEncoding changes one or both of the context's encoding parameters. Supported conversions are described in Table 2 on page PG-34. See *Client Library Reference Manual* for definitions of *DPSNameEncoding* and *DPSProgramEncoding*.

DPSContextFromContextID

```
DPSContext DPSContextFromContextID(ctxt, cid, textProc,
         errorProc)
   DPSContext ctxt;
   ContextPSID cid;
   DPSTextProc textProc;
   DPSErrorProc errorProc;
```

DPSContextFromContextID creates a *DPSContextRec* and returns a *DPSContext* handle for a forked context; it returns *NULL* if it is unable to create these data structures.

The application must call this procedure before attempting to communicate with a forked context. **DPSContextFromContextID** creates the client-side data structures for the context and associates them with the server-side structures previously created by the **fork** operator. *cid* is the context identifier (of type *long int*) that is assigned to the forked context by the PostScript interpreter. *ctxt* is the handle of the context that created the forked context; its *DPSContextRec* will be used as a model for the *DPSContextRec* of the forked context, as described below.

If a *DPSContextRec* has already been created for *cid*, its handle is returned by **DPSContextFromContextID**. Otherwise, a new context record is created according to the following rules:

- If supplied, the *textProc* and *errorProc* arguments are used for the forked context.

- If *textProc* or *errorProc* are *NULL*, the missing values are copied from the *DPSContextRec* of *ctxt*.

- The chaining pointers for the forked context are set to *NULL*.

- All other fields in the new *DPSContextRec* are copied from *ctxt*.

DPSCreateTextContext

```
DPSContext DPSCreateTextContext(textProc, errorProc)
    DPSTextProc textProc;
    DPSErrorProc errorProc;
```

DPSCreateTextContext creates a text context and returns its *DPSContext* handle. When this handle is passed as the argument to a Client Library procedure, all input to the context is passed to *textProc*. If the input is PostScript language in a binary encoding, the input is converted to ASCII encoding before being passed to *textProc*. *errorProc* is used to report any errors (such as *dps_err_nameTooLong*) resulting from converting binary encodings to ASCII encoding. *textProc* is responsible for dealing with errors resulting from handling the text, such as file system or I/O errors.

DPSDefaultTextBackstop

```
void DPSDefaultTextBackstop(ctxt, buf, count)
    DPSContext ctxt;
    char *buf;
    unsigned count;
```

DPSDefaultTextBackstop is the text backstop procedure automatically installed by Display PostScript. Since it is of type *DPSTextProc*, you may use it as your context *textProc*. The text backstop procedure writes text to *stdout* and flushes *stdout*.

DPSDestroyContext

```
void DPSDestroyContext(ctxt)
    DPSContext ctxt;
```

DPSDestroyContext is as defined in *Client Library Reference Manual*, except as it pertains to shared contexts.

Both the client and the server are affected by this procedure. On the client side, **DPSDestroyContext** destroys the *DPSContextRec*. On the server side, it destroys the PostScript execution context and the X resource associated with it. After a call to **DPSDestroyContext**, the *DPSContext* handle for *ctxt* is no longer valid.

If the context is a shared context (that is, a *DPSContextRec* allocated for a context created by another client), only the *DPSContextRec* is destroyed; the interpreter context and resource are unchanged.

For text contexts, **DPSDestroyContext** destroys the *DPSContextRec*.

DPSDestroySpace

```
void DPSDestroySpace(spc)
    DPSSpace spc;
```

DPSDestroySpace is as defined in *Client Library Reference Manual* except for shared spaces.

For spaces created by the client, this procedure destroys the space and the X resource associated with it. PostScript execution contexts that use this space are also destroyed, along with their X resources and *DPSContextRec* records. Finally, the *DPSSpaceRec* is destroyed.

If the space is a shared space (a *DPSSpaceRec* allocated by another client), the space and the X resource are not destroyed. Only the *DPSSpaceRec* is destroyed, along with any *DPSContextRec* records for contexts associated with this space. See section 4.7 on page CLX-37 for a discussion of shared resources.

If the client that created the space destroys it and there are other clients sharing it, the space is destroyed and the sharing clients will experience unpredictable results.

DPSNewUserObjectIndex

```
long int DPSNewUserObjectIndex( );
```

DPSNewUserObjectIndex returns a new user object index. The Client Library is the sole allocator of new user object indices. The application should not attempt to compute them from a previously obtained index. Because user object indices are dynamic, they should not be used as numeric values for computation or saved in long-term storage such as a file. See "User Object Indices" on page CLX-20 for more information.

XDPSContextFromSharedID DPSContext XDPSContextFromSharedID(dpy, cid, textProc,
                errorProc)
       Display *dpy;
       ContextPSID cid;
       DPSTextProc textProc;
       DPSErrorProc errorProc;

XDPSContextFromSharedID creates a *DPSContextRec* for a context that was
created by another client.

cid specifies the context. (*cid* is the context identifier assigned by the PostScript
interpreter, not the X resource ID.) *dpy* is the *Display* that both clients are
connected to. *textProc* and *errorProc* are the context text and error handlers for
the shared context. For information on sharing resources, see section 4.7 on
page CLX-37.

XDPSContextFromXID DPSContext XDPSContextFromXID(dpy, xid)
       Display *dpy;
       XID xid;

XDPSContextFromXID gets the context record for the given X resource ID on
dpy. It returns *NULL* if *xid* is not valid.

XDPSCreateContext DPSContext XDPSCreateContext(dpy, drawable, gc, x, y,
                eventmask,grayramp, ccube, actual,
                extProc, errorProc, space)
       Display *dpy;
       Drawable drawable;
       GC gc;
       int x;
       int y;
       unsigned int eventmask;
       XStandardColormap *grayramp;
       XStandardColormap *ccube;
       int actual;
       DPSTextProc textProc;
       DPSErrorProc errorProc;
       DPSSpace space;

XDPSCreateContext creates a context with a customized colormap; it returns
NULL if there is any error.

dpy, drawable, gc, x, y, textProc, errorProc, and *space* are the same as for
XDPSCreateSimpleContext. *eventmask* is reserved for future extensions and
should be passed as zero.

The colormap specified in *grayramp* and *ccube* must contain a range of uniformly distributed colors. *grayramp* specifies the factors needed to compute a pixel value for a particular gray level. *grayramp* is required. *ccube* specifies the factors needed to compute a pixel value for a particular RGB color. *ccube* is optional; if it is passed as *NULL*, rendering will be done in shades of gray. The colormap specified in *ccube* must be the same as the one specified in *grayramp*. *actual* specifies the upper limit of the number of additional RGB colors the application plans to request, beyond those specified in *ccube* and *grayramp*.

The following restrictions apply:

- *drawable* and *gc* must be on the same screen.

- *drawable* and *gc* must have the same depth *Visual*.

- If the *drawable* is a *Window*, any colormaps specified must have the same *Visual*.

- *grayramp* must be specified; *ccube* is optional; both must be valid.

See section 3.2, "Creating a Context," for additional information.

XDPSCreateSimpleContext

```
DPSContext XDPSCreateSimpleContext(dpy, drawable, gc, x, y,
        textProc, errorProc, space)
    Display *dpy;
    Drawable drawable;
    GC gc;
    int x;
    int y;
    DPSTextProc textProc;
    DPSErrorProc errorProc;
    DPSSpace space;
```

XDPSCreateSimpleContext creates a context with the default colormap; it returns *NULL* if there is any error.

The procedure creates a context associated with *dpy*, *drawable*, and *gc*.

x and *y* are offsets from the *drawable* origin to the PostScript device space origin in pixels.

textProc points to the procedure that will be called to handle text output from the context. *errorProc* points to the procedure that will be called to handle errors reported by the context. *space* determines the private VM of the new context. A *NULL* space causes a new one to be created.

The following restrictions apply:

- *drawable* and *gc* must be on the same screen.

- *drawable* and *gc* must have the same depth *Visual*.

See section 3.2, "Creating a Context," on page CLX-6 for additional information.

XDPSDispatchEvent

```
Bool XDPSDispatchEvent (event)
    XEvent *event;
```

XDPSDispatchEvent checks whether an event is a Display PostScript event and, if so, dispatches it to the appropriate status or output handler, as follows:

- If the event is not a Display PostScript event, **XDPSDispatchEvent** returns *False* and does nothing else.

- If the event is a Display PostScript event, **XDPSDispatchEvent** determines the context from the event, calls the context's status or output handler, and returns *True*.

This procedure is not available in early versions of the Client Library.

XDPSFindContext

```
DPSContext XDPSFindContext(dpy, cid)
    Display *dpy;
    long int cid;
```

XDPSFindContext returns the *DPSContext* handle of a context given its context identifier, *cid*. It returns *NULL* if the context identifier is invalid.

XDPSGetContextStatus

```
int XDPSGetContextStatus(ctxt)
    DPSContext ctxt;
```

XDPSGetContextStatus returns the status of *ctxt*. This procedure does not alter the mask established for *ctxt* by **XDPSSetStatusMask**. For information on status events, see section 3.4 on page CLX-25 and section 6.1 on page CLX-50.

XDPSGetDefaultColorMaps   void XDPSGetDefaultColorMaps (dpy, screen, drawable,
                        colorcube, grayramp)
                Display *dpy;
                Screen *screen;
                Drawable drawable;
                XStandardColormap *colorcube;
                XStandardColormap *grayramp;

XDPSGetDefaultColorMaps returns the colormaps used in creating a simple
context. The display must be specified.

- If *screen* is *NULL* and *drawable* is *None*, the colormaps are retrieved for the
  default screen of the display.

- If *screen* is *NULL* and *drawable* is not *None*, the colormaps are retrieved for the
  drawable's screen.

- If *screen* is not *NULL*, the colormaps are retrieved for that screen.

Either *colorcube* or *grayramp* may be *NULL*, indicating that the colormap is not
needed.

This procedure is not available in early versions of the Client Library.

XDPSIsDPSEvent   Bool XDPSIsDPSEvent (event)
                XEvent *event;

XDPSIsDPSEvent returns *True* if the event is a Display PostScript event and *False*
otherwise.

This procedure is not available in early versions of the Client Library.

XDPSIsOutputEvent   Bool XDPSIsOutputEvent (event)
                XEvent *event;

XDPSIsOutputEvent returns *True* if *event* is a Display PostScript output event and
False otherwise.

The contents of an output event are not defined. If **XDPSIsOutputEvent** returns
True, the event must be passed to **XDPSDispatchEvent**. If the application does
not pass the event to **XDPSDispatchEvent**, the results are undefined.

This procedure is not available in early versions of the Client Library.

XDPSIsStatusEvent

```
Bool XDPSIsStatusEvent (event, ctxt, status)
    XEvent *event;
    DPSContext *ctxt;
    int *status;
```

XDPSIsStatusEvent returns *True* if *event* is a Display PostScript status event and *False* otherwise. If the event is a status event, *ctxt* and *status* are set to that event's context and status. Either *ctxt* or *status* can be *NULL* if the information is not needed.

The contents of a status event is not defined; the returned context and status values are the only way to extract the information from the event.

This procedure is not available in early versions of the Client Library.

XDPSRegisterStatusProc

```
XDPSStatusProc XDPSRegisterStatusProc(ctxt, proc)
    DPSContext ctxt;
    XDPSStatusProc proc;
```

XDPSRegisterStatusProc registers a status event handler, *proc*, to be called when a status event is received by the client for the context specified by *ctxt*. The status event handler may be called by Xlib any time the client gets events or checks for events.

XDPSStatusProc replaces the previously registered status event handler for the context, if any. *proc* handles only status events generated by *ctxt*; if the application has more than one context, **XDPSRegisterStatusProc** must be called separately for each context.

XDPSRegisterStatusProc returns the old status procedure when a new one is registered.

In early versions of the Client Library, this procedure returns *void*.

XDPSSetEventDelivery

```
DPSEventDelivery XDPSSetEventDelivery (dpy, newMode)
    Display *dpy;
    DPSEventDelivery newMode;
```

An application can call **XDPSSetEventDelivery** to change or query how the Client Library delivers events.

XDPSSetEventDelivery always returns the previous event delivery mode for the specified display.

- If *newMode* is *dps_event_query*, **XDPSSetEventDelivery** does nothing else.

- If *newMode* is *dps_event_internal_dispatch*, the Client Library dispatches events internally without passing them to the application. This is the default value.

- If *newMode* is *dps_event_pass_through*, the Client Library stops dispatching events internally and passes them through to the application as normal X events.

This procedure is not available in early versions of the Client Library.

XDPSSetStatusMask

```
void XDPSSetStatusMask(ctxt, enableMask, disableMask,
        nextMask)
DPSContext ctxt;
unsigned long enableMask, disableMask, nextMask;
```

XDPSSetStatusMask sets the status mask for the context, as follows:

- *enableMask* specifies status events for which continuing notification to the client is requested.

- *disableMask* specifies status events for which the client does not want to be notified.

- *nextMask* specifies status events for which the client wants to be notified of the next occurrence only. Setting *nextMask* is equivalent to setting *enableMask* for a status event and, after being notified of the next occurrence, setting *disableMask* for that event.

A given status event type may be set in only one of the three status masks. If an event is set in more than one mask, a protocol error (*Value*) is generated and the context is left unchanged. For more information on status events, see sections 3.4 and 6.1.

XDPSSpaceFromSharedID

```
DPSSpace XDPSSpaceFromSharedID(dpy, sxid)
Display *dpy;
SpaceXID sxid;
```

XDPSSpaceFromSharedID creates a *DPSSpaceRec* for the space identified by an X resource ID, *sxid*, that was created by another client. *dpy* is the *Display* that both clients are connected to. **XDPSSpaceFromSharedID** returns *NULL* if *sxid* is not valid.

XDPSSpaceFromXID
```
DPSSpace XDPSSpaceFromXID(dpy, xid)
    Display *dpy;
    XID xid;
```

XDPSSpaceFromXID gets the space record for the given X resource ID on *dpy*. It returns *NULL* if *xid* is not valid.

XDPSUnfreezeContext
```
void XDPSUnfreezeContext(ctxt)
    DPSContext ctxt;
```

XDPSUnfreezeContext notifies a context that is in the *PSFROZEN* state to resume execution. Attempting to unfreeze a context that is not frozen has no effect.

XDPSXIDFromContext
```
XID XDPSXIDFromContext(Pdpy, ctxt)
    Display **Pdpy;
    DPSContext ctxt;
```

XDPSXIDFromContext gets the X resource ID for the given context record and returns its *Display* in the location pointed to by *Pdpy*. *Pdpy* is set to *NULL* if *ctxt* is not a valid context.

XDPSXIDFromSpace
```
XID XDPSXIDFromSpace(Pdpy, spc)
    Display **Pdpy;
    DPSSpace spc;
```

XDPSXIDFromSpace gets the X resource ID for the given space record and returns its *Display* in the location pointed to by *Pdpy*. *Pdpy* is set to *NULL* if *spc* is not a valid space.

CLX

7 X-Specific Custom PostScript Operators

This section describes the custom PostScript operators for the Display PostScript system extension to the X Window System. The operators are organized alphabetically by operator name. Each operator description is presented in the following format:

operator
$operand_1$ $operand_2$ ... $operand_n$ **operator** $result_1$ ... $result_m$

Detailed explanation of the operator.

Errors   A list of the errors that this operator might execute.

At the head of an operator description, $operand_1$ through $operand_n$ are the operands that the operator requires, with $operand_n$ being the topmost element on the operand stack. The operator pops these objects from the operand stack and consumes them. After executing, the operator leaves the objects $result_1$ through $result_m$ on the stack, with $result_m$ being the topmost element.

The notation '–' in the operand position indicates that the operator expects no operands; a '–' in the result position indicates that the operator returns no results.

Error conditions include the following:

rangecheck   Invalid match: either the *drawable* and *gc* have different depths or they don't have a *Visual* that matches the colormap associated with the context.

stackunderflow Not enough operands on the operand stack.

typecheck   Invalid X resource ID.

undefined   The device associated with the context is not a display device.

clientsync
– **clientsync** –

The **clientsync** operator synchronizes the application with the current context. **clientsync** notifies the current context to stop executing, sets the context status to *FROZEN*, and causes a *PSFROZEN* status event to be generated. To resume execution, call the **XDPSUnfreezeContext** procedure.

For an example of the use of **clientsync**, see section 4.8.2 on page CLX-39.

currentXgcdrawable   – **currentXgcdrawable** gc drawable x y

The **currentXgcdrawable** operator returns the X *gc*, *drawable*, and offset from the origin of the *drawable* to the device space origin for the current context. Results returned by this operator can be input to **setXgcdrawable**. The returned *gc* is a *GContext* identifier, not a *GC* pointer.

Errors: **undefined**

currentXgcdrawablecolor   – **currentXgcdrawablecolor** gc drawable x y colorinfo

The **currentXgcdrawablecolor** operator is similar to the **currentXgcdrawable** operator, except that it also returns an array of 12 integers describing the color cube, gray ramp, and other color variables used for the context. The returned *gc* is a *GContext* identifier, not a *GC* pointer. The *colorinfo* array, described in Table 4, has the form shown in Example 13.

Example 13 *Form of colorinfo array*

```
[maxgrays graymult firstgray maxred redmult maxgreen
    greenmult maxblue bluemult firstcolor colormap actual]
```

Table 4 *Description of colorinfo array values*

Value	Description
maxgrays	Maximum number of gray values. Equivalent to *red_max* field of *XStandardColormap* for the gray ramp.
graymult	Scale factor to compute gray pixel. Equivalent to *red_mult* field of *XStandardColormap* for the gray ramp.
firstgray	First gray pixel value. Equivalent to *base_pixel* field of *XStandardColormap* for the gray ramp.
maxred	Maximum number of red values. Equivalent to *red_max* field of *XStandardColormap*.
redmult	Scale factor to compute color pixel. Equivalent to *red_mult* field of *XStandardColormap*.
maxgreen	Maximum number of green values. Equivalent to *green_max* field of *XStandardColormap*.

greenmult	Scale factor to compute color pixel. Equivalent to *green_mult* field of *XStandardColormap*.
maxblue	Maximum number of blue values. Equivalent to *blue_max* field of *XStandardColormap*.
bluemult	Scale factor to compute color pixel. Equivalent to *blue_mult* field of *XStandardColormap*.
firstcolor	First color pixel value. Equivalent to *base_pixel* field of *XStandardColormap*.
colormap	The colormap that these pixel values are allocated in.
actual	The upper limit of additional RGB colors, as in the *actual* argument to **XDPSCreateContext**.

Errors: **undefined**

currentXoffset   – **currentXoffset** x y

The **currentXoffset** operator returns the *x* and *y* coordinates representing the offset from the origin of the *drawable* to the device space origin for the current context. This operator returns a subset of the variables returned by **currentXgcdrawable**. Its result values can be input to **setXoffset**.

Errors: **undefined**

setXgcdrawable   gc drawable x y **setXgcdrawable** –

The **setXgcdrawable** operator sets the X *gc*, *drawable*, and offset from the origin of the *drawable* to the device space origin for the current context. The specified values override any existing values.

The *gc* operand is a *GContext* identifier, not a *GC* pointer. Use **XGContextFromGC** to extract a *GContext* from a *GC*.

To temporarily change the values specified for **setXgcdrawable**, execute **gsave** before the operator and follow it with **grestore**.

Errors: **rangecheck, stackunderflow, typecheck, undefined**

setXgcdrawablecolor   gc drawable x y colorinfo **setXgcdrawablecolor** –

The **setXgcdrawablecolor** operator changes *gc*, *drawable*, *offset*, and *colorinfo* for the context. The *colorinfo* argument is described under **currentXgcdrawablecolor**.

The *gc* operand is a *GContext* identifier, not a *GC* pointer. Use **XGContextFromGC** to extract a *GContext* from a *GC*.

To temporarily change the values specified for **setXgcdrawablecolor**, execute **gsave** before the operator and follow it with **grestore**.

Errors: **rangecheck, stackunderflow, typecheck, undefined**

setXoffset   x y **setXoffset** –

The **setXoffset** operator sets the default origin for the user space of the current context. This operator is a subset of **setXgcdrawable**.

Errors: **stackunderflow, undefined**

setXrgbactual   red green blue **setXrgbactual** bool

The **setXrgbactual** operator attempts to allocate a new entry in the context's colormap. It takes three floating-point numbers between 0.0 and 1.0 to specify the RGB color, as with **setrgbcolor**. The operator returns *true* if the color was successfully allocated in the colormap; it returns *false* if the color cannot be allocated or if an error occurs. If the operator returns *true*, future requests for the specified color will be rendered using the allocated colormap entry.

Executing **setXrgbactual** is a way of ensuring that the color you request is actually allocated, not dithered. Colors specified by **setXrgbactual** do not count against the number of *actual* colors that are allocated automatically; see "Using XDPSCreateContext" in section 3.2, "Creating a Context." **setXrgbactual** may be called even if the context was created with *actual* set to zero.

setXrgbactual does not change the graphics state in any way; to paint with the specified color, execute **setrgbcolor**.

Errors: **stackunderflow, typecheck, undefined**

CLX

7.1 Single-Operator Procedures

Client Library Reference Manual explains and lists a number of single-operator procedures in section 9, "Single-Operator Procedures." The X Window System implementation of the Display PostScript system provides some additional procedures for the X-specific PostScript operators.

The procedure declarations listed below can be found in *<DPS/dpsops.h>*. *<DPS/psops.h>* contains the analogous definitions without the *ctxt* argument.

Note: *Some early releases of the Display PostScript system did not include these operators.*

Example 14 *Procedure declarations for X-specific PostScript operators*

C language code:

```
extern void DPSclientsync( /* DPSContext ctxt; */ );
extern void DPScurrentXgcdrawable( /* DPSContext ctxt;
                int *gc, *draw, *x, *y; */ );
extern void DPScurrentXgcdrawablecolor( /* DPSContext ctxt;
                int *gc, *draw, *x, *y, colorInfo[ ]; */ );
extern void DPScurrentXoffset( /* DPSContext ctxt;
                int *x, *y; */ );
extern void DPSsetXgcdrawable( /* DPSContext ctxt;
                int gc, draw, x, y; */ );
extern void DPSsetXgcdrawablecolor( /* DPSContext ctxt;
                int gc, draw, x, y, colorInfo[ ]; */ );
extern void DPSsetXoffset( /* DPSContext ctxt;
                int x, y; */ );
extern void DPSsetXrgbactual( /* DPSContext ctxt;
                float r, g, b; int *success; */ );
```

POSTSCRIPT™
Software From Adobe

The Display PostScript System

Adobe Systems Incorporated

pswrap Reference Manual

pswrap Reference Manual

1 About This Manual

pswrap Reference Manual is a guide to the *pswrap* translator. It tells you how to use *pswrap* to create C-callable procedures that contain PostScript™ language code.

Section 2, "About pswrap," introduces the *pswrap* translator.

Section 3, "Using pswrap," tells you how to run *pswrap*, and documents the options in the *pswrap* command line.

Section 4, "Writing a Wrap," tells you how to write wrap definitions for *pswrap*.

Section 5, "Declaring Input Arguments," tells you how to declare input arguments.

Section 6, "Declaring Output Arguments," tells you how to declare output arguments.

Section 7, "Syntax," explains the syntax used in wrap definitions.

Appendix A lists error messages from the *pswrap* translator.

PSW

2 About pswrap

The *pswrap* translator provides a natural way for an application developer or toolkit implementor to compose a package of C-callable procedures that send PostScript language code to the PostScript interpreter. These C-callable procedures are known as *wrapped procedures* or *wraps*. A *wrap* is a procedure that consists of a C declaration with a PostScript language body. A *wrap body* is the PostScript language program fragment in a wrap.

Here's how *pswrap* fits into the Display PostScript system:

- You write the PostScript language programs required by your application, using the *pswrap* syntax to define a C-callable procedure and specify input and output arguments.

- You run *pswrap* to translate these PostScript language programs into wrapped procedures.

- You compile and link these wraps with the application program.

- When a wrap is called by the application, it sends encoded PostScript language to the PostScript interpreter and receives the values returned by the interpreter.

A *pswrap* source file associates PostScript language code with declarations of C procedures; *pswrap* writes C source code for the declared procedures, in effect wrapping C code around the PostScript language code. Wrapped procedures can take both input and output arguments.

- Input arguments are values a wrap sends to the PostScript interpreter as PostScript objects.

- Output arguments are pointers to variables where the wrap stores values returned by the PostScript interpreter.

Wraps are the most efficient way for an application to communicate with the PostScript interpreter.

3 Using pswrap

The form of the *pswrap* command line (UNIX-specific) is:

```
pswrap [-apr] [-o outputCfile] [-h outputHfile] [-s maxstring]
    [inputFile]
```

where square brackets [ ] indicate optional items.

3.1 Command-Line Options

The *pswrap* command-line options are as follows:

inputFile   A file that contains one or more wrap definitions. *pswrap* transforms the definitions in *inputFile* into C procedure definitions. If no input file is specified, the standard input (which can be redirected from a file or pipe) is used. The input file can include text other than procedure definitions. *pswrap* converts procedure definitions to C procedures and passes the other text through unchanged. Therefore, it is possible to intersperse C-language source code with wrap definitions in the input file.

Note: *Although C code is allowed in a* pswrap *input file, it is not allowed within a wrap body. In particular, no CPP macros (for example, #define) are allowed inside a wrap.*

–a   Generates ANSI C procedure prototypes for procedure declarations in *outputCfile* and, optionally, *outputHfile*. The **–a** option allows compilers that recognize the ANSI C standard to do more complete typechecking of parameters. The **–a** option also causes *pswrap* to generate *const* declarations.

Note: *ANSI C procedure prototype syntax is not recognized by most non-ANSI C compilers, including many compilers based on the Portable C Compiler. Use the –a option only in conjunction with a compiler that conforms to the ANSI C Standard.*

–h *outputHFile*   Generates a header file that contains *extern* declarations for non-static wraps. This file can be used in *#include* statements in modules that use wraps. If the **–a** option is specified, the declarations in the header file are ANSI C procedure prototypes. If the **–h** option is omitted, a header file is not produced.

-o *outputCFile*   Specifies the file to which the generated wraps and passed-through text are written. If omitted, the standard output is used. If the **–a** option is also specified, the procedure declarations generated by *pswrap* are in ANSI C procedure prototype syntax.

–p   Specifies that strings passed by wraps are padded so that each data object begins on a long-word (4-byte) boundary. This option allows wraps to run on architectures that restrict data alignment to 4-byte boundaries and improves performance on some other architectures.

PSW

−r   Generates reentrant code for wraps shared by more than one process (as in shared libraries). Reentrant code can be called recursively or by more than one thread. Wraps generated without this option use local static variables, which can be overwritten by recursive calls or multiple threads. Since those variables need to be reused by reentrant wraps, the −r option causes local automatic variables to be used instead. The −r option causes *pswrap* to generate extra code, use it only when necessary.

−s *maxstring*   Sets the maximum allowable length of a PostScript string object or PostScript hexadecimal string object in the wrap body input. A syntax error is reported if a string is not terminated with) or > within *maxstring* characters. *maxstring* cannot be set lower than 80; the default is 200.

3.2   #line Directives

The C code that *pswrap* generates for wrapped procedures usually contains more lines than the input wrap body, so lines in the output file do not correspond to lines in the input file. This circumstance could make bugs that originate in the wrap body difficult to fix with a source-code debugger because the debugger displays C code from the output wrapped procedures, not PostScript language code from the input file.

pswrap solves the problem by using *#line* directives to record input file line numbers along with output file line numbers in the output file. When you use a C source code debugger, the directives refer the debugger to the correct line from the input file.

Note: *Do not use the standard input and standard output streams as pipes to or from pswrap, because the resulting #line directives will be incomplete. pswrap expects both the input and output files to be named on the command line. If no input file is named, the references to input file line numbers will contain no filename; if the output file is not named, the name of the C source file produced by pswrap will be missing.*

pswrap writes diagnostic output to the standard error if there are errors in the command line or in the input. If *pswrap* encounters errors during processing, it reports the error and exits with a nonzero termination status.

4 Writing a Wrap

Example 1 is a sample wrap definition. It declares the **PSWGrayCircle** procedure, which creates a solid gray circle with a radius of 5.0 centered at (10.0, 10.0).

Example 1 *Sample wrap definition*

Wrap definition:

```
defineps PSWGrayCircle( )
    newpath
    10.0 10.0 5.0 0.0 360.0 arc
    closepath
    0.5 setgray
    fill
endps
```

Procedure call:

```
PSWGrayCircle( );
```

PostScript language code equivalent:

```
newpath
10.0 10.0 5.0 0.0 360.0 arc
closepath
0.5 setgray
fill
```

4.1 The Wrap Definition

Following are the rules for defining a wrapped procedure. Each wrap definition consists of four parts:

- *defineps* begins the definition. It must appear at the beginning of a line without any preceding spaces or tabs.

- *Declaration of the C-callable procedure* is the name of the procedure followed by a list in parentheses of the arguments it takes. The arguments are optional. Parentheses are required even for a procedure without arguments. (Wraps do not return values; they are implicitly declared void.)

- *Wrap body* is a PostScript language program fragment, which is sent to the PostScript interpreter. It includes a series of PostScript operators and operands separated by spaces, tabs, and newline characters.

- *endps* ends the definition. Like *defineps*, *endps* must appear at the beginning of a line.

By default, wrap definitions introduce external (that is, global) names that can be used outside the file in which the definition appears. To introduce private (local) procedures, declare the wrapped procedure as static. For example, the **PSWGrayCircle** wrap in Example 1 can be made static by substituting the following statement for the first line:

```
defineps static PSWGrayCircle( )
```

Note: *It is helpful for the application to give wraps names that identify them as such; for example,* **PSWDrawBox**, **PSWShowTitle**, **PSWDrawSlider**, *and so on.*

4.2 Comments

C comments can appear anywhere outside a wrap definition. PostScript language comments can appear anywhere after the procedure is declared and before the definition ends. *pswrap* strips PostScript language comments from the wrap body. Comments cannot appear within PostScript string objects.

Example 2 *Comments in a wrap*

Wrap definition:
```
/* This is a C comment */
defineps PSWNoComment( )
   (/* This is not a comment */) show
   (% Nor is this.) length
   % This is a PS comment
endps
```

Wraps cannot be used to send PostScript language comments that contain structural information (%% and %!). Use another Client Library facility, such as **DPSWriteData**, to send comments.

4.3   The Wrap Body

pswrap accepts any valid PostScript language code as specified in the *PostScript Language Reference Manual, Second Edition.* If the PostScript language code in a wrap body includes any of the following symbols, the opening and closing marks must balance:

{ } Braces (to delimit a procedure)

[ ] Square brackets (to define an array)

( ) Parentheses (to enclose a string)

< > Angle brackets (to mark a hexadecimal string)

Parentheses within a string body must balance or be quoted with \ according to standard PostScript language syntax.

Note: *pswrap does not check a wrap definition for valid or sensible PostScript language code.*

pswrap attempts to wrap whatever it encounters. Everything between the closing parenthesis of the procedure declaration and the end of the wrap definition is assumed to be an element of the PostScript language unless it is part of a comment or matches one of the wrap arguments.

Note: *pswrap does not support the double slash (//) PostScript language syntax for immediately evaluated names. See the PostScript Language Reference Manual, Second Edition for more information about immediately evaluated names.*

PSW

4.3.1 Execution Considerations

A wrap body executes as if the entire body were enclosed in an extra set of braces and followed by the **exec** operator. In other words, the body is put into an executable array which is then executed. This form of execution places a few restrictions on wrap bodies:

- First, **restore** can be used in only two cases:

  1. If the corresponding **save** is executed in the same wrap

     or

  2. If **restore** is the last thing in the wrap and the wrap does not return any values

  In cases other than these two, the executable array on the operand stack causes an invalidrestore error.

- Second, literal composite objects within the wrap body are actually created before any code in the body is executed. If the wrap body changes virtual memory allocation mode, this change does not affect the literal composite objects. For example, if the current VM allocation mode is false, the wrap in Example 3 produces the output "true", "false".

Example 3 *Nested composite objects in a wrap*

Wrap definition:

```
defineps PSWtestshared( )
   true setshared
   3 string scheck ==
   (abc) scheck ==
endps
```

The string "abc" was actually created before any code was executed, so the change to VM allocation mode does not affect it. The same effect occurs with nested executable array objects (sequences within { } braces).

4.4   Arguments

Argument names in the procedure header are declared using C types. For instance, the following example declares two variables, *x* and *y*, of type *long int*.

```
defineps PSWMyFunc(long int x, y)
```

In addition, the following holds true for arguments:

- There can be an unlimited number of input and output arguments.

- Input arguments must be listed before output arguments in the wrap header.

- Precede the output arguments, if any, with a vertical bar |.

- Separate arguments of the same type with a comma.

- Separate arguments of different types with a semicolon.

- A semicolon is optional before a vertical bar or a right parenthesis; these two examples are equivalent:

```
defineps PSWNewFunc(float x, y; int a | int *i)
defineps PSWNewFunc(float x, y; int a;| int *i;)
```

4.5   Input Arguments

Input arguments describe values that the wrap converts to encoded PostScript objects at runtime. When an element within the wrap body matches an input argument, the value that was passed to the wrap replaces the element in the wrap body. Input arguments represent placeholders for values in the wrap body. They are not PostScript language variables (names). Think of them as macro definitions that are substituted at runtime.

For example, the **PSWGrayCircle** procedure can be made more useful by providing input arguments for the radius and center coordinates, as in Example 4.

Example 4 *Wrap with input arguments*

Wrap definition:

```
defineps PSWGrayCircle(float x, y, radius)
  newpath
  x y radius 0.0 360.0 arc
  closepath
  0.5 setgray
  fill
endps
```

Procedure call:

```
PSWGrayCircle(25.4,17.7, 40.0);
```

PostScript language code equivalent:

```
newpath
25.4 17.7 40.0 0.0 360.0 arc
closepath
0.5 setgray
fill
```

The value of input argument *x* replaces each occurrence of *x* in the wrap body. This version of **PSWGrayCircle** draws a circle of a specified size at a specified location.

4.6   Output Arguments

Output arguments describe values that PostScript operators return. For example, the PostScript operator **currentgray** returns the gray-level setting in the current graphics state. PostScript operators place their return values on the top of the operand stack. To return a value to the application, place the name of the output argument in the wrap body at a time when the desired value is on the top of the operand stack. In Example 5, the wrap gets the value returned by **currentgray**.

Example 5 *Wrap with output arguments*

Wrap definition:

```
defineps PSWGetGray(| float *level)
  currentgray level
endps
```

Procedure call:

```
float aLevel;
PSWGetGray(&aLevel);
```

PostScript language code equivalent:

```
currentgray
% Pop current gray level off operand stack
% and store in aLevel.
```

Note: *See section 11, "Runtime Support for Wrapped Procedures," on page CL-64 of the Client Library Reference Manual for a discussion about how pswrap uses* **printobject** *to return results.*

When an element within a wrap body matches an output argument in this way, *pswrap* replaces the output argument with code that returns the top object on the operand stack. For every output argument, the wrap performs the following operations:

1. Pops an object off the operand stack.

2. Sends it to the application.

3. Converts it to the correct C data type.

4. Stores it at the place designated by the output argument.

Each output argument must be declared as a pointer to the location where the procedure stores the returned value. To get a *long int* from a *pswrap*-generated procedure, declare the output argument as *long int* *, as in Example 6.

Example 6 *Output argument as long int*

Wrap definition:

```
defineps PSWCountExecStack(| long int *n)
    countexecstack n
endps
```

Procedure call:

```
long int aNumber;
PSWCountExecStack(&aNumber);
```

PostScript language code equivalent:

```
countexecstack
% Pop count of objects on exec stack
% and return in aNumber.
```

To receive information from the PostScript interpreter, use only the syntax for output arguments described here. Do not use operators that write to the standard output (such as =, ==, **print**, or **pstack**). These operators send ASCII strings to the application that *pswrap*-generated procedures cannot handle.

For an operator that returns results, the operator description shows the order in which results are placed on the operand stack, reading from left to right. When you specify a result value in a wrap body, the result is taken from the top of the operand stack. Therefore, the order in which wrap results are stated must be the reverse of their order in the operator description.

For instance, the PostScript operator description for **currentpoint** returns two values, *x* and *y*:

```
– currentpoint x y
```

Because the *y* value is left on the top of the stack, the corresponding wrap definition must be written

```
defineps PSWcurrentpoint (| float *x, *y)
    currentpoint y x      % Note: y before x.
endps
```

Note: *Putting output parameters in the wrong order is one of the most common errors made with the Display PostScript system.*

5   Declaring Input Arguments

This section defines the data types allowed as input arguments in a wrap. Note that *pswrap* accepts only *pswrap* data types as parameters. Although some *pswrap* data types correspond to C data types, they really are not the same. Also, not all defined C data types have corresponding *pswrap* data types (*long long*, and *signed char*, for example).

In the following list, square brackets indicate optional elements.

- *DPSContext*. If the wrap specifies a context, it must appear as the first input argument. (*DPSContext* is a handle to the context record.)

- One of the following *pswrap* data types (note the *boolean* and *userobject*, data types, which are exclusive to *pswrap*):

```
boolean                  userobject
int                      unsigned [int]
short [int]              unsigned short [int]
long [int]               unsigned long [int]
float                    double
```

- An array of a *pswrap* data type.

- A character string (*char** or *unsigned char**).

- A character array (*char [ ]* or *unsigned char [ ]*). (The square brackets are part of C syntax.)

A string (*char**) passed as input can't be more than 65,535 characters. An array can't contain more than 65,535 elements.

5.1   Sending Boolean Values

If an input argument is declared as *boolean*, the wrap expects to be passed a variable of type *int*. If the variable has a value of zero, it is translated to a PostScript Boolean object with the value *false*. Otherwise, it is translated to a PostScript Boolean object with the value *true*.

5.2 Sending User Object Values

Input parameters declared as type *userobject* should be passed as type *long int*. The value of a *userobject* argument is an index into the **UserObjects** array.

When *pswrap* encounters an argument of type *userobject*, it generates PostScript language code to obtain the object associated with the index, as in Example 7.

Example 7 *Wrap with a userobject argument*

Wrap definition:

```
defineps PSWAccessUserObject(userobject x)
   x
endps
```

Procedure call:

```
long int aUserObject;
   ...
/* assume aUserObject = 6 */
PSWAccessUserObject(aUserObject);
```

PostScript language code equivalent:

```
6 execuserobject
```

If the object is executable, it executes; if it's not, it is pushed on the operand stack.

If you want to pass the index of a user object without having it translated by *pswrap* as described in Example 7, declare the argument to be of type *long int* rather than type *userobject*. Example 8 is a wrap that defines a user object.

Example 8 *Wrap that defines a user object*

Wrap definition:

```
defineps PSWDefUserObject(long int d)
   d 10 dict defineuserobject
endps
```

Procedure call:

```
long int anIndex;
    . . .
/* assume anIndex = 12 */
PSWDefUserObject(anIndex);
```

PostScript language code equivalent:

```
12 10 dict defineuserobject
```

5.3   Sending Numbers

An input argument declared as one of the *int* types is converted to a 32-bit PostScript integer object before it is sent to the interpreter. A *float* or *double* input argument is converted to a 32-bit PostScript real object. These conversions follow the C conversion rules. The *int*, *long* and *short* types correspond to the data sizes in the native C environment. On some architectures, a long integer or double float is 64 bits, but the usable range of values is still 32 bits.

See *The C Programming Language, Second Edition*, B.W. Kernighan and D.M. Ritchie (Englewood Cliffs, N.J., Prentice-Hall, 1988) or *C: A Reference Manual, Second Edition*, Harbison and G. L. Steele, Jr. (Englewood Cliffs, N.J., Prentice-Hall, 1987).

Note: *Since the PostScript language doesn't support unsigned integers, unsigned integer input arguments are converted to signed integers in the body of the wrap.*

5.4   Sending Characters

An input argument composed of characters is treated as a PostScript name object or string object. The argument can be declared as a character string or a character array.

pswrap expects arguments that are passed to it as character strings (*char** or *unsigned char**) to be null terminated (\0). Character arrays are not null terminated. The number of elements in the array must be specified as an integer constant or an input argument of type *int*. In either case, the integer value must be positive.

PSW

5.4.1 Text Arguments

A text argument is an input argument declared as a character string or character array and converted to a single PostScript name object or string object.

The PostScript language interpreter does not process the characters of text arguments. It assumes that any escape sequences (\n, \t, and so on) have been processed before the wrap is called.

To make *pswrap* treat a text argument as a PostScript literal name object, precede it with a slash, as in the **PSWReadyFont** wrap definition in Example 9. (Only names and text arguments are preceded by a slash.)

Example 9 *Using a text argument as a literal name*

Wrap definition:

```
defineps PSWReadyFont(char *fontname; int size)
    /fontname size selectfont
endps
```

Procedure call:

```
PSWReadyFont("Sonata", 6);
```

PostScript language code equivalent:

```
/Sonata 6 selectfont
```

To make *pswrap* treat a text argument as a PostScript string object, enclose it within parentheses. The **PSWPutString** wrap definition in Example 10, shows a text argument, *str.*

Example 10 *Using a text argument as a string*

Wrap definition:

```
defineps PSWPutString(char *str; float x, y)
    x y moveto
    (str) show
endps
```

Procedure call:

```
PSWPutString("Hello World", 72.0, 72.0);
```

PostScript language code equivalent:

```
72.0 72.0 moveto
(Hello World) show
```

Note: *Text arguments are recognized within parentheses only if they appear alone, without any surrounding white space or additional elements. In the following wrap definition, only the first string is replaced with the value of the text argument. The second and third strings are sent unchanged to the interpreter.*

```
defineps PSWThreeStrings(char *str)
    (str) ( str ) (a str)
endps
```

If a text argument is not marked by either a slash or parentheses, *pswrap* treats it as an executable PostScript name object. In Example 11, *paintOp* is treated as executable.

Example 11 *Using a text argument as an executable name*

Wrap definition:

```
defineps PSWDrawPath(char *paintOp)
    0 setgray
    paintOp
endps
```

Procedure call:

```
PSWDrawPath("stroke");
```

PostScript language code equivalent:

```
0 setgray
stroke
```

5.5 Sending Arrays of Numbers or Booleans

Each element in the wrap body that names an input array argument represents a PostScript literal array object that has the same element values. In Example 12, the current transformation matrix is set using an array of six floating-point values.

Example 12 *Wrap with an array argument*

Wrap definition:

```
defineps PSWSetMyMatrix (float mtx[6])
   mtx setmatrix
endps
```

Procedure call:

```
static float anArray[ ] = {1.0, 0.0, 0.0, -1.0, 0.0, 0.0};
PSWSetMyMatrix(anArray);
```

PostScript language code equivalent:

```
[1.0 0.0 0.0 -1.0 0.0 0.0] setmatrix
```

The **PSWDefineA** wrap in Example 13 sends an array of variable length to the PostScript interpreter.

Example 13 *Wrap with a variable-length array argument*

Wrap definition:

```
defineps PSWDefineA (int data[x]; int x)
   /A data def
endps
```

Procedure call:

```
static int d1[ ] ={1, 2, 3};
static int d2[ ] = {4, 5};
   ...
PSWDefineA(d1, 3);
PSWDefineA(d2, 2);
```

PostScript language code equivalent:

```
/A [1 2 3] def
/A [4 5] def
```

5.6 Sending a Series of Numeric or Boolean Values

Occasionally, it is useful to group several numeric or Boolean values into a C array, and pass the array to a wrap that will send the individual elements of the array to the PostScript interpreter, as in Example 14.

Example 14 *Using array elements within a wrap*

Wrap definition:

```
defineps PSWGrayCircle(float nums[3], gray)
    newpath
    \nums[0] \nums[1] \nums[2] 0.0 360.0 arc
    closepath
    gray setgray
    fill
endps
```

Procedure call:

```
static float xyRadius = {40.0, 200.0, 55.0};
PSWGrayCircle(xyRadius, .75);
```

PostScript language code equivalent:

```
newpath
40.0 200.0 55.0 0.0 360.0 arc
closepath
.75 setgray
fill
```

In Example 14,
>   \ *nums*[i]

identifies an element of an input array in the wrap body, where *nums* is the name of an input boolean array or numeric array argument, and i is a nonnegative integer literal. No white space is allowed between the backslash (\) and the right bracket (]).

5.6.1 Specifying the Size of an Input Array

As the previous examples illustrate, you can specify the size of an input array in two ways:

- Give an integer constant size when you define the procedure, as in the **PSWGrayCircle** wrap definition

- Give an input argument that evaluates to an integer at runtime, as in the **PSWDefineA** wrap definition

In either case, the size of the array must be a positive integer with a value not greater than 65,535.

5.6.2　Sending Encoded Number Strings

A number sequence in the PostScript language can be represented either as an ordinary PostScript array object whose elements are to be used successively or as an encoded number string. Encoded number strings are described in section 3.12.5, "Encoded Number Strings," of the *PostScript Language Reference Manual, Second Edition.*

The encoded number string format efficiently passes sequences of numbers, such as coordinates, to PostScript operators that take arrays of operands (**xyshow** and **rectfill**, among others). In this form, the arrays take up less space in PostScript VM. In addition, the operator that consumes them executes faster because the data in an encoded number string, unlike a PostScript array object, does not have to be scanned by the PostScript scanner.

To simplify passing encoded number strings in a wrap, *pswrap* syntax provides the *numstring* data type, which lets you pass PostScript operands as numeric elements in a normal C array. The *pswrap* translator generates code that produces the encoded number string corresponding to this C array.

Note:　*numstring is used only for input. It is invalid as an output parameter in a wrap definition.*

The syntax of the *numstring* declaration is as follows, where braces enclose optional parts (the square brackets enclosing the array size are actual brackets):

```
{modifier} numstring variablename[arraysize] {: scale};
```

The modifier can be *int, long, short,* or *float,* and describes the numbers passed in as a parameter. For example, if a system defines long to be 64-bit integers, the array passed as a parameter should be 64-bit integers. If no modifier is specified, the default is *int.*

Scale applies only to fixed-point types and specifies the number of fractional bits in the number. If it isn't specified, *scale* defaults to zero.

Arraysize and *scale* can be specified as either constants or variables. Any variable that is used must be declared immediately after the *numstring* parameter and must be an integer type.

Example 15 *Examples of numstrings in wrap definitions*

Wrap definitions:

```
defineps PSWNums1(numstring a[5];)
% Array of 5 elements of default format
% Native integer size, zero scale.

defineps PSWNums2(float numstring a[6];)
% Floating point, constant array size.

defineps PSWNums3(float numstring a[n]; int n;)
% Floating point, variable array size.

define PSWNums4 (int numstring a{6}:8)
% Native integer size, constant array size and scale.

defineps PSWNums5(int numstring a[n]:6; int n;)
% Native integer size, variable array size, constant scale.

defineps PSWNums6(long numstring a[n]:s; int n, s;)
% Long integer size, variable array size and scale.
```

Note: *Number string parameters with int, long, or short modifiers are packed into 16- or 32-bit PostScript language number strings. If an integer type is 16 bits or shorter, it converts into a 16-bit number string, otherwise it converts into a 32-bit number string. If an integer type is longer than 32 bits, values will be truncated to 32 bits.*

PSWXShowChars, as shown in Example 16, is a wrap that uses the *numstring* data type to pass an array of user-defined widths to the **xshow** operator.

Example 16 *Wrap with a numstring argument*

Wrap definition:

```
defineps PSWXShowChars(char str[4];
                       long numstring widths[4]:0)
    /Times-Roman 30 selectfont
    100 100 moveto
    str widths xshow
endps
```

Procedure call:

```
char str[4] = "test";
long widths[4] = {7, 10, 9, 7};
    ...
PSWXShowChars(str, widths);
```

PostScript language code equivalent:

```
/Times-Roman 30 selectfont
/str (test) def
/widths <9580040007000000A0000000900000007000000> def
        % encoded number string, hex format,
        % preceded by 4-byte generated header
100 100 moveto
str widths xshow
```

5.7 Specifying the Context

Every wrap communicates with a PostScript execution context. The current context is normally used as the default. The Client Library provides operations for setting and getting the current context for each application. To override the default, declare the first argument as type *DPSContext* and pass the appropriate context as the first parameter whenever the application calls the wrap. Example 17 shows a wrap definition that explicitly declares a context.

Note: *Do not refer to the name of the context in the wrap body.*

Example 17 *Wrap that declares a context*

Wrap definition:

```
defineps PSWGetGray(DPSContext c | float *level)
    currentgray level
endps
```

Procedure call:

```
DPSContext myContext;
float aLevel;
    ...
PSWGetGray(myContext, &aLevel);
```

PostScript language code equivalent:

```
currentgray
% Pop current gray level off operand stack
% and store in aLevel
```

6 Declaring Output Arguments

To receive information from the PostScript interpreter, the output arguments of a wrap must refer to locations where the information can be stored. One of the following can be declared as an output argument:

- A pointer to one of the *pswrap* data types listed previously except *userobject*

- An array of one of these types

- A character string *(char* or unsigned char*)*

- A character array *(char [ ] or unsigned char [ ])*

If an output argument is declared as a pointer or character string, the procedure writes the returned value at the pointed-to location.

For an output argument declared as a pointer, previous return values are overwritten if the output argument is encountered more than once in executing the wrap body.

 For an output argument declared as a character string *(char *)*, the value is stored only the first time it is encountered.

For an output argument declared as an array of one of the *pswrap* data types or as a character array, the wrap fills the slots in the array.

For example, the wrap in Example 18 returns 2 in *nump*, "abc" in *charp*, the array {3,4} in *numarray*, and the string "ghijkl" in *chararray*.

Example 18 *Returning output values more than once*

Wrap definition:

```
defineps PSWreturn( | int *nump, char *charp,
                    int numarray[2], char chararray[6])
    1 nump
    2 nump
    3 numarray
    4 numarray
    (abc) charp
    (def) charp
    (ghi) chararray
    (jkl) chararray
endps
```

Note: *Whenever an array output argument is encountered in the wrap body, the values on the PostScript operand stack are placed in the array in the order in which they would be popped off the stack. When the array bounds have been exceeded, no further storing of output in the array is done. No error is reported if elements are returned to an array that is full.*

You can specify output arguments in the defineps statement in any order that is convenient. The order of the output arguments has no effect on the execution of the PostScript language code in the wrap body.

pswrap does not check whether the wrap definition provides return values for all output arguments, nor does it perform type checking for declared output arguments.

6.1 Receiving Numbers

PostScript integer objects and real objects are 32 bits long. When returned, these values are assigned to the variable provided by the output argument. On a system where the size of an *int* or *float* is 32 bits, pass a pointer to an *int* as the output argument for a PostScript integer object; pass a pointer to a *float* as the output argument for a PostScript real object:

```
defineps PSWMyWrap ( | float *f; int *i)
```

A PostScript integer object or real object can be returned as a *float* or *double*. Other type mismatches cause a **typecheck** error (for example, attempting to return a PostScript real object as an *int*).

6.2 Receiving Boolean Values

A procedure can declare a pointer to a *boolean* as an output argument.

Example 19 *Wrap with a boolean output argument*

Wrap definition:

```
defineps PSWKnown(char *Dict, *x | boolean *ans)
    Dict /x known ans
endps
```

Procedure call:

```
int found;
    ...
PSWKnown("statusdict", "duplex", &found);
```

PostScript language code equivalent:

```
statusdict /duplex known found
```

This wrap expects to be passed the address of a variable of type *int* as its output argument. If the PostScript interpreter returns the value *true*, the wrap places a value of 1 (one) in the variable referenced by the output argument. If the interpreter returns the value *false*, the wrap places a value of 0 (zero) in the variable.

6.3 Receiving a Series of Output Values

To receive a series of output values as an array, declare an array output argument; then write a wrap body in the PostScript language to compute and return its elements, one or more elements at a time. Example 20 declares a wrap that returns the 256 font widths for a given font name at a given font size.

Example 20 *Returning a series of output values*

Wrap definition:

```
defineps PSWGetWidths(char *fn; int size | float wide[256])
  /fn size selectfont
  0 1 255 {
    (X) dup 0 4 -1 roll put
    stringwidth pop wide
  } for
endps
```

Procedure call:

```
float widths[256];
PSWGetWidths("Serifa", 12, widths);
```

PostScript language code equivalent:

```
/Serifa 12 selectfont
0 1 255 {
   (X) dup 0 4 -1 roll put
   stringwidth pop
   % Pop width for this character and insert width
   % into widths array at current element;
   % point to next element.
} for
```

In Example 20, the loop counter is used to assign successive ASCII values to the scratch string ("X"). The **stringwidth** operator then places both the width and height of the string on the PostScript operand stack. (Here it operates on a string one character long.)

The **pop** operator removes the height from the stack, leaving the width at the top. The occurrence of the output argument *wide* in this position triggers the width to be popped from the stack, returned to the application, and inserted into the output array at the current element. The next element then becomes the current element.

The **for** loop (the procedure enclosed in braces followed by **for**) repeats these operations for each character in the font, beginning with the first, 0, and ending with 255th element of the font array.

6.3.1 Receiving a Series of Array Elements

A PostScript array object can contain a series of elements to be stored in an output array. The output array is filled in, one element at a time, until it's full. Therefore, the **PSWTest** wrap defined below returns {1, 2, 3, 4, 5, 6}:

```
defineps PSWTest(| int Array[6])
   [1 2 3] Array
   [4 5 6] Array
endps
```

The **PSWTestMore** wrap defined below returns {1, 2, 3, 4}:

```
defineps PSWTestMore(| int Array[4])
    [1 2 3] Array
    [4 5 6] Array
endps
```

6.3.2   Specifying the Size of an Output Array

The size of an output array is specified in the same manner as the size of an input array. Use a constant in the wrap definition or an input argument that evaluates to an integer at runtime. If more elements are returned than fit in the output array, the additional elements are discarded.

6.4   Receiving Characters

To receive characters from the PostScript interpreter, declare the output argument as either a character string or as a character array.

If the argument is declared as a character string, the wrap copies the returned string to the location indicated. Provide enough space for the maximum number of characters that might be returned, including the null character (\0) that terminates the string. Only the first string encountered will be returned. For example, in the following **PSWStrings** procedure, the string "123" is returned:

```
defineps PSWStrings(| char *str)
    (123) str
    (456) str
endps
```

Character arrays, on the other hand, are treated just like arrays of numbers. In the **PSWStrings2** procedure, the value returned for *str* will be "123456".

```
defineps PSWStrings2(| char str[6])
    (123) str
    (456) str
endps
```

Note: *The string is not null terminated. If the argument is declared as a character array (for example, char s[num]), the procedure copies up to num characters of the returned string into the array. Additional characters are discarded.*

6.5 Communication and Synchronization

The PostScript interpreter can run as a separate process from the application; it can also run on a separate machine. When the application and interpreter processes are separated, the application programmer must take communication into account. This section alerts you to communication and synchronization issues.

A wrap that has no output arguments returns as soon as the wrap body is transferred to the client-server communications channel. In this case, the communications channel is not necessarily flushed. Since the wrap body is not executed by the PostScript interpreter until the communications channel is flushed, errors arising from the execution of the wrap body can be reported long after the wrap returns.

In the case of a wrap that returns a value, the entire wrap body is transferred to the client-server communications channel, which is then flushed. The client-side code awaits the return of output values followed by a special termination value. Only then does the wrap return.

See Appendix A, "Client Library," for information concerning synchronization, runtime errors, and error handling.

7 Syntax

Square brackets, [ ], mean that the enclosed form is optional. Curly brackets, { }, mean that the enclosed form is repeated, possibly zero times. A vertical bar, |, separates choices in a list.

```
Unit =
   ArbitraryText {Definition ArbitraryText}

Definition =
   NLdefineps ["static"] Ident "(" [Args] ["|" Args]")"
   Body
   NLendps

Body =
   {Token}

Token =
   Number | PSIdent | SlashPSIdent
   | "(" StringLiteral ")"
   | "<" StringLiteral ">"
   | "{" Body "}"
   | "[" Body "]"
   | Input Element

Args =
   ArgList {";" ArgList} [";"]

ArgList =
    Type ItemList

Type =
   "DPSContext" | "boolean" | "float" | "double"
   | ["unsigned"] "char"
   | ["unsigned"] ["short" | "long"] "int"
   | ["int" | "long" | "short" | "float"] "numstring"

ItemList =
   Item {"," Item}

Item =
   "*" Ident | Ident ["["Subscript"]"]
   | Ident "["Subscript"]" [Scale]
```

```
Subscript =
    Integer | Ident

Scale =
    ":" Integer | ":" Ident
```

7.1 Syntactic Restrictions

- *DPSContext* must be the first input argument if it appears.

- A simple char argument *(char Ident)* is never allowed; it must be
  * or [ ].

- A simple *Ident* item is not allowed in an output item list; it must be
  * or [ ].

7.2 Clarifications

- *NLdefineps* matches the terminal *defineps* at the beginning of a new
  line.

- *NLendps* matches the terminal *endps* at the beginning of a new line.

- *Ident* follows the rules for C names; *PSIdent* follows the rules for
  PostScript language names.

- *SlashPSIdent* is a PostScript language name preceded by a slash.

- *StringLiteral* tokens follow the PostScript language conventions for
  string literals.

- *Number* tokens follow the PostScript language conventions for
  numbers.

- Integer subscripts follow the C conventions for integer constants.

- *Input Element* is \n[i] where *n* is the name of an input array argument,
  i is a nonnegative integer literal, and no white space is allowed
  between \ and].

Error Messages from the pswrap Translator

The following is a list of error messages the pswrap translator can generate:

input parameter used as a subscript is not an integer

output parameter used as a subscript

char input parameters must be starred or subscripted

hex string too long

invalid characters

invalid characters in definition

invalid characters in hex string

invalid radix number

output arguments must be starred or subscripted

out of storage, try splitting the input file

-s 80 is the minimum

can't allocate char string, try a smaller -s value

can't open file for input

can't open file for output

error in parsing

string too long

usage: pswrap [-s maxstring] [-ar] [-h headerfile]
[-o outfile] [infile]

endps without matching defineps

errors in parsing

errors were encountered

size of wrap exceeds 64K

parameter reused

output parameter used as a subscript

non-char input parameter

not an input parameter

not a scalar type

wrong type

parameter index expression empty

parameter index expression error

end of input file/missing endps

POSTSCRIPT™
Software From Adobe

The Display PostScript System

Adobe Systems Incorporated

Display PostScript Toolkit
for X

TK

Display PostScript Toolkit for X

1 About This Manual

Display PostScript Toolkit for X manual describes the Display PostScript Toolkit for the X Window System. It also contains information about locating PostScript language resources and about the *makepsres* utility.

The Display PostScript Toolkit is a collection of procedures and objects for programmers who use the Display PostScript extension to the X Window System, which is sometimes referred to as DPS/X. The toolkit can be used for context management, user object management, user path handling, and file previewing. It also allows you to preview and choose from currently available fonts by using the font selection panel and the font sampler.

The toolkit is supplemented by procedures for locating PostScript language resources using resource database files and by the *makepsres* utility, which can be used to create the resource database files. These utilities are used by the font selection panel, but can be helpful in other situations as well.

The toolkit library that contains the facilities described in this manual is available from several sources:

- The X Consortium Release 5 contributed software under *contrib/lib/DPS*.

- The Display PostScript System Software Development Kit for the X Window System, available from Adobe Systems.

- On Adobe's public access file server. Using the file server is described in the preface of this book.

TK

- The Display PostScript system release provided by your system vendor. Note, however, that not all system vendors include the Display PostScript Toolkit as part of their release.

1.1 What This Manual Contains

Section 2, "About the Display PostScript Toolkit," introduces the Display PostScript Toolkit.

Section3, "Context Management Procedures," describes context management procedures.

SectionSection 4 documents facilities for working with user objects.

SectionSection 5," introduces a convenient interface for working with user paths.

Section 6, "File Preview Procedures," describes file preview procedures, which simplify rendering PostScript language files into X drawable objects (windows or pixmaps).

Section 7, "The Motif Font Selection Panel," provides information about the font selection panel, which can be used to view and select the fonts available on a workstation.

Section 8, "The Motif Font Sampler," provides information about the font sampler, which can be popped up from the font selection panel for viewing multiple fonts simultaneously.

Appendix A explains how applications can locate PostScript language resources using resource database files.

Appendix B documents the *makepsres* utility, which can be used to create resource database files.

2 About the Display PostScript Toolkit

The toolkit is located in the libraries *libdpstk.a* and *libdpstkXm.a*. The *libdpstkXm.a* library contains the Motif font selection and font sampler dialogs, and the library *libdpstk.a* contains everything else. When compiling an application, you must specify these libraries to the linker before the Display PostScript library *libdps.a*.

- If an application uses the font selection panel, you must specify the toolkit libraries to the linker before the Motif™ library. In that case, you must also link with the resource location library for the PostScript language, which is described in Appendix A. The normal order for libraries is:

    ```
    -ldpstk -ldpstkXm -lpsres -lXm -lXt -ldps -lX11 -lm
    ```

- If the application does not use the font selection panel, linking with *libdpstkXm.a* and Motif is not required. In that case, the normal order for libraries is:

    ```
    -ldpstk -ldps -lX11 -lm
    ```

Note: *The math library, libm.a, is required by some implementations of libdps.a.*

2.1   Common Definitions

The header file *<DPS/dpsXcommon.h>* contains definitions used by various procedures in the Display PostScript Toolkit.

2.1.1   Type Definitions

The type *DPSPointer* is used for pointers of an unspecified type.

DPSPointer   `typedef char *DPSPointer;`

Note: *The definition of DPSPointer is implementation-specific.*

2.1.2   Return Values

Table 1 describes the values returned by the procedures in the Display PostScript Toolkit. These values are all of type *int*.

TK

Table 1 *Toolkit return values*

Return Value	Meaning
dps_status_success	The procedure executed successfully and to completion.
dps_status_failure	The procedure failed. The reason is documented in the description of the procedure.
dps_status_no_extension	The procedure attempted to execute an operation that requires context creation and discovered that the server does not support the Display PostScript extension.
dps_status_unregistered_context	The procedure requires a context registered with the context manager, and the passed context has not been registered.
dps_status_illegal_value	One of the parameters to the procedure has an illegal value.
dps_status_postscript_error	The PostScript language code being handled by the procedure contains an error.
dps_status_imaging_incomplete	The PostScript language code being handled by the procedure did not finish execution within a time-out period.

3 Context Management Procedures

In DPS/X, a context is a server resource that represents all of the execution state needed by the PostScript interpreter to run PostScript language programs. Contexts are described in *Client Library Reference Manual* and in *Client Library Supplement for X*.

This section documents context management procedures provided by the Display PostScript Toolkit. A brief introduction is followed by a table listing all available procedures. The rest of the section lists structures and procedure definitions in alphabetical order.

3.1 Introduction

A PostScript execution context consists of all the information (or state) needed by the PostScript interpreter to execute a PostScript language program. Context management utilities allow different code modules to share PostScript contexts. They make it easy to associate several drawables with one context and to switch between the drawables. They also hide the details of context creation from an application by creating and managing default contexts.

Some libraries provide an encapsulated service—a closed, well-defined task with minimal outside interaction (for example, displaying read-only text). If you are writing a library that provides an encapsulated service, the context management procedures can simplify the interface you provide to applications. For example, the file preview procedures described in section 6, "File Preview Procedures," can use the context management procedures to get a context for previewing a file. The font selection panel described in section 7, "The Motif Font Selection Panel," can use the context management procedures to get a context for previewing fonts. If an application uses both file previewing and the font selection panel, they can share the same context. The shared context is called the *default context* for the application. Context management procedures allow an application that uses the file preview procedures to ignore contexts completely; the application does not even have to know that contexts exist.

Code that uses the context management procedures must include *<DPS/dpsXshare.h>*, which automatically includes *<DPS/dpsXcommon.h>*.

TK

An application can get the shared context for a display by calling
XDPSGetSharedContext. To use the context management procedures
on its own context, the application can register its context with the
context manager by calling **XDPSRegisterContext**. In either case, the
application can then manipulate the context in a number of ways:

- Chain text contexts using **XDPSChainTextContext**.

- Set window system parameters for a context using
  XDPSSetContextParameters, or set individual parameters using
  XDPSSetContextDepth, **XDPSSetContextGrayMap**,
  XDPSSetContextRGBMap, or **XDPSSetContextDrawable**.

- Call **XDPSPushContextParameters** to temporarily set parameters and
  undo the results using **XDPSPopContextParameters**.

- Work with gstate objects (data structures that hold current graphics
  control parameters) by first capturing the current graphics state with
  XDPSCaptureContextGState, and then setting a context to the saved
  gstate object using **XDPSSetContextGState**. Use
  XDPSPushContextGState to temporarily set a context to a gstate
  object and later undo this action with **XDPSPopContextGState**. To
  update or to free a gstate object, **XDPSUpdateContextGState** and
  XDPSFreeContextGState can be called.

- Free contexts that are no longer needed by calling
  XDPSDestroySharedContext, which destroys a shared context and its
  space. **XDPSUnregisterContext** can be called to free context
  information without destroying the context.

3.2 Programming Tips

Capturing the current state with **XDPSCaptureContextGState** and
restoring it later with **XDPSPushContextGState** or
XDPSSetContextGState is more efficient than setting the parameters
each time. However, each gstate object consumes memory, so don't
capture a gstate object unless you expect to return to it. You should also
free gstate objects that are no longer being used, or recycle them with
XDPSUpdateContextGState.

3.3   Procedure Overview

Table 2 *Context management procedures*

Procedure	Functionality
XDPSCaptureContextGState	Captures the current graphics state as a gstate object and returns a handle to it.
XDPSChainTextContext	Enables or disables a chained text context for a context.
XDPSDestroySharedContext	Destroys a shared context for a display and the context's space.
XDPSExtensionPresent	Determines whether a display supports the Display PostScript extension.
XDPSFreeContextGState	Releases a gstate object.
XDPSFreeDisplayInfo	Frees the stored display information for a display.
XDPSGetSharedContext	Returns the shared context for a display.
XDPSPopContextGState	Reverses the effects of **XDPSPushContextGState**.
XDPSPopContextParameters	Reverses the effects of **XDPSPushContextParameters**.
XDPSPushContextGState	Sets a context to a saved gstate object; can be undone by **XDPSPopContextGState**.
XDPSPushContextParameters	Sets context parameters; can be undone by **XDPSPopContextParameters**.
XDPSRegisterContext	Registers a context with the context manager.
XDPSSetContextDepth	Sets the screen and depth for a context.
XDPSSetContextDrawable	Sets the drawable for a context.
XDPSSetContextGrayMap	Sets the gray ramp for a context.
XDPSSetContextGState	Sets a context to a saved gstate object.
XDPSSetContextParameters	Sets context parameters.
XDPSSetContextRGBMap	Sets the RGB map for a context.
XDPSUnregisterContext	Frees context information for a context but doesn't destroy the context.
XDPSUpdateContextGState	Updates a saved gstate object to correspond to the current graphics state.

TK

3.4 Structures

The *XDPSStandardColormap* structure is identical to the *XStandardColormap* structure but allows signed numbers for the multipliers.

XDPSStandardColormap

```
typedef struct {
    Colormap colormap;
    unsigned long red_max;
    long red_mult;
    unsigned long green_max;
    long green_mult;
    unsigned long blue_max;
    long blue_mult;
    unsigned long base_pixel;
    unsigned long visualid;
    unsigned long killid;
} XDPSStandardColormap;
```

The structure is used by **XDPSSetContextRGBMap**, **XDPSSetContextGrayMap**, **XDPSSetContextParameters**, and **XDPSPushContextParameters**.

3.5 Procedures

XDPSCaptureContextGState

```
int XDPSCaptureContextGState (context, *gsReturn)
    DPSContext context;
    DPSGState *gsReturn;
```

XDPSCaptureContextGState captures the current graphics state as a gstate object and returns a reference to it. *DPSGState* is an opaque type. It is legal to set a *DPSGState* variable to integer zero and to test it against zero—**XDPSCaptureContextGState** never returns zero in *gsReturn*.

XDPSCaptureContextGState returns *dps_status_unregistered_context* or *dps_status_success*.

XDPSChainTextContext   `int XDPSChainTextContext (context, enable)`
                  `DPSContext context;`
                  `Bool enable;`

XDPSChainTextContext either enables or disables a chained text context for a context. The first time **XDPSChainTextContext** is called with *enable* set to *True*, it creates the text context. The text context writes its output to the standard output file.

The context must have been registered with **XDPSRegisterContext**.

XDPSChainTextContext returns *dps_status_unregistered_context* or *dps_status_success*.

XDPSDestroySharedContext   `void XDPSDestroySharedContext (context)`
                  `DPSContext context;`

XDPSDestroySharedContext destroys the shared context for a display; it also destroys the context's space.

XDPSExtensionPresent   `Bool XDPSExtensionPresent (display)`
                  `Display *display;`

XDPSExtensionPresent returns *True* if *display* supports the Display PostScript extension, *False* otherwise.

XDPSFreeContextGState   `int XDPSFreeContextGState (context, gs)`
                  `DPSContext context;`
                  `DPSGState gs;`

XDPSFreeContextGState releases a gstate object previously acquired through **XDPSCaptureContextGState**.

XDPSFreeContextGState returns *dps_status_unregistered_context* or *dps_status_success*.

TK

XDPSFreeDisplayInfo void XDPSFreeDisplayInfo (display)
                           Display *display;

XDPSFreeDisplayInfo frees the stored display information for *display*. It
should be used if an application no longer needs to use the Display
PostScript Toolkit on that display, but the application will be
continuing.

XDPSGetSharedContext DPSContext XDPSGetSharedContext (display)
                           Display *display;

XDPSGetSharedContext returns the shared context for *display*. If no
shared context exists, it creates one. **XDPSGetSharedContext** returns
NULL if *display* does not support DPS/X.

The returned context is initially set to use the default colormap on the
default screen with the default depth, but is not set to use any drawable.

XDPSPopContextGState int XDPSPopContextGState (pushCookie)
                           DPSPointer pushCookie;

XDPSPopContextGState restores a context to the state it was in before
the call to **XDPSPushContextGState** that returned *pushCookie*.

XDPSPushContextGState and **XDPSPopContextGState** must be called
in a stack-oriented fashion.

XDPSPopContextGState returns *dps_status_success* or
dps_status_illegal_value.

XDPSPopContextParameters int XDPSPopContextParameters (pushCookie)
                           DPSPointer pushCookie;

XDPSPopContextParameters restores all context parameters to the state
they were in before the call to **XDPSPushContextParameters** that
returned *pushCookie*.

XDPSPushContextParameters and **XDPSPopContextParameters** must
be called in a stack-oriented fashion.

XDPSPushContextGState

XDPSPopContextParameters returns *dps_status_success* or *dps_status_illegal_value.*

```
int XDPSPushContextGState (context, gs, pushCookieReturn)
    DPSContext context;
    DPSGState gs;
    DPSPointer *pushCookieReturn;
```

XDPSPushContextGState sets a context to a saved gstate object. This can be undone by passing the returned *pushCookieReturn* to **XDPSPopContextGState**.

XDPSPushContextGState and **XDPSPopContextGState** must be called in a stack-oriented fashion.

XDPSPushContextGState returns *dps_status_unregistered_context* or *dps_status_success.*

XDPSPushContextParameters

```
int XDPSPushContextParameters (context, screen, depth,
        drawable, height, rgbMap, grayMap, flags,
        pushCookieReturn)
    DPSContext context;
    Screen *screen;
    int depth;
    Drawable drawable;
    int height;
    XDPSStandardColormap *rgbMap;
    XDPSStandardColormap *grayMap;
    unsigned int flags;
    DPSPointer *pushCookieReturn;
```

XDPSPushContextParameters is identical to **XDPSSetContextParameters** but can be undone by passing the returned *pushCookieReturn* to **XDPSPopContextParameters**.

XDPSPushContextParameters and **XDPSPopContextParameters** must be called in a stack-oriented fashion.

XDPSPushContextParameters returns the same values as **XDPSSetContextParameters**.

TK

XDPSRegisterContext

```
void XDPSRegisterContext (context, makeSharedContext)
    DPSContext context;
    Bool makeSharedContext;
```

XDPSRegisterContext registers a context with the context manager and makes it possible to manipulate the context using the procedures in this section.

If *makeSharedContext* is *True*, *context* becomes the shared context for the display. This does not destroy the previous shared context for the display, if there is one.

XDPSSetContextDepth

```
int XDPSSetContextDepth (context, screen, depth)
    DPSContext context;
    Screen *screen;
    int depth;
```

XDPSSetContextDepth sets a context for use with a particular screen and depth.

XDPSSetContextDepth returns *dps_status_unregistered_context* or returns *dps_status_success*. If *screen* is not on the context's display or *depth* is not valid for that screen, **XDPSSetContextDepth** returns *dps_status_illegal_value*.

XDPSSetContextDrawable

```
int XDPSSetContextDrawable (context, drawable, height)
    DPSContext context;
    Drawable drawable;
    int height;
```

XDPSSetContextDrawable sets a context for use with a particular drawable that has the specified *height*. The origin is at the lower left corner. The context must already be set for use with the drawable's screen; see **XDPSSetContextDepth**.

XDPSSetContextDrawable returns *dps_status_unregistered_context* or returns *dps_status_success*. If *height* is less than 1, **XDPSSetContextDrawable** returns *dps_status_illegal_value*.

XDPSSetContextGrayMap

```
int XDPSSetContextGrayMap (context, map)
    DPSContext context;
    XDPSStandardColormap *map;
```

XDPSSetContextGrayMap sets the gray ramp for *context*. The colormap in the *map* structure must be appropriate for the current drawable and depth. This colormap can be **None** when the context is imaging to a pixmap. In that case, the ramps must be set to the values used in the window that will display the pixmap.

If *map* is *NULL*, the default gray ramp for the default screen of the context's display is used. The *flags* parameter of **XDPSSetContextParameters** described below can be used to get the default for a nondefault screen.

The gray ramp is based upon the *base_pixel, red_max,* and *red_mult* fields of the *XDPSStandardColormap* structure; all other *_max* and *_mult* fields are ignored.

XDPSSetContextGrayMap returns *dps_status_unregistered_context* or returns *dps_status_success.*

XDPSSetContextGState

```
int XDPSSetContextGState (context, gs)
    DPSContext context;
    DPSGState gs;
```

XDPSSetContextGState sets a context to a saved gstate object. It returns *dps_status_success* or *dps_status_unregistered_context.*

XDPSSetContextParameters

```
int XDPSSetContextParameters (context, screen, depth,
                    drawable, height, rgbMap, grayMap, flags)
    DPSContext context;
    Screen *screen;
    int depth;
    Drawable drawable;
    int height;
    XDPSStandardColormap *rgbMap;
    XDPSStandardColormap *grayMap;
    unsigned int flags;
```

XDPSSetContextParameters sets any of the context parameters. It uses the following macros to decide which parameters to set.

TK

```
XDPSContextScreenDepth
XDPSContextDrawable
XDPSContextRGBMap
XDPSContextGrayMap
```

flags should be a bitwise *OR* of one or more of these values.

XDPSSetContextParameters returns *dps_status_success* if all requested changes were successfully made. If any parameter is in error, **XDPSSetContextParameters** returns either *dps_status_unregistered_context* or *dps_status_illegal_value* as appropriate. In the case of non-success, no changes were made.

If *flags* requires that a colormap is set and the corresponding *map* parameter is *NULL*, a default map is used. In that case:

- If *screen* is not *NULL*, the default map is the one set on the screen's root window.

- If *screen* is *NULL* and *drawable* is **None**, the default map is the one on the display's default root window.

- If *screen* is *NULL* but *drawable* is not **None**, the default map is the one set on the root window of the screen specified by *drawable*.

XDPSSetContextRGBMap

```
int XDPSSetContextRGBMap (context, map)
   DPSContext context;
   XDPSStandardColormap *map;
```

XDPSSetContextRGBMap sets the RGB color cube for *context*. The colormap in the *map* structure must be appropriate for the current drawable and depth. This colormap can be **None** if the application is rendering to a pixmap. In that case, the ramps must be set to the values used in the window that will display the pixmap.

If *map* is *NULL*, the default RGB cube for the default screen of the context's display is used. The *flags* parameter of **XDPSSetContextParameters** described above can be used to get the default for a nondefault screen.

XDPSSetContextRGBMap returns *dps_status_success* or returns *dps_status_unregistered_context*.

XDPSUnregisterContext   void XDPSUnregisterContext (context)
                                 DPSContext context;

> **XDPSUnregisterContext** frees context information but doesn't destroy a context.

XDPSUpdateContextGState   int XDPSUpdateContextGState (context, gs)
                                 DPSContext context;
                                 DPSGState gs;

> **XDPSUpdateContextGState** updates the saved gstate object to correspond to the current graphics state. The previous setting of the gstate object is no longer accessible.
>
> **XDPSUpdateContextGState** returns *dps_status_unregistered_context* or *dps_status_success.*

4 User Objects

The toolkit procedures described in this section can be used to manage user objects such as user paths. These procedures are recommended for any DPS/X application that uses user objects. User objects are discussed in section 3.7.6 of *PostScript Language Reference Manual, Second Edition.*

The procedures documented in this section are compatible with those described in described in "User Object Indices" in section 3.3 of *Client Library Supplement for X.* An application can combine them as convenient.

Applications that call the procedures documented in this section must include *<DPS/dpsXshare.h>*. The procedures can be used for any context; it is not necessary to register the context first.

4.1 Procedure Overview

Two forms are provided for each user object management procedure, one starting with **DPS** and the other with **PS**. The procedures are identical, except for the first argument: the procedure starting with **PS** uses the current context, while the procedure starting with **DPS** requires a context as its first argument.

Table 3 *User object procedures*

Procedure	Functionality
PSDefineAsUserObj **DPSDefineAsUserObj**	Allocates a user object index and associates it with the item on top of the operand stack
PSRedefineUserObj **DPSRedefineUserObj**	Breaks the association between a user object index and its current object and associates the index with the item on top of the operand stack.
PSReserveUserObjIndices **DPSReserveUserObjIndices**	Reserves a number of user object indices for an application's use.
PSUndefineUserObj **DPSUndefineUserObj**	Breaks the association between a user object index and its current object.

4.2 Procedures

PSDefineAsUserObj
DPSDefineAsUserObj

```
int DPSDefineAsUserObj (context)
    DPSContext context;
```

DPSDefineAsUserObj allocates a user object index and associates it with the item on top of the operand stack. The return value is the user object index.

PSRedefineUserObj
DPSRedefineUserObj

```
void DPSRedefineUserObj (context, userObj)
    DPSContext context;
    int userObj;
```

DPSRedefineUserObj breaks the association between the user object index *userObj* and its current object. It then associates the index with the item on top of the operand stack.

PSReserveUserObjIndices
DPSReserveUserObjIndices

```
int DPSReserveUserObjIndices (context, number)
    DPSContext context;
    int number;
```

DPSReserveUserObjIndices reserves a specified number of user object indices for an application's use. It does not associate these indices with any objects. The return value is the first index reserved; if the return value is *f*, an application can freely use the indices *f* through *f+number–1*.

PSUndefineUserObj
DPSUndefineUserObj

```
void DPSUndefineUserObj (context, userObj)
    DPSContext context;
    int userObj;
```

DPSUndefineUserObj breaks the association between the user object index *userObj* and its current object. Further use of the index is not allowed. Future calls to **DPSDefineAsUserObj** might return the same index with a new association.

TK

5 User Paths

The procedures described in this section provide convenient access to user paths. A *user path* is a PostScript language procedure that consists entirely of path construction operators and their coordinate operands expressed as literal numbers. User paths can also be expressed in a compact, encoded form. The compact form is the format generated by the procedures described in this section.

User paths are described in section 4.6 of *PostScript Language Reference Manual, Second Edition*. Applications that use the utilities described in this section must include *<DPS/dpsXuserpath.h>*.

5.1 Structures and Type Definitions

DPSNumberFormat

```
typedef enum _DPSNumberFormat {
    dps_float,
    dps_long,
    dps_short
} DPSNumberFormat;
```

DPSNumberFormat describes the format of numeric procedure call parameters.

- For floating point, 32-bit, or 16-bit values, use *dps_float*, *dps_long*, or *dps_short*, respectively.

- For 32-bit fixed-point numbers, use *dps_long* plus the number of bits in the fractional part.

- For 16-bit fixed-point numbers, use *dps_short* plus the number of bits in the fractional part.

Note: *You cannot use 64-bit values with the procedures in this section.*

DPSUserPathOp

```
typedef enum _DPSUserPathOp {
    dps_setbbox,
    dps_moveto,
    dps_rmoveto,
    dps_lineto,
    dps_rlineto,
    dps_curveto,
    dps_rcurveto,
    dps_arc,
    dps_arcn,
    dps_arct,
    dps_closepath,
    dps_ucache};

typedef char DPSUserPathOp;
```

DPSUserPathOp enumerates the PostScript operators that define a path.

DPSUserPathAction

```
typedef enum _DPSUserPathAction {
    dps_uappend,
    dps_ufill,
    dps_ueofill,
    dps_ustroke,
    dps_ustrokepath,
    dps_inufill,
    dps_inueofill,
    dps_inustroke,
    dps_infill,
    dps_ineofill,
    dps_instroke,
    dps_def,
    dps_put,
    dps_send
} DPSUserPathAction;
```

DPSUserPathAction enumerates the operators that can be applied to a path. The special action *dps_send* pushes the user path on the stack and leaves it there.

TK

5.2 Procedure Overview

Two forms are provided for each user path procedure, one starting with **DPS** and the other with **PS**. The procedures are identical, except for the first argument: the procedure starting with **PS** uses the current context, while the procedure starting with **DPS** requires a context as its first argument.

A context used with these procedures does not need to be registered with the context management procedures described in section 3, "Context Management Procedures."

Table 4 *User path procedures*

Procedure	Functionality
PSDoUserPath **DPSDoUserPath**	Sends a user path and operates on it, using the operator specified in the *action* parameter.
PSHitUserPath **DPSHitUserPath**	Sends a user path for one of the hit detection operators. The operator is specified in the *action* parameter.

5.3 Procedures

PSDoUserPath
DPSDoUserPath

```
void DPSDoUserPath (ctx, coords, numCoords, numType, ops,
                numOp, bbox, action)
    DPSContext ctx;
    DPSPointer coords;
    int numCoords;
    DPSNumberFormat numType;
    DPSUserPathOp *ops;
    int numOp;
    DPSPointer bbox;
    DPSUserPathAction action;
```

DPSDoUserPath provides a convenient interface to user paths.

coords is an array of coordinates for the operands. Do not include the parameters for the *dps_setbbox* operation in this array.

numCoords provides the number of entries in the *coords* array. The type of the entries in *coords* is defined by the *numType* parameter.

numType describes the number format used in the *coords* and *bbox* parameters.

ops points to an array of operations, as defined by *DPSUserPathOp*.

numOp gives the number of entries in the array pointed to by *ops*.

bbox points to four numbers in the format defined by *numType*.

action describes the PostScript operator that consumes the created user path.

The operator list in the *ops* parameter can, but need not, include a *dps_setbbox* operation. If *dps_setbbox* is not included, **DPSDoUserPath** inserts it at the appropriate place.

Each operator in the *ops* array consumes operands from the *coords* array. The number of coordinates varies for different operands, as shown in Table 5:

Table 5 *Operators and coordinates*

Operator	# of Operands	Description
dps_setbbox	none	see the *bbox* parameter
dps_moveto	2	x, y
dps_rmoveto	2	dx, dy
dps_lineto	2	x, y
dps_rlineto	2	dx, dy
dps_curveto	6	$x_1, y_1, x_2, y_2, x_3, y_3$
dps_rcurveto	6	$dx_1, dy_1, dx_2, dy_2, dx_3, dy_3$
dps_arc	5	x, y, r, ang1, ang2
dps_arcn	5	x, y, r, ang1, ang2
dps_arct	5	x_1, y_1, x_2, y_2, r
dps_closepath	None	
dps_ucache	None	

The following code fragment uses **DPSDoUserPath** to draw a 75-unit circle centered around the point (100,100) with a radius from (100, 100) to (175, 100):

```
static long coords[9] = {100, 100, 75, 0, 360,
                         100, 100, 75, 0};
static DPSUserPathOp ops[3] = {dps_arc, dps_moveto,
                         dps_rlineto};
static long bbox[4] = {25, 25, 175, 175};

DPSDoUserPath (ctxt, (DPSPointer) coords, 9, dps_long,
              ops, 3,
         (DPSPointer) bbox, dps_ustroke);
```

PSHitUserPath
DPSHitUserPath

```
Bool DPSHitUserPath (ctx, x, y, radius, coords, numCoords,
            numType, ops, numOp, bbox, action)
    DPSContext ctx;
    double x, y, radius;
    DPSPointer coords;
    int numCoords;
    DPSNumberFormat numType;
    DPSUserPathOp *ops;
    int numOp;
    DPSPointer bbox;
    DPSUserPathAction action;
```

DPSHitUserPath provides a convenient interface to PostScript operators that test for path intersection without actually painting anything. For more information, consult sections 4.5.3, "Insideness Testing," and 7.3.2, "Hit Detection," of *PostScript Language Reference Manual, Second Edition.*

If *radius* is zero, **DPSHitUserPath** uses the *x/y* form of the operator specified by *action*. If *radius* is nonzero, **DPSHitUserPath** constructs a circular user path centered on *x* and *y* with the specified radius and uses the aperture form of the specified action.

If *action* is *dps_ineofill, dps_infill,* or *dps_instroke,* **DPSHitUserPath** ignores the parameters specifying the user path and tests against the current path. If *action* is *dps_inueofill, dps_inufill,* or *dps_inustroke,* **DPSHitUserPath** uses the parameters specifying the user path to define the user path being tested against. If *action* is anything else, **DPSHitUserPath** returns *False* and does nothing else.

See **DPSDoUserPath** for a description of the *coords*, *numCoords*, *numType*, *ops*, *numOp*, and *bbox* parameters.

The procedure returns the resulting boolean value.

Note: *Calling **DPSHitUserPath** with radius zero and dps_ineofill, dps_infill, or dps_in-stroke as the action is semantically equivalent to calling the DPSineofill, DPSinfill, or DPSinstroke procedure.*

6   File Preview Procedures

The procedures described in this section simplify rendering PostScript language files into X drawable objects (windows or pixmaps). Code that uses the procedures must include *<DPS/dpsXpreview.h>*, which automatically includes *<DPS/dpsXcommon.h>*.

The section starts with a brief introduction to the file preview utilities, followed by structure and type definitions, a procedure overview, and procedure definitions.

6.1   Introduction

The first step is optionally to call **XDPSSetFileFunctions** to supply file access procedures appropriate to the data source:

- **XDPSFileGetsFunc** and **XDPSFileRewindFunc** are the default procedures, suitable for a separate EPS file.

- **XDPSEmbeddedEPSFGetsFunc** and **XDPSEmbeddedEPSFRewindFunc** handle an EPSF section within a longer file.

- The application can also define its own procedures that mimic the behavior of **fgets** and **rewind**. In this case, the image source is not limited to files.

An application can render a file into a pixmap or a window. If the application renders an EPS file into a pixmap, it can use **XDPSCreatePixmapForEPSF** to create an appropriately sized pixmap. The %%BoundingBox comment in the EPS file and the *pixelsPerPoint* parameter to **XDPSCreatePixmapForEPSF** determine the size of the pixmap. **XDPSPixelsPerPoint** can be called for information about the resolution of the specified screen.

The application then calls **XDPSImageFileIntoDrawable** to actually render the file **XDPSImageFileIntoDrawable** can render a file into any X window or pixmap; it is not limited to pixmaps created by **XDPSCreatePixmapForEPSF**.

If the specified display does not support the Display PostScript extension, the image area is filled with a 50% gray stipple pattern, or filled with solid 1's if the *createMask* argument to **XDPSImageFileIntoDrawable** is *True*.

If the display supports the Display PostScript extension, **XDPSImageFileIntoDrawable** starts executing the file, placing the resulting image into the drawable. The setting of *waitForCompletion* determines what happens next:

- If *waitForCompletion* is *True*, **XDPSImageFileIntoDrawable** waits until imaging is complete before it returns.

- If *waitForCompletion* is *False*, **XDPSImageFileIntoDrawable** waits for the amount of time specified by **XDPSSetImagingTimeout**. If imaging is not complete by this time, **XDPSImageFileIntoDrawable** returns *dps_status_imaging_incomplete*.

  If imaging was incomplete, **XDPSImageFileIntoDrawable** temporarily sets the imaging context's status handler so that the variable pointed to by *doneFlag* will become *True* when the imaging completes. The application must then call **XDPSCheckImagingResults** to find the results of imaging. *doneFlag* can only change its state as a result of handling a status event from the DPS/X server.

If **XDPSImageFileIntoDrawable** returns *dps_status_imaging_incomplete*, an application has to wait until **XDPSCheckImagingResults** returns a status that is not *dps_status_imaging_incomplete* before it does anything with the context. The context is otherwise left in an undefined state and imaging might not be correct.

When an application uses **XDPSImageFileIntoDrawable** with *waitForCompletion False*, using pass-through event delivery is highly recommended. There can otherwise be substantial delays between the time *doneFlag* is set and the time the application has an opportunity to test *doneFlag*. See "Event Dispatching" in section 4.8 of *Client Library Supplement for X* for more information.

An application can stop partial imaging by destroying the context with **DPSDestroySharedContext** if it is using the shared context, or with both **DPSDestroyContext** and **XDPSUnregisterContext** if it is not using the shared context.

While **XDPSCreatePixmapForEPSF** requires a correctly formed EPS file to find the bounding box, **XDPSImageFileIntoDrawable** can image any single-page PostScript language file into a drawable.

The following code example shows how to create a pixmap for an EPS file and image the file into that pixmap. This example assumes that *widget* is the widget that will ultimately display the image, *depth* is the depth of that widget, and *file* is the opened EPS file. In this example, the

penultimate parameter to **XDPSImageFileIntoDrawable** is *True*, so
XDPSImageFileIntoDrawable will not return until the imaging is
complete.

Example 1 *Creating a pixmap and executing an EPS file*

C language code:

```
int status;
XRectangle bbox, pixelSize;
Pixmap p;
Bool doneFlag;
float pixelsPerPoint;

pixelsPerPoint = XDPSPixelsPerPoint(XtScreen(widget));

status = XDPSCreatePixmapForEPSF((DPSContext) NULL,
        XtScreen(widget), file, depth, pixelsPerPoint,
        &p, &pixelSize, &bbox);

switch (status) {
  case dps_status_success:
    break;
  case dps_status_failure:
    fprintf(stderr, "File is not EPSF\n");
    exit(1);
  case dps_status_no_extension:
    fprintf(stderr, "Server does not support DPS\n");
    exit(1);
  default:
    fprintf(stderr, "Internal error %d\n", status);
    exit(1);
}

status = XDPSImageFileIntoDrawable((DPSContext) NULL,
        XtScreen(widget), p, file, pixelSize.height,
        depth, &bbox, -bbox.x, -bbox.y, pixelsPerPoint,
        True, False, True, &doneFlag);

switch (status) {
 case dps_status_success:
  break;
 case dps_status_no_extension:
  fprintf(stderr, "Server does not support DPS\n");
  exit(1);
```

```
    case dps_status_postscript_error:
     fprintf(stderr,
            "PostScript execution error in EPSF file\n");
     exit(1);
    default:
     fprintf(stderr, "Internal error %d\n", status);
     exit(1);
   }
```

An EPS file can take a long time to execute. Worse, a poorly written EPS file might contain an infinite loop in its PostScript language code and never finish executing. One way to protect an application that imports EPS files is to use **XDPSImageFileIntoDrawable** with the *waitForCompletion* parameter *False* and allow the user to abort execution. The following code example contains the framework for doing this.

The *waitForCompletion* parameter to **XDPSImageFileIntoDrawable** (located next to last in the parameter list) has the value *False,* so the procedure call can return before the imaging is complete. If **XDPSImageFileIntoDrawable** returns *dps_status_imaging_incomplete,* the example goes into a subsidiary event dispatching loop until *doneFlag* becomes *True.* An application that gives the user a way to abort the execution of the EPS file would add an additional exit criterion to the dispatching loop. The example below assumes that the application has already set up pass-through event dispatching with **XDPSSetEventDelivery.**

Example 2 *Protecting against incorrect EPS files*

```
status = XDPSImageFileIntoDrawable((DPSContext) NULL,
        XtScreen(widget), p, file, pixelSize.height,
        depth, &bbox, -bbox.x, -bbox.y, pixelsPerPoint,
        True, False, False, &doneFlag);

if (status == dps_status_imaging_incomplete) {
  XEvent ev;
  do {
     XtAppNextEvent(app, &ev);
     if (!XDPSDispatchEvent(&ev)) XtDispatchEvent(&ev);
  } while (!doneFlag);
  status = XDPSCheckImagingResults((DPSContext) NULL,
        XtScreen(shell));
}
```

TK

```
switch (status) {

/* ... as before ... */

}
```

6.2 Structures and Type Definitions

XDPSGetsFunction
```
typedef char *(*XDPSGetsFunction) (/*
    char *buf,
    int n,
    FILE *f,
    DPSPointer private*/);
```

XDPSGetsFunction is a procedure type. An *XDPSGetsFunction* mimics the
behavior of the standard C library **fgets** procedure and returns the next
line of a specified file. The *XDPSGetsFunction* returns *NULL* to indicate the
end of the section to be imaged.

XDPSPosition
```
typedef struct {
    long startPos;
    int nestingLevel;
    unsigned long binaryCount;
    Bool continuedLine;
} XDPSPosition;
```

This data structure is used with **XDPSEmbeddedEPSFRewindFunc** and
XDPSEmbeddedEPSFGetsFunc and is described there.

XDPSRewindFunction
```
typedef void (*XDPSRewindFunction) (/*
    FILE *f,
    DPSPointer private */);
```

XDPSRewindFunction is a procedure type. An *XDPSRewindFunction* mimics
the standard C library **rewind** procedure and repositions the specified
file to the beginning of the section to be imaged, normally with **fseek**.
When **XDPSImageFileIntoDrawable** and **XDPSCreatePixmapForEPSF**
start to read lines from a file, they first execute the *XDPSRewindFunction*
procedure.

6.3 Procedure Overview

Table 6 *File preview procedures*

Procedure	Functionality
XDPSCheckImagingResults	Checks the status of the imaging on a specified context.
XDPSCreatePixmapForEPSF	Creates a pixmap for imaging on a specified screen.
XDPSEmbeddedEPSFRewindFunc **XDPSEmbeddedEPSFGetsFunc**	These are **rewind** and **gets** procedures that handle an EPSF section embedded within a longer file.
XDPSFileRewindFunc **XDPSFileGetsFunc**	These are the default **rewind** and **gets** procedures that handle a separate EPS file.
XDPSImageFileIntoDrawable	Images a PostScript language file into a specified drawable.
XDPSPixelsPerPoint	Returns the resolution of a specified screen in pixels per point.
XDPSSetFileFunctions	Defines the procedures used by **XDPSCreatePixmapForEPSF** and **XDPSImageFileIntoDrawable** to reset a file to its beginning and to read the next line of the file.
XDPSSetImagingTimeout	Determines how long, in milliseconds, **XDPSImageFileIntoDrawable** waits before returning after incomplete imaging.

6.4 Procedures

XDPSCheckImagingResults

```
int XDPSCheckImagingResults (context, screen)
    DPSContext context;
    Screen *screen;
```

XDPSCheckImagingResults checks the status of the imaging on *context*.

If *context* is *NULL*, the shared context for *screen*'s display is used. If a non-*NULL* context is passed, it must have been registered with **XDPSRegisterContext**.

XDPSCheckImagingResults returns:

- *dps_status_success* if imaging is complete and successful.

- *dps_status_imaging_incomplete* if imaging is continuing.

- *dps_status_postscript_error* if imaging is complete but the PostScript language file being executed contains an error.

- *dps_status_illegal_value* if the context is not currently involved in previewing.

- *dps_status_unregistered_context* if the context has not been registered with the context manager.

XDPSCreatePixmapForEPSF

```
int XDPSCreatePixmapForEPSF (context, screen, epsf, depth,
                            pixelsPerPoint, pixmapReturn,
                            pixelSizeReturn, bboxReturn)
    DPSContext context;
    Screen *screen;
    FILE *epsf;
    int depth;
    double pixelsPerPoint;
    Pixmap *pixmapReturn;
    XRectangle *pixelSizeReturn;
    XRectangle *bboxReturn;
```

XDPSCreatePixmapForEPSF creates a pixmap for use on the specified screen. The %%BoundingBox comment in the file, scaled by *pixelsPerPoint*, determines the size of the pixmap.

context can be *NULL*. In that case, the shared context for *screen*'s display is used. If *context* is non-*NULL*, it must have been registered with **XDPSRegisterContext**.

XDPSCreatePixmapForEPSF returns one of the status values shown in Table 7.

Table 7 *Status return values for XDPSCreatePixmapForEPSF*

Status	Description
dps_status_success	This value is returned when **XDPSCreatePixmapForEPSF** completes successfully.
dps_status_no_extension	If this value is returned, the procedure still creates a pixmap and returns a suitable size. However, **XDPSImageFileIntoDrawable** will not be able to image to the pixmap since the Display PostScript extension is not present.
dps_status_illegal_value	This status value is returned if *screen* is *NULL*, *file* is *NULL*, or *depth* or *pixelsPerPoint* is less than or equal to 0.
dps_status_failure	This status value is returned if the file specified by *epsf* does not contain a %%BoundingBox comment.

XDPSCreatePixmapForEPSF returns the size of the pixmap in *pixelSizeReturn* (*x* and *y* are zero) and the bounding box (in points) in *bboxReturn*.

XDPSEmbeddedEPSFGetsFunc

```
extern char *XDPSEmbeddedEPSFGetsFunc (buf, n, f, data)
  char *buf;
  int n;
  FILE *f;
  DPSPointer data;
```

XDPSEmbeddedEPSFRewindFunc

```
extern void XDPSEmbeddedEPSFRewindFunc (f, data)
  FILE *f;
  DPSPointer data;
```

XDPSEmbeddedEPSFRewindFunc and **XDPSEmbeddedEPSFGetsFunc** are **rewind** and **gets** procedures that handle an EPS file embedded within a longer file. To preview a separate EPS file, use **XDPSFileRewindFunc** and **XDPSFileGetsFunc**.

TK

An application can pass the **rewind** and **gets** procedures to **XDPSSetFileFunctions**. The *rewindPrivateData* and *getsPrivateData* arguments to **XDPSSetFileFunctions** must both point to the same instance of an *XDPSPosition* structure.

The procedures use the document structuring conventions comments %%BeginDocument and %%EndDocument (DSC version 2.0 or later) to detect the end of the included file and to identify any subsidiary EPSF sections included in the EPSF section being executed.

The application must set the *startPos* in the *XDPSPosition* structure to the first character of the desired EPSF section before calling **XDPSCreatePixmapForEPSF** or **XDPSImageFileIntoDrawable**. The position must be *after* any initial %%BeginDocument comment for this EPSF section.

The *nestingLevel, continuedLine,* and *binaryCount* fields are used internally by the procedures and should not be modified. A call to **XDPSImageFileIntoDrawable** modifies *startPos* to be the first character after the complete EPSF section, or –1 if the EPSF section ended with end-of-file.

XDPSFileGetsFunc

```
extern char *XDPSFileGetsFunc (buf, n, f, private)
    char *buf;
    int n;
    FILE *f;
    DPSPointer private;
```

XDPSFileRewindFunc

```
extern void XDPSFileRewindFunc (f, private)
    FILE *f;
    DPSPointer private;
```

XDPSFileGetsFunc and **XDPSFileRewindFunc** are the default **gets** and **rewind** procedures and are appropriate for an EPSF file that is a separate file. Use **XDPSEmbeddedEPSFRewindFunc** and **XDPSEmbeddedEPSFGetsFunc** while previewing an EPSF section embedded in a longer file.

If an application has installed different procedures for this behavior, **XDPSFileRewindFunc** or **XDPSFileGetsFunc** can be passed to **XDPSSetFileFunctions** to restore the default behavior. The *rewindPrivateData* and *getsPrivateData* pointers should both be *NULL*.

XDPSImageFileIntoDrawable

```
extern int XDPSImageFileIntoDrawable (context,
     screen, dest, file, drawableHeight, drawableDepth,
     bbox, xOffset, yOffset, pixelsPerPoint, clear,
     createMask, waitForCompletion, doneFlag)
  DPSContext context;
  Screen *screen;
  Drawable dest;
  FILE *file;
  int drawableHeight, drawableDepth;
  XRectangle *bbox;
  int xOffset, yOffset;
  double pixelsPerPoint;
  Bool clear, createMask, waitForCompletion, *doneFlag;
```

XDPSImageFileIntoDrawable images a PostScript language file into the *dest* drawable object—that is, into a pixmap or a window.

If *context* is *NULL*, the shared context for the display is used. If a context is passed, it must have been registered with **XDPSRegisterContext**.

drawableHeight and *drawableDepth* describe the drawable object; the height is in X pixels.

bbox describes the bounding box of the imaged area, in points.

The image is offset by *xOffset* and *yOffset*, which are given in points. The offsets are often *–bbox.x* and *–bbox.y*, which shifts the image to the lower left corner of the drawable.

pixelsPerPoint defines the scale factor used to image the PostScript language file.

If *clear* is *True*, the area defined by *bbox* is cleared to white before imaging.

If *createMask* is *True*, the drawable must be 1 bit deep, and becomes a mask that can be used as an X clip mask: each bit that the PostScript interpreter touches during imaging is set to 1. If *clear* is also *True*, all untouched bits within *bbox* are set to 0.

If *waitForCompletion* is *True*, **XDPSImageFileIntoDrawable** waits until imaging is complete before returning. If *waitForCompletion* is *False*, **XDPSImageFileIntoDrawable** waits for the amount of time specified by **XDPSSetImagingTimeout** and then returns *dps_status_imaging_incomplete* if imaging is not complete.

TK

When imaging is complete, agents set up by
XDPSImageFileIntoDrawable set the variable pointed to by *doneFlag* to
True. The application must then call **XDPSCheckImagingResults** to find
the results of imaging. The status of *doneFlag* can only change as a result
of handling a status event from the DPS/X server.

Incorrect imaging can result, and a context can be left in an undefined
state, if anything is done to affect the context between the following
times:

- When **XDPSImageFileIntoDrawable** returns
  dps_status_imaging_incomplete

- When **XDPSCheckImagingResults** returns a status that is *not*
  dps_status_imaging_incomplete

To cancel imaging, the application can destroy the context by calling
DPSDestroySharedContext or by calling both **DPSDestroyContext** and
XDPSUnregisterContext.

When an application uses **XDPSImageFileIntoDrawable** with
waitForCompletion False, using pass-through event delivery is highly
recommended. There can otherwise be substantial delays between the
time *doneFlag* is set and the time the application gets the opportunity to
test *doneFlag*. See *Client Library Supplement for X*, section 5.3, "Use
Pass-Through Event Dispatching," for more information.

If a display does not support the Display PostScript extension, the
image area determined by the *bbox* parameter is filled with a 50% gray
stipple pattern, or is filled with solid 1's if *createMask* is *True*.

XDPSImageFileIntoDrawable returns *dps_status_success*,
dps_status_no_extension, or *dps_status_unregistered_context*, or one of the
following values:

- *dps_status_illegal_value* if *screen* is *NULL*, *drawable* is **None**, *file* is *NULL*,
  or *drawableHeight*, *drawableDepth*, or *pixelsPerPoint* is less than or equal
  to 0.

- *dps_status_postscript_error* if the PostScript language file contains an
  error.

- *dps_status_imaging_incomplete* if *waitForCompletion* is *False* and the
  imaging is not finished within the time-out.

XDPSPixelsPerPoint

```
extern double XDPSPixelsPerPoint (screen)
    Screen *screen;
```

XDPSPixelsPerPoint returns the resolution of *screen*; this value can be passed to **XDPSCreatePixmapForEPSF** or **XDPSImageFileIntoDrawable**.

Note: *If the X server reports incorrect resolution information about the screen, as is the case in some implementations, the incorrect information is propagated by* **XDPSPixelsPerPoint**.

XDPSSetFileFunctions

```
extern int XDPSSetFileFunctions (rewindFunction,
        rewindPrivateData, getsFunction, getsPrivateData)
    XDPSRewindFunction rewindFunction;
    DPSPointer rewindPrivateData;
    XDPSGetsFunction getsFunction;
    DPSPointer getsPrivateData;
```

XDPSSetFileFunctions defines the procedures that **XDPSCreatePixmapForEPSF** and **XDPSImageFileIntoDrawable** use to reset a file to its beginning and to read the next line of the PostScript language file.

The values specified by *rewindPrivateData* and *getsPrivateData* are passed as the *private* parameter to the *rewind* and *gets* procedures, but are otherwise ignored.

The default procedures are suitable for use with a file that contains a single EPSF image. They can be replaced with procedures to handle, for example, an EPSF section embedded within a longer file.

XDPSSetImagingTimeout

```
extern void XDPSSetImagingTimeout (timeout, maxDoublings)
    int timeout, maxDoublings;
```

XDPSSetImagingTimeout determines how long (in milliseconds) **XDPSImageFileIntoDrawable** waits before returning that imaging incomplete. **XDPSImageFileIntoDrawable** first waits for the amount of time specified by *timeout* and then repeatedly doubles the wait until imaging is complete or until *maxDoublings* have occurred.

TK

7 The Motif Font Selection Panel

The font selection panel is a Motif dialog box that allows the end user to choose one of the available Type 1 fonts. It presents the fonts available on the workstation and any fonts that can be located through the *PSRESOURCEPATH* environment variable. (See Appendix A, "Locating PostScript Language Resources.") The user can choose a font by selecting the font family, face, and size, then view the font in the preview window above the selection panels.

From the font selection panel, the user can bring up a font sampler (see section 8, "The Motif Font Sampler"). The font sampler makes it possible to view fonts with certain characteristics—for example, to view all currently available bold italic fonts.

The following sections provide information on the font selection panel and the font sampler, including

- The behavior of the font selection panel and the font sampler.

- The available resources for the font selection panel and the font sampler.

- Callback procedures and associated callback information.

- Procedures for working with the font selection panel and the font sampler.

Note: *An application that creates a font selection panel must merge the contents of the FontSelect defaults file into its own application defaults file. Beginning with the X11R5 release of the X Window System, this can be done with a #include directive in the application defaults file.*

An application normally creates the font selection panel as a child of a shell widget, usually a transient shell. The font selection panel can also be elsewhere in the widget hierarchy. This allows the application to put additional information around the font selection panel. In that case, the application is responsible for popping up and popping down the Font Selection Panel.

The following information lets you use the widget:

- The header file is *<DPS/FontSB.h>*.

- The class pointer is *fontSelectionBoxWidgetClass*.

- The class name is *FontSelectionBox*.

- The *FontSelectionBox* widget is a subclass of *XmManager*.

7.1 Using the Motif Font Selection Panel

This section describes the behavior of the font selection panel in more detail. Information about the resources, callbacks, and procedures that implement the behavior are documented in the following sections. An example of a font selection panel is shown in Figure 1.

Figure 1 *The font selection panel*

7.1.1 Introduction

At the top of the font selection panel, a display region shows the selected font. This region, which is as wide as the panel, is called the *preview window*. The user can resize the preview window by moving the square handle at the lower right corner of the preview window. Below the preview window, the Family list region on the left and the Face list region on the right show the available fonts. Each time the user chooses a font family from the Family list, the Face list is updated appropriately. For example, a Face list for Helvetica might include Bold and Oblique, while a Face list for New Caledonia might include Bold and Italic.

Below the Family list region are a type-in region for selecting a font size and an option button. Below the Face list region are the Sampler button that brings up the font sampler and the Preview button. At the bottom of the font selection panel, the user can choose the OK, Apply, Reset, or Cancel buttons to apply or undo the selection.

7.1.2 The Sampler Button

When the user activates the Sampler button, the font selection panel creates and displays a font sampler as described in Section 8.

7.1.3 The Preview Button

When the user activates the Preview button, the preview window displays the currently selected font name in that font. Typing *p* or *P* into the *size* text field or double-clicking in the Family or Face list is equivalent to activating the Preview button. Previewing can be made automatic with the *XtNautoPreview* resource. See Table 8 for the font selection panel resource set.

7.1.4 The OK Button

When the user activates the OK button, the font selected in the panel is returned to the application and the font selection panel disappears, as described below.

1. Any fonts downloaded for preview which do not correspond to the current selection are undefined.

2. The panel looks for the name of the selected font's AFM (Adobe Font Metric) file if the *XtNgetAFM* resource is *True* and the current settings are for exactly one font.

3. *XtNvalidateCallback* is invoked with the current settings in the panel. *FSBCallbackReason* is *FSBOK*.

   • If the *doit* field in the call data is now *False*, the panel does nothing more and remains on screen without calling *XtNokCallback*.

   • Otherwise, the panel uses the current selections to update the resources *XtNfontName*, *XtNfontSize*, *XtNfontFamily*, *XtNfontFace*, *XtNfontNameMultiple*, *XtNfontFamilyMultiple*, *XtNfontFaceMultiple*, and *XtNfontSizeMultiple* with the current selections.

4. *XtNokCallback* is called with the current settings. *FSBCallbackReason* is *FSBOK*.

5. If the parent of the font selection panel is a shell, the panel pops down the shell.

Note: *If the parent is not a shell, the application should make the font selection panel disappear in its XtNokCallback.*

7.1.5   The Apply Button

When the user activates the Apply button, the font selection panel performs all the operations for the OK button but does not pop down the panel's parent shell. *XtNapplyCallback* is called instead of *XtNokCallback*. *FSBCallbackReason* is *FSBApply* in all callbacks.

7.1.6   The Reset Button

When the user activates the Reset button, the selected font reverts to the one selected when the user last chose Apply or OK, or the one last set by the application, whichever happened most recently.

To accomplish this, the font selection panel performs the following actions:

- First, the panel restores the current settings to those specified by the resources *XtNfontName*, *XtNfontFamily*, *XtNfontFace*, *XtNfontSize*, *XtNfontNameMultiple*, *XtNfontFamilyMultiple*, *XtNfontFaceMultiple*, and *XtNfontSizeMultiple*.

- Then all fonts which were downloaded for preview, but which do not correspond to the current settings, are undefined.

- After that, the panel calls *XtNresetCallback* with the current settings. The settings are identical to those passed to the most recent invocation of *XtNokCallback* or *XtNapplyCallback*, or to the most recent settings specified by the application, whichever happened last. *FSBCallbackReason* is *FSBReset*.

TK

7.1.7 The Cancel Button

When the user activates the Cancel button, the font selection panel performs all operations listed for the Reset button, but calls *XtNcancelCallback* instead of *XtNresetCallback*. *FSBCallbackReason* is *FSBCancel*. If the parent of the font selection panel is a shell, the panel pops down the shell.

Note: *If the parent is not a shell, the application should make the font selection panel disappear in its XtNcancelCallback.*

7.2 Application Control of the Font Panel

The application can set the currently selected font in the font selection panel. It does this either by specifying a font name (for example, "Helvetica-BoldOblique") for the *XtNfontName* resource or by specifying a font family and face (for example "Helvetica" and "Bold Oblique") for the *XtNfontFamily* and *XtNfontFace* resources. The boolean resource *XtNuseFontName* controls whether the font selection panel pays attention to the font name resource or the font family and face resources. The two interface procedures **FSBSetFontName** and **FSBSetFontFamilyFace** provide convenient interfaces to these resources.

The currently selected font size can be set with the *XtNfontSize* resource. This is a floating point resource, and is therefore difficult to set with **XtSetValues**. The interface procedure **FSBSetFontSize** provides the same functionality and is easier to use.

The application can also tell the font selection panel to display the fact that multiple fonts or sizes are currently selected. The boolean resources *XtNfontNameMultiple*, *XtNfontFamilyMultiple*, *XtNfontFaceMultiple*, and *XtNfontSizeMultiple* control this; there are also parameters to the convenience interface procedures that set these resources.

Setting multiple fonts allows some useful interaction techniques. For example, assume that the user has selected a block of text that contains several different fonts. The application sets a multiple font selection in the font selection panel.

- If the user selects a new size but makes no font selection, the application can make all the text in the block the selected size without changing the fonts.

- If the user selects a new font family but not a new font face, the application can convert each face in the block to the corresponding face in the new family by calling **FSBMatchFontFace**.

The callback data passed to the application indicates when there is a multiple font or size selection. A multiple font or size selection can result only from the application's setting a multiple selection that the user does not subsequently change; the user cannot convert a nonmultiple selection into a multiple selection.

7.3   Font Downloading and Resource Database Files

Each implementation of the Display PostScript extension has a directory or set of directories where it looks for Type 1 font outline programs. The fonts described in these programs are the fonts that appear in the font selection panel. The font selection panel can also temporarily download other font programs into the Display PostScript extension.

Generally, users should install new fonts in the normal font outline directory. However, there can be reasons why a user cannot or does not want to do this:

- The user might not have permission to add files to the outline directory.

- The font program might be the user's own private copy, and the outline directory might be shared among different machines.

- The user might have so many font programs available, for example on a file server, that unsophisticated programs would bog down if all the fonts were installed in the outline directory.

The font selection panel uses the *PSRESOURCEPATH* environment variable to locate fonts to download. This environment variable lists directories that contain PostScript language resource database files, and the resource database files in turn list the names of files that contain font programs to download. Appendix A gives full details of these resource database files. When the user chooses a font that is not resident in the server, the font selection panel automatically downloads the font into the Display PostScript extension. This is somewhat slower than using a resident font, but it is otherwise transparent to the user.

In addition to names of font programs, resource database files contain name information about each font, whether it is downloadable or resident in the server. This scheme allows the font selection panel to list

TK

the font without having to look into the font program itself. When no name information is found for a resident font, the font selection panel queries the server for this information, but this query takes much longer than fetching the information from resource database files—up to 100 times longer.

For efficient performance, always be sure to provide resource database files for resident fonts. If creating a font selection panel takes a long time, the reason is probably that resource database files are not available.

7.4 Font Selection Resources

Table 8 *Motif font selection panel resource set*

Name	Class	Default	Type	Access
XtNautoPreview	XmCAutoPreview	True	XtRBoolean	CSG
XtNcontext	XmCContext	NULL	XtRDPSContext	CSG
XtNdefaultResourcePath	XmCDefaultResourcePath	See description	XtRString	CSG
XtNfontFace	XmCFontFace	NULL	XtRString	CSG
XtNfontFaceMultiple	XmCFontFaceMultiple	False	XtRBoolean	CSG
XtNfontFamily	XmCFontFamily	NULL	XtRString	CSG
XtNfontFamilyMultiple	XmCFontFamilyMultiple	False	XtRBoolean	CSG
XtNfontName	XmCFontName	NULL	XtRString	CSG
XtNfontNameMultiple	XmCFontNameMultiple	False	XtRBoolean	CSG
XtNfontSize	XmCFontSize	12.0	XtRFloat	CSG
XtNfontSizeMultiple	XmCFontSizeMultiple	False	XtRBoolean	CSG
XtNgetAFM	XmCGetAFM	False	XtRBoolean	CSG
XtNgetServerFonts	XmCGetServerFonts	True	XtRBoolean	CSG
XtNmakeFontsShared	XmCMakeFontsShared	True	XtRBoolean	CSG
XtNmaxPendingDeletes	XmCMaxPendingDeletes	10	XtRInt	CSG
XtNpreviewOnChange	XmCPreviewOnChange	True	XtRBoolean	CSG
XtNpreviewString	XmCPreviewString	NULL	XtRString	CSG
XtNresourcePathOverride	XmCResourcePathOverride	NULL	XtRString	CSG
XtNsizeCount	XmCSizeCount	10	XtRInt	CSG
XtNsizes	XmCSizes	See description	XtRFloatList	CSG
XtNshowSampler	XmCShowSampler	False	XtRBoolean	CSG
XtNshowSamplerButton	XmCShowSamplerButton	True	XtRBoolean	CSG
XtNundefUnusedFonts	XmCUndefUnusedFonts	True	XtRBoolean	CSG
XtNuseFontName	XmCUseFontName	True	XtRBoolean	CSG

7.4.1 Resource Description

XtNautoPreview   If *True*, the font selection panel previews fonts as soon as the user selects them. If *False*, the user must activate the Preview button. Default is *True.*

XtNcontext	Provides a context to use for previewing and querying the server for fonts. The font selection panel changes the *drawable* and possibly the *depth* for this context. If the context is *NULL*, the panel uses the shared context for the display. Default is *NULL*.
XtNdefaultResourcePath	Provides the default *path* parameter for locating AFM files and fonts that can be downloaded. Default is specified at compilation time. See Appendix A, "Locating PostScript Language Resources," for more information.
XtNfontFace	Provides the selected face name. Relevant only if *XtNuseFontName* is *False*. If *NULL*, the face is selected by the *XtNfaceSelectCallback* resource. Default is *NULL*.
XtNfontFaceMultiple	If *True*, displays a message that multiple faces are selected. Default is *False*.
XtNfontFamily	Provides the selected font family. Relevant only if *XtNuseFontName* is *False*. If *NULL*, no family is selected. Default is *NULL*.
XtNfontFamilyMultiple	If *True*, displays a message that multiple families are selected. Default is *False*.
XtNfontName	Provides the selected font name. Relevant only if *XtNuseFontName* is *True*. If *NULL*, no font is selected. Default is *NULL*.
XtNfontNameMultiple	If *True*, displays a message that multiple families and faces are selected. Default is *False*.
XtNfontSize	Provides selected font size. Default is 12.0. Setting this resource with **XtSetValues** is difficult. Use **FSBSetFontSize** instead.
XtNfontSizeMultiple	If *True*, indicates that multiple sizes are selected. Default is *False*.
XtNgetAFM	If *True*, the font selection panel tries to find an AFM file before calling *XtNokCallback* or *XtNapplyCallback*. Default is *False*.
XtNgetServerFonts	If *True*, list both resident and downloadable fonts. If *False*, list only downloadable fonts. Default is *True*.
XtNmakeFontsShared	*XtNmakeFontsShared* and *XtNundefUnusedFonts* control where fonts are defined and whether the font selection panel undefines fonts that were previewed but not selected.

The possible behaviors for values of *XtNundefUnusedFonts* and *XtNmakeFontsShared* are shown in the following table.

Table 9 *Behaviors for XtNundefUnusedFonts and XtNmakeFontsShared*

Resource Values		
XtNundefUnusedFonts	*XtNmakeFontsShared*	*Behavior*
False	*False*	The panel loads the fonts into private VM and never undefines fonts.
False	*True*	The panel loads the fonts into shared VM and never undefines fonts.
True	*False*	The panel loads the fonts into private VM and undefines unused fonts when the user activates the OK, Apply, Reset, or Cancel buttons, or when there are more unused fonts than specified in the *XtNmaxPendingDeletes* resource.
True	*True*	The panel loads the fonts into private VM. When the user activates the OK or Apply button, all fonts downloaded into private VM are undefined and the selected font is downloaded into shared VM. Fonts are also undefined if the user activates the Reset or Cancel button, or when there are more unused fonts than specified in the *XtNmaxPendingDeletes* resource.

If *XtNmakeFontsShared* is *False*, the application must use the same context as the font selection panel, otherwise loaded fonts will not be available to the application.

Default is *True*.

XtNmaxPendingDeletes If *XtNundefUnusedFonts* is *True*, *XtNmaxPendingDeletes* specifies the maximum number of unused fonts allowed to remain before the font selection panel undefines the least recently loaded font. Making this value too small leads to repeated downloading during typical browsing. Making this value too large leads to excessive server memory use. Default is 10.

XtNpreviewOnChange If *XtNautoPreview* is *False*, *XtNpreviewOnChange* controls whether the font selection panel preview changes when the application changes *fontName*, *fontFamilyName*, *fontFaceName*, or *fontSize*. Default is *True*.

XtNpreviewString Determines the string displayed in the preview window. If *NULL*, displays the font name. Default is *NULL*.

XtNresourcePathOverride	If non-*NULL*, provides a resource path to override the user's *PSRESOURCEPATH* environment variable. Default is *NULL*.
XtNsizeCount	Determines the number of entries in the *XtNsizes* resource. Default is 10.
XtNsizes	Provides a list of sizes to present in the Size menu. Default is 8, 10, 12, 14, 16, 18, 24, 36, 48, 72.
XtNshowSampler	Determines whether the font sampler is shown when the font selection panel pops up. Tracks the popped-up state of the sampler, and can be used to pop the sampler up or down. Default is *False*.
XtNshowSamplerButton	Determines whether or not the button to bring up the font sampler is visible. Default is *True*.
XtNundefUnusedFonts	Default is *True*. A description is given under *XtNmakeFontsShared*.
XtNuseFontName	Determines whether the *XtNfontName* or the *XtNfontFamily* and **XtNfontFace** resources are used to choose the initial font to display. Default is *True*.

7.4.2 Children of the Motif Font Panel

The following resources provide access to the child widgets of the font selection panel. They cannot be changed.

The name of each child widget is the same as the resource name, but without the *Child* suffix.

Table 10 *Motif font selection panel child resource set*

Name	Class	Type	Access
XtNapplyButtonChild	XtCReadOnly	XtRWidget	G
XtNcancelButtonChild	XtCReadOnly	XtRWidget	G
XtNfaceLabelChild	XtCReadOnly	XtRWidget	G
XtNfaceMultipleLabelChild	XtCReadOnly	XtRWidget	G
XtNfaceScrolledListChild	XtCReadOnly	XtRWidget	G
XtNfamilyMultipleLabelChild	XtCReadOnly	XtRWidget	G
XtNfamilyScrolledListChild	XtCReadOnly	XtRWidget	G
XtNokButtonChild	XtCReadOnly	XtRWidget	G
XtNpaneChild	XtCReadOnly	XtRWidget	G
XtNpanelChild	XtCReadOnly	XtRWidget	G
XtNpreviewButtonChild	XtCReadOnly	XtRWidget	G
XtNpreviewChild	XtCReadOnly	XtRWidget	G
XtNresetButtonChild	XtCReadOnly	XtRWidget	G
XtNsamplerButtonChild	XtCReadOnly	XtRWidget	G
XtNseparatorChild	XtCReadOnly	XtRWidget	G
XtNsizeLabelChild	XtCReadOnly	XtRWidget	G
XtNsizeMultipleLabelChild	XtCReadOnly	XtRWidget	G
XtNsizeOptionMenuChild	XtCReadOnly	XtRWidget	G
XtNsizeTextFieldChild	XtCReadOnly	XtRWidget	G

7.5 Callback Procedures

The following sections contain information about callback procedures available for working with the font selection panel. The resource table is followed by a short description of each callback.

Table 11 *Motif font selection panel callback resource set*

Name	Class	Default	Type	Access
XtNapplyCallback	XtCCallback	NULL	XtCallbackList	C
XtNcancelCallback	XtCCallback	NULL	XtCallbackList	C
XtNcreateSamplerCallback	XtCCallback	NULL	XtCallbackList	C
XtNfaceSelectCallback	XtCCallback	NULL	XtCallbackList	C
XtNokCallback	XtCCallback	NULL	XtCallbackList	C
XtNresetCallback	XtCCallback	NULL	XtCallbackList	C
XtNvalidateCallback	XtCCallback	NULL	XtCallbackList	C

XtNapplyCallback Indicates that the user wants to choose the selected options. The font selection panel remains. *XtNapplyCallback* passes a pointer to an *FSBCallbackRec* as call data. Applications typically supply the same procedure for the *XtNapplyCallback* as for *XtNokCallback.*

XtNcancelCallback The font selection panel reverts to the values last set with *XtNfontName, XtNfontFamily, XtNfontFace,* and *XtNfontSize.* The font selection panel goes away after the callback returns. *XtNcancelCallback* passes a pointer to an *FSBCallbackRec* as call data. Applications rarely need to specify *XtNcancelCallback.*

XtNcreateSamplerCallback To create the font sampler itself rather than letting the font selection panel create it an application must provide an *XtNcreateSamplerCallback. XtNcreateSamplerCallback* passes a pointer to an *FSBCreateSamplerCallbackRec* as call data. The application must fill in the *sampler* field with the widget ID of the *FontSampler* widget, and must fill in the *sampler_shell* field with the widget ID of the shell widget that contains the sampler. An application can use this callback procedure to enclose the font sampler in another widget—for example, to display an application icon with the sampler. It can also use this procedure if it has subclassed the font sampler.

XtNfaceSelectCallback After the user chooses a new font family this callback procedure is used to pick the face selection initially provided for the new family. *XtNfaceSelectCallback* passes a pointer to an *FSBFaceSelectCallbackRec* as call data. If, after this callback has been invoked, the *new_face* field is *NULL* or is not in *available_faces*, the font selection panel chooses a face using these rules:

1. If the new family has a face with the same name as the current face, select it.

2. If not, consider similar attributes in the face name, such as Roman-Medium-Regular-Book and Italic-Oblique-Slanted. If a face that is similar to the current face is found, select it.

3. If not, select a face with one of these names, in order: Roman, Medium, Book, Regular, Light, Demi, Semibold.

4. If no matching name is found, select the first face.

Application developers typically specify an *XtNfaceSelectCallback* only if they believe they can perform better face matching than the font selection panel, or if they want to provide a face selection that is entirely different from the panel's selection.

XtNokCallback Indicates that the user wants to choose the selected options. The font selection panel disappears after the callback returns. *XtNokCallback* passes a pointer to an *FSBCallbackRec* as call data. Applications typically use the same procedure for the *XtNokCallback* as for the *XtNapplyCallback*.

XtNresetCallback The font selection panel reverts to the values last set with *XtNfontName*, *XtNfontFamily*, *XtNfontFace*, and *XtNfontSize*. The font selection panel remains. *XtNresetCallback* passes a pointer to an *FSBCallbackRec* as call data. Applications rarely need to specify an *XtNresetCallback*.

XtNvalidateCallback If an application needs to validate a font selection before accepting it, the application should provide an *XtNvalidateCallback*. The font selection panel calls *XtNvalidateCallback* before calling *XtNokCallback* or *XtNapplyCallback*. If *doit* is *False* after the call to *XtNvalidateCallback*, the OK or Apply action is canceled. *XtNvalidateCallback* passes a pointer to an *FSBValidateCallbackRec* structure as call data.

Typical uses for *XtNvalidateCallback* include verifying that exactly one font and size are selected or that an AFM file is available for the selected font. If an application rejects a selection (by setting *doit* to *False*) it should display a message that explains why the selection is rejected.

TK

7.5.1 Callback Information

This section provides the definitions for structures that are used by the callback procedures described in the previous section.

FSBCallbackRec

```
typedef struct {
    FSBCallbackReason reason;
    String family;
    String face;
    float size;
    String name;
    String afm_filename;
    FSBSelectionType family_selection;
    FSBSelectionType face_selection;
    FSBSelectionType size_selection;
    FSBSelectionType name_selection;
    Boolean afm_present;
} FSBCallbackRec;
```

XtNokCallback, XtNapplyCallback, XtNresetCallback and *XtNcancelCallback* (see section 7.5, "Callback Procedures") pass a pointer to an *FSBCallbackRec* structure as call data.

FSBCallbackReason is one of *FSBOK, FSBApply, FSBReset,* or *FSBCancel*.

afm_filename is assigned a value only if the *XtNgetAFM* resource is *True*.

The *..._selection* fields contain *FSBNone* if the user has made no selection, *FSBOne* if the user has made one selection, or *FSBMultiple* if the user has made multiple selections. Multiple selections are possible only if the application has set the corresponding *...Multiple* resource and the user has not modified the selection of that type of information. If the *..._selection* field is *FSBNone* or *FSBMultiple*, the corresponding data field is *NULL* or *0.0*.

afm_present is *True* if *afm_filename* is not *NULL*, and *False* if *afm_filename* is *NULL*.

FSBValidateCallbackRec

```
typedef struct {
    FSBCallbackReason reason;
    String family;
    String face;
    float size;
    String name;
    String afm_filename;
    FSBSelectionType family_selection;
    FSBSelectionType face_selection;
    FSBSelectionType size_selection;
    FSBSelectionType name_selection;
    Boolean afm_present;
    Boolean doit;
} FSBValidateCallbackRec;
```

XtNvalidateCallback passes a pointer to an *FSBValidateCallbackRec* as call data.

All fields in this structure are the same as in *FSBCallbackRec*. The *doit* field is initially *True*.

FSBFaceSelectCallbackRec

```
typedef struct {
    String *available_faces;
    int num_available_faces;
    String current_face;
    String new_face;
} FSBFaceSelectCallbackRec;
```

XtNfaceSelectCallback passes a pointer to an *FSBFaceSelectCallbackRec* as call data.

available_faces is a list of faces available in the newly selected family.

num_available_faces is the length of the *available_faces* list.

current_face is the currently selected face. If this face is one of the available faces, the pointer in *current_face* has the same value as the pointer in the *available_faces* list. Comparing the pointers for equality has the same result as comparing the pointed-to strings.

The callback should fill the *new_face* field with one of the entries in the *available_faces* field.

TK

FSBCreateSamplerCallbackRec

```
typedef struct {
  Widget sampler;
  Widget sampler_shell;
} FSBCreateSamplerCallbackRec;
```

XtNcreateSamplerCallback passes a pointer to an
FSBCreateSamplerCallbackRec as call data.

7.6 Procedures

This section documents the procedures supplied by the font selection
panel. For all the procedures, the *widget* parameter must be a
FontSelectionBox widget or subclass of a *FontSelectionBox* widget.

FSBDownloadFontName

```
Boolean FSBDownloadFontName (w, font_name)
  Widget w;
  String font_name;
```

FSBDownloadFontName attempts to download the font specified by
font_name, using the specified font selection panel's resources to find
the font file and to decide whether to load the font into shared VM.

FSBFindAFM

```
String FSBFindAFM (w, font_name)
  Widget w;
  String font_name;
```

FSBFindAFM returns the name of the AFM file for the specified font
name, using the specified font selection panel's resources to determine
where to look for the file. If no AFM file is found, **FSBFindAFM** returns
NULL.

FSBFindFontFile

```
String FSBFindFontFile (w, font_name)
  Widget w;
  String font_name;
```

FSBFindFontFile returns the name of the font file for the specified font
name, using the specified font selection panel's resources to determine
where to look for the file. If no font file is found, **FSBFindFontFile**
returns *NULL*.

FSBFontFamilyFaceToName   void FSBFontFamilyFaceToName (w, family, face,
                               font_name_return)
         Widget w;
         String family;
         String face;
         String *font_name_return;

FSBFontFamilyFaceToName returns the font name for *family* and *face*. If *family* and *face* are not known to the font selection panel, *font_name_return* is set to *NULL*.

FSBFontNameToFamilyFace   void FSBFontNameToFamilyFace (w, font_name, family_return,
                               face_return)
         Widget w;
         String font_name;
         String *family_return;
         String *face_return;

FSBFontNameToFamilyFace returns the family and face for *font_name*. If *font_name* is not known to the font selection panel, *family_return* and *face_return* are set to *NULL*.

FSBGetFaceList   void FSBGetFaceList (w, family, count_return, face_return,
                      font_return)
         Widget w;
         String family;
         int *count_return;
         String **face_return;
         String **font_return;

FSBGetFaceList returns a list of the faces and a list of associated font names for the fonts specified by *family*. When the lists are no longer needed, the caller should free them with **XtFree**. The caller should not free the entries in the lists.

TK

FSBGetFamilyList

```
void FSBGetFamilyList (w, count_return, family_return)
    Widget w,
    int *count_return;
    String **family_return;
```

FSBGetFamilyList returns a list of the font families known to the font selection panel. When the list is no longer needed, the caller should free it with **XtFree**. The caller should not free the entries in the list.

FSBGetTextDimensions

```
void FSBGetTextDimensions (w, text, font, size, x, y, dx,
        dy, left, right, top, bottom)
    Widget w;
    String text, font;
    double size, x, y;
    float *dx, *dy, *left, *right, *top, *bottom;
```

FSBGetTextDimensions returns information about the size of the text string. It can be used to avoid a potential **limitcheck** error that could result from executing **charpath** on a string.

dx and *dy* return the change in the current point that would result from showing the text at the *x, y* position, using the font at the given size. They are equivalent to the ones that **stringwidth** returns.

left, *right*, *top*, and *bottom* return the bounding box of the imaged text. They are the ones that would result from the following code:

```
(text) false charpath flattenpath pathbbox
```

There is no danger of a **limitcheck** error if the resulting path exceeds the maximum allowed path length.

FSBMatchFontFace

```
Boolean FSBMatchFontFace (w, old_face, new_family,
        new_face_return)
    Widget w;
    String old_face;
    String new_family;
    String *new_face_return;
```

FSBMatchFontFace attempts to find a face in *new_family* that is similar to *old_face*. It uses the same rules as the default *XtNfaceSelectCallback*, with the following results:

- If the font selection panel does not know *new_family*, *new_face_return* is *NULL* and **FSBMatchFontFace** returns *False*.

- If the font selection panel succeeds in finding a close match, it returns the new face in *new_face_return* and returns *True*.

- If the font selection panel cannot find a close match, it stores the closest it can find (a "regular" face or, failing that, the first face) in *new_face_return* and returns *False*.

FSBRefreshFontList

```
void FSBRefreshFontList (w)
    Widget w;
```

FSBRefreshFontList instructs the font selection panel to refresh its font lists. An application should call this procedure only when new fonts have been installed.

FSBSetFontFamilyFace

```
void FSBSetFontFamilyFace (w, font_family, font_face,
        font_family_multiple, font_face_multiple)
    Widget w;
    String font_family;
    String font_face;
    Bool font_family_multiple;
    Bool font_face_multiple;
```

Calling **FSBSetFontFamilyFace** is equivalent to calling **XtSetValues** with the *XtNuseFontName, XtNfontFamily, XtNfontFace, XtNfontFamilyMultiple,* and *XtNfontFaceMultiple* resources. *XtNuseFontName* is set to *False*.

TK

FSBSetFontSize

```
void FSBSetFontSize (w, font_size, font_size_multiple)
    Widget w;
    double font_size;
    Bool font_size_multiple;
```

Calling **FSBSetFontSize** is equivalent to calling **XtSetValues** with the *XtNfontSize* and *XtNfontSizeMultiple* resources.

FSBSetFontName

```
void FSBSetFontName (w, font_name, font_name_multiple)
    Widget w;
    String font_name;
    Bool font_name_multiple;
```

Calling **FSBSetFontName** is equivalent to calling **XtSetValues** with the *XtNuseFontName*, *XtNfontName*, and *XtNfontNameMultiple* resources. *XtNuseFontName* is set to *True*.

FSBUndefineUnusedFonts

```
void FSBUndefineUnusedFonts (w)
    Widget w;
```

FSBUndefineUnusedFonts undefines all fonts that were downloaded for previewing but are not the currently previewed font. Since this happens automatically when the user activates the OK, Apply, Reset, or Cancel button, **FSBUndefineUnusedFonts** should be called only if the application has popped the font selection panel down without waiting for the user to activate the OK or Cancel button.

8 The Motif Font Sampler

The Motif font sampler can be popped up from the font selection panel to view multiple fonts at the same time. This section provides information about:

- Using the font sampler

- Resources (listing and description)

- Callbacks and procedures

By default, the font selection panel creates the font sampler and pops it up and down. The application can intervene using the *XtNcreateSamplerCallback* procedure of the font panel.

The header file is *<DPS/FontSample.h>*.

The class pointer is fontSamplerWidgetClass.

The class name is *FontSampler*.

The *FontSampler* widget is a subclass of XmManager.

8.1 Using the Motif Font Sampler

The font sampler allows the user to view multiple fonts at the same time and to choose among them. It provides a set of filters that narrow the choices to fonts with particular characteristics. Figure 2 shows a font sampler displaying the letters "Abc" using selected filters.

At the top of the font sampler, a text field allows the user to specify the text to be previewed. Below the type-in region is a display area on the left and a selection area containing boxes with toggles on the right. The top box allows the user to select a display criterion; below that are the choices for filtering fonts.

Figure 2 *The font sampler*

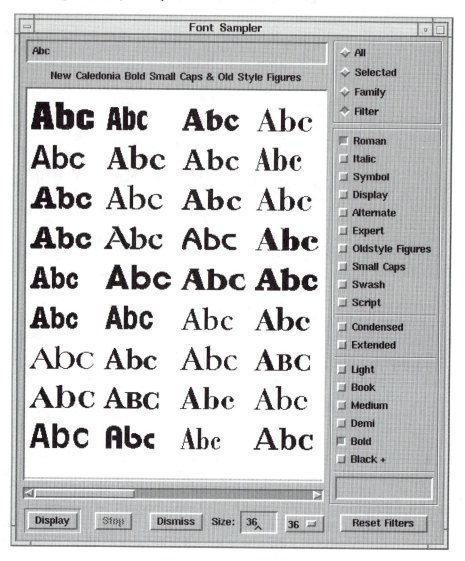

To display a set of fonts the user:

1. Types some text into the text field.

2. Chooses a display criterion and one or more font selection criteria, as described below.

3. Activates the Display button.

If the user activates the Display button during an ongoing display, the font sampler restarts the display. If the user activates the Stop button, any ongoing display is stopped.

To remove the font sampler from the screen, activate the Dismiss button.

8.1.1 Display Criteria

When the user activates the Display button, the font sampler begins to show fonts, using the current display criteria:

- If the All toggle is set, all fonts are displayed.

- If the Selected toggle is set, the font selected in the associated font selection panel is displayed.

- If the Family toggle is set, all fonts in the family selected in the associated font selection panel are displayed.

- If the Filter toggle is set, fonts that match the current set of filters are displayed.

In all cases, the size field and menu control the size of the displayed font.

8.1.2 Font Selection Criteria

The filter check boxes determine which fonts are displayed when the Filter toggle is set. There are four sets of filters:

- The first set describes general classes of fonts: Roman, Italic, Symbol, Small Caps, Script, and so on. (Note that "Roman" in this context means not Italic and not Symbol).

- The second set describes condensed or expanded fonts.

- The third set describes font weights: Light, Medium, Bold, and so on.

- The fourth set is a filter text field that is used for general matching.

A font will be displayed only if it matches one of the check boxes in each set that has any boxes checked. If the filter text field is not empty, the font name must also contain the string in that text field. (For the mathematically minded, the check boxes form a conjunction of disjunctions.)

Consider the following two examples:

- In the first set, the Italic box is checked. In the second set, no boxes are checked. In the third set, the Bold and Demi boxes are checked. The text field is empty. This combination matches any italic font that is either bold or demi. Note that the font sampler does not compare fonts against the filters in the second set, because no boxes are checked in that set.

- In the first set, Roman and Italic are checked. In the second set, Condensed is checked. In the third set, no boxes are checked. The text field contains the string "Garamond". This combination matches all nonsymbol, condensed fonts that have the string "Garamond" in their name.

The filtering process is based on searching for strings in the font's full name. Each check box has a set of strings that it matches. The Italic check box, for example, matches the strings "Italic", "Oblique", "Slanted", or "Kursiv".

Note: *Font naming does not follow a simple set of rules, so the results of a match might be unexpected. For example, if the user selected Symbol, any font that contained the string "Symbol" in its name would be matched, even if the font did not actually contain symbols. Similarly, a font that was "Ultra Condensed" would match the Black+ check box because "Ultra" is one of the strings that matches the Black+ category. (While some fonts use the phrase "Ultra Condensed" to mean very condensed, others use it to mean ultra-heavy and condensed.)*

Any changes to the currently displayed text, the size of the sampled fonts, the check boxes, or the filter text take effect immediately. However, changing the display criteria (All, Selected, Family, and Filtered) does not affect the current display until the user clicks the Display button.

Selecting a filter automatically changes the display type to Filtered.

If the user activates the Reset Filters button, all check boxes are toggled to *off* and the text filter is reset to be empty.

Clicking any mouse button on a displayed font sample displays the font name above the work area. The font becomes selected in the associated font selection panel. The size selected in the font selection panel is not affected by the size selected in the sampler.

8.2 Motif Font Sampler Resources

The following section describes the font sampler resources. The resource set table is followed by a brief description of each resource.

Table 12 *Motif font sampler resource set*

Name	Class	Default	Type	Access
XtNfontSelectionBox	XmCFontSelectionBox	NULL	XtRWidget	C
XtNminimumHeight	XmCMinimumHeight	100	XtRDimension	CSG
XtNminimumWidth	XmCMinimumWidth	100	XtRDimension	CSG
XtNnoFamilyFontMessage	XmCNoFamilyFontMessage	See description	XmRXmString	CSG
XtNnoFontMessage	XmCNoFontMessage	"There are no fonts!"	XmRXmString	CSG
XtNnoMatchMessage	XmCNoMatchMessage	"No fonts match filters"	XmRXmString	CSG
XtNnoRoomMessage	XmCNoRoomMessage	See description	XmRXmString	CSG
XtNnoSelectedFamilyMessage	XmCNoSelectedFamilyMessage	See description	XmRXmString	CSG
XtNnoSelectedFontMessage	XmCNoSelectedFontMessage	See description	XmRXmString	CSG
XtNsizeCount	XmCSizeCount	10	XtRInt	CSG
XtNsizes	XmCSizes	See description	XtRFloatList	CSG

8.2.1 Resource Descriptions

XtNfontSelectionBox Specifies the *FontSelectionBox* widget associated with a *FontSampler* widget. This resource must be specified when the font sampler is created, and cannot be changed.

XtNminimumHeight Specifies the minimum height for the work area. If the user resizes the font sampler and the work area becomes shorter than *XtNminimumHeight,* a vertical scroll bar appears and allows scrolling. Default is 100.

XtNminimumWidth Specifies the minimum width for the work area. If the user resizes the font sampler and the work area becomes narrower than *XtNminimumWidth,* a horizontal scroll bar appears and allows scrolling. Default is 100.

XtNnoFamilyFontMessage Specifies the compound string the font sampler displays if the selected font family has no fonts. This should not happen. Default is "Selected family has no fonts!"

TK

XtNnoFontMessage   Specifies the compound string the font sampler string displays if there are no fonts to be shown. This should not happen. Default is "There are no fonts!"

XtNnoMatchMessage   Specifies the compound string the font sampler displays if no fonts match the selected filters. Default is "No fonts match filters."

XtNnoRoomMessage   Specifies the compound string the font sampler displays if the work area is too small to show a single font sample. Default is "Current size is too large or panel is too small."

XtNnoSelectedFamilyMessage
Specifies the compound string the font sampler displays if no font family is selected but the user chooses to display the selected family. Default is "No family is currently selected."

XtNnoSelectMessage   Specifies the compound string the font sampler displays if no font is selected but the user chooses to display the selected font. Default is "No font is currently selected."

XtNsizeCount   Specifies the number of entries in the *XtNsizes* resource. Default is 10.

XtNsizes   Specifies the list of sizes to present in the menu. Default is 8, 10, 12, 14, 16, 18, 24, 36, 48, 72.

8.2.2   Children of the Motif Font Sampler

The following resources provide access to the descendants of the font selection panel. These resources cannot be changed. All are of type XtRWidget.

Table 13 *Motif Font sampler child resource set*

Name	Class	Type	Access
XtNallToggleChild	XtCReadOnly	XtRWidget	G
XtNareaChild	XtCReadOnly	XtRWidget	G
XtNclearButtonChild	XtCReadOnly	XtRWidget	G
XtNdismissButtonChild	XtCReadOnly	XtRWidget	G
XtNdisplayButtonChild	XtCReadOnly	XtRWidget	G
XtNfilterBoxChild	XtCReadOnly	XtRWidget	G
XtNfilterFrameChild	XtCReadOnly	XtRWidget	G
XtNfilterTextChild	XtCReadOnly	XtRWidget	G

XtNfilterToggleChild	XtCReadOnly	XtRWidget	G
XtNpanelChild	XtCReadOnly	XtRWidget	G
XtNradioBoxChild	XtCReadOnly	XtRWidget	G
XtNradioFrameChild	XtCReadOnly	XtRWidget	G
XtNscrolledWindowChild	XtCReadOnly	XtRWidget	G
XtNselectedFamilyToggleChild	XtCReadOnly	XtRWidget	G
XtNselectedToggleChild	XtCReadOnly	XtRWidget	G
XtNsizeLabelChild	XtCReadOnly	XtRWidget	G
XtNsizeOptionMenuChild	XtCReadOnly	XtRWidget	G
XtNsizeTextFieldChild	XtCReadOnly	XtRWidget	G
XtNstopButtonChild	XtCReadOnly	XtRWidget	G
XtNtextChild	XtCReadOnly	XtRWidget	G

8.3 Callbacks

XtNdismissCallback   *XtNdismissCallback* indicates that the user has dismissed the font sampler. The call data is *NULL*.

8.4 Procedures

FSBCancelSampler
```
void FSBCancelSampler (w)
    Widget w;
```

FSBCancelSampler cancels any display currently in progress. It can be used if the creator of the font sampler disables the sampler. If the user or application pops down the font selection panel, **FSBCancelSampler** does not have to be called; the font selection panel calls the appropriate procedures itself.

Locating PostScript Language Resources

Applications that use the PostScript language need to locate files that describe and contain PostScript language objects. The files may be Adobe Font Metric (AFM) files, font outline files, PostScript language procedure sets, forms, patterns, encodings, or any named PostScript language object. They are collectively referred to as PostScript language resource files, or *resource files*.

In many cases, resource files are installed system-wide—for example, the AFM files for the fonts that reside on a system's PostScript printers. In other cases, resource files are private to a user—for example, private font outlines that a user has purchased or procedure sets for a private application. PostScript language resource database files, or *resource database files*, allow applications to locate resource files uniformly.

This appendix contains information about locating resources, including:

- The structure of resource database files.

- The predefined resource type names.

- Facilities for locating resource database files.

- Procedures and type definitions for locating resources.

- Memory management and error handling.

Appendix B describes the *makepsres* utility, which you can use to create resource database files.

TK

A.1 Resource Database Files

This section describes resource database files, which can be used to locate resource files, including:

- Description of the format

- Information about the different sections

- A sample resource database file

A.1.1 Format of a Resource Database File

The following restrictions and requirements exist for the format of a resource database file:

- No line may exceed 255 characters plus the line termination character.

- A backslash (\) quotes any character. For example, the sequence \ABC represents the characters ABC. In most sections of the file, you may continue any line by ending it with a backslash immediately before the newline character (see section A.1.2, "Components of a Resource Database File").

- A section terminator begins with a period. If you begin any other line with a period, you must precede the period with a backslash.

- All lines in the file are case-sensitive.

- To include comments on any line, precede them with a percent sign. To avoid making a percent sign a comment, precede it with a backslash.

- Trailing blanks and tab characters are ignored everywhere in the file, but they do count toward the 255-character line length limit.

A.1.2 Components of a Resource Database File

A resource database file consists of several components, which must appear in the database in the following order:

- An identifying string (required)

- A list of resource types in this resource database file (required)

- A directory path (optional)

- The data for each resource type (required)

Identifying String Component

The first line of a resource database file must contain either the constant string *PS-Resources-1.0* or the constant string *PSResources-Exclusive-1.0*. The difference between the two is explained in section A.3, "Locating Resource Database Files."

Resource Types Component

The resource types component lists the resource types described by the file. Each line is the name of a single resource type, terminated by a newline character. The resource types component is terminated by a line containing a single period. Any string can be used to identify a resource type; the predefined resource types are defined in section A.2.

Directory Component

The directory component is an optional single line that identifies the directory prefix to be added to all file names in the resource database file. The component consists of a slash (/) followed by the directory prefix. (In operating systems where a slash is the first character of a fully specified path, the line must begin with two slashes.) If the directory component is not present, the directory prefix becomes, by default, the directory containing the resource database file.

Resource Data Components

Each resource type requires a data component. The data components must be presented in the same order as the corresponding identifiers in the resource types component.

Each data component consists of a single line identifying the resource type, followed by lines of resource data for that type, followed by a line containing a single period.

Each line of resource data contains:

TK

- The name of the resource. If the name contains an equal sign, precede the equal sign with a backslash.

- A single or double equal sign (= or = =).

- The name of the file that contains the resource. The file name may be an absolute or relative path name. If relative, it is interpreted relative to the directory prefix as specified above in the directory component description. However, a double equal sign forces the file name to be interpreted as absolute. In that case, the prefix is not used.

For some special predefined resource types the file name is replaced by some other kind of data; see section A.2. In these cases the directory prefix does not apply. (It is as if every line of resource data were specified with a double equal sign.)

A.1.3 Resource Database File Example

This is a sample resource database file for fonts in the Trajan family. The next section describes the resource types used in this example.

```
PS-Resources-1.0
FontOutline        % This section lists resource types
FontPrebuilt
FontAFM
FontFamily
FontBDF
FontBDFSizes
.                  % This line ends resource type listing
//usr/local/PS/resources
FontOutline        % This section lists font outline files
Trajan-Bold=Trajan-Bold
Trajan-Regular=Trajan-Regular
.
FontPrebuilt
Trajan-Bold=Trajan-Bold.bepf
Trajan-Regular=Trajan-Regular.bepf
.
FontAFM
Trajan-Bold=Trajan-Bold.afm
Trajan-Regular=Trajan-Regular.afm
.
FontFamily
Trajan=Bold,Trajan-Bold,Regular,Trajan-Regular
.
FontBDF
```

```
Trajan-Regular18-75-75=Trajan-Regular.18.bdf
Trajan-Regular24-75-75=Trajan-Regular.24.bdf
Trajan-Regular36-75-75=Trajan-Regular.36.bdf
Trajan-Regular48-75-75=Trajan-Regular.48.bdf
Trajan-Bold18-75-75=Trajan-Bold.18.bdf
Trajan-Bold24-75-75=Trajan-Bold.24.bdf
Trajan-Bold36-75-75=Trajan-Bold.36.bdf
Trajan-Bold48-75-75=Trajan-Bold.48.bdf
.
FontBDFSizes
Trajan-Regular=18-75-75,24-75-75,36-75-75,48-75-75
Trajan-Bold=18-75-75,24-75-75,36-75-75,48-75-75
.
```

A.2 Predefined Resource Types

The following table lists the name and contents of the predefined
resource types. Each resource line contains the name of the resource, a
single equal sign, and the name of the file containing the resource or
other relevant information, as described in the table. Examples for
several of the resource types can be found in section A.1.3, "Resource
Database File Example."

Table A.1 *Resource types*

Resource	Contents
FontOutline	The file contains PostScript language character outline programs.
FontPrebuilt	The file contains a set of prebuilt font bitmaps. Currently, only the Display PostScript system uses this format.
FontAFM	The file is an AFM file.
FontBDF	The file contains bitmap font data in Bitmap Distribution Format (BDF).
FontBDFSizes	If the resource type is *FontBDFSizes*, the file name in the resource line is replaced by a list of the *FontBDF* resources in the current file. Each entry consists of the point size, the *x* resolution, and the *y* resolution of the BDF file, separated by a single hyphen (–) character. The entries are separated with a single comma (,) character. Each entry may be appended to the resource name on the line to yield a valid *FontBDF* resource. The directory prefix does not apply to this resource type.

TK

In the sample file in A.1.3, "Resource Database File Example," the line

```
Trajan-Regular=18-75-75,24-75-75,36-75-75,48-75-75
```

indicates that the Trajan-Regular font has four BDF files available, at 18, 24, 36 and 48 points. All files are at 75 dots per inch in x and y. The name of each FontBDF resource is formed by concatenating Trajan-Regular with one of the size specifications, yielding, for example,

```
Trajan-Regular18-75-75
```

FontFamily   If the resource type is *FontFamily*, the file name in the resource line is replaced by a list of *FontOutline* resource names in the current file that belong to this font family. Each resource name is preceded by the face name for the font. The names are separated by a single comma (,) character; use a backslash to quote a comma within a font name. The directory prefix does not apply to this resource type.

In the sample file in section A.1.3, "Resource Database File Example," the line

```
Trajan=Bold,Trajan-Bold,Regular,Trajan-Regular
```

indicates that the Trajan family contains two faces: Bold, with the font name Trajan-Bold, and Regular, with the font name Trajan-Regular. The correspondence between face names and font names is not always as straightforward as in this example.

Form   The file contains a **Form** definition; see section 3.9.2 of *PostScript Language Reference Manual, Second Edition.*

Pattern   The file contains a **Pattern** definition; see section 3.9.2 of *PostScript Language Reference Manual, Second Edition.*

Encoding   The file contains a character set encoding; see section 3.9.2 of *PostScript Language Reference Manual, Second Edition.*

ProcSet   The file contains a named set of PostScript language procedures implementing some piece of an application's prolog.

mkpsresPrivate   The *makepsres* utility generates and manipulates resource database files. This section contains private information stored by *makepsres* to help it in future invocations. For more information about *makepsres*, consult Appendix B.

Further predefined types will be added to represent additional resources as needed.

A.3 Locating Resource Database Files

A user's *PSRESOURCEPATH* environment variable consists of a list of directories separated by colons. (Systems without environment variables must use an alternate way of expressing the user's preference.) Procedures that look for resource database files search each directory named in the *PSRESOURCEPATH* environment variable.

Each component (for example, the font selection panel and the TranScript™ software package) has a default place where it looks for resource files. The default places may be different for each component and are determined in a component-dependent way, usually at system build time.

Two adjacent colons in a *PSRESOURCEPATH* path represent the list of default places in which a component looks for PostScript language resources.

The *PSRESOURCEPATH* variable defaults to "::" if no value is specified. This is the normal value for users who have not installed private resources. Users with private resources should end the path with a double colon if they want their resources to override the system defaults, or begin it with a double colon if they don't want to override system defaults. Colons in the path can be quoted in a system-dependent way; on UNIX® systems, a backslash quotes colons.

A typical *PSRESOURCEPATH* is the following:

```
::/proj/ourproj/PS:/user/smith/ps
```

The sample path above instructs procedures that locate resource database files to first look in the default place, wherever it may be, then to search the directory */proj/ourproj/PS*, and then search the directory */user/smith/ps*. The user does not need to know the location of the default resource database files.

On UNIX systems, resource database files end with the suffix *.upr* (for UNIX PostScript resources). The principal resource database file in a directory is named *PSres.upr*.

- If the first line of a *PSres.upr* file is *PS-Resources-Exclusive-1.0*, the *PSres.upr* file is the only resource database file in its directory.

- If the first line of a *PSres.upr* file is *PS-Resources-1.0*, or if there is no *PSres.upr* file, any file in the same directory with the suffix *.upr* is a resource database file. For example, the sample file shown in A.1.3, "Resource Database File Example," might be called *Trajan.upr*.

If a *PSres.upr* file begins with *PS-Resources-Exclusive-1.0*, the resource location procedures run more quickly since they don't need to look for other *.upr* files. However, users will then have to update *PSres.upr* whenever new resources are installed.

A.4 Type Definitions and Procedures for Resource Location

If you are writing an application or a library that needs to locate PostScript language resource files, use the resource location library *libpsres.a*. This library contains procedures that locate and parse resource database files and return lists of resource files. The header file for *libpsres.a* is *<DPS/PSres.h>*.

Resource location procedures represent resource types as character strings. This allows matching of arbitrary strings in the resource type list of a resource database file. Several variables are available for matching:

```
extern char *PSResFontOutline, *PSResFontPrebuilt,
    *PSResFontAFM,*PSResFontBDF, *PSResFontFamily,
    *PSResFontBDFSizes,*PSResForm, *PSResPattern,
    *PSResEncoding, *PSResProcSet;
```

The variables evaluate to the appropriate character string; for example, the value of *PSResFontOutline* is "FontOutline". Using the variables instead of the strings themselves allows the compiler to find spelling errors within your application that would otherwise go undetected.

In the following procedure definitions, the phrase *resource location procedure* refers to **ListPSResourceFiles**, **EnumeratePSResourceFiles**, or **ListPSResourceTypes**, but not to **CheckPSResourceTime**.

A.4.1 Type Definitions

PSResourceEnumerator

```
typedef int *(PSResourceEnumerator)(/*
    char *resourceType,
    char *resourceName,
    char *resourceFile,
    char *private*/);
```

A *PSResourceEnumerator* procedure is used with
EnumeratePSResourceFiles.

PSResourceSavePolicy

```
typedef enum {
    PSSaveReturnValues,
    PSSaveByType,
    PSSaveEverything
} PSResourceSavePolicy;
```

PSResourceSavePolicy enumerates the save policies used by
SetPSResourcePolicy.

A.4.2 Procedures

CheckPSResourceTime

```
int CheckPSResourceTime (psResourcePathOverride,
                                defaultPath)
    char *psResourcePathOverride;
    char *defaultPath;
```

CheckPSResourceTime checks whether the access times of directories in
a path have changed since the directories were read in.

psResourcePathOverride provides a path that overrides the environment
resource path. On UNIX systems, it replaces the *PSRESOURCEPATH*
environment variable. The value is usually *NULL*. To quote colons in the
path, use a backslash.

defaultPath is the path that is inserted between adjacent colons in the
resource path. It may be *NULL*.

* If either path value differs from that used in the previous call to any
  procedure in this library, **CheckPSResourceTime** returns 1.

TK

- If neither path has changed since the previous call to the library, **CheckPSResourceTime** determines whether the modification time for any directory described in the paths is more recent than the latest modification time when the directories were scanned for resource files and, if so, returns 1. Otherwise **CheckPSResourceTime** returns 0.

CheckPSResourceTime does not free storage and cannot make invalid storage that was previously returned by **ListPSResourceFiles** or **ListPSResourceTypes**.

If **CheckPSResourceTime** returns 1, the caller can then call

```
FreePSResourceStorage(1)
```

This forces future calls to resource location procedures to reload all resource databases.

EnumeratePSResourceFiles

```
void EnumeratePSResourceFiles (psResourcePathOverride,
        defaultPath, resourceType, resourceName,
        enumerator, private)
char *psResourcePathOverride;
char *defaultPath;
char *resourceType;
char *resourceName;
PSResourceEnumerator enumerator;
char *private;
```

EnumeratePSResourceFiles lists PostScript language files giving applications complete control over saving file names. Applications that do not need this level of control should use **ListPSResourceFiles** instead.

EnumeratePSResourceFiles calls the procedure specified by *enumerator* for each resource that matches the *resourceType* and (if non-*NULL*) *resourceName*. The enumerator procedure has to copy the resource name and resource file into nonvolatile storage before returning. The *resourceType* parameter is passed to the enumerator for information only; it does not have to be copied. If the enumerator procedure returns a nonzero value, **EnumeratePSResourceFiles** returns without enumerating further resources.

EnumeratePSResourceFiles causes minimal state to be saved—for example, which resource files contain which types of resources. To free the saved state, call

```
FreePSResourceStorage(1)
```

psResourcePathOverride provides a path that overrides the environment resource path. On UNIX systems, it replaces the *PSRESOURCEPATH* environment variable. The value is usually *NULL*. To quote colons in the path, use a backslash.

defaultPath is the path inserted between adjacent colons in the resource path. The value may be *NULL*.

resourceType indicates the type of resource desired.

resourceName indicates the requested resource name. If the name is *NULL*, the procedure returns a list of all resource names for the type in *resourceType*.

enumerator provides a procedure that is called for each resource name.

private specifies data to be passed uninterpreted to the enumerator.

FreePSResourceStorage

```
void FreePSResourceStorage (everything)
    int everything;
```

The subroutine library normally keeps internal state to avoid reading directory files each time. Calling **FreePSResourceStorage** frees any storage currently used.

- If *everything* is nonzero **FreePSResourceStorage** completely resets its state. No information is retained.

- If *everything* is zero, **FreePSResourceStorage** allows the library to keep minimal information, normally about which files in the search path contain which resource types.

Calling a resource location procedure with a different value of *psResourcePathOverride* or of *defaultPath* from the previous call implicitly makes the call

```
FreePSResourceStorage(1)
```

FreePSResourceStorage invalidates any string pointers returned by previous calls to **ListPSResourceFiles** or **ListPSResourceTypes**.

ListPSResourceFiles ```int ListPSResourceFiles (psResourcePathOverride,
                defaultPath, resourceType, resourceName,
                resourceNamesReturn, resourceFilesReturn)
            char *psResourcePathOverride;
            char *defaultPath;
            char *resourceType;
            char *resourceName;
            char **resourceNamesReturn;
            char **resourceFilesReturn;```

ListPSResourceFiles lists PostScript language resource files.

psResourcePathOverride provides a path that overrides the environment resource path. On UNIX systems, it replaces the *PSRESOURCEPATH* environment variable. The value is usually *NULL*. To quote a colon in the path, use a backslash.

defaultPath is the path that is inserted between adjacent colons in the resource path. *defaultPath* may be *NULL*.

resourceType indicates the type of resource desired.

resourceName indicates the desired resource name. If *resourceName* is *NULL*, **ListPSResourceFiles** returns a list of all resource names of type *resourceType*.

resourceNamesReturn returns a list of the resource names.

resourceFilesReturn returns a list of the resource file names as absolute path names. Backslash quotes are removed from all strings, with the exception of backslashes that precede commas in the file name. This supports comma quoting for the *FontFamily* resource type.

The *resourceNamesReturn* and *resourceFilesReturn* arrays always have the same number of entries, equal to the return value.

The *resourceNamesReturn* and *resourceFilesReturn* arrays should be freed with **PSResFree** when they are no longer needed. The individual strings should not be freed. They remain valid until a resource location procedure is called with a different value of *psResourcePathOverride* or *defaultPath*, or until **FreePSResourceStorage** is called.

If a particular resource name occurs more than once in the same or in different resource directories, all occurrences are returned, in the following order:

- All resources for a particular directory entry in the resource search path occur before any entries for a later directory.

- For a particular directory, all resources found in *PSres.upr* files occur before any entries found in subsidiary resource directory files.

ListPSResourceFiles returns the number of entries in the *resourceNamesReturn* array. A return value of 0 means that no resources meeting the specification could be found. In that case, *resourceNamesReturn* and *resourceFilesReturn* are not modified.

Applications that need complete control over saving the file names should use **EnumeratePSResourceFiles**.

ListPSResourceTypes

```
int ListPSResourceTypes (psResourcePathOverride,
       defaultPath, resourceTypesReturn)
   char *psResourcePathOverride;
   char *defaultPath;
   char **resourceTypesReturn;
```

Applications can call **ListPSResourceTypes** to determine which resource types are available.

psResourcePathOverride provides a path that overrides the environment resource path. On UNIX systems, that path replaces the *PSRESOURCEPATH* environment variable. The value is usually *NULL*. To quote colons in the path, use a backslash.

defaultPath is the path that is inserted between adjacent colons in the resource path. The value may be *NULL*.

resourceTypesReturn returns a list of resource types.

The *resourceTypesReturn* array should be freed with **PSResFree** when it is no longer needed. The individual strings should not be freed; they remain valid until a resource location procedure is called with a different value of *psResourcePathOverride* or of *defaultPath*, or until **FreePSResourceStorage** is called with *everything* nonzero.

The returned resource types are merged to result in a nonduplicating list. The special type *mkpsresPrivate* is never returned.

TK

ListPSResourceTypes returns the number of entries in the *resourceTypesReturn* array. A return value of 0 means that no resource types could be found. In that case, *resourceTypesReturn* is not modified.

SetPSResourcePolicy

```
void SetPSResourcePolicy (policy, willList, resourceTypes)
    PSResourceSavePolicy policy;
    int willList;
    char **resourceTypes;
```

An application can use **SetPSResourcePolicy** to provide the resource library with information about the expected pattern of future calls to **ListPSResourceFiles**.

policy determines the save policy used. It is of type *PSResourceSavePolicy* and may be one of the following:

- *PSSaveEverything*. The first time **ListPSResourceFiles** or **ListPSResourceTypes** is called with a particular set of values for *psResourcePathOverride* and *defaultPath*, it reads all resource directory files in the specified paths and caches all the information in them. Future calls will use the cache and not read the file system.

- *PSSaveByType*. **ListPSResourceFiles** saves information about the resource types in *resourceTypes*. Calls to **ListPSResourceFiles** for resource types not in the *resourceTypes* list may or may not save values. In that case, it is undefined whether and how much information is saved.

- *PSSaveReturnValues*. **ListPSResourceFiles** saves the returned strings but may save little else. Subsequent calls usually access the file system. It is undefined whether and how much other information is saved, but applications can expect it to be minimal.

You cannot completely disable saving since the saved strings are returned by **ListPSResourceFiles**.

willList is nonzero if the application expects to list resources by passing *NULL* to **ListPSResourceFiles** in the *resourceName* parameter.

resourceTypes is a *NULL*-terminated list of the resource types the application expects to use, or *NULL*.

Note that *willList, policy,* and *resourceTypes* are just hints;
ListPSResourceFiles works correctly regardless of their values. It may,
however, work more slowly.

Calling **SetPSResourcePolicy** more than once changes the future
behavior of **ListPSResourceValues** but has no effect on the previously
saved state.

Applications that need complete control over saving the names can use
EnumeratePSResourceFiles instead of **ListPSResourceFiles**.

A.5   Memory Management and Error Handling

An application using the resource location library may provide its own
implementation of **malloc**, **realloc**, and **free** by assigning values to the
external variables *PSResMalloc, PSResRealloc,* and *PSResFree.*

PSResMallocProc
```
typedef char *(*PSResMallocProc)(/*
    int size */);

extern PSResMallocProc PSResMalloc;
```

PSResReallocProc
```
typedef char *(*PSResReallocProc)(/*
    char *ptr,
    int size */);

extern PSResReallocProc PSResRealloc;
```

PSResFreeProc
```
typedef void (*PSResFreeProc)(/*
    char *ptr */);

extern PSResFreeProc PSResFree;
```

The procedures must provide the following additional semantics
beyond that supplied by the system allocation routines:

- **PSResMalloc** and **PSResRealloc** must never return *NULL*; if they return
  at all they must return the storage. They must not return *NULL* even
  if passed a zero size.

- **PSResFree** must return if passed *NULL*, and do nothing else.

- **PSResRealloc** must allocate storage if passed a *NULL* pointer.

The default routines give an error message and terminate if they are unable to allocate the requested storage.

If the resource location library encounters a resource database file that does not conform to the standard format, a warning handler is called. The default warning handler prints a warning message with the file name on *stderr* and continues, ignoring information it cannot parse. A different warning handler can be installed by assigning a value to the external variable *PSResFileWarningHandler*.

PSResFileWarningHandlerProc

```
typedef void (*PSResFileWarningHandlerProc)
  (/* char *fileName,
      char *extraInfo*/);

extern PSResFileWarningHandlerProc
    PSResFileWarningHandler;
```

The makepsres Utility

The *makepsres* utility creates resource database files. Resource database files can be used to locate PostScript language resources that are used by the font selection panel and other Adobe software. If an application needs to locate PostScript language resources, it uses the facilities described in Appendix A, "Locating PostScript Language Resources."

This appendix provides information about the *makepsres* utility in a format similar to a UNIX manual page.

To invoke *makepsres* in the default mode, type:

```
makepsres
```

Resource installation scripts should invoke *makepsres* automatically.

B.1 Overview of Functionality

The complete command line syntax for *makepsres* is:

```
makepsres [options] directory ...
```

makepsres creates a resource database file containing all the resources in all directories specified on the command line.

- If the list of directories contains "–", *makepsres* reads from *stdin* and expects a list of directories separated by space, tab, or newline.

- If the list of directories is empty, it is taken to be the current directory.

- If all specified directories have a common initial prefix, *makepsres* extracts it as a directory prefix in the new resource database file.

TK

makepsres uses existing resource database files to assist in identifying files. By default, *makepsres* creates a new resource database file containing all of the following that apply:

- Resource files found in the directories on the command line.

- Resource files pointed to by the resource database files in the directories on the command line.

- Resource entries found in the input resource database files. These entries are copied if the files they specify still exist and are located in directories not specified on the command line.

makepsres uses various heuristics to identify files. A file that is of a private resource type or that does not conform to the standard format for a resource file must be specified in one of the following ways:

- Be identified by the user by running *makepsres* in interactive mode

- Have been preloaded into a PostScript resource database file used for input

- Begin with the following line:

    ```
    %!PS-Adobe-3.0 Resource-<resource-type>
    ```

If you run *makepsres* in *discard mode* (using the **–d** command line option), it does not copy resource entries from the input resource database files. In that case, the output file consists only of entries from the directories on the command line. The input resource database files are only used to assist in identifying files.

If you run *makepsres* in *keep mode* (using the **–k** command line option), it includes in the output file all resource entries in the input resource database files, even entries for files that no longer exist or are located in directories specified on the command line.

B.2 Command Line Options

–o *filename*   Writes the output to the specified file name. "**–o** –" writes to *stdout*. If the **–o** option is not specified, *makepsres* creates a *PSres.upr* file in the current directory and writes the output to that file.

–f *filename*	Uses information from the specified file to assist in resource typing. The file must be in PostScript resource database file format (see A.1.1, "Format of a Resource Database File"). Multiple –f options may be specified. "–f –" uses *stdin* as an input file and may not be used if "–" is specified as a directory on the command line. It is not necessary to use –f for files that are in a directory on the command line.
–dir *filename*	Specifies that *filename* is a directory. This option is only needed if the directory name can be confused with one of the command line options.
–d	Specifies discard mode. If **–d** is used, *makepsres* does not copy resource entries from the input resource database files. In that case, the output file consists solely of entries from the directories on the command line. The input resource database files are only used to assist in identifying files.
–e	Tells *makepsres* to mark the resulting *PSres.upr* file as exclusive. This option makes the resource location library run more quickly since it does not have to look for other resource database files. It becomes necessary, however, to run *makepsres* whenever new resources are added to the directory, even if the resources come with their own resource database file.
–i	Specifies interactive mode. In interactive mode, the user is queried for the resource type of any file encountered by *makepsres* that it cannot identify. If **–i** is not specified, *makepsres* assumes an unidentifiable file is not a resource file.
–k	Specifies keep mode. If **–k** is used, *makepsres* includes all resource entries from the input resource database files in the output. This includes entries for files that no longer exist.
–nr	Specifies nonrecursive mode. *makepsres* normally acts recursively: it looks for resource files in subdirectories of any specified directory. If **–nr** is used, *makepsres* does not look in subdirectories for resource files.
–nb	Does not back up the output file if it already exists.
–p	Specifies no directory prefix. If **–p** is used, *makepsres* does not try to find a common directory prefix among the specified directories.
–q	Ignores unidentifiable files instead of warning about them; "be quiet."
–s	Specifies strict mode. If **–s** is used, *makepsres* terminates with an error if it encounters a file it cannot identify.

TK

Index

Symbols

A

B

INDEX

INDEX

INDEX

INDEX

Colophon

This book was prepared using SPARCstation™, DECstation®, and Macintosh® computers with FrameMaker® and Adobe Illustrator™ software. The type used is from the ITC Stone® family. Heads are set in ITC Stone Sans Semibold and the body text is set in ITC Stone Serif, ITC Stone Serif Italic, and ITC Stone Sans Semibold. Code examples are in Lucida® Sans Typewriter, a Type 1 font from Bigelow & Holmes Inc.

Author and Engineer—Paul J. Asente

Technical Writer—Rick Palkovic

Editor—Amy Davidson

Key Contributors—David Lister (engineering), Yvonne Tornatta (technical writing).

Special thanks to Ken Fromm, author of the applications and accompanying text in *Programming the Display PostScript System with NeXTstep*, the predecessor to the current volume, and to all the contributors to that volume.

Reviewers—Larry Baer, Bill Bilodeau, Scott Byer, Perry Caro, Jeff Chien, David DiGiacomo, Bennett Leeds, Jon Ferraiolo, Gordon Hamachi, Freddy Jensen, Anna Kjos, Sherri Nichols, Paul Rovner, Ed Taft, Darin Tomack, Gale Tyson.

Other Contributors—Ed Brakeman (project coordination), Renate Kempf (technical writing), T. Maria Massoni (administrative services), Libby Vincent (technical editing), Nancy Winters (cover design).

Publication Management—Amy Davidson

Project Management—Dano Ybarra

Engineering Management—Jim Sandman

11